FocusPrep™

FOCUS	FOUNDATION	PRACTICE

PSAT 10 and SAT®

MATH WORKBOOK

for the Redesigned PSAT 10, PSAT/NMSQT, and SAT

Vivek Raghuram

1st EDITION

Published by:

>Gift Of Logic, Inc
>http://www.GiftOfLogic.com

Copyright © 2015 GiftOfLogic, Inc. All rights reserved. No part of this publication can be reproduced, stored in a retrieval system, transmitted in any form or by any means, electronic, mechanical, photocopying, recording or otherwise, without the written permission of the publisher.

FocusPrep™ is an imprint of Gift Of Logic, Inc.

Licensing: This book is licensed for use by one student only. Use of this book in a group setting (classroom, workshops, camps, etc.) is illegal.

ISBN-13: 978-1512330793
ISBN-10: 1512330795

7/15, 6/17

Disclaimer:
PSAT 8/9, PSAT 10, PSAT/NMSQT, and SAT are registered trademarks of College Board. College Board does not endorse the materials presented in this workbook. Although every precaution has been taken in the preparation of this book, neither the author nor the publisher shall have any liability to any person or entity with respect to any loss or damage caused or alleged to be caused directly or indirectly by the information contained in this book.

TABLE OF CONTENTS

ORIENTATION & FOCUS		4
CHAPTER 1	**PROBLEM SOLVING & DATA ANALYSIS**	9
Lesson 1	Numbers and Operations	10
Lesson 2	Factors and Multiples	24
Lesson 3	Word problems	31
Lesson 4	Ratio, Rate, and Variation	37
Lesson 5	Percentages	49
Lesson 6	Unit Conversions	55
Lesson 7	Scatterplots	61
Lesson 8	Graphs and Tables	68
Lesson 9	Growth and Decay	84
Lesson 10	Statistics	93
Lesson 11	Population and Sample	105
Lesson 12	Counting	122
Lesson 13	Probability	131
Lesson 14	Extended Thinking	141
CHAPTER 2	**HEART OF ALGEBRA**	158
Lesson 15	Linear Equations	159
Lesson 16	System of Linear Equations	169
Lesson 17	Linear Inequalities	179
Lesson 18	System of Linear Inequalities	185
Lesson 19	Linear Models and Graphs	189
Lesson 20	Absolute Equalities and Inequalities	196
CHAPTER 3	**PASSPORT TO ADVANCED MATH**	201
Lesson 21	Polynomials and Quadratic Equations	202
Lesson 22	Linear - Quadratic Systems	217
Lesson 23	Functions and Transformations	223
Lesson 24	Radicals and Fractional Exponents	245
CHAPTER 4	**ADDITIONAL TOPICS IN MATHEMATICS**	257
Lesson 25	Lines and Angles	258
Lesson 26	Triangles	263
Lesson 27	Pythagorean Theorem	273
Lesson 28	Circles	283
Lesson 29	Polygons	292
Lesson 30	Volume of Solids	300
Lesson 31	Complex Numbers	308
Lesson 32	Trigonometry	315
Lesson 33	Radians	328
APPENDIX		334
Lesson 34	Calculator	335
Lesson 35	Blueprint Problems-1	342

©GiftOfLogic http://www.GiftOfLogic.com

ORIENTATION & FOCUS	
PSAT 10 and PSAT/NMSQT	SAT

The College Board introduced the Redesigned PSAT 10 and PSAT/NMSQT starting October 2015 and the Redesigned SAT starting March 2016. You need to **orient** yourself correctly so that you know what tests are available, when to take them, what content areas are tested, and the details of the format and duration of these tests. Once you have oriented yourself, you need to **focus** on the lessons to stay on track and prepare comprehensively. Please read the following questions and answers.

Q1 How do I **orient** myself to face the Redesigned PSAT 10, PSAT/NMSQT, and SAT?

A1 Begin your **orientation** by familiarizing yourself with the SAT suite of assessments shown below. Then, read the questions and answers below to get the details of the redesigned tests. The College Board has redesigned the PSAT 10 and SAT tests to make them more meaningful for college success. These tests are different from older PSAT 10 and SAT tests – in content, format, duration, difficulty level, and scores. The following table shows important information about them. Contact your school counselor for test availability in your school. Visit the College Board website for up to date information. Note that only the SAT test is used for college admissions – the rest are available from grades 8-10 to practice for the SAT. The table below shows the entire suite of PSAT and SAT assessments and the corresponding grades when you take these tests.

SAT SUITE OF ASSESSMENTS				
Grade	When	Tests	Registration	Purpose
NEW PSAT 8/9				
8	Fall or Spring	PSAT 8/9	contact counselor	to track college readiness
9	Fall or Spring	PSAT 8/9	contact counselor	to track college readiness
REDESIGNED PSAT/NMSQT and PSAT 10				
10	Fall	PSAT/NMSQT	contact counselor	check college readiness; National Merit Qualifier
10	Spring	PSAT 10	contact counselor	check college readiness
11	Fall	PSAT/NMSQT	contact counselor	check college readiness; National Merit Qualifier
REDESIGNED SAT				
11	Spring	SAT	register online	college admission
12	Fall	SAT	register online	college Admission

Q2 How many questions are there in the Redesigned PSAT 10 and Redesigned SAT?

A2 The breakup of the Redesigned PSAT 10 and SAT is shown below.

REDESIGNED PSAT 10 and PSAT/NMSQT		
Section	Questions and Duration	Score Range
Reading	48 questions 60 minutes	160-760
Writing	44 questions 35 minutes	
Math	48 questions 70 minutes 2 sections (calculator and no-calculator)	160-760
Total	2 hours 45 minutes No negative scoring	320-1520

REDESIGNED SAT		
Section	Questions and Duration	Score Range
Reading	52 questions 65 minutes	200-800
Writing	44 questions 35 minutes	
Essay (optional)	1 question 50 minutes	2-8
Math	58 questions 80 minutes 2 sections(calculator and no-calculator)	200-800
Total	3 hours + 50 minutes for optional Essay No negative scoring	400-1600

Q3 What is the syllabus for the Redesigned PSAT and SAT <u>Math section</u>?

A3 SAT Math problems are drawn from four content areas: Problem Solving and Data Analysis, Heart of Algebra, Passport to Advanced Math, and Additional Topics in Math. There will be two math sections – a CALCULATOR section and a NO CALCULATOR section. Each of these sections has problems in specific areas of Math as shown below.

REDESIGNED PSAT 10 and PSAT/NMSQT -- MATH SECTION		
Section	Time	Questions
CALCULATOR SECTION	45 minutes	31 questions 27 Multiple Choice + 4 GRID IN 16 Problem Solving and Data Analysis 8 Heart of Algebra 6 Passport to Advanced Math 1 Additional Topics in Mathematics
NO CALCULATOR SECTION	25 minutes	17 questions 13 Multiple Choice + 4 GRID IN 8 Heart Of Algebra 8 Passport to Advanced Math 1 Additional topics in Mathematics
Total	70 minutes (1 hour 10 minutes)	48 questions

REDESIGNED SAT -- MATH SECTION		
Section	Time	Questions
CALCULATOR SECTION	55 minutes	38 questions 30 Multiple Choice + 8 GRID IN 17 Problem Solving and Data Analysis 11 Heart of Algebra 7 Passport to Advanced Math 3 Additional Topics in Mathematics
NO CALCULATOR SECTION	25 minutes	20 questions 15 Multiple Choice + 5 GRID IN 8 Heart Of Algebra 9 Passport to Advanced Math 3 Additional topics in Mathematics
Total	80 minutes (1 hour 20 minutes)	58 questions

Q4 How do I **focus** and prepare with a strong **foundation** for the PSAT 10, NMSQT, and SAT?

A4 This math workbook has **35 lessons** to give you **focus and foundation** on the four content areas of PSAT 10 & SAT: **Problem Solving and Data Analysis, Heart of Algebra, Passport to Advanced Math, and Additional Topics in Mathematics**. Within each of these four areas, there are several lessons. These lessons and their content broadly mirror the details outlined in the blueprint for the redesigned test specifications published by the College Board. Each lesson has practice problems that are classified as **CALCULATOR and NO CALCULATOR**. Each lesson contains multiple choice questions and student produced response questions (GRID IN). The following table shows the FocusPrep lessons in each content area.

Content Area	FocusPrep Lessons	
Problem Solving and Data Analysis	Lesson 1	Numbers and Operations
	Lesson 2	Factors and Multiples
	Lesson 3	Word problems
	Lesson 4	Ratio, Rate, and Variation
	Lesson 5	Percentages
	Lesson 6	Unit Conversions
	Lesson 7	Scatterplots
	Lesson 8	Graphs and Tables
	Lesson 9	Growth and Decay
	Lesson 10	Statistics
	Lesson 11	Population and Sample

	Lesson 12	Counting
	Lesson 13	Probability
	Lesson 14	Extended Thinking
Heart of Algebra	Lesson 15	Linear Equations
	Lesson 16	System of Linear Equations
	Lesson 17	Linear Inequalities
	Lesson 18	System of Linear Inequalities
	Lesson 19	Linear Models and Graphs
	Lesson 20	Absolute Equalities and Inequalities
Passport to Advanced Math	Lesson 21	Polynomials and Quadratic Equations
	Lesson 22	Linear- Quadratic Systems
	Lesson 23	Functions and Transformations
	Lesson 24	Radicals and Fractional Exponents
Additional topics in Mathematics	Lesson 25	Lines and Angles
	Lesson 26	Triangles
	Lesson 27	Pythagorean Theorem
	Lesson 28	Circles
	Lesson 29	Polygons
	Lesson 30	Volume of Solids
	Lesson 31	Complex Numbers
	Lesson 32	Trigonometry
	Lesson 33	Radians
Appendix Blueprint problems are similar to the ones in the blueprint published by the College Board. Provided to boost your confidence.	Lesson 34	Calculator
	Lesson 35	Blueprint Problems-1

Q5 How long will it take for me to complete all the lessons?

A5 FocusPrep recommends a **8-week plan** to complete the lessons as shown in the table below. You need to focus on developing a strong foundation in these lessons. You can complete the lessons sooner if you are able to, but don't rush - progress with confidence.

Week 1 Problem Solving and Data Analysis	Lesson 1	Numbers and Operations
	Lesson 2	Factors and Multiples
	Lesson 3	Word problems
	Lesson 4	Ratio, Rate, and Variation
	Lesson 5	Percentages
Week 2 Problem Solving and Data Analysis	Lesson 6	Unit Conversions
	Lesson 7	Scatterplots
	Lesson 8	Graphs and Tables
	Lesson 9	Growth and Decay
	Lesson 10	Statistics
Week 3	Lesson 11	Population and Sample
	Lesson 12	Counting

Problem Solving and Data Analysis	Lesson 13	Probability
	Lesson 14	Extended Thinking
Week 4 Heart of Algebra	Lesson 15	Linear Equations
	Lesson 16	System of Linear Equations
	Lesson 17	Linear Inequalities
	Lesson 18	System of Linear Inequalities
	Lesson 19	Linear Models and Graphs
	Lesson 20	Absolute Equalities and Inequalities
Week 5 Passport to Advanced Math	Lesson 21	Polynomials and Quadratic Equations
	Lesson 22	Linear- Quadratic Systems
	Lesson 23	Functions and Transformations
	Lesson 24	Radicals and Fractional Exponents
Week 6 Additional Topics in Mathematics	Lesson 25	Lines and Angles
	Lesson 26	Triangles
	Lesson 27	Pythagorean Theorem
	Lesson 28	Circles
Week 7 Additional Topics in Mathematics	Lesson 29	Polygons
	Lesson 30	Volume of Solids
	Lesson 31	Complex Numbers
Week 8 Additional Topics in Mathematics Practice solving blueprint problems	Lesson 32	Trigonometry
	Lesson 33	Radians
	Lesson 34	Calculator
	Lesson 35	Blueprint Problems-1

Q6 How are the lessons structured?

A6 Each lesson has a Review, Practice, and Answer section.

- The **Review section** begins with a checklist of key questions for the lesson in a box titled FocusPrep CheckList. This is followed by topic material presented in an easy-to-digest **QuickReview™ format**. This question and answer format will help you review the math concepts and formulas quickly and remember them for a long time. After reviewing the questions and answers, proceed to the Practice section.

- The **Practice section** has several questions that are marked as either CALCULATOR SECTION or NO CALCULATOR SECTION. If the problem is a Multiple Choice type, circle the answer. If it is a GRID IN type question, write the answer below the question. Proceed to check your answers from the Answer section that immediately follows.

- The **Answer section** shows the answer key and detailed explanation along with tips and alerts relevant to the problem.

CHAPTER 1 PROBLEM SOLVING AND DATA ANALYSIS	
Lesson	**Title**
Lesson 1	Numbers and Operations
Lesson 2	Factors and Multiples
Lesson 3	Word problems
Lesson 4	Ratio, Rate, and Variation
Lesson 5	Percentages
Lesson 6	Unit Conversions
Lesson 7	Scatterplots
Lesson 8	Graphs and Tables
Lesson 9	Growth and Decay
Lesson 10	Statistics
Lesson 11	Population and Sample
Lesson 12	Counting
Lesson 13	Probability
Lesson 14	Extended Thinking

PROBLEM SOLVING AND DATA ANALYSIS		
Lesson 1	Numbers and Operations	Review

FOCUSPREP CHECKLIST

- What are the different types of numbers?
- What are the properties of Real numbers?
- What are the operations involving exponential numbers?
- What are special operators?
- Workout practice problems in Numbers and Operations

Q1 How are numbers classified?

A1 Numbers are classified as Real Numbers or Complex Numbers. Real numbers are in turn classified as rational and irrational numbers. Complex Numbers are new to SAT and are covered in a separate lesson.

Real numbers:

Rational Numbers: Numbers that can be expressed in the form of $\frac{a}{b}$, $b \neq 0$

Natural Numbers (also called Counting numbers) : 1,2,3,4,5…
Whole Numbers: 0, 1, 2,… Even numbers: 0,2,4,… Odd numbers 1,3,5,…
Integers: …, -5, -4, -3, -2, -1, 0, 1, 2, 3, 4, 5 …
Fractions: $\frac{2}{3}$, $\frac{5}{9}$
Decimals $0.58, 0.374$, 204.56 , $0.6\bar{6}$ (repeating decimal)

Irrational Numbers: Numbers that **cannot** be expressed in the form of $\frac{a}{b}$, $b \neq 0$
Example: $\sqrt{2}$, π are irrational numbers.

Complex Numbers: These are represented as $a + bi$, where i is the imaginary number. Complex numbers are new to SAT and are covered in a separate lesson.

Q2 What is a number line? Why is it important?

A2 All real numbers can be placed on the number line, shown below.

relative size of numbers, and their signs. The negative numbers are on the left of 0, and the positive numbers are on the right of 0. The numbers increase going from left to right. For example, -4 is greater than -5, -3 is greater than -4, and 0 is greater than -3. Similarly, 4 is greater than 3 and 10 is greater than 4. When numbers are added, subtracted, multiplied, or divided, the resulting numbers fall on the number line. Think of two positive numbers a and b such that $a < b$ and place them on the number line. Now place $-a$ and $-b$ on the number line and verify if $-a < -b$ or $-a > -b$. Verify whether $-2a > -2b$. Number lines help to verify answers to these questions.

Q3 What are the operation rules regarding positive and negative Real numbers?

A3 When you operate on numbers that have positive and negative signs, certain rules must be followed.

Adding numbers	When adding two negative numbers, add the numbers and place a negative sign.	$3 + 4 = 7$ $-3 + (-4) = -(3 + 4) = -7$
Subtracting numbers	When subtracting two numbers, subtract the small number from the large number and place the sign of the large number.	$4 - 3 = 1$ $3 - 4 = -1$
Multiplying numbers	The following sign rules apply for multiplying real numbers. $$(+) \cdot (+) = +$$ $$(+) \cdot (-) = -$$ $$(-) \cdot (+) = -$$ $$(-) \cdot (-) = +$$	$3 \cdot 4 = 12$ $3 \cdot (-4) = -12$ $-3 \cdot 4 = -12$ $-3 \cdot (-4) = +12$
Dividing numbers	The following sign rules apply for dividing real numbers. $$\frac{(+)}{(+)} = +$$ $$\frac{(+)}{(-)} = -$$ $$\frac{(-)}{(+)} = -$$ $$\frac{(-)}{(-)} = +$$	$\frac{12}{4} = 3$ $\frac{12}{-4} = -3$ $\frac{-12}{4} = -3$ $\frac{-12}{-4} = +3$
Comparing numbers	if $a < b$ and $c > 0$ then $ac < bc$ if $a < b$ and $c < 0$ then $ac > bc$ Note that the inequality has changed from $<$ to $>$ when you multiply by the same negative number c on both sides. If $c = -1$, then you have the following rule: if $a < b$ then $-a > -b$	$2 < 5$; so $2 \cdot 3 < 5 \cdot 3$ $-4 < -2$; so $-4 \cdot 3 < -2 \cdot 3$ $2 < 5$; so $2 \cdot (-1) > 5 \cdot (-1)$ i.e $-2 > -5$

Q4 What are the arithmetic properties of Real numbers?

A4 Commutative, Associative, and Distributive properties are described in the table below.

Property	Meaning	Example
Commutative	$a + b = b + a$ $a \cdot b = b \cdot a$ Two numbers can be added or multiplied in any order; this rule does not apply to subtraction and division. $a - b \neq b - a; \frac{a}{b} \neq \frac{b}{a}$	$2 + 3 = 3 + 2$ $3 \cdot 5 = 5 \cdot 3$ $2 - 3 \neq 3 - 2$ $\frac{2}{3} \neq \frac{3}{2}$
Associative	$a + (b + c) = (a + b) + c$ $a \cdot (b \cdot c) = (a \cdot b) \cdot c$ Three numbers can be added or multiplied in any order; this rule does not apply to subtraction and division. $a - (b - c) \neq (a - b) - c$ $\frac{a}{b-c} \neq \left(\frac{a}{b}\right) - c$	$7 + (8 + 9) = (7 + 8) + 9$ $7 \cdot (8 \cdot 9) = (7 \cdot 8) \cdot 9$ $7 - (8 - 9) \neq (7 - 8) - 9$ $\frac{7}{8-9} \neq \frac{7}{8} - 9$
Distributive	$a \cdot (b + c) = (a \cdot b) + (a \cdot c)$ $a \cdot (b - c) = (a \cdot b) - (a \cdot c)$ Multiplication is distributive over addition and subtraction.	$7 \cdot (8 + 9) = 7 \cdot 8 + 7 \cdot 9$ $7 \cdot (8 - 9) = (7 \cdot 8) - (7 \cdot 9)$

Q5 What comparison operations can be performed on Real numbers?

A5 Real numbers can be compared as follows using symbols:

Comparison symbol	Meaning	Example
>	Greater than	$n > 4$
<	Less than	$n < 6$
=	Equal to	$n = 6$
≥	Greater than or equal to	$n \geq 89$
≤	Less than or equal to	$n \leq 77$
≠	Not equal to	$n \neq 5$

Q6 What is PEMDAS?

A6 When you perform arithmetic operations on a series of numbers, use the PEMDAS rule from left to right to decide which operation to perform first. PEMDAS stands for Parenthesis, Exponents, Multiplication, Division, Addition, and Subtraction.

<u>Example:</u> $6-(4 \div 2) \cdot 3^2 = 6 - 2 \cdot 3^2 = 6 - 2 \cdot 9 = 6 - 18 = -12$; parenthesis first and then exponent, and then multiplication, and then subtraction.

<u>Example:</u> $2 - (4 \div 2) + 6 \cdot 3 = 2 - 2 + 6 \cdot 3 = 2 - 2 + 18 = 18$; parenthesis first and then multiplication.

Q7 What are fractions? What are the operations regarding fractions?

A7 Fractions are real numbers that represent parts of a whole. They are of the form $\frac{a}{b}, b \neq 0$, typically with $b > a$. For example, if you ate 3 slices out of 8 slices of pizza, you ate $\frac{3}{8}$ of the pizza. Fractions with $b < a$, such as $\frac{9}{5}$ are called improper fractions. Operations involving fractions are shown in the table below.

Adding fractions	$\frac{a}{b} + \frac{c}{b} = \frac{a+c}{b}$	$\frac{3}{7} + \frac{2}{7} = \frac{3+2}{7} = \frac{5}{7}$
	$\frac{a}{b} + \frac{c}{d} = \frac{ad+bc}{bd}$	$\frac{3}{7} + \frac{2}{5} = \frac{3 \cdot 5 + 2 \cdot 7}{7 \cdot 5} = \frac{29}{35}$
Subtracting fractions	$\frac{a}{b} - \frac{c}{b} = \frac{a-c}{b}$	$\frac{3}{7} - \frac{2}{7} = \frac{3-2}{7} = \frac{1}{7}$
	$\frac{a}{b} - \frac{c}{d} = \frac{ad-bc}{bd}$	$\frac{3}{7} - \frac{2}{5} = \frac{3 \cdot 5 - 2 \cdot 7}{7 \cdot 5} = \frac{1}{35}$
Multiplying fractions Follow the multiplication sign rules for real numbers.	$\frac{a}{b} \cdot \frac{c}{d} = \frac{ac}{bd}$ $(+) \cdot (+) = +$ $(+) \cdot (-) = -$ $(-) \cdot (+) = -$ $(-) \cdot (-) = +$	$\frac{3}{7} \cdot \frac{2}{5} = \frac{3 \cdot 2}{7 \cdot 5} = \frac{6}{35}$ $\frac{3}{8} \cdot -\frac{4}{5} = -\frac{3}{10}$ $-\frac{1}{2} \cdot -\frac{1}{3} = +\frac{1}{6}$
Reciprocal of a fraction.	$\frac{1}{\frac{a}{b}} = \frac{b}{a}$	$\frac{1}{\frac{5}{6}} = \frac{6}{5}$

Dividing fractions Follow the division sign rules for real numbers	$\dfrac{a}{b} \div \dfrac{c}{d} = \dfrac{a}{b} \cdot \dfrac{d}{c}$ $(+)/(+) = +$ $(+)/(-) = -$ $(-)/(+) = -$ $(-)/(-) = +$	$\dfrac{\frac{3}{7}}{\frac{2}{5}} = \dfrac{3}{7} \cdot \dfrac{5}{2} = \dfrac{15}{14}$ $-\dfrac{\frac{2}{5}}{\frac{3}{5}} = -\dfrac{2}{5} \cdot \dfrac{5}{3} = -\dfrac{2}{3}$
Comparing fractions	If $a > b$, then $\dfrac{a}{d} > \dfrac{b}{d}$ provided $d > 0$ To compare $\dfrac{a}{b}$ and $\dfrac{c}{d}$, convert both fractions to the same denominator and then compare.	$\dfrac{4}{5} > \dfrac{2}{5}$; because denominator is same and not negative and $4 > 2$, larger the numerator, larger the fraction $\dfrac{4}{8} > \dfrac{4}{9}$; numerator is same, and $8 < 9$; larger the denominator, smaller the fraction
Reducing fractions	Factorize the numerator and denominator and cancel the common factors.	$\dfrac{8}{24} = \dfrac{2 \cdot 4}{6 \cdot 4} = \dfrac{2}{6} = \dfrac{2}{2 \cdot 3} = \dfrac{1}{3}$ OR $\dfrac{8}{24} = \dfrac{8}{8 \cdot 3} = \dfrac{1}{3}$

Q8 What are decimals? What are the operations regarding decimals?

A8 Decimals are obtained by dividing the numerator of a fraction by its denominator. For example, the fraction of $\dfrac{1}{2}$ is written as 0.5. The fraction $\dfrac{10}{30}$ can be converted to decimal form as 0.333. Use your calculator whenever possible to convert difficult fractions to decimals. For example, the fraction $\dfrac{2}{7}$ can be converted to the decimal 0.286 by using a calculator. Operations on decimals are similar to operations on real numbers.

Adding decimals	When adding two negative decimals, add the numbers and place a negative sign.	$22.45 + 45.20 = 67.65$ $-22.45 - 45.20 = -67.65$
Subtracting decimals	Line up the decimals and subtract. Apply the appropriate signs.	$4.6 - 2.5 = 2.1$ $2.5 - 4.6 = -(4.6 - 2.5) = -2.1$

Multiplying decimals	Multiply the numbers without considering the decimals and then account for the decimal places. Apply the multiplication sign rules for real numbers. $(+) \cdot (+) = +$ $(+) \cdot (-) = -$ $(-) \cdot (+) = -$ $(-) \cdot (-) = +$	$-2.2 \cdot 1.1 = -2.42$ $-1.2 \cdot -2.3 = +2.76$
Dividing decimals	If possible, multiply the numerator and denominator by a multiple of 10 and then simplify. Apply the division sign rules for real numbers. $(+)/(+) = +$ $(+)/(-) = -$ $(-)/(+) = -$ $(-)/(-) = +$	$\frac{2.2}{1.1} = \frac{2.2 \cdot 10}{1.1 \cdot 10} = \frac{22}{11} = 2$

Q9 What is an exponential number?

A9 Numbers written in the form b^x are called exponential numbers. b is called the base and x is called the exponent. b and x can be any real number(integers, fractions, decimals, and they can be positive or negative). b^x is read as b raised to the power of x. For example, 10^3 is read as 10 raised to the power of 3.

Examples: 5^4; 3^{-5}, $7^{\frac{2}{3}}$; $3^{4.2}, 15.6^4, 27^{\frac{1}{3}}, (-3)^2, 8^{\frac{1}{2}}$.

Q10 What are the mathematical rules regarding exponential numbers?

A10 Rules regarding exponential numbers are summarized in the following table. Radicals such as the square root, cube root, etc. are covered in a separate lesson.

Rule	Meaning	Example
$b^0 = 1$	Any non-zero number raised to the power of 0 is defined as 1, 0^0 is undefined.	$100^0 = 1$; $87^0 = 1$
$a^m \cdot a^n = a^{m+n}$	The product of two exponential numbers with the same base is equal to the base raised to the sum of the exponents.	$6^3 \cdot 6^4 = 6^{3+4} = 6^7$ $6^3 \cdot 6^{-4} = 6^{3+(-4)} = 6^{-1}$ This is true only if the base is the same.
$\frac{a^m}{a^n} = a^{m-n}$	The quotient of two exponential numbers with the same base is equal to the base raised to the difference of the exponents.	$\frac{6^5}{6^4} = 6^{5-4} = 6^1$ This is true only if the base is the same.
$(a^m)^n = a^{mn}$	When an exponential number is raised to another exponent, multiply the exponents	$(6^3)^2 = 6^{3 \cdot 2} = 6^6$ $(6^8)^{\frac{1}{2}} = 6^{8 \cdot \frac{1}{2}} = 6^4$

$(ab)^m = a^m b^m$	Two numbers multiplied and raised to a power is the same as the two numbers raised separately to the same power and then multiplied.	$(8 \cdot 7)^4 = 8^4 \cdot 7^4$ conversely $8^4 \cdot 7^4 = (8 \cdot 7)^4$
$a^{-m} = \dfrac{1}{a^m}$ when $m = 1$, $a^{-1} = \dfrac{1}{a}$	A number raised to a negative power equal to -1 is the same as its reciprocal.	$6^{-1} = \dfrac{1}{6}$ $6^{-4} = \dfrac{1}{6^4}$
Fractional Exponents	Numbers can be raised to fractional powers such as $\dfrac{1}{2}, \dfrac{2}{3}$ etc	$5^{\frac{1}{2}}, 6^{\frac{2}{3}}$
Square root	A positive number raised to a power of $\dfrac{1}{2}$ is called its square root, represented by the radical $\sqrt{}$ symbol.	$9^{\frac{1}{2}} = \sqrt{9} = +3$ $7^{\frac{1}{2}} = \sqrt{7}$
Multiplying and dividing square roots.	$\sqrt{a}\sqrt{b} = \sqrt{ab}$ $\dfrac{\sqrt{a}}{\sqrt{b}} = \sqrt{\dfrac{a}{b}}$	$\sqrt{8} \cdot \sqrt{3} = \sqrt{24}$ $\dfrac{\sqrt{9}}{\sqrt{3}} = \sqrt{\dfrac{9}{3}} = \sqrt{3}$
Cube root	A positive number raised to a power of $\dfrac{1}{3}$ is called its cube root, represented by $\sqrt[3]{}$ symbol.	$8^{\frac{1}{3}} = \sqrt[3]{8}, \quad 45^{\frac{1}{3}} = \sqrt[3]{45}$

Q11 What are special operators?

A11 Special operators are operators that are defined in the problem itself. They use special symbols.

<u>Example</u>: If $a♣b = \dfrac{a+b}{a-b}$, what is $3♣4$?

Solution:
Use the definition of the operator ♣. $3♣4 = \dfrac{3+4}{3-4} = -7$

<u>Example</u>: If $a♣b = \dfrac{a+b}{b-a}$, what is $3♣(4♣5)$?

Solution:
Evaluate the value of the expression in the parenthesis by using the definition of the operator ♣.

$4♣5 = \dfrac{4+5}{5-4} = 9$

$3♣(4♣5) = 3♣9 = \dfrac{3+9}{9-3} = \dfrac{12}{6} = 2$

PROBLEM SOLVING AND DATA ANALYSIS
Lesson 1 | Numbers and Operations | Practice

NO CALCULATOR SECTION

1. 2^{16} is equal to

   (A) 4^4
   (B) 4^8
   (C) 8^4
   (D) 8^3

2. $(3^4)^6 =$
   (A) 3^{10}
   (B) 3^{24}
   (C) 3^2
   (D) 3^{-2}

3. $\frac{1}{(3^4)^6} =$
   (A) 3^{-10}
   (B) 3^{24}
   (C) 3^{-24}
   (D) 3^{-2}

4. If $3^{p-2} = 81$, $p^2 =$
   GRID IN

NO CALCULATOR SECTION

5. If $a^m b^m = 16^m$, $\frac{4}{ab}$
   (A) 4
   (B) $\frac{1}{4}$
   (C) $\frac{1}{2}$
   (D) 16

6. If $x^m = 16^m$ and $2^8 = 16^y$, $xy =$
   (A) 8
   (B) 16
   (C) 32
   (D) 64

7. If $x^m = 16$ then $16^3 =$
   (A) x^{2m}
   (B) x^{3m}
   (C) $x^{\frac{m}{3}}$
   (D) x^{m-3}

8. If $\frac{x^m}{x^n} = x^2$ and $x^m x^n = x^4$ then $m \cdot n =$
   (A) 1
   (B) 2
   (C) 3
   (D) 4

NO CALCULATOR SECTION

9. $\sqrt{4}\sqrt{64} =$
(A) $\frac{1}{4}$
(B) 4
(C) 16
(D) 32

10. If $A = x \cdot y$, $3x \cdot 4y =$
(A) 2A
(B) 3A
(C) 4A
(D) 12A

11. $18^m 9^n =$
(A) $9^m 2^{m+n}$
(B) $9^m 2^n$
(C) $9^{m-n} 2^n$
(D) $9^{m+n} 2^m$

12. If $\frac{1}{a^n} \div \frac{1}{b^n} = 15^n$, then $b =$
(A) a
(B) $3a$
(C) $12a$
(D) $15a$

NO CALCULATOR SECTION

13. $\frac{\sqrt[3]{8}}{\sqrt{8}} =$
(A) $\frac{1}{\sqrt{2}}$
(B) $\frac{2}{\sqrt{2}}$
(C) $\frac{\sqrt{2}}{2}$
(D) $\frac{1}{2\sqrt{2}}$

14. $\frac{8^{\frac{2}{3}}}{27^{\frac{4}{3}}} =$
(A) $\frac{2}{81}$
(B) $\frac{4}{81}$
(C) $\frac{2}{27}$
(D) $\frac{4}{27}$

15. How many positive integer values of x satisfy the inequality $\sqrt{x} < 8$?
(A) 7
(B) 8
(C) 63
(D) 64

16. If x is a positive integer and $1 < \sqrt{x} < 3$, the minimum value of $10 - x$ is
GRID IN

NO CALCULATOR SECTION

17. If $\frac{1}{2} \cdot x = \frac{1}{3} \cdot y$, then $\frac{x}{y} =$

(A) $0.2\overline{2}$
(B) $0.3\overline{3}$
(C) $0.5\overline{5}$
(D) $0.6\overline{6}$

18. John shared a 12-slice pizza equally with two of his friends. After his friends ate their share, he ate two thirds of his share. What fraction of the pizza is still left?

(A) $\frac{1}{9}$

(B) $\frac{2}{9}$

(C) $\frac{5}{9}$

(D) $\frac{7}{9}$

19. One third of the cars available for sale in a dealership are used cars. If there are 20 new cars, how many cars are there in the dealership?

(A) 5
(B) 10
(C) 15
(D) 30

NO CALCULATOR SECTION

20. A recipe for one full cake calls for one fourth cup of sugar. If three eights cup of sugar is used, how many cakes were made?

(A) $\frac{3}{2}$

(B) $\frac{5}{2}$

(C) $\frac{7}{2}$

(D) $\frac{1}{3}$

21. One half of a container is filled with water and one eighth of it is filled with milk. If the remaining space can hold 12 gallons of oil, what is the size of the container in gallons?

(A) 8
(B) 16
(C) 32
(D) 64

22. When 4 gallons of gasoline are pumped into a tank that is half full, the tank becomes three fourths full. How many gallons of gasoline does the tank have now?

(A) 4
(B) 8
(C) 12
(D) 16

NO CALCULATOR SECTION

23. A cylindrical bucket has water up to half its height. One fourth of this water was used to water a tree. If 5 gallons of water were used to water the tree, then how much water is left in the bucket?
(A) 10
(B) 15
(C) 40
(D) 80

24. In a pet care facility, two thirds of the animals are dogs and one sixth are cats. If there are 20 animals that are neither dogs nor cats, how many cats are there in the facility?
(A) 20
(B) 80
(C) 100
(D) 120

25. When Jenny finished reading one third of one half of a novel, there were still 40 pages unread. How many pages are there in the novel?
(A) 40
(B) 48
(C) 58
(D) 60

26. After reading one half of a novel and ten percent more, there are still 40 more pages to read. How many pages does the novel have?
(A) 40
(B) 80
(C) 100
(D) 120

NO CALCULATOR SECTION

27. A school that originally had 12 teachers now has only 10. Due to this change, the student to teacher ratio has increased by 5. How many students are there in the school?
(A) 100
(B) 200
(C) 300
(D) 350

28. If a positive integer n is odd, then all of the following are odd EXCEPT
(A) $n(n+2)$
(B) $n(n+1)$
(C) n^2
(D) $n^2 + 2$

29. In the rational number $\frac{2x-1}{2x+1}$, x can take any value EXCEPT
(A) -0.5
(B) 0.5
(C) 0
(D) 1

30. $\frac{9}{8} \cdot \frac{8}{7} \cdot \frac{7}{6} \cdot \frac{6}{5} \cdot \frac{5}{4} \cdot \frac{4}{3} \cdot \frac{3}{2} \cdot \frac{2}{1} =$
(A) 0
(B) 1
(C) 8
(D) 9

31. If $a♣b = \frac{a+b}{a-b}$, and $c♠d = -\frac{c}{d}$ what is the value of $(3♣4)♠11$?
GRID IN

PROBLEM SOLVING AND DATA ANALYSIS

Lesson 1 — Numbers and Operations — Answers

#	Explanation	Comments
1 B	Notice that the answers have different bases, 4, and 8. This gives you a clue to simplify this exponential number to a number with base of 4 or 8. $$2^{16} = 2^{2 \cdot 8} = (2^2)^8 = 4^8$$	Use $a^{mn} = (a^m)^n$
2 B	$(3^4)^6 = 3^{4 \cdot 6} = 3^{24}$	Use $(a^m)^n = a^{mn}$
3 C	$\frac{1}{(3^4)^6} = \frac{1}{3^{24}} = 3^{-24}$	Use $\frac{1}{(a^m)^n} = \frac{1}{a^{mn}} = a^{-mn}$
4 36	$3^{p-2} = 81 = 9^2 = 3^4$ $p - 2 = 4;\, so\, p = 4 + 2 = 6$ $p^2 = 6^2 = 36$	
5 B	$a^m b^m = 16^m$ $(ab)^m = 16^m$ $ab = 16$ $\frac{4}{ab} = \frac{4}{16} = \frac{1}{4}$	Use $a^m b^m = (ab)^m$
6 C	$x^m = 16^m \text{ and } 2^8 = 16^y$ $x^m = 16^m;\, so\, x = 16$ $2^8 = (2^4)^y = 2^{4y}$ $so\, 4y = 8;\, y = 2$ $xy = 16 \cdot 2 = 32$	Pause for a second to observe the given facts and the question; question asks for the product of x and y, and you have two equations—one for x and one for y; so, proceed to find x and y and then xy.
7 B	$x^m = 16$ $16 = x^m$ $16^3 = (x^m)^3 = x^{3m}$	
8 C	$\frac{x^m}{x^n} = x^2$ $x^{m-n} = x^2;\, so\, m - n = 2$ $x^m x^n = x^{m+n} = x^4;\, so\, m + n = 4$ $m - n = 2;$ $m + n = 4;$ adding these equations, you get $2m = 6;$ $m = 3;$ $n = m - 2 = 3 - 2 = 1$ So, $m \cdot n = 3 \cdot 1 = 3$	Get the m and n from the two equations and find the product.
9 C	$\sqrt{4} \cdot \sqrt{64} = 2 \cdot 8 = 16$	
10 D	$A = x \cdot y,$	The question may look confusing, but pause

		$3x \cdot 4y = 12\,xy = 12A$	for a few seconds to observe the question to get a clue.
11	D	$18^m 9^n = (2 \cdot 9)^m 9^n = 2^m 9^m 9^n = 2^m 9^{m+n}$	
12	D	$\dfrac{\frac{1}{a^n}}{\frac{1}{b^n}} = 15^n \quad \dfrac{b^n}{a^n} = 15^n;$ $\left(\dfrac{b}{a}\right)^n = 15^n;\ \dfrac{b}{a} = 15;\ b = 15a$	
13	A	$\dfrac{\sqrt[3]{8}}{\sqrt{8}} = \dfrac{(2^3)^{\frac{1}{3}}}{\sqrt{2 \cdot 4}} = \dfrac{2^1}{2\sqrt{2}} = \dfrac{1}{\sqrt{2}}$	
14	B	$\dfrac{8^{\frac{2}{3}}}{27^{\frac{4}{3}}} = \dfrac{(2^3)^{\frac{2}{3}}}{(3^3)^{\frac{4}{3}}} = \dfrac{2^2}{3^4} = \dfrac{4}{81}$	
15	C	$\sqrt{x} < 8$ squaring both sides; $x < 64$ there are 63 positive integers less than 64 (1 to 63)	
16	2	$1 < \sqrt{x} < 3$, Squaring all sides, $1 < x < 9$ So the minimum values of $10 - x$ is when x is maximum; maximum x value is 8. So $10 - 8 = 2$ is the minimum value of $10 - x$.	Note that $1 < x < 9$; so the maximum integer value of x is 8.
17	D	$\dfrac{1}{2} \cdot x = \dfrac{1}{3} \cdot y$ $\dfrac{x}{y} = \dfrac{1}{3} \cdot 2 = \dfrac{2}{3} = 0.6\overline{6}$	$0.6\overline{6}$ is a repeating decimal.
18	A	John shared the pizza with two of his friends – so his share is $\frac{1}{3}$ of the whole. He ate $\frac{2}{3}$ of his share – so, what is remaining is $\frac{1}{3}$ of his share of the whole pizza = $\frac{1}{3} \cdot \frac{1}{3} = \frac{1}{9}$.	Note that the number of slices of pizza does not matter. It has been given to confuse you. You need to calculate the fraction of the total pizza left – not the fraction of his share – that will be $1 - \frac{2}{9} = \frac{7}{9}$.
19	D	The total number of cars = used cars + new cars $$u = \dfrac{1}{3}(u + 20)$$ $3u = u + 20;\ 2u = 20;\ u = 10;\ n = 20;$ total number of cars = used + new = $10 + 20 = 30$	This is a tricky question; information about used cars is given in fractions and info about new cars is given as an integer. Set up the equation carefully and solve.
20	A	$\frac{1}{4}$ cup of sugar gets you 1 cake $\frac{3}{8}$ cup of sugar = $\frac{1}{\frac{1}{4}} \cdot \frac{3}{8} = \frac{3}{2}$ cakes	See the lesson on Ratio, Rate, and Variation to learn how to setup a direct proportion.
21	C	Let the container hold c gallons $\frac{1}{2}$ is water; $\frac{1}{8}$ is milk. Remaining is $1 - (\frac{1}{2} + \frac{1}{8}) = 1 - \frac{5}{8} = \frac{3}{8}$ of the containter. $\frac{3}{8}$ c = 12 gallons; so c= $12 \cdot \frac{8}{3} = 32$ gallons	Get the clue from the statement "if the remaining space can hold 12 gallons".
22	C	Let the tank capacity be t gallons.	Note the tank levels carefully; the information is given in fractions; set up the

	$\frac{3}{4}t - \frac{1}{2}t = 4$ $\frac{1}{4}t = 4$ $t = 16$ When the tank is $\frac{3}{4}$ full, it has $\frac{3}{4} \cdot 16 = 12$ gallons	equation and know that you still have to calculate how much gasoline is there in the tank when it is $\frac{3}{4}$ full.
23 B	Let b be the capacity of the bucket; water is filled to $\frac{1}{2}$ b. $\frac{1}{4}$ of this water is used for the tree; so $\frac{1}{4} \cdot \frac{1}{2} b = \frac{1}{8} b = 5$; so, b = 40 gallons; originally the bucket had $\frac{1}{2} b = \frac{1}{2} \cdot 40 = 20$ gallons; Now it has $20 - 5 = 15$ gallons.	Pay attention to fractions.
24 A	$\frac{2}{3}$ are dog, $\frac{1}{6}$ are cats, 20 are neither; So $1 - (\frac{2}{3} + \frac{1}{6}) = 1 - \frac{5}{6} = \frac{1}{6}$. So, $\frac{1}{6}$ ·total animals = 20. So, total animals = $6 \cdot 20 = 120$; cats = $\frac{1}{6} \cdot 120 = 20$ cats	Note that the remaining fraction has to be found and equated to 20.
25 B	Let n be the number of pages in the novel $\frac{1}{3} \cdot \frac{1}{2} \cdot n = \frac{1}{6} n$; remaining is $1 - \frac{1}{6} = \frac{5}{6} \cdot n = 40$; $n = 6 \cdot \frac{40}{5} = 48$ pages	Pages that have been read is given in fraction; pages yet to be read is given; find the remaining fraction and equate to 40.
26 C	Let p be the number of pages in a novel After reading $0.5p + 0.1p = 0.6p$, 40 more page are yet to be read – so the remaining pages are $1 - 0.6 p = 0.4p = 40$; $p = \frac{40}{0.4} = \frac{400}{4} = 100$	Calculate the remaining number of pages in decimals.
27 C	Let s be the number of students. When there were 12 teachers, ratio is $\frac{s}{12}$. When there are 10 teachers, ratio is $\frac{s}{10}$. so $\frac{s}{10} - \frac{s}{12} = 5$ $\frac{(12s - 10s)}{120} = 5$ $\frac{2s}{120} = 5$; $s = 5 \cdot \frac{120}{2} = 300$ students	
28 B	Eliminate each answer choice by plugging in an odd number; only $n(n + 1)$ will be an even number.	Pay attention to problems that have EXCEPT in them. The answer choice that does not obey the facts in the question is the correct answer.
29 A	The definition of rational number is $\frac{a}{b}$ where $b \neq 0$; so $2x + 1 \neq 0$ or $x \neq -1/2$	
30 D	$\frac{9}{8} \cdot \frac{8}{7} \cdot \frac{7}{6} \cdot \frac{6}{5} \cdot \frac{5}{4} \cdot \frac{4}{3} \cdot \frac{3}{2} \cdot \frac{2}{1}$ Except 9 and 1, all numbers cancel out Answer is 9/1	Pause and observe the pattern.
31 $\frac{7}{11}$	$a♣b = \frac{a+b}{a-b}$, and $c♠d = \frac{-c}{d}$; $(3♣4)♠11=?$ $(3♣4) = \frac{3+4}{3-4} = -7$. Continuing on, $-7♠11 = -\frac{-7}{11} = \frac{7}{11}$	Pay attention to the definition of the special operation and the symbol of the special operators. There are two different special operators.

PROBLEM SOLVING AND DATA ANALYSIS

| Lesson 2 | Factors and Multiples | Review |

FOCUSPREP CHECKLIST

- What are the divisibility rules for 2, 3, 4, 5, 6, 9, and 10?
- What is the difference between a Factor and a Multiple?
- What are Prime numbers and Composite numbers?
- What are Prime factors? How do I Prime factorize?
- How do I calculate the LCM and GCF?
- Workout practice problems in Factors and Multiples, LCM and GCF

Q1 How do I find out if a number is divisible by 2, 3, 4, 5, etc.

A1 Divisibility rules are shown in the table below.

Divisibility rule for	Rule	Example
2	If the number is even, then it is divisible by 2; A number is even if it ends with either 0,2,4,6 or 8.	1216 is even since it ends with a 6. So it is divisible by 2. 1315 is not divisible by 2.
3	If the sum of the digits of a number is divisible by 3, then it is divisible by 3	453 is divisible by 3 since 4+5+3=12 is divisible by 3.
4	If the last 2 digits of a number are divisible by 4, then it is divisible by 4	552 is divisible by 4 since 52 (last 2 digits) is divisible by 4.
5	If the last digit of a number is 0 or 5, then it is divisible by 5	5095 is divisible by 5 since the last digit is a 5.
6	If a number is divisible by 2 and 3, then it is divisible by 6	1236 is divisible by 2 and 3, so it is divisible by 6.
9	If the sum of the digits of a number is divisible by 9, then it is divisible by 9	189 is divisible by 9 since 1+8+9=18 is divisible by 9.
10	If the last digit of a number is 0, then it is divisible by 10	1010 is divisible by 10, 1005 is not divisible by 10.

Q2 What is the difference between a factor and a multiple?

A2 Factor: A number n is a factor of number x, if the number n divides x without leaving a remainder.
Example: 1,3, and 5 are factors of 15. Each of these factors will divide 15 without leaving a remainder.

Multiple: The multiples of a number x are $x, 2x, 3x, ...$
Example: The multiples of 6 are 6,12,18, etc.

Q3 What are Prime numbers and Composite numbers?

A3 A prime number is a number that has only two factors, 1 and itself. For example, the factors of 11 are 1 and 11, the factors of 13 are 1 and 13, and the factors of 97 are 1 and 97. 11,13, and 97 are examples of prime numbers. By convention, 1 is neither a prime number nor a composite number.

A composite number is a number that has more than two factors. For example, the factors of 12 are 1,2,3,4,6 and 12. There are more than two factors, so it is composite. Note that some of the factors are prime and some are not.

Q4 What is LCM? How do I find it?

A4 LCM is acronym for Least Common Multiple. You can find the LCM of two (or more) numbers by writing the multiples of the two numbers and finding the least multiple that is common to all numbers.

Example: Find the LCM of 12 and 18.
Multiples of 12 are 12, 24, **36**,...
Multiples of 18 are 18, **36**, ..
The first common multiple is 36 and since this is the least common multiple of 12 and 18, the LCM of 12 and 18 is 36.

Q5 What is GCF? How do I find it?

A5 GCF is acronym for Greatest Common Factor. You can find the GCF of two numbers by writing the factors of the two numbers and finding the greatest factor that is common to both numbers.

Example: Find the GCF of 12 and 18.
Factors of 12 are 1,2,3,4,**6**,12
Factors of 18 are 1,2,3,**6**,9

The last common factor is 6 and since this is the greatest common factor of 12 and 18, the GCF of 12 and 18 is 6.

Q6 What does Prime Factorization mean?

A6 Prime factorization is the process of converting a number to a product of prime numbers. Keep breaking the number down to its factors until you cannot anymore.

Example: Prime factorize 28:
Solution: $28 = 2 \cdot 14 = 2 \cdot 7 \cdot 2$. So, $2 \cdot 2 \cdot 7$ is the prime factorization of 28.

Example: Prime factorize 35:
Solution: $35 = 5 \cdot 7$

Example: Prime factorize 156:
Solution: $156 = 2 \cdot 78 = 2 \cdot 3 \cdot 26 = 2 \cdot 3 \cdot 2 \cdot 13$

PROBLEM SOLVING AND DATA ANALYSIS

| Lesson 2 | Factors and Multiples | Practice |

NO CALCULATOR SECTION

1. When a number n is divided by 7, the quotient is 2 and the remainder is x. In terms of n, x is =
(A) $n - 7$
(B) $n - 14$
(C) $n + 7$
(D) $n + 14$

2. The prime factorization of 36 is
(A) $4 \cdot 3^2$
(B) $2^2 \cdot 3^2$
(C) $2^3 \cdot 3^2$
(D) $2^2 \cdot 3^3$

3. Which of the following is true?

I. All even numbers are divisible by 3
II. Some even numbers are divisible by 3
III. No even number is divisible by 3

(A) I only
(B) II only
(C) III only
(D) I and II only

NO CALCULATOR SECTION

4. Maria wants to cut a rope that is 20 feet long into several equal pieces with no rope left over. How many pieces will she have if the length of each piece is the greatest integer possible?
(A) 2
(B) 4
(C) 5
(D) 10

5. Scott has two ropes of length 20 feet and 36 feet respectively. He wants to cut the ropes into several pieces of equal length with no rope left over. What is the most number of pieces he can have if the length of each piece is the greatest integer possible?
(A) 3
(B) 4
(C) 14
(D) 18

6. Stephanie wants to cut two ribbons of length 18 feet and 24 feet respectively into several strings of equal length with no ribbon left over. What is the total number of strings she will have if the strings need to be of maximum length?
(A) 3
(B) 6
(C) 7
(D) 12

©GiftOfLogic http://www.GiftOfLogic.com

NO CALCULATOR SECTION

NO CALCULATOR SECTION

7. The fifth graders at Stinson Elementary are going to the Zoo. The boys have to be in a group of 7 and the girls have to be in a group of 5. If the same number of boys and girls went to the Zoo, what is the least number of students that went to the zoo?
GRID IN

9. The PE teacher at Mockingbird High School needs to split 15 boys and 20 girls into groups such that there are the same number of boys and girls in each group. A group can have boys or girls but not both. If the greatest number of students are there in each group, how many groups are possible?
GRID IN

8. The sixth graders at Otto Middle School are going to the Museum. The boys have to be in a group of 11 and the girls have to be in a group of 22. If the same number of boys and girls went to the Museum, what is the least number of boys that went to the Museum?
GRID IN

10. If p is an even integer, then the remainder when $2p + 1$ is divided by 2 is
GRID IN

	PROBLEM SOLVING AND DATA ANALYSIS	
Lesson 2	Factors and Multiples	Answers

#	Explanation	Comments
1 B	when a number n is divided by 7, the quotient is 2 and the remainder is x. So, $n = 7 \cdot 2 + x$; $x = n - 14$	
2 B	When a number has been prime factorized, it has to be represented with a prime base. Choice A is not correct since it has 4 in its prime factorization and 4 is not prime. Test the other choices to see if they multiply to 36. $2^2 3^2 = 36$	
3 B	All even numbers are NOT divisible by 3; 4 is not divisible by 3. No even number is divisible by 3 is false; 12 is an even number that is divisible by 3. So, choice B is the correct answer – some even numbers are divisible by 3.	
4 A	A 20 feet long rope needs to be cut equally with the condition that each piece is the greatest length possible. The factors of 20 are 1,2,4,5,10,20. If the length is 20 feet, then there is no cut required but the question states that she wants to cut the rope into several pieces. If she cuts the rope such that each length is 10 feet, then there will be $\frac{20}{10} = 2$ pieces of rope.	After listing the factors, apply the constraints – in this problem, there should be several pieces left after the cut – so 20 is not a valid choice for the length.
5 C	Factors of 20 are 1,2,4,5,10,20 Factors of 36 are 1,2,3,4,6,9,18,36 The GCF of 20 and 36 is 4. He should cut the 20 feet and 36 feet ropes into pieces that are 4 units long. So, he will have $\frac{20}{4} = 5$ pieces and $\frac{36}{4} = 9$ pieces, a total of $5 + 9 = 14$ pieces.	
6 C	The two ribbons are 18 feet and 24 feet long. If the cut strings need to be maximum length, then the GCF of 18 and 24 will yield that length. Note that the string must be of equal length. Factors of 18 are 1,2,3,6,18 Factors of 24 are 1,2,3,4,6,12,24 GCF of 18 and 24 is 6. So, each ribbon must be cut such that the length of the strings are 6 feet each. The question asks for the total number of strings - she will have 3 strings after cutting the 18 feet string ($\frac{18}{6} = 3$), and 4 more strings after cutting the 24 feet string ($\frac{24}{6} = 4$) – so a total of 3+4=7 strings	Don't just calculate the GCF and think you got the answer. Make sure you understand what the question is – it may require you to use the GCF.
7 70	Boys have to be in group of 7; girls in group of 5 Same number of boys and girls went to the zoo Multiples of 7 are 7,14,21,28,35,..	Know when to use LCM and when to use GCF.

©GiftOfLogic http://www.GiftOfLogic.com

	Multiples of 5 are 5,10,15,20,25,30,35,… LCM of 7 and 5 is 35. So, 35 boys and 35 girls went to the zoo; boys in group of 7 and girls in groups of 5. Totally 35+35=70 students went to the zoo	
8 22	This is a LCM question; Multiples of 11 are 11,22,33,… Multiples of 22 are 22,44,66, LCM= 22 22 boys and 22 girls went to the zoo.	This question forces you to use the LCM.
9 7	This is a GCF question; Factors of 15 are 1,3,5,15 Factors of 20 are 1,2,4,5,20 GCF is 5. Each group has 5 boys or 5 girls. So, the total number of groups = $\frac{15}{5} + \frac{20}{5} = 3 + 4 = 7$	This question forces you to use the GCF.
10 1	p is an even integer when $p = 0,2,4,6..$ etc, $2p + 1\ is$ 1,5,9,13,…etc so, when $2p + 1$ is divided by 2, the remainder is always 1.	

PROBLEM SOLVING AND DATA ANALYSIS

Lesson 3 — Word Problems — Review

FOCUSPREP CHECKLIST

- How do I translate word problems from English to Math?
- Workout practice Word problems

Q1 What are Word problems?

A1 Word problems are problems that describe real life situations verbally. You have to convert them to mathematical form using variables, constants, etc. and then apply mathematical principles to solve the problem.

Q2 What should I know before doing Word problems?

A2 The following table shows statements and their equivalent mathematical expressions. When you solve a word problem, you can use the first letter of the person or thing to write the math expression. For example, if the phrase is "John is eight years older than Mary", use J for John and M for Mary. Naming variables like this will help you to avoid confusion when dealing with them.

Topic	Word problem	Math expression
Addition	John is eight years older than Mary	$J = M + 8$
	John ate three more apples than Mary	$J = M + 3$
	John has four more dollars than Brandi	$J = B + 4$
	When 3 is added to a number you get 9	$X + 3 = 9$
	The sum of two numbers is 19	$X + Y = 19$
	A number increased by 10 is equal to 50	$X + 10 = 50$
Subtraction	John is six years younger than Mary	$J = M - 6$
	John's age is six years less than Mary's	$J = M - 6$
	John's age is 6 less 4	$J = 6 - 4 = 2$
	John ate three apples less than Mary	$J = M - 3$
	John has 7 dollars less than Linda	$J = L - 7$
	100 less than the weight of the box is 20	$w - 100 = 20$
	The difference of two numbers is 250	$X - Y = 250$
	55 subtracted from a number yields 22	$X - 55 = 22$
	A number when decreased by 40 gives 80	$X - 40 = 80$
	John's salary was reduced by 100	$S = J - 100$
Multiplication	Area of a carpet is 3 by 4.	$A = 3 \cdot 4 = 12$
	The product of 6 and a number is 24	$6 \cdot n = 24$
	The cost of a red shirt is twice the cost of a blue shirt	$r = 2 \cdot b$
Division	8 people shared the cost of a cake equally	$\dfrac{c}{8}$
	A number, when divided by 6, yields 3 without a remainder	$\dfrac{x}{6} = 3$
	A number, when divided by 6, yields 3 with a remainder of 1	$x = 6 \cdot 3 + 1$

	A number m multiplied by 5 is the same the number n divided by 6	$m \cdot 5 = \dfrac{n}{6}$
	The quotient is 7 when a number is divided by 8	$\dfrac{n}{8} = 7$
Fraction	One half of all the money was spent on movies	$M = \dfrac{1}{2} \cdot T$; where T=Total, M=movies
	One half of one third of 24 is your share	$\dfrac{1}{2} \cdot \dfrac{1}{3} \cdot 24$
	Two thirds of this 24 gallon tank is empty	$\dfrac{2}{3} \cdot 24 = 16$
Percentage	The shirt is discounted by 20% off the price.	$D = \dfrac{20}{100} \cdot P = 0.2\, P$ D = Discount P=Price
	X is 22 percent of Y	$X = \dfrac{22}{100} \cdot Y = 0.22Y$
	Four percent of a number is 10	$0.04 \cdot x = 10$
	The price (p) of the sweater was increased by 12%	$p + \dfrac{12}{100}p = 1.12p$
	The price (p) of the sweater was decreased by 12%	$p - \dfrac{12}{100}p = 0.88p$
Limits	The new car will cost at least $20,000	$c \geq 20000$
	The new car will cost at most $20,000	$c \leq 20{,}000$
	The red watch costs more than the blue watch	$r > b$
	The red watch costs less than the blue watch	$r < b$
Combination	20 plus a number equals 13 minus the number.	$20 + x = 13 - x$
	20 plus a number equals the number less 13.	$20 + x = x - 13$
	x is twice as much as y	$x = 2y$
	20 percent of a number is greater than 100	$0.2\, x > 100$
	Six times a number increased by two is 15	$6x + 2 = 15$
	The difference of three times and two times a number is 99	$3x - 2x = 99$
	One fourth of the difference between x and 2 is 9	$\dfrac{1}{4} \cdot (x - 2) = 9$
	The square of a number is 121	$x^2 = 121$
	The square of 2 more than a number is 9	$(x + 2)^2 = 9$
	Price of the watch plus 10 is hundred dollars or less	$p + 10 \leq 100$

PROBLEM SOLVING AND DATA ANALYSIS		
Lesson 3	Word Problems	Practice

NO CALCULATOR SECTION

1. If the ratio of 7 less than a number and 7 more than the number is 2, what is the number?
(A) −21
(B) −7
(C) 7
(D) 14

2. The sum of two numbers x and y is at least 10 and at most 50. This fact can be expressed as
(A) $10 < x + y < 50$
(B) $10 \leq x + y < 50$
(C) $10 < x + y \leq 50$
(D) $10 \leq x + y \leq 50$

3. If 12 times a number is 40 more than 2 times the number, the number is
(A) 1
(B) 2
(C) 3
(D) 4

4. In a game, Mark scored 3 more than twice what Nancy scored. Nancy scored 2 less than 4 times what Olivia scored. If Olivia scored 2 points, what did Mark score?
(A) 10
(B) 12
(C) 15
(D) 18

NO CALCULATOR SECTION

5. Andy is as old today as John was 10 years ago. Which one of the following choices is true?
I Andy is older than John
II John is older than Andy
III John is 20 years old
(A) I only
(B) II only
(C) III only
(D) II and III only

6. If one fourth of the difference between a number and 2 is 9, the number is
(A) 36
(B) 37
(C) 38
(D) 40

7. Paula and Olivia have a total of $60. Olivia has three times as much as Paula. How much does Paula have?
(A) 5
(B) 10
(C) 15
(D) 20

8. If 0.05 percent of a number is 1, then 2 percent of the number is
(A) 10
(B) 20
(C) 30
(D) 40

NO CALCULATOR SECTION

9. If the square of 2 more than a number is 9, the number could be
(A) -5
(B) -4
(C) -3
(D) -1

10. Tim had $100 in his bank account at the beginning of the month. During the month, he withdrew w dollars and deposited d dollars. If the deposit was twice as much as the withdrawal, then how much did he deposit if he had a balance of $150 at the end of the month?
GRID IN

11. If the square of the sum of two numbers is the same as the square of the difference of the two numbers, then one of the numbers must be
GRID IN

12. If the radius of a circle is doubled, by what factor will the area increase by?
GRID IN

13. The length of a rectangle is increased by 10 percent. By how much percent should the width be decreased if the area is to be kept the same?
(A) 0.91
(B) 1.1
(C) 9
(D) 11

14. A cab driver charges $5 for the first 0.75 miles, $8 for the subsequent 0.25 miles, and $2 for each additional mile. How many miles can you travel in the cab if you paid $50?
GRID IN

15. Playing golf costs a one-time $50.25 deposit and an additional 25.75 dollars per game. How many full games can be played for $1500?
GRID IN

CALCULATOR SECTION

PROBLEM SOLVING AND DATA ANALYSIS
Lesson 3 — Word Problems — Answers

#	Explanation	Comments
1 A	Let x be the number; $$\frac{x-7}{x+7} = 2$$ $x - 7 = 2(x+7) = 2x + 14$ $x = -21$	Set the ratio carefully; note the phrases "7 less than" and "7 more than"
2 D	"Sum of x and y is at least 10" is expressed as $10 \leq x + y$; Sum of x and y is at most 50 is expressed as $x + y \leq 50$; combining them, you get $10 \leq x + y \leq 50$	Note the difference between $<$ and $\leq, >,$ and $\geq$ signs.
3 D	The word problem can be translated to math as $12x = 2x + 40$ $10x = 40; x = 4$	
4 C	Let m be the score for Mark and n be the score for Nancy and o be the score for Olivia. "Mark scored 3 more than twice what Nancy scored" can be translated to math as $m = 3 + 2n$. "Nancy scored 2 less than 4 times what Olivia scored" can be translated as $n = 4o - 2$; "Olivia scored 2 points" can be translated to $o = 2$. Put all these equations together and solve. $m = 2n + 3$ $n = 4o - 2$ $o = 2$ $m = 2n + 3 = 2(4o - 2) + 3 = 8o - 4 + 3$ $= 8 \cdot 2 - 4 + 3 = 15$	Using variables like $m, n,$ and o to correspond to the Mark, Nancy, and Olivia will help you to stay focused on the problem. If you use variables like $x, y,$ and z then you will waste time trying to figure out what each variable represents.
5 B	Note that the problem talks about their ages today and 10 years ago. Let a be Andy's age today and j be John's age today. "Andy is as old today as John was 10 years ago" can be translated to $a = j - 10$, since John was $j - 10$ years old 10 years ago. So, John is older than Andy. Choice B is true. In problems of the Roman Numeral type, you must also evaluate other choices. Choice A is false. Choice C is false since you cannot infer that John was 20 years old. Only choice B is correct.	In problems with choices given in Roman Numerals, evaluate all the choices and then select your answer choice.
6 C	"one fourth of the difference between a number and 2 is 9" can be translated to $\frac{1}{4} \cdot (x - 2) = 9$. $x - 2 = 9 \cdot 4 = 36; x = 38$	You could argue that this equation could be set up as $\frac{1}{4} \cdot (2 - x) = 9$; when in doubt, go with the most straight forward math translation. The problem says "difference between a number and 2", with "number" mentioned first and then "2" mentioned after that. So go with $x - 2$.

©GiftOfLogic http://www.GiftOfLogic.com

7 C	"Paula and Olivia have a total of $60" can be translated to $p + o = 60$; "Olivia has three times as much as Paula" can be translated to $o = 3p$ Solve by substitution; $p + o = p + 3p = 60$ $4p = 60$ $p = 15$	
8 D	0.05 percent of a number is 1 $\frac{0.05}{100} x = 1$ $x = \frac{100}{0.05}$ 2 percent of the number = $\frac{2}{100} \cdot \frac{100}{0.05} = \frac{2}{0.05} = \frac{200}{5} = 40$	x percent of y is translated as $\frac{x}{100} \cdot y$
9 A	square of 2 more than a number is 9 can be translated as $(x + 2)^2 = 9$ $x + 2 = \pm 3$ $x = -2 + 3 = 1$ or $-2 - 3 = -5$ Choice A is -5, and is the correct answer.	If you arrive at two solutions, and only one solution is in the answer choice, pick that choice.
10 100	Initial amount = 100, withdraw w and deposit d Balance = 150, $d = 2w$ $100 - w + d = 150$ $100 - w + 2w = 150$ $100 + w = 150$ $w = 50$; so $d = 2w = 100$	
11 0	$(x + y)^2 = (x - y)^2$ $x^2 + 2xy + y^2 = x^2 - 2xy + y^2$ $4xy = 0; xy = 0$ Since $xy = 0$, either x or y must be 0.	
12 4	$A = \pi r^2$ After the radius is doubled, $A = \pi (2r)^2 = 4\pi r^2$ The question asks by what factor does the area increase- this is the same as asking "how many times" – new area/ old area= factor = $\frac{4\pi r^2}{\pi r^2} = 4$.	By what "factor" something has increased or decreased – is the same as finding the ratio of the new quantity to the old quantity. For example if the price of bread increased from $4 to $5, it increased by a factor of $\frac{5}{4} = 1.25$. Note that this is NOT the same as calculating the percentage increase or decrease.
13 C	Old area $A = l \cdot w$ New area $\acute{A} = 1.1l \cdot \acute{w}$ Old area= new Area	Note that the question asks "by how much percent should the width be decreased." This is different from asking "by what factor

35

		$lw = 1.1l\,\acute{w}$ $w = 1.1\,\acute{w}$ $\acute{w} = \dfrac{1}{1.1}w = 0.91\,w$; use calculator So, the old width w has to be reduced to $0.91\,w$ This is a percentage decrease of $\dfrac{0.91w - 1w}{w} \cdot 100 = 9\%$	should the width be decreased "
14 19.5		$5 for the first 0.75 miles; $8 for the next 0.25 miles, $2 each additional mile. How many miles can you travel for $50? Let m me the miles traveled for $50; m miles can be broken down, based on each fare segment; this must to add up to m miles; $m = 0.75 + 0.25 + (m - 1)$; The first mile is included in the m. Now apply the fares to each segment $5 + 8 + (m - 1) \cdot 2 = 50$ $13 + 2m - 2 = 50$ $2m = 39$ $m = 19.5\ miles$	In these "cab driver" type of problems, first break down the total miles that you are calculating based on the fare segments and then apply the fares to each segment; this will help you avoid making mistakes; review the answer to this question to see how this is done.
15 56		Let n be the number of games that you can play for $1500; the total cost of playing n games must be less than or equal to 1500. $50.25 + 25.75n <= 1500$ $25.75n <= 1500 - 50.25 = 1449.75$ $n = 56.30$ Since the question asks "how many full games" can be played, the answer is 56.	

PROBLEM SOLVING AND DATA ANALYSIS
Lesson 4 — Ratio, Rate, and Variation — Review

FOCUSPREP CHECKLIST

- What is a Ratio? Is it the same as a proportion?
- What is a Rate?
- What are Direct and Inverse variations?
- How do I solve problems with direct and inverse variations?
- Workout practice problems in Ratio, Rate, and Variation

Q1 What is a Ratio? What is a proportion?

A1 The ratio of two quantities a and b is defined as the quotient of $\frac{a}{b}$ where $b \neq 0$. Proportion is the fraction of one quantity with respect to the whole. From this fraction, you can calculate the percentage.

Example: There are 50 boys and 20 girls in a class. So, the ratio of boys to girls is $\frac{50}{20}$ which can be simplified as $\frac{5}{2}$. The proportion of boys in the class is $\frac{5}{7} \cdot 100$ and the percentage of boys in the class is $\frac{5}{7} \cdot 100 = 71.43\%$.

Example: There are 700 students in a school. The ratio of boys to girls is $5:2$. How many boys are there?
Solution: The proportion of boys with respect to the whole is $\frac{5}{5+2} = \frac{5}{7}$. So the number of boys = $\frac{5}{7} \cdot 700 = 500$.

Q2 Can ratios be reduced like fractions?

A2 Since ratios are fractions, you can reduce them: $\frac{A}{B} = \frac{2}{6}$ can be reduced to $\frac{A}{B} = \frac{1}{3}$. For example, if the ratio of boys to girls is $50:20$, you can reduce it to $5:2$ without loss of meaning.

Q3 How do I specify ratios between three quantities?

A3 If you have two ratios P:Q and Q:R involving three quantities P, Q, and R, then the ratio of the three quantities is P:Q:R. Note that Q must be the same number in both ratios.
Example: P:Q = 1:3 Q:R = 3:4, since Q=3 in both ratios, the ratio P:Q:R = 1:3:4

Example: P:Q = 1:4 Q:R = 8:16 What is P:Q:R? What percentage of the whole is R?
Solution: Since Q is not the same in both ratios, you make it the same by reducing Q:R from 8:16 to 4:8. Now P:Q = 1:4 and Q:R = 4:8. So P:Q:R = 1:4:8. R is $\frac{8}{1+4+8} = \frac{8}{13}$ of the whole or $\frac{8}{13} \cdot 100 = 61.5\%$ of the whole.

Q4 In what context can I expect to see problems on ratios?

A4 You will encounter ratios in problems typically in Social and Scientific contexts.
Examples : in Physics- Velocity = distance/ time; Current = Voltage/ Resistance; in Economics - Per capita income=Total Income / population ; in Business: P/E ratio= Stock Price/ Earnings.

Q5 What is a Rate?

A5 Rate is the change of one quantity with respect to unit-change of another and is expressed in the form of a ratio.
Examples: speed= 20 miles/hour; snow accumulation = 3 inches/hour; Taxi rate= $10/mile; Phone call charge= $0.20/minute; mowing rate=1/3 lawn/hr.

Examples:
If a man can paint 8 houses in 2 days – his rate of work is 8 houses/2 days = 4 houses/day.
If Tom takes 5 hours to mow a lawn, his rate of work is $\frac{1}{5}$ lawn/hr
If a car travels 100 miles in 2 hours, its rate of distance covered (speed) is 100/20=50 miles/hr
If a contractor charges $800 for 8 hours of work, his rate of pay is 800/8=$100/hr

You can see the different units of measure in the numerator and denominator. Problems involving Rate appear in distance problems, machine capacity problems, work rate problems, and direct and inverse relation problems.

Q6 What does a typical distance problem look like?

A6 **Example**: Tim drives from home to work at the rate of 20 miles/hour and drives back to home at the rate of 30 miles/hour. If he drives for 3 hours in total, how much distance does he travel?
Solution: Speed=s=$\frac{distance}{time}$ =$\frac{d}{t}$; $t = \frac{d}{s}$, where d is the one-way distance from home to work. You know the speed and time; you know that total time $t = 3$ hrs= time to work+ time to home. So $3 = \frac{d}{20} + \frac{d}{30}$; $3 = \frac{50d}{600} = \frac{d}{12}$; $d = 36$; but this is one way distance; so the total distance = $2d = 2 \cdot 36 = 72$ miles.

Q7 When are variables said to be in <u>DIRECT</u> relationship (or direct variation)?

A7 Two variables are in direct relationship(variation) when one increases as the other increases, maintaining a constant ratio at all times. For example, when P is in DIRECT variation with Q, $\frac{P}{Q} = k$, where k is the constant of proportionality. For example, the more hours a contractor works, the more money he makes – so the money he makes is in DIRECT variation with the hours that he works.

If four numbers a, b, c, d are in DIRECT proportion, then $\frac{a}{b} = \frac{c}{d}$.

Q8 When are variables in an <u>INVERSE</u> relationship (or inverse variation)?

A8 Two variables are in inverse variation when one increases as the other decreases. For example, when P is in INVERSE variation with Q, then $P = \frac{k}{Q}$ or $PQ = k$, where k is the constant of proportionality. For example, if more men are available to do a job, then it will take less time to finish the job - so the number of men available and the time taken to finish the job are in INVERSE variation.

Q9 What is the procedure for solving DIRECT and INVERSE variation problems?

A9 DIRECT and INVERSE variation problems can appear in work rate problems, capacity problems, labor problems etc. Follow these steps to solve the problem.
Step 1: Identify the variables involved and their relationship (DIRECT or INVERSE)
Step 2: Write the information with the unknown quantity x that you are trying to find at the bottom right as shown below.

a   c
b   x

Step 3: Setup the ratio for DIRECT or INVERSE variation and solve for the unknown variable.
DIRECT variation: $\frac{a}{b} = \frac{c}{x}$ or $\frac{b}{a} = \frac{x}{c}$
INVERSE variation: **Flip only one** of the ratios: $\frac{a}{b} = \frac{x}{c}$ or $\frac{b}{a} = \frac{c}{x}$
Step 4: Cross multiply and solve for x.

Q10 What does a typical labor problem look like?

A10 <u>Example</u>: Tim will take 3 hours to paint one room. How long will he take to paint 2 rooms?
<u>Solution</u>: step 1: identify the variables and their relation- time to paint and number of rooms.
Clearly, if he takes 2 hours to paint 1 room, he is going to take more time to paint 2 rooms. So, the time and number of rooms are in DIRECT variation.
step 2: Write the given information so that the quantity you are trying to find is at the bottom right.
1 room   3 hours
2 rooms x hours
step 3: setup the ratio for DIRECT variation
$\frac{1}{2} = \frac{3}{x}$. Cross multiply to get $x = 3 \cdot 2 = 6$

<u>Example</u>: 20 men can do a job in 3 hours. How many men are needed to do the same job in 2 hours?
<u>Solution</u>: step 1: Identify variables and relation: number of men and time to do the job. Less time to do the job means more men are needed –so, they are in inverse relationship. step 2: write the information such that the quantity that you are trying to find is on the bottom right.

3 hours   20 men
2 hours x men
step 3: setup the ratio for INVERSE variation, remember to <u>flip</u> one of the ratios.

$$\frac{3}{2} = \frac{x}{20}$$

$$x = \frac{3}{2} \cdot 20 = 30$$

$x = 30$; so 30 men are required to do the job in 2 hours.

Q11 What does a typical capacity problem look like?

A11 Capacity Problems involve rate at which machines output certain products. Pay attention to unit of time in the question (seconds,minutes,hours). Also verify whether the problem is a direct or inverse relation/variation problem.

Example: A machine has a capacity to make 300 buttons/hour. How many buttons can it make in 45 minutes?

Solution step 1: identify variables and relation - number of buttons and time; more time, more buttons – DIRECT variation step 2: write the info in correct format so that the quantity you are trying to find is at bottom right; all quantities of the same type should be in the same units; for example time should be in minutes.

    60 minutes 300 buttons
    45 minutes x buttons

step 3: setup the ratio for direct relation

$\frac{60}{45} = \frac{300}{x}$; cross multiply

$$x = \frac{45}{60} \cdot 300 = 225$$

Q12 Can rate problems have 3 variables? How do I solve them?

A12 Rate problems can have 3 variables – for example, number of men, number of jobs, and time. You need to know how to calculate the work rate per hour and how to set up direct and inverse relations. Remember that for inverse relationships, flip the numbers in only one ratio and then cross multiply.

Example: 4 men can do 1 job in 3 hours. What fraction of a job can be completed by 1 man in 8 hours?
Solution:

4 men – 1 job – 3 hrs;
1 man- x job – 8 hrs;

The work rate of 4 men is $\frac{1}{3}$ job/hr; so work rate of 1 man is $\frac{\frac{1}{3}}{4} = \frac{1}{12}$ job/hr; The question is what portion of the job can 1 man do in 8 hours? You know 1 man can do $\frac{1}{12}$ job/hr.

1 hour $\frac{1}{12}$ job
8 hours x job

Set up the direct relation ratio

$$\frac{1}{8} = \frac{\frac{1}{12}}{x} = \frac{1}{12x}$$

$$12x = 8; \quad x = \frac{8}{12} = \frac{2}{3}$$

So, in 8 hours, he will do $\frac{2}{3}$ job.

Example: 4 men can do 1 job in 3 hours. How long will it take 1 man to finish 2 jobs?

4 men – 1 job - 3 hrs

1 man- 2 jobs – x hrs

The work rate of 4 men is $\frac{1}{3}$ job/hr; work rate of 1 man is $\frac{\frac{1}{3}}{4} = \frac{1}{12}$ job/hr;

$\frac{1}{12}$ job   1 hour

2 jobs x hours

Set up a DIRECT variation equation:

$$\frac{\frac{1}{12}}{2} = \frac{1}{x}$$

$$\frac{1}{24} = \frac{1}{x}$$

$$x = 24$$

So, 1 man will take 24 hours for 2 jobs;

Example: 4 men can do 1 job in 3 hours. How many men will it take to do 2 jobs in 4 hours?

4 men – 1 job – 3 hrs

x men - 2 jobs – 4 hrs;

4 men-1 job- 3 hrs;

so 4 men – 2 jobs – 6 hours, since they are doing double the work

But, you need to find how many men can do 2 jobs in 4 hours. Since the 2 jobs need to be done in less time – 4 hours instead of 6, more men will be needed. This is INVERSE variation. Setup the ratio as follows. Remember to flip one ratio, since this is an INVERSE relation.

6 hrs 4 men

4 hrs x men

$\frac{6}{4} = \frac{x}{4}$; so $x = 6$ men

PROBLEM SOLVING AND DATA ANALYSIS

Lesson 4 | Ratio, Rate, and Variation | Practice

NO CALCULATOR SECTION

1. If the four numbers $\frac{1}{40}, \frac{1}{80}, \frac{1}{70}, \frac{1}{x}$ form a proportion, what is the value of x?
(A) 6
(B) 7
(C) 14
(D) 140

2. If 20 men can build a home in 360 days, how many men are needed to build the home in 150 days?
(A) 6
(B) 12
(C) 24
(D) 48

NO CALCULATOR SECTION

3. George takes 3 hours to mow a lawn. Jacob takes 6 hours to mow the same lawn. How long will it take if both of them mow 3 lawns together?
(A) 3
(B) 6
(C) 9
(D) 12

4. A piece of ribbon is cut into three pieces that have lengths in the ratio 7:8:9. The length of the ribbon is 96 centimeters. Each centimeter is worth 75 cents. How much does the smallest piece of ribbon cost in <u>dollars</u>?
(A) 2.10
(B) 19.00
(C) 21.00
(D) 27.00

NO CALCULATOR SECTION

5. If x is an integer such that $-3 \leq x \leq 0$ and k is an integer such that $-8 \leq k \leq 17$. What is the largest possible value of $\frac{x}{k}$?

(A) $-\frac{3}{8}$

(B) 3

(C) $\frac{3}{17}$

(D) $\frac{3}{8}$

6. Machine A can make 8 toys in one hour. Machine B can make 9 toys in 30 minutes. If each machine works simultaneously, how many toys will be made after 90 minutes?
(A) 26
(B) 29
(C) 36
(D) 39

NO CALCULATOR SECTION

7. Bob drives from home to a shopping center at 30 miles/hr and returns back at 20 miles/hr. If he takes 60 minutes for the round trip, how much distance in miles did he drive in total?
(A) 12
(B) 24
(C) 600
(D) 720

8. If $\frac{x}{z} = \frac{3}{4}$, then what is $\frac{100x}{32z}$?

(A) $\frac{32}{75}$

(B) $\frac{3}{4}$

(C) $\frac{25}{32}$

(D) $\frac{75}{32}$

NO CALCULATOR SECTION

9. The number of pencils that Pam has is inversely proportional to the number of erasers that she has. When she has 120 pencils, she has 2 erasers. How many erasers will she have when she has 80 pencils?
(A) 1
(B) 2
(C) 3
(D) 4

Gums	Mint
1000	50
1250	40

10 The number of Bubble Gum and Mint candies sold are related as shown in the table. If 2500 Bubble gums are sold, how many Mint candies will be sold?
(A) 10
(B) 20
(C) 25
(D) 40

NO CALCULATOR SECTION

11. The length of a rectangle of x units is increased by 10% and its width of y units is increased by 15%. What is the ratio of the area of the old rectangle to the area of the new rectangle?
(A) 1:1.0265
(B) 1:1.265
(C) 1:1.562
(D) 1.625:1

12 A farmer loads bags of rice, wheat, and corn into his truck. The ratio of the weight of rice to that of wheat is 2 to 3.1. The ratio of the weight of wheat to that of corn is 6.2 to 1. Which of the following loadings, in pounds, is possible?
(A) Rice 200, Wheat 410, Corn 620
(B) Rice 400, Wheat 310, Corn 100
(C) Rice 200, Wheat 310, Corn 620
(D) Rice 400, Wheat 620, Corn 100

CALCULATOR SECTION

13. Rachel invested $100 at a bank that gives a simple interest of 3% per year. She invested another $100 at a Credit Union that gives her a simple interest of 5% per year. After one year, what is the ratio of her balance at the bank to that of her balance at the credit union?
(A) 0.6
(B) 0.66
(C) 0.89
(D) 0.98

14 The ratio of poor people to rich people in a town in the year 1990 was 6 to 1. The same ratio in the year 2000 was 10 to 3. What is the percent increase of rich people in the town from 1990 to 2000?
(A) 2.67
(B) 6.69
(C) 8.79
(D) 9.23

CALCULATOR SECTION

15. A box contains two red balls, five green balls, and eight blue balls. The number of red balls is directly proportional to the number of green balls. The number of green balls is inversely proportional to the number of blue balls. If the number of green balls is increased to twenty, then what is the ratio of red balls to blue balls?
GRID IN

PROBLEM SOLVING AND DATA ANALYSIS
Lesson 4 — Ratio, Rate, and Variation — Answers

#		Explanation	Comments
1	D	If four numbers, A, B, C and D form a proportion, then $\frac{A}{B} = \frac{C}{D}$. In this question, the numbers are fractions. $$\frac{\frac{1}{40}}{\frac{1}{80}} = \frac{\frac{1}{70}}{\frac{1}{x}}$$ $$\frac{80}{40} = \frac{x}{70}; \quad x = 140$$	4 numbers a,b,c,d are in direct proportion if $\frac{a}{b} = \frac{c}{d}$.
2	D	20 men – 360 days 150 days – how many men; step1: days and men – less days will require more men – inverse variation; step 2: write the facts down with unknown quantity at bottom right 360 days 20 men 150 days x men step3: setup the equation for inverse relation; flip one of the ratios. $$\frac{x}{20} = \frac{360}{150}$$ $$x = \frac{360}{150} \cdot 20 = 48 \text{ men}$$	While setting up the equation for INVERSE variation, remember to flip one of the ratios. See review section for solved examples.
3	B	George takes 3 hrs/lawn; his rate of work is $\frac{1}{3}$ lawn/hr Jacob takes 6 hrs/lawn; his rate of work is $\frac{1}{6}$ lawn/hr If they work together, they will mow $\frac{1}{3} + \frac{1}{6} = \frac{1}{2}$ lawn/hr $\frac{1}{2}$ lawn – 1 hr 3 lawns – x hrs DIRECT relation $$\frac{\frac{1}{2}}{3} = \frac{1}{x}$$ $$\frac{x}{2} = 3$$ $$x = 6 \text{ hrs}$$	Calculating the rate of work is important to solve this problem.
4	C	You have to find the cost of $\frac{7}{24}$ of the 96 centimeter ribbon. $\frac{7}{24} \cdot 96 = 28$ centimeters. $28 \cdot 75 = 2100$ cents. Converting this to dollars gives $21.00.	The smallest portion of a ribbon that is cut in the ratio of 7:8:9 is $\frac{7}{7+8+9} = \frac{7}{24}$.
5	B	The largest possible value of $\frac{x}{k}$ is obtained when $x = -3$ and $k = -1$. This makes the fraction equal to $\frac{-3}{-1} = 3$.	

©GiftOfLogic http://www.GiftOfLogic.com

6	D	Machine A: 8 toys in 60 minutes Machine B: 9 toys in 30 minutes, meaning 18 toys in 60 minutes. Totally 8+18=26 toys in 60 minutes. The question is how many toys in 90 minutes. 60 minutes 26 toys 90 minutes x toys More time, more toys ; so DIRECT variation $\frac{60}{90} = \frac{26}{x}$ $60x = 26 \cdot 90$ $x = 26 \cdot \frac{90}{60} = 26 \cdot \frac{3}{2} = 39$	
7	B	Speed=distance/time; so time=distance/speed; you know the speed for the two segments ; let d be the distance from home to shopping center. Total time t= 1 hr = time to shopping + time to home; $1 = \frac{d}{30} + \frac{d}{20} = \frac{50}{600}d$; so $d = 12$ miles. Remember that this is just one-way; so the total distance= $2 \cdot 12 = 24$ miles.	Remember to keep the unit of time as hours – the equation must have 1 hour – not 60 minutes – since the speed is in miles/hour.
8	D	Take a few seconds to just "look" at the problem to see if there is any pattern or trick that you can identify. If $\frac{x}{z} = \frac{3}{4}$, then $\frac{100x}{32z} = \frac{100}{32} \cdot \frac{x}{z} = \frac{100}{32} \cdot \frac{3}{4} = \frac{75}{32}$	Always pause for a few seconds to observe anything tricky or spot a pattern; this will help you move forward with the correct strategy.
9	C	Since the number of pencils is inversely proportional to the number of erasers, you can write pencils · erasers = k; so pencils · erasers = k =120 · 2 = 240. Now, when she has 80 pencils, 80 · erasers = $k = 240$; so the number of erasers that she will have is $\frac{240}{80} = 3$.	If p is in inverse variation with q, then $pq = k$. That is, if p increases, then q will decrease so that the product of p and q is still equal to k.
10	B	Note that the problem says that the sales of gums and mint are related – but you need to find out if they are in direct or inverse relation. Observe that as gums increase, mints decrease. Now check if their product is a constant; 1000 · 50=50000=1250 · 40=50000. So, the constant of proportionality is k=50000. So, when 2500 bubble gums are sold, 2500 · mints = 50000; or mint=$\frac{50,000}{2500} = 20$.	If the data is in a table, visually observe if the two quantities are in direct or inverse relation. If they are in inverse relation, their product will be constant; if they are in direct relation, then their ratio will be constant.
11	B	x increased by 10% is $1.1x$; y increased by 15% is $1.15y$. So, the new area is $1.1 \cdot 1.15\, y = 1.265\, xy$. The ratio is $\frac{xy}{1.265\, xy} = 1:1.265$	x increased by 10% is $x + \frac{10}{100} \cdot x = x + 0.1x = 1.1x$
12	D	Note that there are three quantities- rice, wheat, and corn $\frac{rice}{wheat} = \frac{2}{3.1}$ and $\frac{wheat}{corn} = \frac{6.2}{1}$	Review how to compare three quantities. Though the problem looks complex, once you simplify

	To be able to compare, bring the wheat portion to 6.2 in the rice/wheat ratio. $\frac{rice}{wheat} = \frac{4}{6.2}$ and $\frac{wheat}{corn} = \frac{6.2}{1}$; therefore, rice:wheat:corn = 4:6.2:1 Now, a possible loading of the truck in pounds will have to satisfy this ratio - be 400, 620 and 100 (multiply all the items by 100)	the ratios, the problem is solved easily.
13 D	Use the calculator. The balance after one year at the bank =100 + 0.03 ·100 = $103 The balance after one year at the credit union =100 + 0.05 ·100 = $105 The ratio = $\frac{103}{105}$=0.98.	
14 C	In 1990 $\frac{poor}{rich} = \frac{6}{1}$; so the percentage of rich people=$\frac{1}{7}$ · 100 = 14.29% In 2000, $\frac{poor}{rich} = \frac{10}{3}$; so the percentage of rich people= $\frac{3}{13}$ · 100= 23.08% So, the percentage increase is 23.08-14.29=8.79%	Starting with a ratio, learn to calculate proportion of one part with respect to the whole and then its percentage of the whole.
15 4	Initially: red 2 green 5 blue 8. Note that red and green are directly proportional- so $\frac{red}{green} = \frac{2}{5}$ and green and blue are inversely proportional – so, initially, green · blue =5·8=40 and this inverse relationship must be maintained. Now, the number of green balls is increased to 20; so the number of red and blue balls must be different in order to maintain the direct and inverse relationship. So, $\frac{new\ red}{20} = \frac{2}{5}$; so $new\ red = 8$ new green · new blue=40 20·new blue=40 new blue=2 So $\frac{new\ red}{new\ blue} = \frac{8}{2} = 4$	Review the direct and inverse relationship fundamentals.

PROBLEM SOLVING AND DATA ANALYSIS

Lesson 5 | Percentages | Review

FOCUSPREP CHECKLIST

- How do I calculate a percentage increase or decrease?
- How do I convert a fraction, or a decimal to a percentage?
- How do I convert a ratio to a percentage?
- Workout practice problems in Percentages

Q1 What is a Percentage?

A1 Percent means "for every 100." "cent" means centum, which is Latin for 100.

Q2 How do I convert a fraction or a decimal to a percentage?

A2 Fraction to percentage: Multiply by 100. $\frac{2}{3}$ converted to percentage is $\frac{2}{3} \cdot 100 = 66.67\%$
Decimal to percentage: Multiply by 100. 0.25 converted to percentage is $0.25 \cdot 100 = 25\%$

Q3 How do I convert a percentage to a fraction or a decimal?

A3 Percentage to fraction: Divide by 100. $25\% = \frac{25}{100} = \frac{1}{4}$
Percentage to decimal: Divide by 100. $25\% = \frac{25}{100} = 0.25$

Q4 How do I convert a ratio to a percentage?

A4 If the ratio of boys to girls is $\frac{2}{5}$, then the percentage of boys= $\frac{2}{2+5} = \frac{2}{7} \cdot 100 = 28.57\%$. The percentage of boys is NOT $\frac{2}{5} \cdot 100 = 40\%$. The percentage of girls= $\frac{5}{2+5} = \frac{5}{7} \cdot 100 = 71.43\%$.

Q5 How do I calculate the percentage increase or percentage decrease?

A5 If a quantity a becomes quantity b, then the percentage increase or decrease is given by the formula $\frac{(b-a)}{a} \cdot 100$. If $b > a$, then the percentage is positive and indicates an increase; If $b < a$, then the percentage is negative and indicates a decrease.

Example: Sales of an automobile was 2000 last year and 3000 this year. What is the percentage change?
Solution: $\frac{3000-2000}{2000} \cdot 100 = 50\%$. Since the percentage change is positive, it indicates an increase in sales.

Example: Sales of an automobile was 3000 last year and 2000 this year. What is the percentage change?
Solution: $\frac{2000-3000}{3000} \cdot 100 = -33.33\%$. Since the percentage change is negative, it indicates a decrease in sales.

Q6 What kind of problems can I encounter with percentages?

A6 Problems regarding percentages can appear in algebra, geometry, banking, taxes, science, census, etc. – wherever there are two numbers and you want to figure out how much increase or decrease there has been relative to the first number as a percentage. You can expect to encounter percentage problems in data analysis involving tables and graphs.

Q7 How do percentages relate to sale price, cost price, profits, and discounts?

A7 Get familiar with these terms as you will encounter them frequently. Suppose a product costs c dollars to make and the product is sold for s dollars. The profit is $s - c$ dollars and profit as a percentage is $\frac{s-c}{c} \cdot 100$.

Example: Suppose a product that is sold for $20 is discounted by 20%. What is the discount and the new sales price?
Solution: The discount is 20% $= \frac{20}{100} \cdot 20 = 4$. The new sales price is old sales price-discount = 20-4= 16; Another way to quickly arrive at the answer is to figure out that if the discount is 20%, then the remaining 80% is the new sales price $-$ so $\frac{80}{100} \cdot 20 = 16$.

Example: A toy costs $50. The tax is 8.25%. What is the sale price of the toy?
Solution: The sale price is cost + tax = $50 + \frac{8.25}{100} \cdot 50 = 50 + 0.0825 \cdot 50 = 50 + 4.13 = 54.13$

Q8 A shopkeeper increases the price of a shirt by 10% and then increases it again by 10% of the new price. Should he instead be increasing the price once by 20% if he wants more profit?

A8 Solution: Assume that the shirt is originally sold at $ s. He increases by 10% - so the price now is 1.1s. He increased it again by 10% of this new price – so the price now is 1.1s · 1.1 = 1.21s. If he increased it just once by 20%, he would be selling the shirt for 1.2s, which is less than 1.21s. So he should not be increasing it by 20% if he wants to have more profit.

Q9 What should I be aware of with regard to word problems involving percentages?

A9 Watch out for phrases such as "what is the percentage increase", "what is the percentage decrease", "what is the change in percentage", "what percentage of", etc.

Example: What percentage of 20 is 10? $\frac{x}{100} \cdot 20 = 10; x = 50\%$
What percentage is 3 of 20? $3 = \frac{x}{100} \cdot 20; x = 15\%$

PROBLEM SOLVING AND DATA ANALYSIS		
Lesson 5	Percentages	Practice

CALCULATOR SECTION

1. A small zoo has lions, tigers, and cheetahs only. The ratio of lions to tigers is 1:2 and the ratio of tigers to cheetahs is 3:7. What percentage of the zoo population is made of lions?
(A) 12.04%
(B) 13.04%
(C) 15.38%
(D) 20%

2. If the length and width of a rectangle are doubled, the area will increase by what percentage?
(A) 4%
(B) 20%
(C) 300%
(D) 400%

CALCULATOR SECTION

3. If the radius of a circle is halved, then by what percentage does the area decrease by?
(A) 25%
(B) 50%
(C) 75%
(D) 100%

4. If $x = 4y$, where x and y are positive integers, then what percent of x is y?
(A) 15
(B) 25
(C) 40
(D) 100

CALCULATOR SECTION

5. Lisa donated $1600 for charity in 2014. If there are 52 paychecks in one year, and she gets $1200 in each of her paychecks, what percentage of her salary does Lisa donate?
(A) 2.56
(B) 2.65
(C) 6.5
(D) 7.5

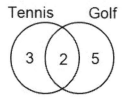

6. The Venn diagram above shows students who play tennis and golf. What percentage of tennis players play golf as well?
(A) 40.00
(B) 42.86
(C) 71.42
(D) 100

CALCULATOR SECTION

7. At a car dealership, sales of model-A were 100 cars in 2010, and sales increased at the same percentage for the next two years. The sales of model-B were 1600 in 2010, but the sales decreased by the same percentage for the next two years. If the percentage increase in sales of model-A cars is the same as the percentage decrease in sales of model-B cars, and the total number of model-A cars sold in 2012 is the same as model-B cars, what is the percentage increase or decrease?
GRID IN

8. A sculpture worth $5000 loses 5% of its value for 2 years and then loses 6% of its value for two more years. Another sculpture loses its value by 7% for two years and then by 9% for two more years. If the value of the two sculptures is the same after the four years of losses, what is the value of the second sculpture?
GRID IN

PROBLEM SOLVING AND DATA ANALYSIS
Lesson 5 — Percentages — Answers

#	Explanation	Comments
1 B	You have three animals and the ratios linking them; $\frac{lions}{tigers}=\frac{1}{2}$; $\frac{tigers}{cheetahs}=\frac{3}{7}$ To find the percentage of lions, you need to represent the ratios in lions: tigers: cheetahs format. Since the tigers are not in the same quantity in the two ratios (2 and 3), you need to make them the same. The least common multiple of 2 and 3 is 6. So, make lions/tigers as $\frac{3}{6}$ and tigers/cheetahs=$\frac{6}{14}$. This gives us lions: tigers: cheetahs=3:6:14. So, the percentage of lions is $\frac{3}{3+6+14} \cdot 100 \cong 13.04\%$	Review the lesson on ratios to learn how to work with ratios involving three quantities and how to bring them into the a:b:c format. Doing this is critical to answer a problem of this type. Be prepared to encounter problems that have a mix of ratios, variations, and percentages.
2 C	Let length = l and width= w, Area= $l \cdot w$ New length = $2l$ New width=$2w$, New Area = $2l \cdot 2w = 4\,lw$. The percentage increase = $\frac{4lw-lw}{lw} \cdot 100 = 300\%$	Note that percentage increases can be more than 100. Review the percentage increase and decrease formula.
3 C	Area = $\pi \cdot r^2$ New area = $\pi \cdot \left(\frac{r}{2}\right)^2 = \pi \cdot \frac{r^2}{4}$ The percentage decrease is $\frac{\frac{\pi r^2}{4}-\pi r^2}{\pi r^2} \cdot 100 = \frac{\frac{1}{4}-1}{1} \cdot 100 = -75\%$	When you apply the percentage formula, if you get a negative percentage, don't be alarmed - negative percentage indicates that there is a decrease in quantity.
4 B	$x = 4y$; What percentage of x is y? so $y = \frac{1}{4}x = 0.25\,x = \frac{25}{100}x = 25\%$ of x	This problem highlights conversion from fraction to decimal to percentage.
5 A	percentage donation = donation/salary · 100 Lisa's salary = 52 · 1200= 62400 Her donation = 1600; In percentage, $\frac{1600}{62400} \cdot 100 = 2.56\%$	Be careful while entering large numbers like 62400. Don't miss any zeros!
6 A	Total # of tennis players = 3+2 = 5 Total Number of players who play both golf and tennis=2 Percentage = $\frac{2}{5} \cdot 100 = 40\%$	
7 60%	Let the increase in percentage of model-A cars and decrease in percentage of model-B cars=$x\%$. Make a table to show the sales of the two models.	This is a harder problem; setup the equation carefully.

©GiftOfLogic http://www.GiftOfLogic.com

Year	Model-A	Model-B
2010	100	1600
2011	$100(1+x)$	$1600(1-x)$
2012	$100(1+x)(1+x)$	$1600(1-x)(1-x)$

You know that in 2012 the sales is the same for the two models. So
$100(1+x)^2 = 1600(1-x)^2$

$$\frac{(1+x)^2}{(1-x)^2} = \frac{1600}{100} = 16$$

$$\left[\frac{1+x}{1-x}\right]^2 = 16$$

$$\left[\frac{1+x}{1-x}\right] = \pm 4$$

If $x = +4, 1 + x = 4 - 4x$
$5x = 3$
$x = \frac{3}{5} = 0.6 = \frac{60}{100} = 60\%$

So the percentage increase of model-A and percentage decrease of model-B=60%.

Verify your answer: for model-A, starting with 10 in 2010, the sales in 2012 is $100(1.6)^2$. For model-B, starting from 1600 in 2010, the sales in 2012 is $1600(1-0.6)^2 = 256$.

If $x = -4, 1 + x = -4 + 4x, x = -\frac{5}{3} = -166.67\%$. This cannot be a solution since the sales of model-A increased and so x must be positive.

| 8 5538 | 5% decrease in value for two years = 95% of value. 6% decrease in value for two years = 94% of value. 7% decrease in value for two years = 93% of value. 9% decrease in value for two years = 91% of value.

Value of the first sculpture after 4 years = $5000 \cdot 0.95 \cdot 0.95 \cdot 0.94 \cdot 0.94$ = \$3987.25.
Let x be the value of the second sculpture.
Value of the second sculpture after 4 years =
$x \cdot 0.93 \cdot 0.93 \cdot 0.91 \cdot 0.91 = 0.72x$
You know that the value of the two sculptures are the same after 4 years; So, $0.72x = 3987.25; x = \$5537.84 \cong \$5538$. | Be careful with decreasing percentages and discounts – if the value of a sculpture x decreases by 7%, then its new value is 100-7=93% of the old value=$0.93x$. If this new value again decreases by 7%., then the new value will again be multiplied by 93%= $0.93x \cdot 0.93 = x \cdot 0.93 \cdot 0.93$ |

	PROBLEM SOLVING AND DATA ANALYSIS	
Lesson 6	Unit Conversions	Review

FOCUSPREP CHECKLIST

- What is Unit of Measurement?
- How do I convert one unit to another?
- Workout practice problems in Unit Conversions

Q1 What is an Unit Of Measurement?

A1 Unit of Measurement refers to the unit that is used to measure length, weight, speed etc. For example, the unit of measurement of length is feet, miles, kilometers, etc.; the unit of measurement of weight is pound, kilogram, ton, etc.; and the unit of measurement of time is seconds, minutes, month, week, etc.

Q2 What is unit conversion?

A2 Unit conversion is the process of converting measurements from one unit to another. For example, you convert feet to inches by using the fact that $1\ feet\ =\ 12\ inches$.

So, $3\ feet\ =\ 3\ \cancel{feet}\cdot 12\frac{inches}{\cancel{feet}} = 36\ inches$. Notice that you started with feet and ended with inches.

Q3 Do I need to remember unit conversion tables for SAT?

A3 You need to know the basic conversion data regarding measurements of lengths, weight, and time in order to answer questions quickly. However, any required conversion information will be given in the problem itself. Browse through the table below to familiarize yourself with some common conversions.

Length	1 feet = 12 inches
	1 mile = 1760 yards
	1 yard = 3 feet
Volume	1 gallon= 4 quarts
	1 quart= 2 pints
	1 pint = 2 cups
	1 cup = 8 fluid ounces
Time	1 year = 12 months
	1 year = 52 weeks
	1 week = 7 days
	1 day = 24 hours
	1 hour = 60 minutes
	1 minute= 60 seconds
Mass	1 ton = 2000 pounds
	1 pound = 16 ounces
Density	Pounds per cubic feet $\frac{lbs}{ft^3}$
Pressure	Pounds per square inch $\frac{lbs}{in^2}$
Money	1 US Dollar = 100 cents

©GiftOfLogic http://www.GiftOfLogic.com

Q4 When will I need to convert units?

A4 You need to convert units when information is provided in one unit and a question is asked where the answer will be in another unit.

Example: John spent 2 hours and 30 minutes studying for an exam. How many seconds did he study?
Solution: Convert 2 hours to minutes => $2 \;\cancel{hrs} \cdot 60 \frac{minutes}{\cancel{hr}} = 120$ minutes
Add 30 minutes => 120+30=150 minutes. Convert to seconds = $150 \;\cancel{minutes} \cdot 60 \frac{seconds}{\cancel{minute}} =$ 9000 seconds.

Example: Sometimes, you may be introduced to a new item and its unit of measurement that you may not have come across in your life. For example, a Watt-Hour is how the electricity consumed is measured. A 40 Watt appliance that is operated for 25 hours consumes 40 · 25=1000 Watt Hours of electricity.

Q5 What is Kilo, Mega, etc.?

A5 When the magnitude of the item being measured is very high, it is customary to represent these numbers in terms of Mega, Kilo etc.
  Tera = 10^{12} ; example: 3 Tera Bytes = $3 \cdot 10^{12}$ Bytes
  Giga = 10^9 ; example: 1 Giga Byte = 10^9 Bytes
  Mega = 10^6 ; example: 2 Mega Bytes = $2 \cdot 10^6$ Bytes
  Kilo = 10^3; example: 1 Kilo Byte = 10^3 Bytes; 3 Kilo Meters= $3 \cdot 10^3 = 3000 \; m$

Q6 Where am I most likely to make mistakes during unit conversion?

A6 You are most likely to make a mistake when you are converting a unit two or more times to get to your final unit and did not properly cancel out the units.

Example: How many hours are there in 3 weeks?
Solution: If you are not careful, you might calculate it as 3 · 24 and end up with a wrong answer. A week does not have 24 hours. Carefully write out the units from beginning to end.
$3 \;\cancel{weeks} \cdot 7 \frac{\cancel{days}}{\cancel{week}} \cdot 24 \frac{hours}{\cancel{day}} = 504 \; hours$. Note that after cancelling the units in the numerator and denominator, you are left with hours only in the numerator. This is the unit of measure you want in your answer.

Q7 What are some examples of unit conversion problems?

A7

Example
A carpenter earns $20/day. If he works for 3 days/week for 3 weeks in a month, how much does he earn in one month? $\frac{\$20}{\cancel{day}} \cdot \frac{3 \;\cancel{days}}{\cancel{week}} \cdot \frac{3 \;\cancel{weeks}}{month} = \frac{\$180}{month}$

Example
There are 5 cities in a state, 9 schools in each city, 200 students in each school. How many students are there in the state?
$\frac{5 \;\cancel{cities}}{state} \cdot \frac{9 \;\cancel{schools}}{\cancel{city}} \cdot \frac{200 \; students}{\cancel{school}} = \frac{9000 \; students}{state}$

PROBLEM SOLVING AND DATA ANALYSIS

Lesson 6 — Unit Conversions — Practice

CALCULATOR SECTION

1. There are 14 books in Sonia's shelf. There are 20 chapters in each book, 6 lessons in each chapter, and 5 pages in each lesson. Sonia has so far read 10 books fully, and 3 lessons each from 4 other books. How many pages are yet to be read?
(A) 1170
(B) 2340
(C) 2430
(D) 4680

2. A 20 Watt bulb burning for 50 hours consumes 20 · 50=1000 Watt-Hours or 1 Kilowatt-Hour(KWh). If the Simpson household consumes 200 KWh in January, this consumption is equivalent to how many 20 Watt bulbs burning for 8 hours?
(A) 650
(B) 1050
(C) 1250
(D) 2500

CALCULATOR SECTION

3. 50 painters can paint 3 buildings in 6 days. Painters are paid $20/hour each day and they work for 8 hours per day. If more painters are hired to paint 2 buildings in 1 day, how much money will be needed to pay them?
(A) 12,000
(B) 14,000
(C) 16,000
(D) 32,000

4. 100 people planned to run to raise funds for a charity. Twenty percent of them ran 3 miles, two fifth ran 6 miles, and the rest ran 9 miles. For every mile run, they raised $20. What was the total amount raised for the charity?
(A) 3600
(B) 7200
(C) 13,200
(D) 24,600

CALCULATOR SECTION

5. A cable company provides Internet data transmission speeds of 1.5 MBPS, where 1 MBPS=1 Million Bits Per Second. If a file is 100 Mega Bytes and 1 Byte=8 Bits, how many minutes will it take to download half the file?
(Mega= 10^6)
(A) 4.44
(B) 5.44
(C) 6.44
(D) 6.68

6. A city that is facing a water shortage developed a plan to restrict water usage as follows:

Family size	Permitted Usage
Less than 3	20 gallons/day/family
3 to 5	25 gallons/day/family
More than 5	28 gallons/day/family

In the city, there are 700 families of 2 people each, 800 families of 4 people each, and 1000 families of 6 people each. If a TGAL represents thousand gallons, how many TGALs of water can be used by the residents of this city in one day?
GRID IN

CALCULATOR SECTION

7. After an empty rectangular wooden crate was filled with some material that has a density of 8 lb/ft^3, the mass increased by 2400 lbs. If this material is replaced by another material that has a density of 17 lb/ft^3, what will the mass of the crate increase by? Density = $\frac{mass}{volume}$
GRID IN

8. Water is pumped from three lakes to an empty water tank every day according to the following information.

Lake	Pumping rate	Pumping Hours
Lake 1	20 gallons/hr	2 hrs
Lake 2	30 gallons/hr	3 hrs
Lake 3	40 gallons/hr	5 hrs

Water is drained from the tank every day at the rate of 40 gallons/hr for 5 hours. How much water will be in the tank after 15 days?
GRID IN

PROBLEM SOLVING AND DATA ANALYSIS

Lesson 6 — Unit Conversions — Answers

#	Explanation	Comments
1 B	Note that the question asks- "how many pages are yet to be read?" Sonia has read 10 books = 10 books $\cdot \frac{20 \text{ chapters}}{\text{book}} \cdot \frac{6 \text{ lessons}}{\text{chapter}} \cdot \frac{5 \text{ pages}}{\text{lesson}} = 6000$ pages. 3 lessons each from 4 books = 12 lessons $\cdot \frac{5 \text{ pages}}{\text{lesson}} = 60$ pages So, totally, Sonia has read 6000+60= 6060 pages. The total number of pages in all the books = 14 books $\cdot 600 \frac{\text{pages}}{\text{book}} = 8400$ pages. The pages that she is yet to read is $8400 - 6060 = 2340$.	Verify that the units cancel out and pay attention to what units you are left with at the end.
2 C	One 20 Watt bulb burning for 8 hrs = $20 \cdot 8 = 160$ Watt-Hrs. Let b be the number of 20 Watt bulbs that will burn for 8 hrs that will be equivalent to 200KWh. $b \cdot 160$ Watt $-$ Hrs $= 160b$ Watt $-$ Hrs $\qquad = 200{,}000$ Watt $-$ Hrs $b = \frac{200{,}000}{160} = 1250$ bulbs.	Make sure you are comparing the same units on both sides – convert Kilo Watt-Hours to Watt Hours. 1 Kilo=1000.
3 D	50 painters can paint 3 buildings in 6 days. Painters are paid $20/hour each day and they work for 8 hours per day. If more painters are hired to paint 2 buildings in 1 day, how much money will be needed to pay them? 1 painter is paid $20/hr $\cdot$ 8 hrs/day = $160/day Now you need to find how many painters are needed to paint 2 buildings in 1 day. 50 painters – 3 bldgs – 6 days So 50 painters – 1 bldg = $\frac{6 \text{ days}}{3 \text{ bldgs}} \cdot 1$ bldg $= 2$ days This means 50 painters – 2 bldgs = $2 \cdot 2 = 4$ days So if 50 painters – 2 bldgs – 4 days how many painters- 2 bldgs – 1 day ? since you want to paint the 2 bldgs in less time(1 day instead of 4 days), you will need more painters; the number of painters is inversely proportional to the number of days; 4 days 50 painters 1 day x painters So setup INVERSE relation; flip one of the ratios; $\frac{x}{50} = \frac{4}{1}$ $x = 50 \cdot 4 = 200$ painters. So, now each painter needs to be paid $160/day; therefore total to be paid = $160/day/painter . 200 painters = $32000/day.	This problem combines unit conversion with a labor rate problem. Review the lesson on ratios and variation to get familiar with rate problems.

©GiftOfLogic http://www.GiftOfLogic.com

4 C	20% of 100=20 persons $20 \text{ persons} \cdot \frac{3 \text{ miles}}{\text{person}} = 60 \text{ miles}$ $\frac{2}{5} \cdot 100 = 40$, $40 \text{ persons} \cdot \frac{6 \text{ miles}}{\text{person}} = 240 \text{ miles}$ The rest = $100 - (20 + 40) = 40$ persons; $40 \text{ persons} \cdot 9 \frac{\text{miles}}{\text{person}} = 360 \text{ miles}$ Total miles = $60 + 240 + 360 = 660$ miles. Total fund raised=$\frac{\$20}{\text{mile}}$ $660 \text{ miles} = \$13,200$		
5 A	Note carefully that the speed is in MegaBits per second but the file size is in MegaBytes. data speed=1.5 M Bits/s Half the file size = $\frac{100}{2}$ M Bytes = 50 M Bytes = =50 $M \text{ Bytes} \cdot 8 \frac{Bits}{byte}$ = 400 M Bits Let T be the time in seconds that it takes to download half the file. 1.5 M Bits – 1 secs 400 M Bits – $\frac{400}{1.5} \cdot 1 \text{ sec} = 266.66 \text{ secs} = \frac{266.66 \text{ secs}}{60 \text{ secs/minute}} =$ 4.44 minutes	Use M for mega to simplify the calculation. Be careful, Bytes and Bits sound similar but are different – 1 Byte=8 Bits.
6 62	Correlate the text with the information in the table. 700 families of 2 consume $700 \text{ families} \cdot 20 \frac{gallons}{day-family} =$ 14000 gallons/day 800 families of 4 consume $800 \cdot 25 = 20000$ gallons/day 1000 families of 6 consume $1000 \cdot 28 = 28000$ gallons/day Total consumption=14000+20000+28000=62000 gallons/day 1000 gallons = 1 TGAL, so 62000 gallons = 62000 gallons/1000 gallons $\cdot$ 1 TGAL = 62 TGALs.	20 gallons/day/family must be written as $20 \frac{gallons}{day-family}$ in order to cancel the units correctly. Practice how to cancel the units.
7 2700	When the density of the filled material is 8 lb/ft³ the mass is 2400 lbs. Density = $\frac{mass}{volume}$ $8 \frac{lb}{ft^3} = \frac{2400 \text{ lb}}{volume}$ volume=$\frac{2400 \text{ lb}}{8 \text{ lb}/ft^3} = 300 \text{ ft}^3$ Now the density of the new material is 16 So, $17 = mass/300$ Mass= $17 \frac{lb}{ft^3} \cdot 300 ft^3 = 5100$ lbs The mass will increase by $5100 - 2400 = 2700$ lbs.	
8 1950	The daily influx to the tank from the 3 lakes= $20 \cdot 2 + 30 \cdot 3 + 40 \cdot 5 = 330$ gallons/day; The drainage from the tank = 40 gallons/hr $\cdot$ 5 hrs = 200 gallons - this is the drainage per day as well – so 200 gallons/day. So, the net addition to the tank = 330-200=130 gallons/day. The amount of water in the tank after 15 days = $130 \frac{gallons}{day} \cdot 15 \text{ days} = 1950$ gallons	

Lesson 7	PROBLEM SOLVING AND DATA ANALYSIS Scatterplots	Review

> **FOCUSPREP CHECKLIST**
> - What is a scatterplot?
> - How do I fit a curve in a scatterplot?
> - What is a positive and a negative correlation?
> - Workout practice problems in Scatterplots

Q1 What is a Scatterplot?

A1 A scatterplot is a type of graph that is used to verify if there is a correlation between two sets of data. The correlation can be a positive correlation, a negative correlation, or there may not be any correlation at all between the two sets.

Q2 How do scatterplots look?

A2 Scatterplots with positive correlation, negative correlation, and no correlation are shown below.

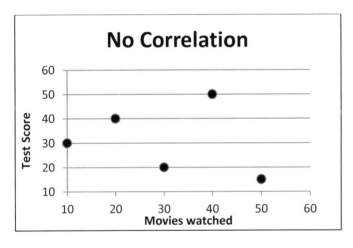

This scatterplot shows that test scores do not depend on the number of movies watched.

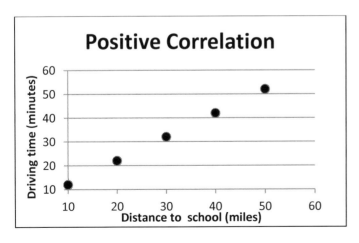

This scatter plot shows a positive correlation between the distance to school and the driving time. As the distance to school increases, the driving time increases.

©GiftOfLogic   http://www.GiftOfLogic.com

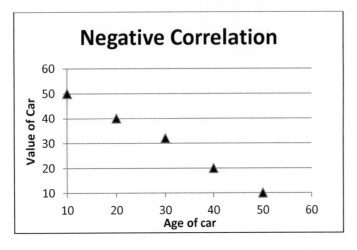

This scatterplot shows a negative correlation between the age of a car and its value. As the car gets older, its value decreases.

Q3 Can scatterplots be used to compare values of two sets of data of the same type?

A3 Scatterplots can also be used to plot data with the same units (scores, dollar value, etc.)

In this scatter plot, both the x axis and y axis represent the scores. The x coordinate of each point represents Jack's score and the y coordinate represents Mary's score.

You can infer from this scatterplot that there were 4 tests in total and Mary scored more than Jack in 3 tests.

Q4 I find a positive correlation between the two variables in my scatterplot. How do I fit a curve?

A4 You can fit several types of curves into a scatterplot depending on the type of correlation.

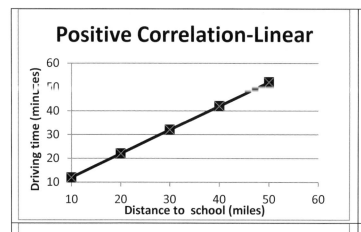

In this scatterplot, a straight line can be fit to connect the points.

You can model this line as $y = mx + b$ where m is the slope and b is the y-intercept.

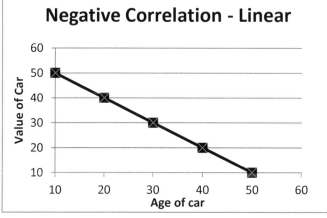

In this scatterplot, a straight line can be fit to connect the points. Note that the line has a negative slope. You can model a straight line as $y = mx + b$ where m is the slope and b is the y-intercept.

Sometimes, you may not be able to fit a line connecting all the points. In that case, connect as many points as possible. Sometimes, you may only be able to fit a line in such a way that all the points lie on either side of the line but none of them lie on the line.

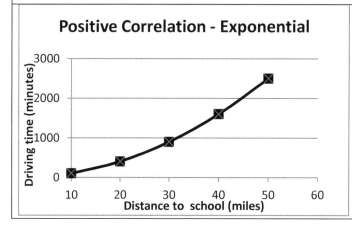

In this scatterplot, an exponential curve can be fit to connect the points.

Exponential curves take the form of $y = ab^x$.

Review the lesson on Growth and Decay for more information on Exponential functions.

PROBLEM SOLVING AND DATA ANALYSIS

Lesson 7 — Scatterplots — Practice

CALCULATOR SECTION

1. The scatterplot above shows the scores of two students in five games. A student with a higher score wins. What percentage of games did Ashley win?
(A) 20%
(B) 40%
(C) 60%
(D) 90%

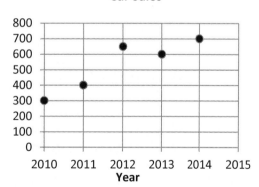

2. The scatterplot above shows the car sales at a dealership. How many cars can the dealer expect to sell in 2015?
(A) 700
(B) 750
(C) 800
(D) 850

CALCULATOR SECTION

3. A botanist did a survey to find out how much time people spend every week in their gardens. The scatterplot above shows the results of the survey. Which of the following is true?

(A) The total number of people spending 3 and 4 hours at the garden is the same as the total number of people spending 0 hours at the garden.
(B) More than half of the respondents spend less than 3 hours at the garden.
(C) 5 respondents spend more than five hours at the garden.
(D) Everyone surveyed spends at least one hour at the garden.

4. The scores obtained by students in a geography test are shown in the scatterplot above. What is the average score for this test?
(A) 55
(B) 57.62
(C) 63.05
(D) 67.62

©GiftOfLogic   http://www.GiftOfLogic.com

CALCULATOR SECTION

Use the scatterplot above to answer questions 5 and 6 below.

5. A hydrologist began tracking the water level in a dam as soon as heavy rain started. The plot of the water level after four hours of rain is shown above. Which of the following functions best describes the relationship between the water level (w) and the time (t)?

(A) $w = 2^t$
(B) $w = 2.5^t$
(C) $w = 3^t$
(D) $w = 5^t$

6. Assuming that the rain continues for several hours, what would be the water level (ft) in the dam after 5 hours?
(A) 32
(B) 52.52
(C) 97.66
(D) 243

NO CALCULATOR SECTION

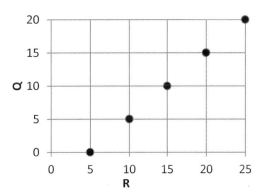

7. A materials engineer is testing three properties P, Q, and R of a new alloy. All of them have the same units of measurement. Scatterplots showing the relation between P and Q and the relation between Q and R are shown above. Which of the following models best describe the relation between P and R?

(A) $P = 7 - 2R$
(B) $P = 2R - 7$
(C) $P = R + 5$
(D) $P = R - 5$

8. If the property $Q = 6$ units, then what is the ratio of R to P?
GRID IN

PROBLEM SOLVING AND DATA ANALYSIS
Lesson 7 — Scatterplots — Answers

#		Explanation	Comments
1	C	List out the score pairs of Abby and Ashley. They are (10,30), (20.40,),(30,20),(40,50),(50,15). From this list it is clear that Ashley won 3 games out of a total of 5 games. So the percentage is $\frac{3}{5} \cdot 100 = 60\%$	Remember that a scatterplot can be used to compare values of the same type - in this problem it is the scores of two students.
2	C	**Car Sales** (scatterplot with years 2010–2015 on x-axis, sales 0–800 on y-axis, with fitted line) Fit a curve connecting the points. Except for 2012 (outlier), you can connect the data using a straight line. In this line, observe that there is an increase in sales of 100 units for every 1 year increment. So, from a car sale of 700 units in 2014, the dealer can expect to sell 100 more cars in 2015. The answer is 700+100=800	When you fit a line, you may not be able to connect all the points. It is possible that in some problems, none of the points fall on the line. In that case, draw a line such that it divides the points on either side of the line, as much as possible. You can then find the slope of the line and extrapolate the data.
3	B	There are a total of 85 respondents (25+20+15+10+10+5+0). A total of 60 survey respondents spend less than 3 hours (0,1 and 2 hours) at the garden (25+20+15). This is more than half the respondents.	
4	D	The average score is the sum of all scores divided by the number of students. From the scatterplot, you can see that 35 students obtained a score of 55, 25 students got 65 and so on. So, the average is calculated as (35 · 55+25 · 65+25 · 75+10 · 80+ 5 · 85+5 · 90)/105 =67.62	Note carefully that there are multiple students who have the same scores.
5	C	When you fit a curve on the data points, it appears that the curve is exponential. To find the function that fits the curve, create a table with x and y points and see if you can find a model or plug in the choices to see which one fits the data. From the scatterplot, you get the following table of values for t and w. | t	0	1	2	3	4
---	---	---	---	---	---
w			9	27	81		The water level at $t = 0$ and $t = 1$ are not clearly readable but other points are readable. When the answer choices list the models, apply them against the data.

©GiftOfLogic http://www.GiftOfLogic.com

	Since the curve appears to be exponential, try the exponential choices against the data. When $t = 2, 3,$ and 4 you can see that $w = 3^t$. So the model is $w = 3^t$.		Note that the general form of an exponential model/function is $y = ab^x$.
6 D	After 5 hours, the water level would be $w = 3^5 = 243$ ft.		
7 D	First, find the relationship between P and Q by listing the scatterplot values for P and Q. 	Q	1	2	3	4	5	 	P	5	7	9	11	13	 The relation can be expressed as $P = 2Q + 3$. Now find the relation between Q and R. 	R	5	10	15	20	25	 	Q	0	5	10	15	20	 The relation between Q and R is $Q = R - 5$. The question asks for the relationship between P and R. You have $P = 2Q + 3$ and $Q = R - 5$. So, $P = 2(R - 5) + 3 = 2R - 10 + 3 = 2R - 7$		Note that you need to extract the models out of the data in the scatterplots and then derive a new model connecting P and R. When making the table, place the variable in the x axis in the first row and the variable in the y axis in the second row, so that as you visually browse through the values in the x axis, you may get an idea about the model values in the y axis.
8 0.73	When $Q = 6, R = Q + 5 = 6 + 5 = 11$ $P = 2Q + 3 = 2 \cdot 6 + 3 = 15$ The ratio of R to P $= \frac{11}{15}$.		

PROBLEM SOLVING AND DATA ANALYSIS

Lesson 8 — Graphs and Tables — Review

> **FOCUSPREP CHEKLIST**
> - What are the different types of graphs?
> - What are the different parts of a graph?
> - Workout practice problems in Graphs and Tables

Q1 What are the different types of graphs?
A1 Graphs such as Bar Graphs (vertical or horizontal), Line Graphs, Circle Graphs, and Pictographs will appear in the problems. Related data may be presented in tables and in textual descriptions of data.

Q2 What kind of questions are asked in problems with graphs and tables?
A2 You will be asked to calculate percentage increase and decrease, make inferences from data, extrapolate to the next data point, calculate difference between two data points, correlate information from multiple graphs, calculate ratio between two values obtained from the graphs, correlate data in graphs and tables, etc.

Q3 What are the parts of a graph?
A3 Pay careful attention to the different parts of a graph described below. A sample graph is shown.

<u>Title:</u> Title will indicate the subject of the graph – what exactly is being plotted. For example, Rainfall, Rocket Speed, Test Scores, Tiger Population, etc. Sometimes, title will indicate the scale and unit of measure of the numbers – for example Population (millions), Students (thousands), Water Level (ft).

<u>X axis label:</u> The X axis label indicates the data that is plotted on the X axis. The label will indicate the unit of measure. For example, Time (minutes), Speed (miles/hr) etc.

<u>X axis major and minor units:</u> You need to figure this out yourself from the value labels and their increment. Sometimes, you will be required to read a data point that falls between two major units. Minor units, if present, are the ticks between two major unit labels on the X-axis.

<u>Y axis label:</u> The Y axis label indicates the data that is plotted on the Y axis. The label will indicate the unit of measure. For example, Salary (US$), Temperature (Fahrenheit).

<u>Y axis major and minor units:</u> You need to figure this out yourself from value labels and their increment. Sometimes, you will be required to read a data point that falls between two major units on the Y-axis. Minor units, if present, are the ticks between two major unit labels on the Y-axis.

<u>Legend:</u> When more than one data series is shown in the graph, the legend shows the description of the data series and their corresponding markers. Read the legend carefully to identify the marker that corresponds to the relevant data series. Markers are typically shapes like squares, diamonds, circles, etc.

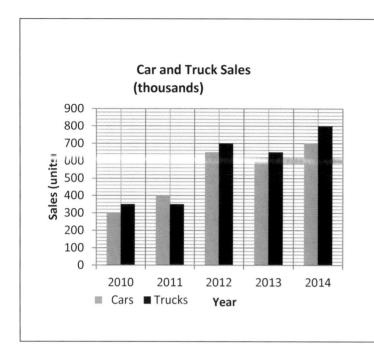

Title: Car and Truck Sales; thousands refers to the scale of the numbers in the Y-axis. For example, the sales of cars in 2010 = 300,000. Read 300 from the graph and multiply by 1000.
X-axis label: Year
Y-axis label: Sales (units) (in thousands)
Legend (shown at bottom): Grey bars indicate Cars and Black bars indicate Trucks
Y-axis major unit: 100 units (increment is 100 for every horizontal line)
Y-axis minor unit: 100/5=20; the gap between two major unit labels is split into 5 sections by minor grid lines
X-axis major unit: 1 year
X-axis minor unit: Not relevant for bar graphs

Q4 What are the different graphs used for and how do they look?

A4 Several types of graphs are shown and described below.

Scatterplots are used for identifying the correlation between data. Scatterplots are reviewed in a separate lesson.	
Line Graphs are used for showing the progression of a series over time or some other variable.	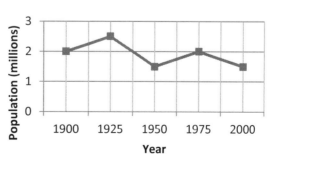

Dotted Line Graphs are used to show the progression of multiple series over time or some other variable.	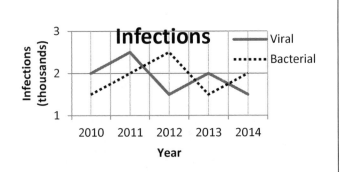
Bar graphs show the data values in bars so that it is easy to visualize the difference in data values. They can appear in horizontal or vertical formats.	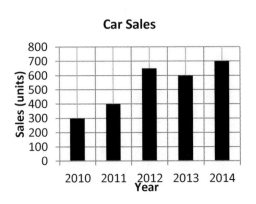
Stacked Bar Graphs are used to show the values of two sets of data on top of each other so that they can be compared using their relative heights. Pay attention to the legend to identify the correct bar that corresponds to a series. Grey bar indicates Cars and Black bar indicates Trucks.	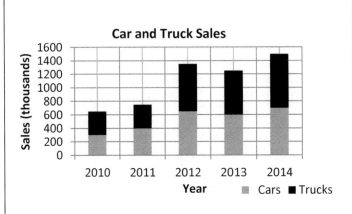
Circle Graphs, also called Pie Graphs or Pie Charts, are used to show the percentage of the parts with respect to the whole.	

Pictographs represent data using pictures. The legend will indicate the numeric quantity that corresponds to each picture. Half sized pictures may also appear in this graph. You should account for all pictures in the pictograph.	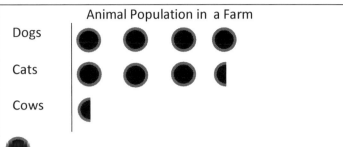
Tables are used when the data is best represented in rows and columns.	
Histograms are bar graphs showing the distribution of data. In the histogram shown, the x-axis shows the cars owned and the y-axis shows the frequency. 10 people did not own a car, 70 people owned 2 cars, nobody owned 5 cars and 20 people owned 6 cars. There are 175 data points – so the median is the 88th data point – which is 2 cars. The mean of the distribution is $$\frac{0 \cdot 10 + 1 \cdot 40 + 2 \cdot 70 + 3 \cdot 20 + 4 \cdot 15 + 6 \cdot 20}{175} = 2.4$$	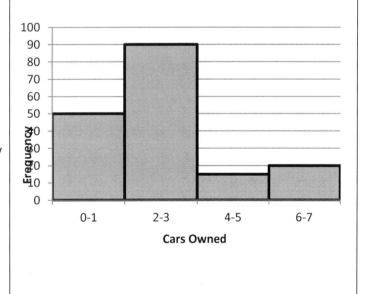
Histograms can also show the frequency of **grouped data**. The groupings are called buckets or bins. This histogram shows the cumulative frequency of 4 groups of car ownership. From this histogram, you cannot tell how many people owned 2 cars only or 3 cars only, but you can tell that a total of 90 people own either 2 cars or 3 cars. You cannot calculate the mean but you can tell that the median could be either 2 or 3 depending on the value of the 88th data point (175/2=87.5).	

PROBLEM SOLVING AND DATA ANALYSIS
Lesson 8 — Graphs and Tables — Practice

CALCULATOR SECTION

CALCULATOR SECTION

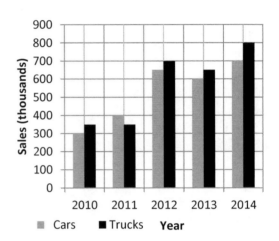

Questions 1 and 2

1. The graph above shows the car sales at a dealership. Between which two years did the car sales increase the most percentage?
(A) 2010-2011
(B) 2011-2012
(C) 2012-2013
(D) 2013-2014

Questions 3 and 4

3. The graph above shows the car and truck sales at a dealership. From 2010 to 2014 what is the approximate ratio of total cars sold to total trucks sold?
(A) 0.65
(B) 0.93
(C) 1.08
(D) 1.80

2. How much more or less is the percentage increase from 2013 to 2014 when compared to the percentage increase from 2010 to 2011?
(A) 12.67%
(B) 14.67%
(C) 16.67%
(D) 33.33%

4. In which year did the sales of trucks exceed the sales of cars the most?
(A) 2010
(B) 2011
(C) 2012
(D) 2014

CALCULATOR SECTION

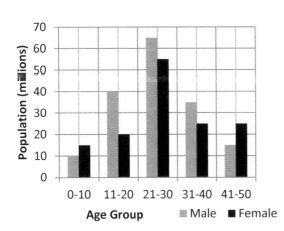

Questions 5 and 6

5. The bar graph above shows the population of different age groups in Space City. In which age group is the difference between male and female population the least?
(A) 0-10
(B) 21-30
(C) 31-40
(D) 41-50

6. How much more is the population of the 31-40 age group compared to the population of the 41-50 age group, in millions?
(A) 10
(B) 20
(C) 30
(D) 40

CALCULATOR SECTION

Age	Male	Female
0-10	10	15
11-20	40	20
21-30	65	55
31-40	35	25
41-50	15	15

7. The table above shows the male and female animal population in a zoo. Which of the following graphs displays the data accurately?

A)

B)

C)

CALCULATOR SECTION

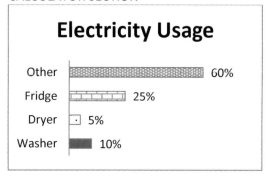

8. Electricity consumption at the McDonald household is shown above. Which of the following circle graphs most accurately depicts the data above?

(A)

(B)

(C)

(D)

CALCULATOR SECTION

9 MORGANTOWN POPULATION DATA

Age	Male	Female
0-25	3000	4000
25-50	5800	6200
50-75	800	1200

Questions 9 and 10.

9. The table above shows the population breakdown of Morgantown. What is the ratio of male population to female population in the 25-75 age group? Express your answer to the nearest hundredths place.
GRID IN

10. How many more people are there in the 25 to 50 age group than there are in the other age groups combined?
(A) 2000
(B) 3000
(C) 6000
(D) 7000

CALCULATOR SECTION

VOLCANO HIGH SCHOOL			
	Score 0-50	Score 51-100	Total
Boys		40	
Girls	30		
Total		120	200

Questions 11 and 12

11. The table above shows partial information about the scores of boys and girls in a History test. How many boys scored in the 0-50 range?
(A) 30
(B) 40
(C) 50
(D) 120

12. What is the ratio of boys to girls at Volcano High School?
(A) 0.60
(B) 0.82
(C) 0.92
(D) 1.22

CALCULATOR SECTION

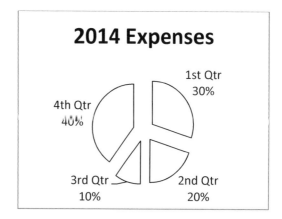

An expense of $20 million in four quarters of 2014 for a cellphone manufacturing company is shown above. A further breakdown of each quarter is shown below.

Expense Breakdown by Category				
	1st Qtr	2nd Qtr	3rd Qtr	4th Qtr
Salary	30%	25%	25%	25%
Materials	60%	65%	70%	40%
Legal	10%	10%	`5%	35%

13. How much expense did the cell phone company incur in 2014 for materials only?
(A) 2 million
(B) 4 million
(C) 10.8 million
(D) 12.8 million

14. What amount, expressed in millions was spent for paying employee salary in the 3rd quarter?
GRID IN

CALCULATOR SECTION

Restaurant Bill

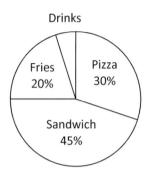

15. A restaurant bill is split up as shown above. If $12 was spent on Pizza, how many dollars was spent on Drinks?
GRID IN

TopTalent High School

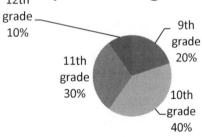

16. The students in four grades in the TopTalent High School are shown above. If the difference between the total number of students in 11th and 12th grades and the total number of students in the 9th and 10th grades is 100, how many students are there at the school?
(A) 100
(B) 200
(C) 300
(D) 500

CALCULATOR SECTION

Alicia's Portfolio

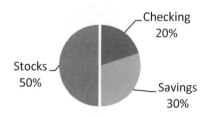

17. Alicia's portfolio of $500,000 is shown above. If she reduces her Stocks to 20% and deposits the amount in her savings account, what percent of her portfolio now will be in Savings?
(A) 50
(B) 60
(C) 70
(D) 90

Cab Ridership by ZipCode

18. A cab company's ridership in various zip codes is shown above. If the total ridership is 3000, what is the ridership in zip code 90214?
(A) 1125
(B) 1375
(C) 1750
(D) 2025

CALCULATOR SECTION

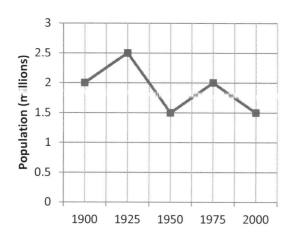

Population of Pearl City

Questions 19 and 20

19. The percentage decrease in population from 1925 to 1950 is more than the percentage decrease from 1900 to 2000 by what percent?
(A) 10
(B) 15
(C) 25
(D) 40

20. From 2000 to 2014, the population increased at the same percentage as the population decrease from 1925 to 1950. What is the population in millions in 2014?
(A) 2.1
(B) 1.2
(C) 1,500,000
(D) 2,100,000

CALCULATOR SECTION

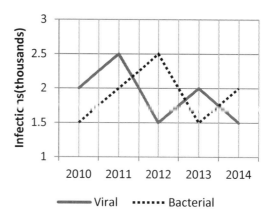

Viral vs. Bacterial Infections in Danger County – thousands

21. The set of numbers that indicates the infections at the three points in time when they were the same is which one of the following?
(A) 2.2, 1.8, 1.8
(B) 2200, 1800, 1700
(C) 1500, 2500, 1500
(D) 1.5, 2.5, 1.5

22. The temperature readings for five hours in two cities are shown above. What is the ratio of difference in maximum and minimum temperatures of Apex to Abyss?
(A) 0.1
(B) 0.5
(C) 0.7
(D) 0.8

CALCULATOR SECTION

= 10 students

23. The production of tiles in a company for three months is shown above. How many more tiles must be made during the rest of the year to reach a target of 100,000 tiles?
(A) 5,000
(B) 10,000
(C) 15,000
(D) None of the above

25. The pictograph above shows the number of students advised by two professors for their PhD thesis. If twenty students of professor A switch to professor B, which one of the following pictographs will accurately describe the switch?

= 40 animals

A)

B)

24. The number of dogs, cats, and lizards in a pet shop is shown above. What is the ratio of cats to dogs to lizards?
(A) 9:7:2
(B) 7:9:1
(C) 2:7:9
(D) 7:2:9

C)

D)

	PROBLEM SOLVING AND DATA ANALYSIS	
Lesson 8	Graphs and Tables	Answers

#	Explanation	Comments
1 B	There is an increase in car sales between 2010-2011, 2011-2012 and 2013-2014. Calculate the increase in sales for these three years 2010-2011 400-300/300 · 100 = 33.33% 2011-2012 650-400/400 · 100 = 62.50% 2013-2014 700-600/600 · 100 = 16.66% So, the car sales increased the most in 2011-2012.	Review the lesson on percentages. Note carefully that the question asks for percentage increase. This is different from asking "between which two years did the car sales increase the most?" – in which case you have to only calculate the sales numbers but not the percentage.
2 C	Note that the question asks "how much more or less". Based on our calculation, you see that the percentage increase for 2013-2014 is less than the percentage increase for 2010-2011 by $16.66 - 33.33 = -16.67$. The negative sign is accounted for when the question asks "more or less".	
3 B	Total number of cars sold= 300+400+650+600+700 =2650 Total number of trucks sold= 350+350+700+650+800 =2850 The ratio of cars to trucks = $\frac{2650}{2850} = 0.93$	Numbers between the major units must be carefully read.
4 D	Looking at the bar graphs, it is clear that in 2010, 2012, and 2014, the sales of trucks exceeded cars. In 2010, trucks-cars= 350-300=50 In 2012, trucks-cars= 700-650=50 In 2014, trucks-cars= 800-700=100 So, in 2014, the number of trucks sold exceeded the cars the most.	
5 A	Look at the age groups to see where the difference might be the least. Age group 11-20 has a large difference and so it is not going to have the least difference. For age groups 0-10, 21-30 and 41-50, the difference seems to be the same. For age groups 0-10, the difference is 15-10=5 For age groups 21-30, the difference is 65-55=10 For age groups 31-40, the difference is 35-25=10 For age groups 4-50, the difference is 25-15=10 So the difference is the least in age group 0-10.	
6 B	Population of 31-40 age group = 35+25=60 Population of 41-50 age group = 15+25=40 The difference=60-40=20.	Remember to add both male and female populations.
7 B	Pay careful attention to the axes labels. Choice A has the data values from the table plotted correctly in the bar graph but the x axis data points are 0-10, 10-20, etc. – this is	This problem correlates a table and a graph.

©GiftOfLogic http://www.GiftOfLogic.com

	incorrect; the correct axis data points must be 0-10, 11-20, 21-30 and so on. Choice B has the correct axis values and title. Choice C is incorrect because the Y axis says Population (thousands) whereas the table does not indicate that the values are in thousands.	
8 A	You need to answer this question by carefully looking at the data label, values, and the shading pattern for the data point. Note that the question is presented as a bar graph but the answers are in circle graphs. "Other" is the largest data point with 60%, whereas Dryer is the least with 5%. 60% must translate to more than half the circle in the circle graph. Choices A and B have the shaded portion corresponding to 'other' drawn with a little more than 50%. Within choices A and B, look for the one with Dryer being smaller than the Washer. This indicates that the correct choice is A.	Note that each of the bars has a pattern – this pattern must be represented in the circle graphs. Choice C has 60% represented by a dark-shade pattern but the dark-shade pattern corresponds to a Washer in the bar graph which is only 10%. Both percentages and shades must match when representing bar graphs as circle graphs.
9 0.89	Male population in the 25-75 age group = 5800+800=6600 Female population in the 25-75 age group =6200+1200=7400 The ratio = 6600/7400=0.89	
10 B	Population in the 25-50 age group = 5800+6200 =12000 "other age groups combined" – indicates age groups 0-25 and 50-75. Population in the 0-25 age group = 3000+4000 =7000 Population in the 50-75 age group = 800+1200=2000 Population in the 0-25 and 50-75 age groups = 7000+2000=9000 So, there are 12000-9000=3000 more people in the 25-50 age group than in the other groups combined.	Pay close attention to the age groups that you are comparing.
11 C	You need to look at the totals and work backwards. There are 200 students in total. 120 of them scored in the 51-100 range. So 200-120=80 students scored in the 0-50 range. Of these, 30 students are girls. So, 80-30=50 are boys in the 0-50 score range.	Familiarize yourself with problems where you to work backwards starting with the totals.
12 B	You need to find the number of girls. You know that there are 200 students and 90 boys (from previous problem). So 200-90=110 are girls. So the ratio of boys to girls is 90/110 =0.82	

VOLCANO HIGH SCHOOL			
	Score 0-50	Score 51-100	Total
Boys	**50**	40	**90**
Girls	30		**110**
Total	**80**	120	200

13 C	Note that you need to find the material expenses for 2014, which means for all four quarters. Carefully note that the table gives the material expense percentages for each of the four quarters, but this percentage is quarter specific. For example, 60% of 1st quarter expense was spent on materials, but the first quarter expense itself is obtained from the circle graph – 30% of 20 million. So, the total material expense is calculated by adding up the material expense for each of the 4 quarters. 1st quarter material expense = $\frac{60}{100} \cdot \frac{30}{100} \cdot 20 = 3.6$ million 2nd quarter material expense = $\frac{65}{100} \cdot \frac{20}{100} \cdot 20 = 2.6$ million 3rd quarter material expense = $\frac{70}{100} \cdot \frac{10}{100} \cdot 20 = 1.4$ million 4th quarter material expense = $\frac{40}{100} \cdot \frac{40}{100} \cdot 20 = 3.2$ million So the total is $3.6 + 2.6 + 1.4 + 3.2 = 10.8$ million	Circle graph and Table are correlated/linked in this problem.
14 0.5	From the table, the salary for 3rd quarter is 25% of expenses of 3rd quarter. From the circle graph, the expense for 3rd quarter is 10% of total expense of $20 million. $\frac{25}{100} \cdot \frac{10}{100} \cdot 20 = 0.5$ million	
15 2	Note that the percentage of Drinks portion is not indicated in the graph. Let the total bill be x. Pizza is 30% of the total bill. $12 was spent on pizza. So, Pizza=$12 = \frac{30}{100} \cdot x$ $x = \frac{1200}{30} = 40$ = total bill. The circle graph does not indicate what percentage is Drinks. Since the total percentage must be 100%, Drinks makes up $100 - (30 + 20 + 45) = 5\%$ of the total bill. So $\frac{5}{100} \cdot 40 = 2$.	Read the question carefully – how much was spent on drinks is different from what percentage was spent on drinks. This question does not ask for pizza percentage.
16 D	Let the total number of students be x. Total number of students in 11th and 12th grades = $0.3x + 0.1x = 0.4x$ Total number of students in 9th and 10th grades = $0.2x + 0.4x = 0.6x$ Difference = 100. $0.6x - 0.4x = 100$ $0.2x = 100$ $x = \frac{100}{0.2} = 500$	
17 B	Note that Alicia has 50% of her portfolio in stocks but she reduces her stocks to 20%, This means she sells 30%. So, $\frac{30}{100} \cdot 500,000 = 150,000$ and this amount is deposited in the saving account. Savings account before this deposit was 30% = $\frac{30}{100} \cdot 500000 = 150,000$. Now with the additional deposit, savings account = $150,000 + 150,000 = 300,000$. This new savings total is $\frac{300,000}{500,000} \cdot 100 = 60\%$ of her portfolio	A person's financial portfolio is a list of accounts where money is saved – checking accounts, saving accounts, stocks, bonds, etc.

18 A	Note that the cab ridership in zip code 90212 is x% and in zip code 90214 is $3x$%. The total ridership is 3000. The percentages must add up to 100. $12 + 18 + 20 + x + 3x = 100$ $4x = 50; x = 12.5$ In zip code 90214, the ridership share= $3x = 3 \cdot 12.5\% = \frac{37.5}{100} \cdot 3000 = 1125$	
19 B	Population in 1925 is 2.5 (million) and Population in 1950 is 1.5 (million). Percentage decrease = $\frac{1.5-2.5}{2.5} \cdot 100 = 40\%$ Population in 1900 is 2 (million) and Population in 2000=1.5 (million). Percentage decrease = $\frac{1.5-2}{2} \cdot 100 = 25\%$ So, the answer to this question is 40-25=15%	In this question, you have to calculate 2 percentages and then find the difference of these percentages.
20 A	Note that the question talks about 2000-2014 – this is not in the graph. The population decrease from 1925 to 1950=$\frac{1.5-2.5}{2.5} \cdot 100 = 40\%$. From 2000 to 2014, the population increased at 40%. So the population in 2014= $1.5 + \frac{40}{100} \cdot 1.5 = 2.1$ million Note that the question asks for the population in millions. So, the answer is 2.1, not 2,100,000.	Be alert to questions that extrapolate data to points that are not shown in the graph.
21 B	Read the question carefully. It asks for the set of numbers that indicates the actual number of infections. It does not ask for the answer in thousands. When the viral and bacterial infections were the same, the infections were 2.2, 1.8 and 1.7, in thousands. So, the actual number of infections is $2.2 \cdot 1000, 1.8 \cdot 1000, 1.7 \cdot 1000$ respectively. (2200,1800,1700) is the answer.	
22 D	For Apex city, the maximum temperature is 40 and the minimum is 20. For Abyss city, the maximum temperature is 40 and the minimum is 15. So the ratio of the difference in temperature in Apex to that in Abyss = $\frac{40-20}{40-15} = 0.8$	
23 A	Note that the pictograph's legend indicates that one picture represents 10,000 tiles. Note also that there are half tiles as well. Each half tile represents 5000 tiles. Totally there are 9.5 tiles. $9.5 \cdot 10000 = 95,000$ tiles. To reach a target of 100,000 tiles, it must make 100,000-95,000=5000 tiles	
24 B	Dogs= 4.5·40=180; Cats=3.5·40=140; Lizards=0.5·40=20 Cats:Dogs:Lizard = 140:180:20 This ratio can be simplified as 7:9:1 by dividing them by 20. Note that the ratio calls for cats to be the first item in the ratio.	Pay attention to the order of items in the ratio.

| 25 C | When 20 students switch from professor A to professor B, professor A will have 50-20=30 students and professor B will have 40+20=60 students. Since each picture represents 10 students, now the students will be represented by 3 pictures for professor A and 6 pictures for professor B. | Read the legend to figure out how many students correspond to one picture in the pictograph. |

PROBLEM SOLVING AND DATA ANALYSIS
Lesson 9 — Growth and Decay — Review

FOCUSPREP CHECKLIST

- How are linear growth and linear decay modeled?
- How are exponential growth and an exponential decay modeled?
- Workout practice problems in Growth and Decay

Q1 What does Linear Growth and Linear Decay mean?

A1 Linear growth is increase and linear decay is decrease at the same rate from one time period to another. When plotted, the linear growth is a straight line with a positive slope and a linear decay is a straight line with negative slope.

For example, if a reservoir gets rain at a constant rate, then its level will grow linearly with a positive slope as shown. On the other hand if the reservoir is drained at a constant rate, it will decay (decrease) linearly with a negative slope as shown.

Q2 How are linear growth and decay modeled?

A2 Linear growth and decay are modeled using a linear equation of the type $y = mx + b$ where y is the dependent variable, x is the independent variable, m is the slope, and b is the y intercept.

Q3 How is a linear model developed from scratch?

A3 Depending on whether the data is in a table or graph, follow the steps below to create a linear model.

Step 1:
If the data is in a scatterplot graph, draw a line of best fit that connects the points as much as possible. Sometimes, points may be above or below the line of best fit. If the data is in a table, you do not need to draw a scatterplot. Proceed to step 2.

Step 2: Pick two data points $(x_1, y_1), (x_2, y_2)$ from the table or the graph, and calculate the slope m using $\frac{y_2 - y_1}{x_2 - x_1}$.

Step 3: If the data is in a graph, find the y-intercept (b) from the graph and then use the slope intercept formula $y = mx + b$ to create the linear model. Verify the model for different values of x.

If the data is in a table, use the point slope formula $y - y_1 = m(x - x_1)$ to develop the linear model. Some examples of linear models are: $y = 2x$, $y = 4.5x + 3.25$, $y = -8.92x + 1000$. Verify the model for different values of x.

Q4 What does correlation coefficient mean?

A4 Correlation coefficient r indicates how well the line fits the data. It can take a value from -1 to 1. ($-1 \leq r \leq 1$). $r = 0$ indicates no fit, $r = 1$ indicates perfect fit with positive slope, and $r = -1$ indicates perfect fit with negative slope. If the slope is positive, r is positive, and if the slope is negative, r is negative.

Q5 After developing the linear model, how do I use it?

A5 After a linear model of the form $y = mx + b$ is developed, it is used for making **predictions** for future values. In the following two examples, you will develop a linear model from a table and a graph. The process is slightly different in each case.

Example: The water level in a reservoir increases every hour as shown. Develop a linear model that fits the data. What will be the water level in the reservoir at 15 hrs? When will the water level be 420 ft?

Time (hr)	0	1	2	3
Level (ft)	100	110	120	130

Solution: Note that the problem asks you to develop a linear model. So you can start off by assuming that the model will be of the form $y = mx + b$ and go on to find m and b.

Calculate the slope using any two data points:

Using $(x_1, y_1) = (1,110)$ and $(x_2, y_2) = (2,120)$, $m = \frac{y_2 - y_1}{x_2 - x_1} = \frac{120 - 110}{2 - 1} = 10$

Use the point slope formula to develop the linear model. Pick any point say $(x_1, y_1) = (3,130)$. $y - y_1 = m(x - x_1)$. So, $y - 130 = 10(x - 3)$. Simplifying, you get the linear model: $y = 10x + 100$. Verify the model for different values of x. When $x = 2$, $y = 10 \cdot 2 + 100 = 120$.

Using this model $y = 10x + 100$, where y is the level of reservoir and x is the time in hours, you can calculate the water level in the reservoir at $t = 15\ hrs$. $y = 10(15) + 100 = 250$ ft.

Using this model, you can also, predict when the water level in the reservoir will reach 420 feet. Substitute 420 into the model.

$420 = 10x + 100$. $x = \frac{320}{10} = 32$ hours. The water level will be 420 feet after 32 hours.

Example The same problem discussed above is given in the form of a scatterplot graph. Find the linear model.

Solution: Step 1: Draw a line of best fit through the points. In this case, the line passes through all the points. In problems where all the data points do not fall on a line, draw a line that connects as many points as possible. A line of best fit may also approximately divide the points such that about half of them are above and half of them are below the line.

Step 2: Pick two points and find the slope. $(x_1, y_1) = (1,110)$, $(x_2, y_2) = (2,120)$. So the slope $m = \frac{y_2 - y_1}{x_2 - x_1} = \frac{120 - 110}{2 - 1} = 10$.

Step 3: Read the y-intercept= $b = 100$. So, the linear model = $y = mx + b = 10x + 100$. Verify the model. For $x = 3$, $y = 10 \cdot 3 + 100 = 130$. This point falls in the line. So, in both examples, the same model is obtained.

Q6 What does Exponential growth mean?

A6 Exponential growth or decay is much quicker than linear growth or linear decay. For example if something doubles or triples in value from one time period to another, then this growth is much faster than linear growth. Certain things (such that the value of a car) can decrease (decay) exponentially. When plotted, the exponential growth is a curve. Bacteria is famous for growing exponentially – for every time period, it will double in quantity over the previous time period.

Q7 How do I model exponential growth or decay?

A7 Exponential growth or decay are modeled as $y = a \cdot b^x$
   When $a > 0$ and $b > 1$ it is Exponential growth model
   When $a > 0$ and $0 < b < 1$ it is Exponential decay model

When $a = 1, b = 2$, the model becomes $y = 2^x$; A table that shows the values of this model is shown below. The value of y doubles over its previous value. Compare this with linear model $y = 2x$ where the values of y do not double over their previous values. Also, note carefully the graphs of linear and exponential functions. A table and a graph of an exponential decay model is also shown.

Linear Growth $y = 2x$				
x	0	1	2	3
y	0	2	4	6

Exponential Growth $y = 2^x$				
x	0	1	2	3
y	1	2	4	8

Exponential Decay $y = 0.5^x$				
x	0	1	2	3
y	1	0.5	0.25	0.125

Q8 Apart from $y = 2^x$ are there other exponential models?

A8 While $y = 2^x$ is a popular exponential growth model, there are other exponential growth models and exponential decay models that are different.

Recall that the general form of an exponential model is $y = ab^x$. In this model, b is the base and x is the exponent. b can take on any value greater than zero other than 1. For example, when $b = 3$, you have $y = 3^x$, when $b = 4$, $y = 4^x$ and these are exponential growth models too. Similarly, when $b < 1$, say when $b = 0.8$, $y = 0.8^x$ – this is an example of an exponential decay model.

Q9 In exponential models, is b always given?

A9 Not necessarily – you will have to calculate b sometimes, and it is easy to do so.

Example
The value of some antique furniture grows at the rate of 18% every year. What is an exponential model that will model this growth?

Answer
At the beginning, assume that the value of the furniture is P dollars.

After 1 year, the value would be $P + \frac{18}{100} \cdot P = 1.18\, P$

After 2 years, the value would be $1.18P + \frac{18}{100} \cdot 1.18\, P = 1.18 \cdot P(1+0.18) = P \cdot 1.18^2$

After n years, the value would be $P \cdot 1.18^n$. This is the model that describes the growth in value of the antique furniture. This is an exponential model too, since it is of the form $y = a \cdot b^x$.

Note that the general formula for an exponential model, $y = ab^x$ can be expanded to include more details about calculating b (in cases where b is not given explicitly) as follows:
$y = a(1 \pm r)^t$ where a is the initial value, r is the rate of increase or decrease, and t is the time period.

Example
The value of a car decreases exponentially at the rate of 20% every year. If its initial value is $20,000, what will be the value of the car after 3 years?

Using $y = a(1 \pm r)^t$, $y = 20000(1 - 0.2)^t = 20000 \cdot 0.8^t$. After 3 years, the value of the car will be $20000 \cdot 0.8^3 = \$10,240$. Use your calculator to find this value correctly.

PROBLEM SOLVING AND DATA ANALYSIS
Lesson 9 — Growth and Decay — Practice

CALCULATOR SECTION

1. A physics professor performs an experiment to measure the friction of a wooden surface. He applies forces on a brick and measures the displacement of the brick. His measurements are shown below.

Force and Displacement

Force f	0	10	15	20
Displacement d	0	3	4	4.5

Which of the following models best describes the displacement as a function of the force applied on the brick?
- A) $d = 0.3f$
- B) $d = 0.2f$
- C) $d = 0.2f + 1$
- D) $d = 0.3f + 1$

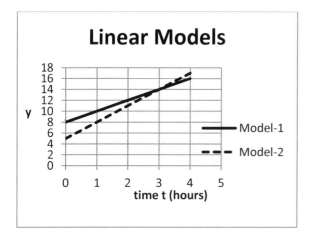

2. Two linear models are graphed above. How many hours after both the linear models have the same value will Model-2 have a value of 62?
GRID IN

CALCULATOR SECTION

An ornithologist spends a significant amount of money to restore a marshy land in order to attract more birds. His recordings for 5 months after the restoration are as follows.

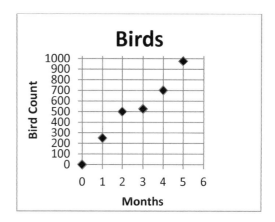

3. What is the average monthly increase in the number of birds visiting the marshland?
GRID IN

4. A nurse was tasked to inject 250 mL of saline water into a patient at the rate of 10 mL every 5 minutes. After how many minutes will the entire saline solution be injected into the patient?
GRID IN

CALCULATOR SECTION

5. The value of a boat that Jim bought for $50,000 depreciates according to the table below.

BOAT'S VALUE IN THOUSANDS

Year y	0	1	2	3
Value v	50	40	32	25.60

Which of the following models describes the depreciation value of the boat, in thousands, over time accurately?
  A) $v = 50 \cdot 0.8^y$
  B) $v = 50 \cdot 1.2^y$
  C) $v = 0.8^y$
  D) $v = 1.2^y$

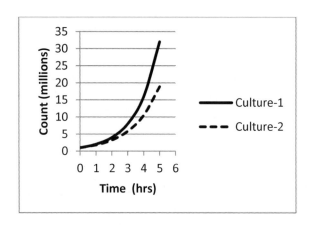

6. Bacterial culture-1 is modeled as $y = 2^x$ and bacterial culture-2 is modeled as $y = 1.8^x$ as shown in the graph. What is the difference in the bacterial count after 7 hours of growth?
A) 6.12 thousand
B) 61.22 thousand
C) 66.78 million
D) 76.84 million

CALCULATOR SECTION

7. Money deposited in the Bank of Generous will get you a 5% interest compounded yearly whereas the Bank of Stingy offers only 3% interest compounded yearly. If $3500 is deposited in both banks, what will be the difference in amounts in the two banks after 8 years? Express your answer to the nearest whole number.
GRID IN

8. Brandi has to payback a loan of $300,000 at the rate of 8% of the original loan every year. How many years will she take to pay off her loan?
GRID IN

#	Explanation	Comments
1 C	Note that the question stem says ".. best describes".

In this problem, you are given a table and a set of linear models. You do not have to develop the models from scratch by using the point slope formula. Fit the model to the data and see which model "best fits" the data. Choice C, $d = 0.2f + 1$ fits the data at 3 points accurately but on the 4th point, $d = 0.2 \cdot 20 + 1 = 5$, which is very close to 4.5. Other models do not fit the data points closely. | In this problem, you don't need to develop the linear model from scratch since the models are given in the answer choices. |
| 2 16 | The question is – how many hours after the models have the same value does model 2 have a value of 62?
From the graph, it is clear that the models have the same value at 3 hrs. Now, find when the model-2 will have a value of 62. y intercept=$b = 5$, pick any 2 points to find the slope, $(x_1, y_1) = (0,5)$ and $(x_2, y_2) = (1,8)$.
slope = $(8 - 5)/(1 - 0) = 3$. So, the model-2 is $y = 3t + 5$. You need to find when y will be equal to 62. $62 = 3t + 5$; $t = \frac{57}{3} = 19$ hrs.
So with the models being the same at 3 hours, it will take $19 - 3 = 16$ more hours for model-2 to have a value of 62. | Pay attention to the legend – when there are multiple models in the graph, they can be shown as dashed lines. |
| 3 200 | What is the average monthly increase in the number of birds? This is the same as the slope of the line. Since this is a scatterplot, draw a line of best fit as shown.

Birds

Bird Count vs Months since restoration

Pick 2 points, $(0,0)$ and $(1,200)$. The slope is $\frac{200 - 0}{1 - 0} = 200$. | Draw a line of best fit connecting the data points. Not all points will always fall on the line. About half the points are above and the other half are below the line. That is the best fit you can get for these points.

For linear models, the average increase or decrease in y for corresponding increase in x is the slope of the line. Be alert for questions that test your understanding of this concept. |

4 125	250mL initially; injection rate is 10 mL/5mins = 2mL/minute. So, imagine a linear decay model that starts at y intercept of 500 and with negative slope of -2. Slope is -2 because the injection rate is 2 – so the saline depletion rate is -2 mL/min. $s = 250 - 2t$ or $-2t + 250$ is the linear model, where s is the saline left. When the entire solution is injected, $s = 0$; so $0 = 250 - 2t$ $2t = 250$ $t = \dfrac{250}{2} = 125$ mins		
5 A	Note that the values are in thousands. Note that the value of the boat at $y = 0$, is 50. Plug in the models to the data. When $y = 0$, the value given by the first 2 models is $v = 50 \cdot 0.8^0 = 50$. Since the value decays, the model is likely to be choice A which is $50 \cdot 0.8^x$. Use your calculator to plug in the other data points; $y = 1, 2,$ and 3 and verify that the model gives you the value v of the boat correctly. $50 \cdot 0.8^1 = 40, 50 \cdot 0.8^2 = 32, 50 \cdot 0.8^3 = 25.60$.	Learn to use your calculator to find exponential values such as $50 \cdot 0.8^3$ quickly and accurately.	
6 C	The graph does not have values at $t = 7$ hours, but the textual information gives you the model. At $t = 7$, culture-1 has 2^7 and culture-2 has 1.8^7. So the difference is $2^7 - 1.8^7 = 66.78$. Note that the graph provides useful information about the scale of the bacterial count – it is in millions. So, the answer is 66.78 million.		
7 737	Since money is compounded yearly, this is a case of exponential growth. Recall that the formula for growth is $P(1 + r)^t$. So, 3500 will become $3500(1.05)^8$ in one bank and $3500(1.03)^8$ in another bank. The difference is $3500(1.05^8 - 1.03^8) = \$737.40 \cong \$737$.	Pay attention to parenthesis – the correct answer is not $3500(1.08 - 1.03)^8$.	
8 12.5	Note that the problem says she has to pay at the rate of 8% of the loan every year. This indicates a linear decay(decrease) in the amount of 8% of 300,000= $0.08 \cdot 300,000 = 24,000/year$. So, the linear model is: balance= $300000 - 24000t$. When the amount is paid in full, the balance is 0. $300000 - 24000t = 0$ $24000 \cdot t = 300,000$ $t = \dfrac{300000}{24000} = 12.5$ years	Read the problem carefully but don't assume anything other than what is stated. The linear model can have large numbers in them and that should not be an issue.	

Lesson 10	PROBLEM SOLVING AND DATA ANALYSIS	Review
	Statistics	

> **FOCUSPREP CHECKLIST**
> - How do I calculate the mean, median, mode, and range?
> - How do I calculate the weighted average?
> - What is standard deviation? How is it calculated?
> - How do I read a box and whisker plot?
> - Workout practice problems in Statistics

Q1 How are the mean, median, mode, and range of a set of numbers calculated?

A1 For a set of numbers, $x_1, x_2, x_3 \ldots x_n$ you can calculate the following:

Mean: (Average, or Arithmetic mean) = $\frac{x_1+x_2+x_3+ \ldots x_n}{n}$

For example, the mean of 1, 2, 3, 4, 5 is $\frac{1+2+3+4+5}{5} = \frac{15}{5} = 3$

Median: The middle number in the set, when the set is arranged in ascending order. If there is even number of items, then there will be two numbers in the middle. In that case, the median is the average of the two middle values. For example, if there are four numbers in a list, the median is the average of the 2nd and 3rd numbers. The median of 1, 2, 3 is 2, the middle number in the set, and the median of 1,2,3,4 is $\frac{2+3}{2} = 2.5$, the average of the 2nd and 3rd numbers in the set.

Mode: The number that appears the most number of times. You can have no mode, one mode or multiple modes. For example, in the set 1,3,3,4 the mode is 3 whereas in the set 1,2,2,3,3 the mode is both 2 and 3. In the set 1,2,3 there is no mode.

Range: The difference between the largest and the smallest number of a data set.

Q2 What does the median indicate?

A2 The median of a set of numbers indicates the value above and below which equal numbers of values exist. For example, the values of 4 toys are $10, $20, $30 and $40. The median is $\frac{20+30}{2} = 25$. This indicates that half the toys are below $25 and half are above $25. In Beverly Hills, the median price of homes is $3 million. This means that 50% of the homes there are below $3 million and 50% are above $3 million.

Q3 What does weighted average mean? When will I need to use it?

A3 Weighted average is also called Expected Value. When you know the frequency of specific data values, you can find which data value can be "expected". If there are n values, $v1, v2, v3 \ldots$ and each value occurs $n1, n2, n3\ldots$ times respectively, then

Weighted Average (Expected value) = $\frac{v1 \cdot n1 + v2 \cdot n2 + \cdots}{n1+n2+\cdots}$

Q4 What is central tendency and how is it measured?

A4 Central tendency is a number that indicates the central value of data. It can be the mean or median or mode of the data set, depending on the type of data and the distribution of data. When the data does not have outliers, the mean is a good indicator of central tendency. When the data has outliers, the median is a good indicator of central tendency. When a data is categorical, the mode (the value that occurs most number of times than other values) is a good indicator of central tendency.

Example 1: Mean is the central tendency: The ages of 5 adults are: 28,37,49,61,75. The data values are close and do not have outliers. The mean is 50 and is a good indicator of central tendency.

Example 2: Median is the central tendency: The ages of 5 adults are: 23,25,28,92,99. Three data values are less than 30 and two values in nineties are very high outliers. The mean is 53.4 and the median is 28. Two adults are older than 28 and two are younger than 28. The median is a better measure of central tendency in this case. When there are outliers, the median is a better indicator of central tendency.

Example 3: Mode is the central tendency: Students in a daycare were asked which tour they wanted to take and the results were as follows: Zoo: 10 Waterpark: 25 Movie: 12 Museum: 16. In this scenario, the waterpark option is the best measure of central tendency since most students want to go there. Mean or Median will not make sense in deciding the central tendency for this data. Mode is a good indicator of central tendency in situations where you have to choose between several options.

Q5 What are the measures of spread (variance) of data?

A5 The range, standard deviation, and quartile are the commonly used measures of variance.

Q6 What is standard deviation and how is it calculated?

A6 The standard deviation of a set of numbers indicates how much deviation is there from the mean, on an average, considering all data in the set. It is an important measure of the spread or variance of data from the mean. It is represented by the Greek symbol Sigma, written as σ.

For a set of n numbers, $x_1, x_2, x_3 \ldots x_n$ where $\bar{x}$ as the mean, the standard deviation is calculated as follows:

$$\sigma = \sqrt{\frac{(x_1-\bar{x})^2+(x_2-\bar{x})^2+(x_3-\bar{x})^2+\cdots(x_n-\bar{x})^2}{n}}$$

Calculating σ is easy – take the difference of each value from the mean, square and sum them, and then average the sum over the number of data values n.

The variance is the number inside the square root. It is written as σ^2.

$$\text{Variance} = \sigma^2 = \frac{(x_1-\bar{x})^2+(x_2-\bar{x})^2+(x_3-\bar{x})^2+\cdots(x_n-\bar{x})^2}{n}$$

The standard deviation is the square root of variance. The College Board says that you **will not** be required to calculate standard deviation, but you are expected to know what it is and answer questions about it. It is important to know how it is calculated so that you can be better prepared to answer questions.

Remember that when the data is clustered around the mean, the standard deviation is close to 0, whereas if the data is spread out, the standard deviation is greater than 0. Learning to calculate standard deviation using the calculator can be valuable sometimes even though SAT questions will not ask you to calculate it. See the calculator section for instructions.

Example 1: The heights of 5 students in a school are as follows: 6, 5, 4, 7, 6. What is the standard deviation of this set of data?

Solution:

Calculate the mean: $\bar{x} = \frac{6+5+4+7+6}{5} = 5.6$

Calculate the variance: $\sigma^2 =$
$\frac{(6-5.6)^2+(5-5.6)^2+(4-5.6)^2+(7-5.6)^2+(6-5.6)^2}{5} = \frac{(0.4^2)+(-0.6)^2+(-1.6)^2+(1.4)^2+(0.4)^2}{5} = 1.04$

Calculate the standard deviation: $\sigma = \sqrt{1.04} = 1.02$.

Example 2: In a high school, the average height of students is 5 feet and the standard deviation is 0 feet. This means that there is no deviation from the mean and so all the students are 5 feet tall.

Example 3: In a high school, the average height of students is 5 feet and the standard deviation is 2 feet. This means that the average deviation of the height of students from their mean height is 2 feet.

Example 4: A high school math teacher wishes that all of her students have almost the same scores in a test. Which one of the following choices of mean and standard deviation will satisfy the teacher's wish?
  (A) Mean 75, Standard Deviation = 1.21
  (B) Mean 52, Standard Deviation = 0.52
  (C) Mean 75, Standard Deviation = 5.67
  (D) Mean 69, Standard Deviation = 22.78

Solution: Choice B is the answer. If the students have almost the same scores, then the mean $\bar{x}$ will be almost the same as the individual scores, so $(x_1 - \bar{x})^2$ will be almost 0. So, the standard deviation will be close to 0. The standard deviation in choice b is 0.52 which is the closest to 0.

Q7 How do I calculate the standard deviation using a calculator?

A7 The College Board says that you will **not** be required to calculate standard deviation. Regardless, it is easy to do so using your calculator. Refer to the calculator section for instructions. Knowing how to calculate standard deviation using your calculator can be of help.

Q8 What is an outlier? How does it impact the mean, median, and standard deviation?

A8 An outlier is a value that is very high or very low compared to other values in the data set. Scatterplots and box and whisker plots are used to visually identify outliers in data.

Example 1: In the data set 1,45,48,52,61 the value of 1 is an outlier since it is very much less than rest of the data.

Example 2: In the data set 1,50,53,59,500 the values of 1 and 500 are outliers since they are very distant from the rest of the data.

If you remove the outlier and analyze data, you will see that the mean and standard deviation are impacted significantly but the median is not impacted significantly. In Example 2, the mean with the outliers is 132.6 whereas the mean without the outliers is 54. The median with outliers is 53 and the median without the outliers is also 53. The standard deviation with the outliers is 184.76 whereas it is 3.74 without the outliers.

Q9 What is a quartile?

A9 Quartiles are numbers that divide a list of numbers into four parts. There are three quartiles for any data set. The first quartile Q1, the second quartile Q2, and the third quartile Q3. The second quartile is the median of the data set. The first quartile is the median of the lower half of the data set. The third quartile is the median of the upper half of the data set. In terms of percentiles, the first quartile is the 25th percentile, the second quartile is the 50th percentile, and the third quartile is the 75th percentile. The first quartile is also called the lower quartile and the third quartile is also called the upper quartile. The interquartile range is Q3 − Q1, that is, the difference between the first and third quartiles. Data that falls in the interquartile range are above the 25th percentile and below the 75th percentile.

Example 1: Consider the data set 1,5,8,10. The median of the data set is (5+8)/2= 6.5. The median of the lower half is (1+5)/2=3. The median of the upper half is (8+10)/2=9. So, the first quartile Q1 is 3, the second quartile Q2 is 6.5 and the third quartile Q3 is 9. The interquartile range is Q3-Q1=0-3=6.

Example 2: Consider the data set 1,5,8,10,15. The median of the data set is 8. The median of the lower half is (1+5)/2=3. The median of the upper half is (10+15)/2=12.5. So, the first quartile is 3, the second quartile is 8 and the third quartile is 12.5. In terms of percentiles, the third quartile value of 12.5 corresponds to 75th percentile. This means that 75% of the data values are below 12.5.

Q10 What is a box and whisker plot used for?

A10 A box plot is used to show the distribution of data. It shows the minimum value, the first quartile, second quartile, third quartile, and the maximum value of the data. The quartiles are shown in a box and the minimum and maximum values are shown in lines that look like whiskers. The range of the data is the difference between the maximum and minimum values.

When two data sets are compared, two box plots are presented together.

Example: The box plot below shows the data obtained from the Electricity bills (in Dollars) of two families over a 12 month period. Several questions can be answered from this box plot as shown below.

- Which family had the lowest electricity bill?
    Family 2–$100
- Which family had the highest electricity bill?
    Family 1– $700
- 50% of the bills of Family 2 were below what amount?
    $300–50% corresponds to the second quartile.
- What is the median expenditure on electricity for Family 1?
    $500–read the dollar value for the second quartile(50th percentile).
- What percentage of bills of Family 1 is above $200?
    100%–all the values are above the minimum value.
- What is the range of expenditures for Family 2?
    Range=max-min=600-100=500
- What percentage of bills for Family 2 is between 200 and 500 dollars?
    75% of bills are below $500 and 25% of bills are below $200. So, 75-25=50% of bills are between 200 and 500 dollars.

PROBLEM SOLVING AND DATA ANALYSIS
Lesson 10 — Statistics — Practice

CALCULATOR SECTION

1. The scores of a student in four tests are 50, 51, 52, and 53 respectively. How much should the student score in the fifth test if the average score in five tests has to be 54?
(A) 44
(B) 54
(C) 64
(D) 74

2. The average of three consecutive numbers starting with $x - 4$ is which one of the following?
(A) $x - 1$
(B) $x - 2$
(C) $x - 3$
(D) $x - 4$

3. The average of three numbers is 5. When a fourth number is added to the list, the average increases to 7. What is the value of the fourth number?
(A) 7
(B) 8
(C) 12
(D) 13

CALCULATOR SECTION

4. The average of six numbers is 15. When one number is removed, the average is 10. What is the value of the number that was removed?
(A) 15
(B) 20
(C) 35
(D) 40

5. Each of the 50 ducks in Alpha Zoo weighs 5 pounds. Each of the 40 ducks in the Beta Zoo weighs 8 pounds. What is the average weight of the ducks in both Zoos combined?
(A) 5.33
(B) 6.33
(C) 7.33
(D) 8.33

6. 50 employees in a company own an average of 2 cars each whereas the remaining 25 employees own an average of 3 cars each. What is the average number of cars owned by all the employees of the company?
(A) 1.53
(B) 1.73
(C) 2.13
(D) 2.33

CALCULATOR SECTION

7. The average of three numbers x, y, z is m. The average of y and z is n. What is the value of x in terms of m and n?
(A) $\frac{2n}{3m}$
(B) $2n + 3m$
(C) $3m - 2n$
(D) $6mn$

8. If $\frac{a}{b} = \frac{1}{4}$ and $\frac{c}{b} = \frac{3}{4}$, what is the average of a and c?
(A) $\frac{b}{2}$
(B) $\frac{b}{3}$
(C) $\frac{b}{4}$
(D) $\frac{b}{5}$

9. The median and mode are the same in which of the following choices?
(A) 11,12,13,14,15
(B) 11,12,12,14,15
(C) 11,12,13,14,14
(D) 11,11,13,14,15

CALCULATOR SECTION

Set-1: 105,106,107,108,110
Set-2: 45,46,47,47,49

10. The range of Set-1 is more than the range of Set-2 by
(A) 1
(B) 2
(C) 4
(D) 6

11. Consider the two statements below and indicate which one of the answer choices is true.

I: The average height of 50 students can be calculated by adding the average heights of two sets of 25 students each.

II: The average height of each of two sets of 25 students can be used to calculate the average height of 50 students.

(A) I only
(B) II only
(C) I and II
(D) None of the above

CALCULATOR SECTION

12. The smallest number in a data set is 5 and the range of the data set is 15. What is the largest number in the data set?
(A) 5
(B) 10
(C) 15
(D) 20

13. A shoe store recorded the following information.

Size	5	6	7
Sales (number of shoes)	85	62	21

If you randomly select a shoe that was sold, it can be expected to be of which size? (round up to the next size)
(A) 5
(B) 6
(C) 7
(D) None of the above

14. If Jana drives 6 hours at a speed of 60 miles/hour and 9 hours at a speed of 62 miles/hour, what is her average speed in miles/hour during her 15 hours of driving?
(A) 51.20
(B) 58.46
(C) 61.20
(D) 64.30

CALCULATOR SECTION

15. If x is the average of all the angles of a triangle and y is the average of all the angles of a rectangle, then $x + y =$
(A) 60
(B) 90
(C) 150
(D) 180

16. A survey asking people how many cars they owned resulted in the following histogram.

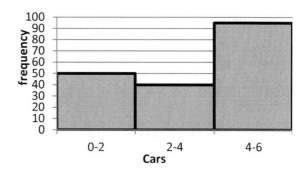

Which of the following could be the median number of cars owned by those surveyed?
(A) 1
(B) 2
(C) 5
(D) 6

CALCULATOR SECTION

17. For a given set of data, which of the following is least affected by the addition of an outlier?
(A) Standard Deviation
(B) Mean
(C) Median
(D) Range

18. The mean score in a Geography test is 74 and the standard deviation is 10. A trophy will be given to students who are at least two standard deviations more than the mean. What is the least one must score to get a trophy?

(A) 64
(B) 74
(C) 84
(D) 94

19. The interquartile range of a data set with a lower quartile of 10 and an upper quartile of 22 is
(A) 10
(B) 12
(C) 22
(D) 32

20. An opinion poll stated that 30% of the citizens of Culver City will vote for Stacy as the new governor of their state. The margin of error of the poll is ±4% with a 95% confidence level. If the poll in conducted again, what is the least percent of votes that Stacy can expect to get?
(A) 10
(B) 26
(C) 30
(D) 34

CALCULATOR SECTION

Set-1: 105,106,107,108,110
Set-2: 11,26,47,59,84

21. Considering the two sets above, which of the following statements below is true?

(A) Set-1 has a higher standard deviation
(B) Set-2 has a higher standard deviation
(C) Set-2 has two modes
(D) Set-1 has a range of 105

$$11,22,33,44,55$$

22. The standard deviation of the data shown above is
(A) 10.29
(B) 11
(C) 15.56
(D) 33

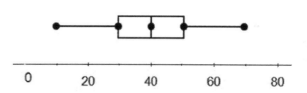

23. The minimum temperature readings in a city for 365 days are shown in the box plot above. The range and interquartile range for this data are
(A) range=60, IQR=30
(B) range=60, IQR=40
(C) range=60, IQR=60
(D) range=60, IQR=20

PROBLEM SOLVING AND DATA ANALYSIS
Lesson 10 — Statistics — Answers

#	Explanation	Comments
1 C	Let x be the score that he needs in the fifth test. $$\frac{50 + 51 + 52 + 53 + x}{5} = 54$$ $x = 54 \cdot 5 - 206 = 270 - 206 = 64$	This is a standard problem involving averages.
2 C	Starting with $x - 4$, three consecutive numbers are one more than the previous number $$x - 4, x - 4 + 1, x - 4 + 2$$ $$x - 4, x - 3, x - 2$$ The average is $\frac{x-4+x-3+x-2}{3} = \frac{3x-9}{3} = x - 3$	Some problems require you to know that for a given number x, the preceding numbers are $x - 1, x - 2$, etc and the succeeding numbers are $x + 1, x + 2$, etc.
3 D	Let a, b, c be the three numbers. $\frac{a+b+c}{3} = 5$; So, $a + b + c = 15$ Let d be the fourth number. Average of four numbers is 7. $\frac{a+b+c+d}{4} = 7$; So, $a + b + c + d = 28$. Substituting $a + b + c = 15$ in the above equation, you get $15 + d = 28$; $d = 28 - 15 = 13$.	
4 D	$\frac{a+b+c+d+e+f}{6} = 15$ $a + b + c + d + e + f = 6 \cdot 5 = 90$ Let f be the number that is removed; average is now 10; $\frac{a+b+c+d+e}{5} = 10$. $a + b + c + d + e = 50$ Substituting this equation in the first one, you get $50 + f = 90$, $f = 90 - 50 = 40$	When an item is removed, remember to reduce the denominator by 1 when calculating the average.
5 B	Average weight= weight of all ducks/ total ducks $= \frac{50 \cdot 5 + 40 \cdot 8}{50 + 40} = \frac{250+320}{90} = \frac{570}{90} = 6.33$	Remember to account for the ducks in both zoos.
6 D	$\frac{50 \cdot 2 + 25 \cdot 3}{50 + 25} = \frac{100 + 75}{75} = \frac{175}{75} = 2.33$	
7 C	$\frac{x+y+z}{3} = m$; So, $x + y + z = 3m$ $\frac{y+z}{2} = n$; $y + z = 2n$; substituting this in the above, you get $x + 2n = 3m$; $x = 3m - 2n$	
8 A	Note that the answers choices show the average of a and c in terms of b. $\frac{a}{b} = \frac{1}{4}$; $a = \frac{b}{4}$; $\frac{c}{b} = \frac{3}{4}$; $c = \frac{3}{4}b$; so $\frac{a+c}{2} = \frac{1}{2}\left(\frac{b}{4} + \frac{3b}{4}\right) = \frac{b}{2}$	

©GiftOfLogic   http://www.GiftOfLogic.com

9 B	In A, median=13 mode=none In B, median=12 mode=12 – both are 12 In C, median=13 mode=14 In D, median=13 mode=11	Review the definition of median and mode.
10 A	Range of set 1= 110-105=5 Range of set 2= 49-45=4 Range of set 1 is more than range of set 2 by 5-4=1	Review the definition of range.
11 B	I. is false – you cannot add averages of two sets of numbers to get the average of the combined set. II. is correct – the average height of each of two sets of 25 students <u>can be used</u> to calculate the average height of 50 students.	If the average height of one set of 25 students is a, then then the sum of their heights is 25a. If the average height of another set of 25 students is b, then the sum of their heights is 25b. You can use this to calculate the average height of 50 students as (25a+25b)/50.
12 D	Range=largest number – smallest number 15=largest number-5 Largest number=15-5=10	
13 B	The expected value is the weighted average= $\frac{5 \cdot 85 + 6 \cdot 62 + 7 \cdot 21}{85 + 62 + 21} = 5.6 \cong 6$	
14 C	Calculate the total distance. Average speed for the entire trip is distance / time for the entire trip $= \frac{60 \cdot 6 + 62 \cdot 9}{6+9} = 61.20$	
15 C	A triangle has 3 angles that add up to 180. So, x=average of the 3 angles= $\frac{180}{3} = 60$. A rectangle has 4 angles that add up to 360. So y=average of the 4 angles=$\frac{360}{4} = 90$. Hence, $x + y = 60 + 90 = 150$.	
16 C	There are 50 respondents for 0-2 cars, 40 respondents for 2-4 cars, and 95 respondents for 4-6 cars. So, totally there are 185 respondents. The median of 185 data points is the 185/2=93rd. Since there are 50 data points for 0-2 cars and 40 data points for 2-4 car range, a total of 90, the 93rd data point will lie in the 4-6 car range. You cannot accurately identify the median since the histogram only shows grouped frequency and not the frequency for the individual number of cars. The 93rd respondent could own either 4 cars or 5 cars. Since choice C is 5, it is the correct answer. Not that choice D is 6 but 6 is not included in any of the bars shown.	Note that the buckets in histograms can sometimes be single values instead of a range. For example, they could be just 0 car, 1 car, 2 cars etc. These are the simple type of histograms. When they have a grouped range like 0-2 cars, 2-4 cars, etc. they are called frequency distribution histograms. Note that since the x-axis labels overlap, like 0-2, 2-4,4-6 each bar in the histogram does not include the right limit of their range. That is, the bar for 0-2 shows the frequency for 0 and 1 cars owned, but not for 2 cars owned. Similarly, the bar for 2-4 cars shows the frequency for 2 and 3 cars owned, but not for the right limit of 4 cars.

17 C	Addition of an outlier will affect the mean, standard deviation, and range the most. It will affect the median the least.	
18 D	Two standard deviations from the mean is 74+20=94. So, one must score 94 to get a trophy.	
19 B	Interquartile is the difference of upper and lower quartiles. 22-10=12.	
20 B	The margin of error is 4%. This means that the next time the poll is conducted, Stacy can expect at least 30-4=26% of the votes and at most 30+4=34% with a confidence level of 95%.	Know how to work with the Margin of Error.
21 B	Set-1 does not have a large standard deviation since the data is clustered close to the average of about 107. The data in set-2 is widely distributed and hence has a large standard deviation. Set-2 does not have 2 modes and set-1 does not have a range of 105.	
22 C	Use your calculator to find the standard deviation of 15.56 for this data set.	
23 D	Range is max-min=70-10=60. Interquartile range is 50-30=20.	

PROBLEM SOLVING AND DATA ANALYSIS

Lesson 11 | Population and Sample | Review

FOCUSPREP CHECKLIST

- What are the different types of studies?
- What is the difference between an observational study and an experimental study?
- How is data collected for a survey?
- What is the difference between a population and a sample?
- What is a two-way frequency table?
- How do I identify the association of variables?
- Workout practice problems in Population and Sample

Q1 What are the different types of scientific studies?

A1 The two types of scientific studies are a) Observational study and b) Experimental study. Scientists design their studies using one of these methods and then collect data and analyze them using statistics. The goal of these studies is to be able to make conclusions that are statistically significant.

Q2 What are the elements of a study?

A2 A study has several elements: a) type – observational or experimental b) subjects – the people or things that are studied c) treatment – specific action applied on the subjects in the case of experimental studies only and d) response – the variable whose outcome is measured.

Q3 What is the difference between an observational study and an experimental study?

A3 An observational study and an experimental study are two different types of studies.

In an observational study, the scientist only observes the subjects and records the information. No treatment is applied to the subjects – that is, no specific experiment is performed on the subjects. Polls and Surveys are examples of observational studies. They are just data gathering exercises.

Example: A research scientist wants to measure the effect of gender on the color of cars purchased. He designs a survey asking people in his zip code what their gender is and the color of their car.

In an experimental study, the subjects are divided into a control group on which no treatment is applied and an experimental group on which treatment is applied and the response is measured from both groups. Experimental studies aim to find cause and effect relationships.

Example: A drug company claims that it has developed a drug to reduce blood sugar. To test this claim, a researcher conducts an experimental study on 50 patients. He divided them into 2 groups of 25 patients each. He does not administer the real drug on the first group (control group) but gives them a fake drug (placebo), and administers the drug on the second group. He then measures the blood sugar of all the patients from both groups and analyses them. The measurements from the control group are used as a baseline to compare the results from the experimental group.

Q4 What do Population and Sample mean? How are they related?

A4 A population is the entire set of values that are being considered for study. A sample is a small subset of the population. For example, all the students in a school can be considered as population whereas the students in one specific class can be considered as a sample.

Q5 What is the difference between a population parameter and a sample statistic?

A5 The goal of a research study is to measure a population parameter. Since a population is too large to conduct a survey on, the survey is conducted on a small sample. The sample statistic (such as mean, median, standard deviation, etc) is then used to make an estimate of the population parameter. So, you have sample mean, sample median, etc and population mean, population median, etc. The population parameters are also called as true mean, true median, etc.

Example: A study aimed to find many families in the country have pets. It surveyed 1000 families and asked them if they have pets. In this example, the number of families in the country that have pets is the population parameter. The number of families that have pets in the sample of 1000 families is the sample statistic.

Q6 What is a survey?

A6 A survey aims to collect information about certain parameters of a population. Since it is often difficult to survey the entire population, a small sample of the population is selected randomly for the survey and its statistics are analyzed and used to make inferences about the entire population. A follow-up survey is a survey that is done in addition to the first survey to find out specific information about the population.

Q7 How is a survey done? How are the results documented?

A7 A survey is done by collecting sample data using unbiased, random sampling. Sampling results are recorded in tables and then analyzed.

Example: A school district administrator wants to find how well the students would perform in a math test. There are 50,000 students in the school district. He picks 300 students randomly and gives them the test. He then calculates the average score obtained by the 300 students.

In this example, the population is made of 50,000 students and the sample is made of 300 students.

Q8 Are surveys accurate?

A8 Errors do creep into surveys due to a variety of reasons – misunderstanding of survey questions, biased survey questions, etc. A survey is said to be biased if these mistakes happen. Errors in surveys are reported in terms of margin of error.

Q9 What statistical measures are used to analyze the results of a survey?

A9 Basic statistical measures such as the mean, median, mode, range, and standard deviation of the sample are used to analyze the results of a sample survey. These sample statistics, along with margin of error and confidence level are used to make estimates/projections of population parameters.

Q10 What is a margin of error? What is a confidence interval? What is a confidence level?

A10 Since the sample sizes are small compared to the population, the sample statistic cannot be applied directly to the population parameter. If a sample survey says that a candidate will get 78% of the votes in a city, you cannot say that he will get 78% of the votes in the country as well. You must take the margin of error and confidence level into account.

A correct survey result will be published as follows: An unbiased poll conducted to predict who will win the election found that the Green party candidate will win 78% of the votes. The poll has a margin of error of ±3% and has 95% confidence level.

The Margin of Error in this survey is ±3%. This means that the confidence interval is 75 to 81 (78 − 3 to 78 + 3). The confidence level is 95%. This means that if the poll is conducted several times, 95% (confidence level) of the time the candidate will get votes in the (confidence interval) range of 75% (78 − 3) to 81% (78 + 3).

Q11 What does a two way table mean?

A11 A two way table categorizes data from a survey in rows and columns. By analyzing the results using a two way table, you can find if the variables are associated or not.

Example: The two-way table below shows the grade of students and the language spoken by them. The cells indicate the number of students in a particular grade speaking a particular language. The totals row and column sum up the data in two ways. Hence it is called a two way table. This table has two categories- grades and language. Each category is broken down into 2 groups- 9th and 10th grades and Spanish and French.

Grade	Spanish	French	Total
9	3	1	4
10	3	2	5
Total	4	5	9

Q12 What does frequency distribution mean?

A12 Data collected from survey is summarized and analyzed in frequency distribution tables and charts such as bar charts and histograms. For example, after doing a survey to find out how many cans of beverage the students in a class drink every week, you can summarize the data in a frequency distribution table and a histogram as follows.

Survey : How many cans of beverage do you drink every week?							
2	0	1	3	5	8	1	0

Frequency Distribution Table	
Cans (Buckets)	Total Number of students
0-3 (0,1,2 cans)	5
3-6 (3,4,5 cans)	2
6-9 (6,7,8 cans)	1

The histogram below showing the frequency distribution of data. Pay attention to the x-axis labels in histograms. In the histogram, the labels show groupings of beverage cans in 0-3, 3-6, and 6-8 range. The first bar represents cans from 0-2 only but not 3. The second bar shown is for groups 3-5 only, but not 5 and so on. Histograms that appear in SAT also follow this convention.

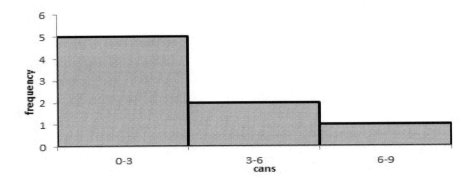

Q13 How do I calculate the mean and median from a histogram?

A13 If the histogram has grouped values in the x-axis such as 0-3, 3-6, etc then you cannot find the mean but you can estimate it. In the histogram above, there are 5 students who drink 0-3 cans – so, since we cannot say how many drank 0 or 1 or 2 cans, we can estimate that all 5 of them drank at least 0 cans. Similarly, we can estimate that 2 students drank at least 3 cans each, and 1 student drank at least 6 cans. So, the average number of cans consumed can be estimated to be at least $\frac{5 \cdot 0 + 2 \cdot 3 + 1 \cdot 6}{8} = 1.5$.

The median can also be estimated. There are 5+2+1=8 students. So there are 8 data values. The median is therefore the average of the 4th and 5th data values. Since there are 5 students in the 0-3 can group, the 4th and 5th students are in this group. So, the median will be in this group. We cannot accurately say what the median is, but we can be sure it will be between 0 and 3.

In the following histogram, the x-axis labels are not grouped. So, the mean and median can be calculated accurately as shown.

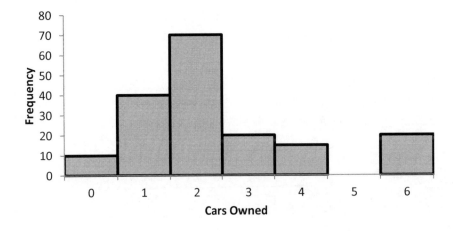

Mean = $\frac{10\cdot 0+ 40\cdot 1+ 70\cdot 2 + 20\cdot 3+15\cdot 4+20\cdot 6}{165} = 2.545$

There are 165 data values. So the median is the value of the 165/2=82.5=83rd data point. From the histogram, you can see that there are 10 people with 0 cars, and 40 people with 1 car – a total of 50 people. There are 70 people with 2 cars – a total of 50+70=120 people. So, the 83rd data point falls in this bar that corresponds to 2 cars. So, the median of this data set is 2.

Q14 How do I calculate the mean and standard deviation from a frequency table?
A14

You are not required to calculate standard deviation or mean from a frequency table but knowing how it is calculated can give you valuable insights. Review the lesson on Statistics for calculation of mean and standard deviation for a set of numbers. If the numbers appear several times and are presented in a frequency table, the mean and standard deviation are calculated as follows. The column f shows the frequency of data x. Calculate the column values and calculate the mean and standard deviation.

x	f	$f \cdot x$	$x - \bar{x}$	$(x - \bar{x})^2$	$f \cdot (x - \bar{x})^2$
1	8	8	-0.76	0.58	4.64
2	5	10	0.24	0.06	0.6
3	4	12	2.24	5.01	6.01
	17	30		5.65	11.25

Mean= $\bar{x} = \frac{f1\cdot x1+f2\cdot x2+\cdots fn\cdot xn}{f1+f2+\cdots fn} = \frac{30}{17} = 1.76$.

Standard Deviation $= \sqrt{\frac{f1\cdot(x1-\bar{x})^2+f2\cdot(x2-\bar{x})^2+\cdots}{f1+f2+\cdots fn}} = \sqrt{\frac{11.25}{30}} = 0.61$

Q15 In a two-way table, how do I calculate the marginal probability, the joint probability and the conditional probability?

A15 Consider the data collected from a survey showing the number of people who speak Spanish and don't speak Spanish and their gender. There are two categories of data – Gender and Language. The goal of the survey is to find if there is an association between gender and people's opinion of sports.

Gender	Like sports	Don't like sports
Male	13	7
Female	3	27

Add a Total row and a Total column and calculate the row and column totals. Then, calculate the marginal, joint, and conditional probabilities as shown in the table below. Using these probabilities (also called distributions) you can make several inferences regarding the sample data.

Gender	Like sports	Don't like sports	Total
Male	13 (13/50=26%) joint (13/20=65%) conditional	7 (7/50=14%) joint (7/20=35%) conditional	20 (20/50=40%) marginal
Female	3 (3/50=6%) joint (3/30=10%) conditional	27 (27/54=54%) joint (27/30=90%) conditional	30 (30/50=60%) marginal
Total	16 (16/50=32%) marginal	34 (34/50=68%) marginal	50 (grand total) marginal

Marginal probability is the ratio of the marginal total with respect to the grand total.
40% of those surveyed are male; 60% of those surveyed are male.
32% of those surveyed like sports; 68% of those surveyed do not like sports.

Joint probability is the ratio of the cell value with respect to the grand total.
Of those surveyed, 26% are males who like sports; 14% are male who don't like sports.
Of those surveyed, 6% are females who like sports; 54% are females who don't like sports.
Sum of joint probabilities in all cells = 1 (100%)

Conditional probability is the ratio of the cell value with respect to the row total. It is used to find the association of categorical variables (gender and choice of sports).

65% of males like sports; 35% of males do not like sports.
10% of females like sports, 90% of females do not like sports.

SAT problems will not mention whether the probabilities are marginal, joint, or conditional, but you can understand what kind of probability you have to use from the context of the question.

Q16 How do I find out if the variables in a two-way table are dependent or independent?

A16

If the conditional probabilities are the same in all the cells in a column, then the two categorical variables are independent (no association). If the conditional probabilities in a column are equal, then the marginal probability of that column will also be the same.

In the above example, since the conditional probabilities are not the same, the variables are dependent on each other. When there is dependence between two categorical variables, they are said to be related or associated.

The following example illustrates how conditional probability is used to determine independence (no association) or dependence (association) of categorical variables.

Example:

The number of students in a college taking Arts and Science classes are shown in the table below:

Gender	Arts	Science	Total
Male			88
Female			62
Total	100	50	150

A research scientist wants to know if the gender of the student is associated with the choice of classes taken. How many male students should take classes in Arts so that there is no association between gender and class choice?

Solution:

If there must be no association between the categorical variables (gender and class choice), then the conditional probabilities must be the same in both cells in one column. It should also be equal to the marginal probability of the variable in that column. For example, if a student takes Arts classes, then the conditional probability of the Arts student being male or female must be the same in the Arts column. The marginal probability that a student will take Arts classes (compared to all the students) should also have the same probability.

The two conditional probabilities and one marginal probability of the Arts column must be the same for no association to exist. If they are different, then there is an association.

In the totals row, you have $\frac{100}{150} = 0.67$. In the male row, if there are m male students that take Arts classes, then $\frac{m}{88}$ is the conditional probability. So, $\frac{m}{88} = \frac{100}{150} = 0.67$ if there should not be any association. This gives $m = 59$ students.

Summary:

A two way table shows categorical information about two variables. Each variable is divided into two groups. For example Gender is one variable that is divided into Male and Female groups. Class choice is another categorical variable that is divided into Arts and Science groups.

A two-way table has $2 \cdot 2 = 4$ cells. Additional cells are added to show the row totals and column totals. Probabilities can be calculated in marginal context, joint context, and conditional context.

Marginal probability:
  What is the probability that a randomly selected student is an Arts student?
  What is the probability that a randomly selected student is a female student?
Joint probability:
  What is the probability that a randomly selected student is a male student taking an Arts class?
  What is the probability that a randomly selected student is a female student taking a Science class?
Conditional probability:
  What is the probability that a randomly selected male student will take an Arts class?
  What is the probability that a randomly selected female student will take a Science class?
Association of variables:
Procedure to find whether there is an evidence of association of the two categorical variables:
  1) Pick one column.
  2) Find the conditional probability of the two cells in that column (cell value/row total)
  3) If the conditional probabilities of the two cells are equal there is **no association.** If they are not equal, there is an **evidence of association**.
  4) Use the fact that all three probabilities (two conditional and one marginal) in any one column must all be the same (in order not to have an association) to find any data that is not given. Refer to the above example to learn how to find missing data.

	PROBLEM SOLVING AND DATA ANALYSIS	
Lesson 11	Population and Sample	Practice

CALCULATOR SECTION

A company that specializes in marketing research conducted a random survey in the state of Texas to find how many people agree that fracking (a method by which shale rock is broken to release natural gas) is necessary to meet the state's energy demand. The response was tabulated as shown below.

Survey Response (in thousands)

Age Group	Fracking OK	Fracking NOT OK	Not Sure	Total
16-25	8,259	2,345	925	11,529
25-50	7,680	5,250	89	13,019
50+	2,344	4,232	10	6,586
Total	18,283	11,827	1024	31,134

1. Based on the survey results, which age group does not like fracking the most?

    (A) 16-25
    (B) 25-50
    (C) 50+
    (D) 75+

2. A follow-up survey was done on the 16-25 age group to find out how many women like fracking by randomly selecting 700 people from this group. 435 respondents in this follow-up survey indicated that they are women. Based on the results of the follow-up survey and the results of the initial survey, which of the following is most likely to be an accurate estimate of how many women in the state of Texas think fracking is ok?

    (A) About 3 million women in the state of Texas think fracking is OK.
    (B) About 5 million women in the state of Texas think fracking is OK.
    (C) About 7 million women in the state of Texas think fracking is OK.
    (D) About 4 million women in the state of Texas think fracking is OK.

CALCULATOR SECTION

A soda manufacturing company conducted a random survey to find out how many boys and girls like their two brands of soda. The response was tabulated as shown below.

Age Group	Soda-1	Soda-2	Neither	Total
1-10	8,259	2,345	925	11,529
11-18	7,680	5,250	89	13,019
Total	15,939	7,595	1014	24,548

3. Based on the survey results, what percentage of 11-18 students like Soda-1 or Soda-2?
    (A) 40.32
    (B) 58.99
    (C) 92.31
    (D) 99.32

4. Of all those that like Soda-1, what percentage are in the 1-10 age group?
    (A) 48.18
    (B) 51.82
    (C) 62.25
    (D) 71.59

5. What percentage(rounded to the nearest hundredths) of those surveyed like neither soda?
GRID IN

6. A follow-up survey of boys and girls that like neither soda was conducted to find out a correlation between their weight and the reason for their dislike of soda. The average weight of the 125 boys and girls randomly surveyed in this follow-up is 85 pounds. What is most likely to be the average weight of the 1014 boys and girls that do not like soda?
GRID IN

CALCULATOR SECTION

The results of the 2010 Census taken at the city of Ventura is shown below.

Age	Asian	African	White	Hispanic
0-10	1300	2400	2000	850
11-25	2500	850	2255	4400
26-50	525	1050	1450	1940
51-100	727	550	650	640

7. What percentage of those in the 0-25 age group is African or White?
   (A) 28.74
   (B) 37.63
   (C) 45.33
   (D) 66.38

8. What percentage of Hispanic population is in the 26-100 age group?
   (A) 8.17
   (B) 24.78
   (C) 32.95
   (D) 41.38

9. A random sample of 26-50 year olds indicates that 35% of them have a Bachelor's degree. Based on this survey result, which one of the following can be inferred?

   (A) 35% of Asian American people in Ventura county have a Bachelor's degree.
   (B) 35% of Asian African American people in Ventura county have a Bachelor's degree.
   (C) 35% of Whites in Ventura county have a Bachelor's degree.
   (D) About 1738 people in the 26-50 age group have a Bachelor's degree.

10. A frequency distribution histogram showing Age buckets and Population will show which one of the following population for the 26-50 age group?
    (A) 655
    (B) 2567
    (C) 4965
    (D) 10,005

CALCULATOR SECTION

A survey done among 9th and 10th graders to find out how many learn Spanish and French produced the following results. The grade of the respondent and the language is listed adjacent to each other.

Grade	Language	Grade	Language	Grade	Language
9	Spanish	10	French	9	Spanish
10	French	9	French	10	Spanish
9	Spanish	10	Spanish	10	French

Questions 10 and 11 refer to the table above

11. How many 9th graders surveyed speak Spanish?
(A) 1
(B) 2
(C) 3
(D) 4

12. Which of the following two way tables represents the data shown above?

(A)
Grade	Spanish	French	Total
9	3	1	4
10	2	3	5
Total	5	4	9

(B)
Grade	Spanish	French	Total
9	2	3	5
10	3	1	4
Total	5	4	9

(C)
Grade	Spanish	French	Total
9	3	3	6
10	2	1	3
Total	5	4	9

(D)
Grade	Spanish	French	Total
9	1	3	4
10	3	2	5
Total	4	5	9

CALCULATOR SECTION

13. The table below shows the data collected from a survey that tried to find if there is an association (dependence) between types of soda by and age groups of students.

Age Group	Soda-1	Soda-2	Total
1-10	80	120	200
11-18	120	280	400
Total	200	400	600

Based on the survey results, the following conclusions can be made.

(A) There is an association between the age groups and the types of soda consumed
(B) There is no association between the age groups and the types of soda consumed
(C) The association between age groups and types of soda cannot be found from the data
(D) More data is required to find an association between age groups and types of soda

14. A two way table prepared after a survey was done on the response to headache tablets on children is shown below.

Age Group	Useful	Not useful	Total
1-10	80	120	200
11-18	120	180	300
Total	200	300	500

Based on the survey results, the following conclusions can be made.

(A) There is an association between the age groups and opinion
(B) There is no association between the age groups and opinion
(C) The association between age groups and opinion cannot be found from the data
(D) More data is required to find an association between age groups and opinion

CALCULATOR SECTION

15. Two lab tests were conducted on 12 guinea pigs. Each of them was placed in a sound proof cage. In Lab Test-1 a low decibel sound was sent into the cage through a small hole in the cage. The time it took for each guinea pig to recognize the sound was noted in seconds. In Lab Test-2 a high decibel sound was sent into the cage and the time it took for each guinea pig to recognize the sound was noted. The results are shown in the dot plots below. Which of the following inferences can be made?

(A) Lab Test-1 has a higher standard deviation than Lab Test-2
(B) Lab Test-2 has a higher standard deviation than Lab Test-1
(C) Both tests have the same standard deviation
(D) More students should take the tests in order to compare the standard deviations

CALCULATOR SECTION

16.

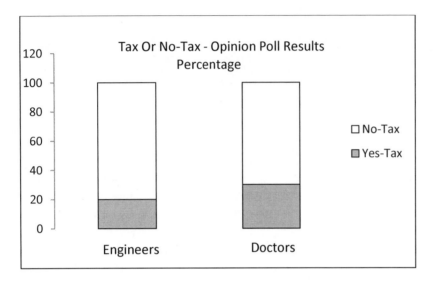

An opinion poll was conducted from Doctors and Engineers to decide if they support or oppose new taxes on their profession. The results are shown in percentages in the stacked bar chart. Which of the following inferences can be drawn from the opinion poll?

(A) Both Engineers and Doctors support taxes equally
(B) More Engineers than Doctors were polled
(C) There is no relation between professionals and their opinion on taxes
(D) There appears to be a relation between professionals and their opinion on taxes

17. A pharmaceutical company wants to test the effect of its back pain drug on 50 test subjects who work in warehouses. Which of the following choices represent the best plan of action to achieve reliable results?

(A) The company must go to warehouses across the country and observe 50 warehouse workers with back pain
(B) The company should select 50 warehouse workers from one warehouse in New York city, and administer the drug on them
(C) The company must randomly select 50 warehouse workers from the country and administer the drug on them
(D) The company must perform a controlled experiment on 50 warehouse workers with back pain selected randomly from the country, and administer the drug only to 25 of them while giving a placebo drug (that does nothing) to the rest

		PROBLEM SOLVING AND DATA ANALYSIS	
Lesson 11		Population and Sample	Answers

#		Explanation	Comments
1	C	Even though age group 25-50 has more people that do not like fracking, as a percentage of their group, it is only 40.3% (5250/13019) whereas the age group 50+ is the one where 64.25% (4232/6586) of the respondents say they don't like fracking.	In this problem, you need to use the percentage to decide.
2	B	Follow-up survey was done on 700 people and 435 reported they are women; Percentage of women in 16-25 age group= $\frac{435}{700} \cdot 100 = 62\%$. Total of 8259 people say fracking is OK- so 62/100 ·8259 – about 5120·1000 – all numbers in the table are in thousands – approximately 5 million women think fracking is OK.	Follow-up survey is a survey that is done in addition to the main survey to find out specific information about the population.
3	D	The question asks what percentage like soda – which means both soda1- and soda-2 must be taken into account. Soda-1+ soda-2= 7680+5250=12,930. Percentage= $\frac{12930}{13019} \cdot 100 = 99.32\%$	
4	B	Total that like soda-1 is 15,939. Of these, 1-10 age group has 8259. So, the percentage is $\frac{8259}{15939} \cdot 100$=51.82%	
5	4.13	1014 like neither soda; 24,548 surveyed. $\frac{1014}{24548} \cdot 100$=4.13%	
6	85	1014 do not like soda. Sample of 125 students has an average weight of 85 lbs. So, this statistic of the sample can be applied to the population and you can say that the average weight of 1014 boys and girls will also be 85 lbs.	A statistic of the sample can be used to make an inference about the population, provided that the sample is not biased.
7	C	<table><tr><td>Age</td><td>Asian</td><td>African</td><td>White</td><td>Hispanic</td><td></td></tr><tr><td>0-10</td><td>1300</td><td>2400</td><td>2000</td><td>850</td><td>6550</td></tr><tr><td>11-25</td><td>2500</td><td>850</td><td>2255</td><td>4400</td><td>10005</td></tr><tr><td>26-50</td><td>525</td><td>1050</td><td>1450</td><td>1940</td><td>4965</td></tr><tr><td>51-100</td><td>725</td><td>550</td><td>650</td><td>640</td><td>2565</td></tr><tr><td></td><td></td><td></td><td></td><td>7830</td><td></td></tr></table> Question is about the 0-25 group – this is 0-10 group + 11-25 group. African =2400+850=3250 White=2000+2255=4255. Total African or White= 3250+4255=7505.	Add additional columns or rows to place your subtotals there.

		Total in the 0-25 group=6550+10005=16555. So, the percentage is 7505/16555 ·100=45.33%	
8	C	The age range in this question is 26-100, which is 26-50 + 51-100. Total Hispanic population in 26-100 age group =1940+640=2580. Total Hispanic population is 7830. So, the percentage is 2580/7830 ·100=32.95%	
9	D	Random sample of 26-50 year olds indicate 35% of them have a Bachelor's degree. So, you can conclude that 35% of the total 26-50 year olds – 35/100 · 4965=1737.75 $\cong$ 1738 people have Bachelor's degree. Note that other choices are not true because you don't know the breakdown of the random sample among Asian, African, White, and Hispanic separately to make this inference.	Make inferences carefully by considering the type of sample obtained.
10	C	The frequency histogram showing age group 26-50 on the x-axis will correspond to a population frequency of 525+1050+1450+1940.	See the lesson on graphs and tables and statistics for a review of histograms.
11	C	Count the number of Spanish speaking 9th graders; there are 3 of them.	Get familiar with the way the survey results are recorded.
12	A	There are a total of 9 students in the survey chart; there are 3 Spanish and 1 French 9th graders, 10 Spanish and 3 French 10th graders. So table 1 is the correct choice.	Familiarize yourself with two way tables.
13	A	<table><tr><th>Age Group</th><th>Soda-1</th><th>Soda-2</th><th>Total</th></tr><tr><td>1-10</td><td>80 (80/200=0.4)</td><td>120</td><td>200</td></tr><tr><td>11-18</td><td>120 (120/400=0.3)</td><td>280</td><td>400</td></tr><tr><td>Total</td><td>200</td><td>400</td><td>600</td></tr></table> To check if an association exists between Age Groups and Soda types, calculate the conditional distributions for any soda type. Since the distributions are not the same, an association exists between the variables. Age group seems to have an effect on what types of soda is consumed.	Remember that when the conditional distributions are the same in any column, then there is no association/dependence/ relation.
14	B	Calculate the conditional distribution as shown for one column as shown. Across age groups, the opinions have the same probability – 0.4. This indicates no association. <table><tr><th>Age Group</th><th>Useful</th><th>Not useful</th><th>Total</th></tr><tr><td>1-10</td><td>80 80/200=0.4</td><td>120</td><td>200</td></tr><tr><td>11-18</td><td>120 120/300=0.4</td><td>180</td><td>300</td></tr><tr><td>Total</td><td>200 200/500=0.4</td><td>300</td><td>500</td></tr></table>	If the conditional probabilities are the same across different groups of the same variable (age group in this case), there is no association between the variables (age group and opinion)
15	A	You are asked to compare the standard deviation of two sets	

		of data. In Test-1, several data values are at 60 and 61 and a few values are at 55. So the average is likely to be between less than 60. This means that the standard deviation will be a higher number. In Test-2, the mean is likely to be about 59, since the values are distributed evenly around 59. Since the data is evenly spread, the standard deviation is most likely less than the standard deviation of test-1 Alternatively, plugging in the values from the dot-plots into the calculator shows that Test-1 has a standard deviation of 2.69, and test 2 has a standard deviation of 2.58	
16	D	Note that this question does not show you a two-way table of data but instead summarizes it and shows the percentages in a stacked bar chart. The categorical variables are Professions and Opinions. The groups within Professions are Engineers and Doctors and the groups within Opinions are Yes-Tax and No-Tax. The Engineers bar shows that 20% of them voted Yes and 80% voted No. The Doctors bar shows that 30% voted Yes and 70% voted No. Recognize that these percentages are the same as conditional probabilities of these groups with respect to the other groups. For example, 20% of Engineers say Yes to tax. This means that the probability that a randomly selected Engineer will say Yes to tax is 20% or 0.2. For an association (relation) to exist between professions and opinions, the conditional probabilities must be the same. Since the conditional probabilities for Yes-Tax are 0.2 for Engineers and 0.3 for Doctors, there seems to be a relation between professions and taxes in that the doctors seems to be more inclined to accept more taxes than engineers.	In questions that ask if relations exist, first recognize the two categories and the groups within their categories. Then identify the conditional probabilities of one group across other groups. In this problem, find the conditional probability of Yes-Tax across Engineers and Doctors. If they are the same, there is no relation between the categories. If they are different, there is a relation between the categories.
17	D	Choice A is incorrect since an observational study that does not apply any treatment (drug) is not going to tell you how effective the drug is. Choice B is incorrect, since the 50 warehouse workers from New York city alone is not an unbiased sample. Choice C is incorrect, since some of the 50 warehouse workers from across the country may not have back pain before the drug was administered on them. Choice D is correct, since a controlled experiment on 50 workers with back pain, is likely to give reliable results about the efficiency of the drug.	Expect questions like this that give you the goal of the study and ask you which of the given choices is the best study design that will yield reliable results. Remember that surveys should be unbiased, and samples must be taken at random to yield best results. Polls and Surveys are observational studies. Experimental studies apply treatment on the subjects to find if there is a cause and effect relationship. They also have a control group on which treatment is not applied.

PROBLEM SOLVING AND DATA ANALYSIS		
Lesson 12	Counting	Review

FOCUSPREP CHECKLIST

- What are the different ways of counting?
- What are the Addition and Multiplication principles of counting?
- What is the Permutation formula and when do I use it?
- What is the Combination formula and when do I use it?
- Workout practice problems in Counting

Q1 What are the different ways of counting?
A1 There are several different ways to count - making up a list, using the multiplication or addition counting principles, placing the numbers in a Venn Diagram, using the Permutations formula nPr and using the Combinations formula nCr.

Q2 What are the types of counting problems?
A2 Examples of counting problems include finding the number of ways in which officers can be selected from available candidates, finding the number of ways in which a team can be formed, problems involving Venn diagrams, license plate problems, phone number problems, etc.

Q3 What is the Multiplication Principle of Counting?
A3 The Multiplication Principle of Counting states that when one task can be done in m ways and another task can be done in n ways, both tasks can be done in $m \cdot n$ ways.

Example: There are 5 ways to go from New York to London. There are 3 ways to go from London to Beijing. How many ways are there to go from New York to Beijing?

Solution: For each of the 5 ways from New York to London, you can take one of the 3 ways to go from London to Beijing. Using the multiplication principle of counting, there are $5 \cdot 3 = 15$ ways to go from New York to Beijing.

Q4 What is the Addition Principle of Counting?
A4 The Addition principle of counting states that when one task can be done in m ways and another task can be done in n ways, and both tasks can be done in k ways, then there are $m + n - k$ ways of doing both tasks.

Problem: From a standard deck of playing cards, if you pick one card only, in how many ways can you pick a Diamond or a card with an odd number?
Solution: There are 4 suits of cards – each suit has 13 cards. So, the Diamond suit has 13 cards. In each of the 4 suits, there are 4 odd numbered cards (3,5,7,9). So, totally there are $4 \cdot 4 = 16$ odd numbered cards. The number of cards that are both odd numbered and Diamond is 4. So, by the addition counting principle, there are $13 + 16 - 4 = 25$ ways to pick a card that is either a Diamond or an odd numbered card.

Q5 How do I use Venn diagrams to solve counting problems?

A5 Venn diagram problems will describe two sets or three sets of information. Pay very careful attention while placing numbers inside the diagrams. For example, in the 2-set Venn diagram below, the number of English speakers is 3+2=5 and this includes the number of English only speakers(3) and the number of English speakers that speak Spanish(2). Also note that some speakers may speak neither English nor Spanish and they also have to be accounted for. In this 2-set example, 2 people speak neither English nor Spanish and are placed outside the circles.

2-set Venn Diagrams

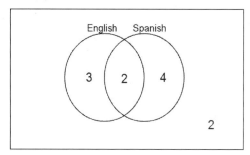

3-set Venn Diagrams

The 3-set Venn Diagram below shows three sets of data and how they are related. Note the meaning of each area of the Venn Diagram carefully. For example, there are 13 people who speak English(4+2+3+4), 4 people who speak English only, 2 people who speak English and Spanish but not French, 3 people who speak English, Spanish, and French, and 4 people who speak English and French but not Spanish.

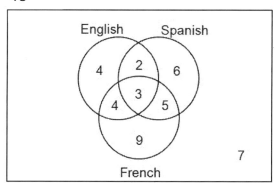

Q6 What is the factorial of a number n?

A6 Factorial of a number n is represented by $n!$ and is defined as $n! = n \cdot (n-1) \cdot (n-2) \cdot (n-3) \cdot \ldots 3 \cdot 2 \cdot 1$ Note that $n! = n \cdot (n-1)! = n(n-1)(n-2)!$ and so on.
Examples:
$4! = 4 \cdot 3 \cdot 2 \cdot 1 = 24$.
$6! = 6 \cdot 5! = 6 \cdot 5 \cdot 4!$

Q7 What is the Permutation formula? When do I use it?

A7 The Permutation formula helps you to find out the number of ways you can select r items from the available n items, where the order of items selected matters. It is represented as nPr and is calculated as $nPr = \frac{n!}{(n-r)!}$

Problem: From five letters A,B,C,D,E in how many ways can two letters be selected if the order of selection matters?

Solution:: Using the permutation formula, $n = 5, r = 2$, $nPr = 5P2 = \frac{5!}{(5-2)!} = \frac{5!}{3!} = \frac{5 \cdot 4 \cdot 3!}{3!} = 20$ ways.
Note that since ordering matters in permutation problems, AB and BA are separate selections and are counted as two separate selections. See below for the same problem where the order of selection does not matter. You can work out more Permutation problems in the practice section.

Q8 What is the Combination formula? When do I use it?

A8 The Combination formula helps you to find out the number of ways you can select r items from n available items, where the order of items selected does not matter. It is represented as nCr and is calculated as $nCr = \frac{n!}{r!(n-r)!}$

Problem: From five letters A,B,C,D,E in how many ways can two letters be selected if the order of selection is not important.

Solution: Using the Combination formula, $n = 5, r = 2, nCr = \binom{5}{2} = \frac{5!}{2!(5-2)!} = \frac{5!}{2!3!} = \frac{5 \cdot 4 \cdot 3!}{2!3!} = \frac{20}{2} = 10$ ways. As you can see, in this answer using Combination formula, AB and BA are considered one selection and are counted only once. You can work out more Combination problems in the practice section.

PROBLEM SOLVING AND DATA ANALYSIS

| Lesson 12 | Counting | Practice |

CALCULATOR SECTION

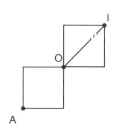

1. In the figure above, how many ways are there to go from A to I?
(A) 2
(B) 3
(C) 5
(D) 6

2. There are 6 highways from A to B, 3 train routes from A to B, and 4 ferry routes from B to C. In how many ways can you go from A to C?
(A) 12
(B) 24
(C) 36
(D) 48

3. There are 5 pencils and 6 crayons in a box. If you pick one item only, in how many ways can you choose a pencil or a crayon?
(A) 5
(B) 6
(C) 11
(D) 30

CALCULATOR SECTION

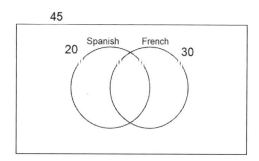

20 students in a class learn Spanish and 30 students learn French. There are 45 students in the class as shown in the Venn diagram.

Questions 4, 5 and 6 refer to the above diagram

4. How many students learn both Spanish and French?
(A) 5
(B) 6
(C) 20
(D) 30

5. How many students learn French but not Spanish?
(A) 10
(B) 20
(C) 25
(D) 30

6. How many students learn neither French nor Spanish?
(A) 0
(B) 5
(C) 10
(D) 20

CALCULATOR SECTION

In a housing community, 15 people play Tennis, 20 people play Soccer, and 25 people play Baseball. 5 People play Tennis and Soccer but not baseball. 4 people play Tennis and Baseball but not Soccer. 6 people play Soccer and Baseball but not Tennis. There are 35 people in the housing community.

Questions 7-10 refer to the problem above.

7. How many people play all three games?
(A) 3
(B) 4
(C) 5
(D) 9

8. How many people play Soccer and Baseball?
(A) 4
(B) 9
(C) 10
(D) 11

9. How many people play only one game?
(A) 1
(B) 4
(C) 10
(D) 15

CALCULATOR SECTION

10. A student council plans to fill three positions, namely the President, Vice President, and Treasurer. Eight students stand for elections to these three positions. In how many ways can the positions be filled?
(A) 256
(B) 336
(C) 408
(D) 512

11. The license plate for a special vehicle will consist of three letters, picked from A to Z. Letters can be repeated. How many license plates can be given out for this special vehicle?
(A) 15,600
(B) 17,576
(C) 18,200
(D) 18,576

12. The license plate for a special vehicle will consist of three letters, picked from A to Z. Letters cannot be repeated. How many license plates can be given out for this special vehicle?
(A) 10,630
(B) 12,200
(C) 15,600
(D) 16,500

CALCULATOR SECTION

Student ID				
0				

13. A student ID will be created with 5 digits chosen from 0 to 9. The first number must be 0 and the second number must be less than 4. The numbers cannot be repeated. What is the maximum number of students that can be issued an ID under this scheme?
GRID IN

14. From a class of 15 boys and 8 girls, in how many ways can a team of 5 students be selected?
(A) 22,500
(B) 33,250
(C) 33,649
(D) 41,249

15. From pool of 10 Robotic Engineers and 7 Biotechnology Engineers, a team needs to be created that has 3 Robotic Engineers and 2 Biotechnology Engineers. How many teams can be created?
GRID IN

CALCULATOR SECTION

16. The picture above needs to be shaded such that each of the four sections is shaded with a different color that is picked from a 5 color palette set. In how many ways can the above picture be colored?
GRID IN

17. xxx-xxx

A cell phone company wants to issue phone numbers to its customers in the format above where X stands for any number from 0-9. The last digit must always be 0 and numbers cannot be repeated. How many customers can be issued a number in the above format?
(A) 10,250
(B) 12,150
(C) 15,020
(D) 15,120

PROBLEM SOLVING AND DATA ANALYSIS

Lesson 12 — Counting — Answers

#	Explanation	Comments
1 D	In this figure, you can go from A to O in 2 ways and O to I in 3 ways – so you can go from A to I in $2 \cdot 3 = 6$ ways.	An easy way to solve these type of problems is to count the ways from the starting point to a mid point and from midpoint to the destination and then multiply.
2 C	6 highways from A to B 3 train routes from A to B 4 ferry routes from B to C Totally 6+3=9 ways to go from A to B; 4 ways to go from B to C – so $9 \cdot 4=36$ ways to go from A to C.	Use the multiplication principle of counting. Be careful not to do $6 \cdot 3 \cdot 4=72$; read the question carefully.
3 C	5 pencils, 6 crayons, only one item is picked 1 pencil can be picked in 5 ways (one of the 5 pencils) 1 crayon can be picked in 6 ways(one of the 5 crayons) 0 ways to choose both a pencil and a crayon, since only one item is picked. Totally 5+6-0=11 ways to choose 1 pencil or 1 crayon.	Use the addition principle of counting.
4 A	Let x be the number of students who learn both. $20 - x$ learn Spanish; x learn both, $30 - x$ learn French; 45 total; So $20 - x + x + 3 - x = 45$; $50 - x = 45$; $x = 50 - 45 = 5$.	
5 C	The question is "how many students learn French but not Spanish" – this is the same as asking "how many learn French only" – see the diagram – the answer is $30 - x = 30 - 5 = 25$	
6 A	How many learn neither French nor Spanish? All the areas of the Venn diagram add up to 45. 15+5+25=45. So, all 45 students learn either French or Spanish or both. Nobody learns anything other than French and Spanish. So, the answer is 0.	

7 C	35
	
	Tennis Soccer
	15 20
	   6-x 5 9-x
	         x
	      4 6
	         15-x
	                25
	         Baseball
		Place the numbers accurately in the Venn diagram. Understand the meaning of each area of the Venn diagram.

	Let x be the number of people who play all the games. Place the numbers from the problem in the Venn diagram. Those who play tennis only is $15 - 5 - 4 - x = 6 - x$. Those who play soccer only is $20 - 5 - 6 - x = 9 - x$. Those who play baseball only is $25 - 4 - x - 6 = 15 - x$. There are totally 35 people. Set up an equation. $6 - x + 5 + x + 4 + 9 - x + 6 + 15 - x = 35$ $45 - 2x = 35$ $2x = 10$ $x = 5$; So 5 people play all the games.	
8 D	Soccer + Baseball = $x + 6 = 5 + 6 = 11$.	
9 D	People who play only one game= those who play tennis only+ those who play soccer only + those who play baseball only = 1+4+10=15.	
10 B	8 students want to stand for 3 positions; So, the number of ways these positions can be filled is $8P3 = \frac{8!}{(8-3)!} = \frac{8!}{5!} = \frac{8 \cdot 7 \cdot 6 \cdot 5!}{5!} = 8 \cdot 7 \cdot 6 = 336$ ways.	Note that you need to figure out if this is a permutation or combination problem. In this problem, 3 positions are filled – so it matters who is in what position – when position matters, it is a Permutation problem. Remember the "P" in Permutation as "Position Matters".
11 B	Three letters are picked from A to Z. So, that is 26 letters to pick from. Problem says that the letters can be repeated – so you can have AAA, AAB, or ABA, etc . The first letter can be picked in 26 ways; second letter in 26 ways, and the third letter in 26 ways. So, totally $26 \cdot 26 \cdot 26 = 17{,}576$ 3-letter plates can be given out for this vehicle.	
12 C	This is similar to the previous problem but the letters cannot be repeated – that is you cannot have AAB, ABB etc. So, this is a pure permutation problem – of selecting 3 letters from 26 letters – so the answer is $26P3 = 15{,}600$	Learn how to calculate nPr and nCr using your calculator.
13 1008	There are 10 numbers available form 0-9 1st number = 0 2nd number - must be less than 4 = 0,1,2,3 – but numbers cannot be repeated and 0 has been taken – so 3 numbers are allowed in 2nd spot – numbers 1,2,3 3rd number – so far 2 numbers are taken – so you have 10-2=8 numbers available for 3rd spot 4th number – 8-1=7 numbers available for 4th spot 5th number = 7-1=6 numbers available for 5th sport Totally, you have $1 \cdot 3 \cdot 8 \cdot 7 \cdot 6 = 1008$ numbers available.	This is a permutation problem with constraints; find the possibilities for each spot and then multiply. When you count the available numbers from 0-9, don't forget to count 0.

14 C	15 boys 8 girls = 23 students 5 students can be selected in 23C5 ways=33,649	Note that the problem says there are 15 boys and 8 girls but the team can have boys and girls in any numbers such that the team has exactly 5 students ; do the next problem to see a variation of this problem.
15 2520	10 robotic and 7 biotech engineers available 3 robotic and 2 biotech engineer team 3 robotic engineers can be selected in 10C3 ways – note that order does not matter – this is a combination problem – 2 biotech engineers can be selected in 7C2 ways So the total number of teams is 10C3 · 7C2= 120·21=2520 teams.	
16 120	4 areas in the figure – when you color the first area, 5 colors are available; when you color the second area 4 colors are available, and so on. Only one color can be used in each area. So, for the 4 areas, there are $5 \cdot 4 \cdot 3 \cdot 2 = 120$ ways to color	
17 D	Six spots in the phone number. Available numbers =0-9 = 10 numbers; Last digit is 0 and numbers cannot be repeated – so 10-1=9 numbers available for each of the 5 spots. 1st spot – 9 ways; 2nd spot – 8 ways etc.; last spot is 0. Totally 9 · 8 · 7 · 6 · 5 · 1=15,120	

PROBLEM SOLVING AND DATA ANALYSIS		
Lesson 13	Probability	Review

FOCUSPREP CHECKLIST

- How do I calculate the probability of an event?
- What are dependent and independent events?
- While selecting objects, what does "with replacement" mean?
- What does conditional probability mean? How do I calculate it?
- How do I calculate the Geometric probability?

Q1 What is a sample space?

A1 The set of all possible outcomes of an experiment is called Sample space.
Example: A coin is tossed. The sample space = {Heads, Tails}
Example: A student is selected and gender is noted. The sample space = {Boy, Girl}

Q2 How is the probability of an event defined?

A2 The Probability of an event is defined as the ratio of the number of favorable outcomes of the event to the total number of possible outcomes of the event.
If A is an event, then the probability of event A= $P(A) = \frac{favorable\ outcomes\ of\ event\ A}{possible\ outcomes\ of\ event\ A}$

Example: A die is rolled. What is the probability that the number 3 will be on the top?
Solution: Number of favorable outcomes= 1 (there is only one way the number 3 will be on top)
Number of possible outcomes=6 (any one of 1,2,3,4,5,6 could be on top)
So, the probability=$\frac{1}{6}$.

Example: A die is rolled. What is the probability that a number less than 3 will be on the top?
Solution: Number of favorable outcomes= 2 (when the numbers 1 or 2 are on the top)
Number of possible outcomes=6 (any one of 1,2,3,4,5,6 could be on top)
So, the probability=$\frac{2}{6} = \frac{1}{3}$

Q3 How do I find the number of favorable outcomes and number of possible outcomes?

A3 Depending on the problem, you can find this by listing and counting, using the addition and multiplication principles of counting, or by using permutation or combination formulas discussed in the lesson on Counting.

Q4 What are the minimum and maximum values of probability of an event?

A4 Minimum value = 0. This is the case when the number of favorable outcomes is 0 which will be true when the event cannot occur at all.
Maximum value = 1. This is the case when the number of favorable outcomes is equal to the number of possible outcomes. For any event A, $0 \leq P(A) \leq 1$

Q5 What is the complement of an event?

A5 The complement of an event A is the probability of it <u>NOT</u> occurring. If $P(A)$ is the probability of an event A, then the probability that the event will not happen (complement) is $P(A') = 1 - P(A)$. Note that $P(A) + P(A') = 1$.

Q6 How do I calculate the probability when two events are involved?

A6 When two events, event A and event B are possible, then only event A can occur or only event B can occur or both event A and event B can occur.

- The probability that either event will occur is $P(A \cup B) = P(A) + P(B) - P(A \cap B)$.
- The probability that both events will occur is $P(A \cap B) = P(A) \cdot P(B)$ if they are independent events.
- The probability that both events will occur is $P(A \cap B) = P(A) \cdot P(B|A)$ if they are dependent events. $P(B|A)$ is called <u>conditional probability</u> of event B given that event A has occurred.

Q7 What are independent and dependent events?

A7 Two events A and B are <u>independent</u> if one event does not affect the sample space of another event. Two events A and B are <u>dependent</u> if one event affects the sample space of another event.

Example (Independent Events):
Consider a set S={1,2,3,4,5,6,7,8,9}. Pick a number from set S and replace it (put it back into the set). Now, pick another number. What is the probability that the first number picked is even and the second number picked is odd?

Solution: Let event A= the number picked is even and event B= number picked is odd. The probability of picking an even number= $P(A) = \frac{4}{9}$ (4 even numbers and 9 numbers in all). After picking the first number, it is replaced (returned back to the sample space) and so the sample space still has 9 numbers when you go to pick the second number. Picking the first number and picking the second number are independent events – they do not depend on each other. So, $P(B) = \frac{5}{9}$ since there are 5 odd numbers. The probability the first number is even <u>and</u> the second number is odd is
$$P(A \cap B) = P(A) \cdot (B) = \frac{4}{9} \cdot \frac{5}{9} = \frac{20}{81}.$$

Example (Dependent Events):
Consider a set S={1,2,3,4,5,6,7,8,9}. Pick a number from set S. Now, pick another number. What is the probability that the first number picked is even and the second number picked is odd?

Solution: The probability that the number picked is even = $P(A) = \frac{4}{9}$ (4 even numbers and 9 numbers in all). After picking the first number, sample space is reduced by 1 and so it now has 9-1= 8 numbers available for picking when you go to pick the second number. Picking the first number and picking the second number are dependent events – one affects the sample space of the other. So, The probability that the second number picked is odd is = $p(B) = \frac{5}{8}$ since there are 5 odd numbers. The probability the first number is even and the second number is odd is $P(A \cap B) = P(A) \cdot P(B|A) = \frac{4}{9} \cdot \frac{5}{8} = \frac{20}{72} = \frac{5}{18}$. P(B|A) means the probability of event B given that event A has occurred. P(B|A) is referred to as the conditional probability. For independent events, $P(A \cap B) = P(A) \cdot P(B)$. For dependent events, $P(A \cap B) = P(A) \cdot P(B|A)$. Pay attention to the sample space available when you calculate the probability. Sample space is the list of all possible outcomes.

Q8 What are mutually exclusive events?

A8 Two events A and B are mutually exclusive if they cannot occur at the same time. In this case, $P(A \cap B)=0$.

Example: Toss a coin. Event A= you get a Head   Event B= you get a Tail. What is the probability of getting a head and a tail?

Solution: Sample space(outcome) of event A ={Head} and sample space (outcome) of event B={Tail}. You cannot get a head and tail at the same time. The two events are mutually exclusive. So, the number of favorable outcomes=0. Hence P(Head and Tail) = P(A∩B)=0.

Q9 What does selection with replacement mean?

A9 After you select a specific item from a larger set, if you return it back to the set, then it is called "replacement". For example, say you have 3 balls and you select 1 ball first and then another ball. After selecting the first ball, if you put it back, then it is called "replacement". In that case, the first ball that you selected is available for selecting again when you go to pick the second ball. This is important to note and will affect the probability calculations. Problem statements will indicate if the items are selected with replacement. If they don't then you can assume that the items selected are NOT available for selection again. This will affect the sample space available and you will need to use conditional probability in your calculation.

Q10 What does Geometric probability mean? Where is it used?

A19 Geometric probability is used when you have to calculate probability with respect to an area. For example, what is the probability that a dart thrown on a dart board will fall on the inner ring?

$$\text{Geometric Probability} = \frac{\text{Favorable Target Area}}{\text{Total Possible Area}}$$

Q11 What is a deck of cards made of?

A11 A deck (full set) of cards has a total of 52 cards split into 4 suits – Club ♣, Diamond ♦, Heart ♥ and Spade ♠. Each suite has 13 cards. So, totally there are $4 \cdot 13 = 52$ cards. The 13 cards in each suit consist of one King, one Queen, one Jack, one Ace and 9 cards that are numbered 2,3,4,5,6,7,8,9,10. The cards in Diamond and Heart suites are red in color. The cards in Spade and Club suites are black in color. Remembering this information will help you solve probability problems involving playing cards.

PROBLEM SOLVING AND DATA ANALYSIS

Lesson 13 — **Probability** — **Practice**

CALCULATOR SECTION

1. A box has 3 red balls, 4 green balls, and 5 blue balls. What is the probability that a ball picked at random will be a green ball?
(A) $\frac{1}{4}$
(B) $\frac{1}{3}$
(C) $\frac{1}{2}$
(D) 1

2. A box has 3 red balls and 4 green balls. What is the probability that two balls picked randomly one after the other are both red in color?
(A) $\frac{1}{8}$
(B) $\frac{1}{7}$
(C) $\frac{1}{2}$
(D) 1

3. A box has 3 red balls and 4 green balls. What is the probability that two balls picked randomly are both of the same color?
(A) $\frac{1}{7}$
(B) $\frac{2}{7}$
(C) $\frac{3}{7}$
(D) $\frac{4}{7}$

CALCULATOR SECTION

4. In a college, the probability that students will chose a science major is $\frac{3}{5}$ and the probability that they will choose an arts major is $\frac{2}{5}$. If a student can choose only one major, what is the probability of choosing a science major or an arts major?
(A) $\frac{6}{25}$
(B) $\frac{2}{5}$
(C) $\frac{3}{5}$
(D) 1

The Panthers Music team has 6 bassoon players Andrea, Betty, Cindy, Darlene, Emma, and Frank. The coach wants to pick 2 players for a statewide competition.

Questions 5-7 refer to the information above

5. What is the probability that Andrea will be selected for the competition?
GRID IN

6. What is the probability that Andrea and Betty will be selected for the competition?
GRID IN

CALCULATOR SECTION

7. What is the probability that Andrea will go with Betty or Cindy will go with Darlene to the competition?
GRID IN

A,G,L,O

8. If the set of letters above are rearranged to create new sets, then what is the probability that a set will have letters in the following order: G,O,A,L

(A) $\frac{1}{72}$

(B) $\frac{1}{60}$

(C) $\frac{1}{25}$

(D) $\frac{1}{24}$

9. If the letters O,D,G are placed randomly in the three cells in the table above, what is the probability that the cells will read G,O,D from left to right?

(A) $\frac{1}{6}$

(B) $\frac{1}{3}$

(C) $\frac{1}{4}$

(D) $\frac{1}{2}$

CALCULATOR SECTION

Set M = {30,40,50}
Set N= {5,10,15}

10. Two numbers m and n are chosen randomly, one from each set M and N shown above. What is the probability that $\frac{m}{n}$ is an integer?
GRID IN

Set N = {1,2,3,4,5,6,7,8,9,10}

11. What is the probability that a number selected randomly from the set above is a perfect square?

(A) $\frac{1}{6}$

(B) $\frac{1}{5}$

(C) $\frac{1}{4}$

(D) $\frac{3}{10}$

12. Alex has 6 red toys and 8 green toys in a box. He picks one toy at random, notes the color and puts it back in the box. He then picks another toy at random again. What is the probability that the second toy is green?
GRID IN

CALCULATOR SECTION

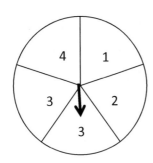

13. If the spinner above is spun twice, what is the probability that you will get a 3 in one spin and a number that is not 3 in the other spin?

(A) $\frac{3}{25}$

(B) $\frac{4}{25}$

(C) $\frac{6}{25}$

(D) $\frac{8}{25}$

14. If a coin is tossed once, the probability of getting Heads is $\frac{1}{2}$. If the coin is tossed twice, what is the probability of getting a Heads both times?
GRID IN

CALCULATOR SECTION

15. A piggy bank has 2 quarters and 3 dimes. If two coins are picked at random one after the other, what is the probability that they add up to more than 35 cents?

(A) $\frac{1}{20}$

(B) $\frac{1}{10}$

(C) $\frac{1}{4}$

(D) $\frac{1}{2}$

16. The probability of seeing a lion at the zoo is $\frac{1}{6}$. How many animals cannot be in the zoo?

(A) 6
(B) 12
(C) 20
(D) 24

17. Two cards are selected from a deck of cards. What is the probability that you will select a 3 in the Hearts suit and a 5 in the Spades suit?

A) $\frac{1}{2704}$

B) $\frac{1}{2652}$

C) $\frac{1}{15}$

D) $\frac{1}{8}$

CALCULATOR SECTION

18. In the figure above, a rectangle is divided into 4 equal parts. If a stone is thrown randomly on the rectangle, what is the probability that it will land on the shaded portion?
(A) 0.2
(B) 0.25
(C) 0.5
(D) 0.75

19. In the figure of a circular swimming pool shown above, the arc of shaded portion makes 30° at the center of the circle. If a bird falls into the pool, what is the probability that it will fall into the shaded region of the pool?

(A) $\frac{1}{12}$

(B) $\frac{1}{10}$

(C) $\frac{1}{4}$

(D) $\frac{1}{2}$

CALCULATOR SECTION

20. The figure above shows a dart board. The outer square is 10 inches wide and the inner square is 8 inches wide. If a dart is thrown at the board, what is the probability that it will fall on the shaded area between the outer and the inner square?

(A) $\frac{8}{25}$

(B) $\frac{9}{25}$

(C) $\frac{2}{5}$

(D) $\frac{3}{5}$

PROBLEM SOLVING AND DATA ANALYSIS
Lesson 13 — Probability — Answers

#	Explanation	Comments
1 B	Favorable outcomes for green=4 Total outcomes=12 P(green) = $\frac{4}{12} = \frac{1}{3}$	If a problem like this is confusing, think what the probability will be if all the balls were green – obviously it will be 1 – since all the balls are not green, the probability is going to be a fraction less than 1 – so it is the number of green balls that helps you to get to the answer.
2 B	First note that the problem does not state that the first ball was replaced(put back). So you have to assume that it was not replaced. P(first is red and second is red)= P(first is red) · P(second is red|first is red). (this is conditional probability) P(first is red)= $\frac{3}{7}$ After first red ball is picked, you have only 2 red balls and 4 green balls left. P(second is red)= $\frac{2}{6} = \frac{1}{3}$ So P(first is red and second is red)= $\frac{3}{7} \cdot \frac{1}{3} = \frac{1}{7}$	Review how conditional probability is calculated.
3 C	3 red and 4 green; pick 2 balls P(2 balls are of same color)=? 2 balls will be of same color if they are Red,Red OR Green,Green P(red,red)= $\frac{3}{7} \cdot \frac{2}{6} = \frac{1}{7}$ P(green,green)= $\frac{4}{7} \cdot \frac{3}{6} = \frac{2}{7}$ P(red,red) or P(green,green)= $\frac{1}{7} + \frac{2}{7} = \frac{3}{7}$	
4 D	P(science)=$\frac{3}{5}$ P(arts)=$\frac{2}{5}$ It is given that a student cannot choose both majors – so P(arts and science)=0. P(science or arts)= P(science) + P(arts)-P(arts and science) =$\frac{3}{5} + \frac{2}{5} - 0 = 1$.	
5 $\frac{1}{3}$	From 6 players – pick 2 for team Total possibilities = $6C2 = \frac{6!}{4!2!}$=15 teams Out of these, Andrea will be in 5 teams (one with each of the other players). So, the probability of Andrea getting selected = $\frac{5}{15} = \frac{1}{3}$.	
6 $\frac{1}{15}$	From 6 players – pick 2 for team Total possibilities = $6C2 = \frac{6!}{4!2!}$=15 teams	

©GiftOfLogic http://www.GiftOfLogic.com

	Out of these, Andrea and Betty will be in 1 team only. So, the probability of Andrea getting selected = $\frac{1}{15}$.	
7 $\frac{2}{15}$	From 6 players – pick 2 for team Total possibilities = $6C2 = \frac{6!}{4!2!}$ =15 teams Out of these, Andrea and Betty will be selected in 1 way and Cindy and Darlene can be selected in 1 way – total of 2 ways So, the probability is $\frac{2}{15}$	
8 D	Note that there are 4 letters – Only one way to get G,O,A,L (that is when G is in 1st spot, O is in 2nd spot, A is in 3rd spot, L is in 4th spot). Possible ways to rearrange the letters = 4·3·2·1=24 ways. So, the P(getting GOAL)=$\frac{1}{24}$.	
9 A	Possible ways=3 · 2 · 1 = 6 ways Favorable ways=1 when the word GOD is in the cells. Probability= $\frac{1}{6}$	
10 $\frac{7}{9}$	Favorable ways to have $\frac{m}{n}$ as integer= (30,5), (30,10), (30,15), (40,5), (40,10), (50,5), (50,10) = 7 ways Possible ways to pick 1 from M and 1 from N=3·3=9. So, probability that $\frac{m}{n}$ is an integer = $\frac{7}{9}$.	List out the possibilities to get the favorable outcomes.
11 D	Favorable outcome= 1,4,9 as these are the only three perfect squares; possible outcomes=10. So, the probability=$\frac{3}{10}$	
12 $\frac{4}{7}$	This is a problem of replacement – that is, the sample space is not affected. When he goes to pick the second toy, he has 6+8=14 toys available. There are 8 green toys. So, probability the second toy is green is =$\frac{8}{14} = \frac{4}{7}$	In probability problems, read carefully to see if there is replacement of items picked or not.
13 C	What is the probability that you will get a 3 in one spin and a number that is not 3 in the other – note the "and" in the question. P(3 in first spin) = $\frac{2}{5}$ (since there are two 3s and 5 numbers in total) P(not 3 in second spin) =P(1,2,4)=$\frac{3}{5}$ P(3 in first spin and not 3 in second spin)=$\frac{2}{5} \cdot \frac{3}{5} = \frac{6}{25}$	
14 $\frac{1}{4}$	P(Heads in toss 1 and heads in toss 2)= $\frac{1}{2} \cdot \frac{1}{2} = \frac{1}{4}$	
15 B	Two coins will add up to more than 35 if both of them are quarters. The probability of picking 2 quarters is $\frac{2}{5} \cdot \frac{1}{4} = \frac{1}{10}$.	
16 C	P(lions in the zoo)=$\frac{1}{6}$. If there are 6 animals, you can find 1 lion, if there are 12 animals, you can find 2 lions, etc. If there are 20 animals, then the number of lions=1/6 ·20 – and this is not possible since the number of lions cannot be in	

		fractions. So, the number of animals has to be in multiples of 6. Only choice C is not a multiple of 6.	
17	B	There are 52 cards in the deck with 13 of each suite. To select a 3 of Hearts, the probability is $\frac{1}{52}$ since there is only one 3 of Hearts. After selecting this card, there will be only 51 cards left (the first card is not replaced). The probability of selecting 5 of Spades is $\frac{1}{51}$. So the answer is $\frac{1}{52} \cdot \frac{1}{51} = \frac{1}{2652}$.	Figure out carefully if it is a problem of selection with replacement or not.
18	B	Since the rectangle is divided into equal parts, the shaded area is one fourth of the rectangle. So the geometric probability = target area/total area = $\frac{0.25A}{A} = 0.25$.	
19	A	Arc of shaded portion = 30° of the circle; since the entire circle is 360°, the shaded portion is $\frac{30}{360} = \frac{1}{12}$ of the total area. So, the probability= target area/total area = $\frac{\frac{1}{12}A}{A} = \frac{1}{12}$	A 30° piece of a circle is not equal to 30% of the area of a circle. Since 360° corresponds to the full area of a circle, a 30° sector is equal to $\frac{30}{360} = \frac{1}{12}$ of the area of a circle.
20	B	Outer square=10 inches; Inner square=8 inches P(dart will fall in shaded area) =shaded area/total area= $\frac{10^2 - 8^2}{10^2} = \frac{100 - 64}{100} = \frac{36}{100} = \frac{9}{25}$.	

PROBLEM SOLVING AND DATA ANALYSIS

| Lesson 14 | Extended Thinking | Review |

FOCUSPREP CHECKLIST

- What is an Extended Thinking problem?
- What are the contexts for ET-problems?
- What problem solving skills are important for solving ET problems?
- What is a good strategy to crack an ET-problem?
- Workout practice problems in Extended Thinking

ET=Extended Thinking

Q1 What is the Extended Thinking Problem (ET-Problem)?

A1 An Extended Thinking problem is a problem where your problem solving skills will be put to test in solving a challenging problem. A problem scenario may be presented and you may be asked two or more questions that build on each other. That is, you may have to use the answer to one question to solve another question. No answer choices will be provided for these questions – you will need to GRID IN the answers yourself.

ET-Problems can be in the area of **Problem solving or Data analysis or both.** A SAT problem will NOT be clearly marked as an Extended Thinking problem. After completing this lesson, you will have a good strategy to solve these types of problems.

Q2 What is a good strategy to crack ET-Problems?

A2 The following strategy will help you to gain confidence in solving ET-problems.

- General Knowledge - Acquire general knowledge and financial literacy.
- Context Awareness - Familiarize yourself with different contexts.
- Problem Solving Skills - Acquire important problem solving skills.
- Core Lessons - Workout all lessons in Problem Solving and Data Analysis chapter.
- Workout ET-practice problems at the end of this lesson.

The following table outlines a four step strategy that you may want to follow to gain confidence in solving ET-Problems.

Extended Thinking Problem Solving Strategy	
1 General Knowledge	**2 Context Awareness**
Having a general knowledge of the real world will come in handy and help you avoid surprises when you encounter them in the ET-problems. Credit Cards, Debit Cards, Foreign exchange Currency conversions, Simple and Compound Interest Rate Formulas, Computer memory, Bits and Bytes, etc. are reviewed in detail in this lesson.	The ET-Problem can appear in any context – following are some specific contexts: Science, Social Studies, Sports, Commerce, Economics, Meteorology, Chemistry, Physics, Business, Transportation, Accounting, Manufacturing, Environment, Medicine, Investing, Government, Financial Literacy, etc. Read a variety of articles with a keen eye on numbers and formulas.

3 Key Problem Solving Skills	4 Lessons
The following skills will come in handy while solving ET-problems: Diagramming, Venn Diagrams, Modeling, Guessing and Checking, Finding Patterns, Making a table, Making a list. These skills are reviewed below with examples. Note that these skills may help you to solve just one part of the ET problem. For other parts, you may have to use common skills such as setting up algebraic equations/inequalities and solving them. Which skill you will need to use depends on the problem.	The following are some lessons that will come in handy while solving ET-problems. Workout the problems in these lessons to gain confidence in solving ET-problems. Ratios, Percentages, Unit Conversions, Direct and Inverse variation, Linear Equalities, Linear Inequalities, Permutations, Combinations, Probability, Linear and Exponential models. Lessons in the Problem Solving and Data Analysis chapter cover most of these topics. Refer to the table of contents for other topics such as setting up inequalities, linear and exponential growth and decay, etc.

Q3 What general knowledge may be useful while solving ET-problems?

A3 Keep an eye on news that you encounter everyday where math is significantly involved. Following are some useful topics that will come in handy. As you encounter other topics, keep notes.

- **Credit Cards:** These cards have a limit, say $20,000. This limit is the amount offered to you for credit. You pay with a credit card while making purchases. When the bill arrives, it will ask you to pay the full purchased amount or pay a minimum amount and the remainder in subsequent months at a specific interest rate. At any time, if you try to charge more than the available balance, your request will be denied. Visa, MasterCard, Discover, and American Express are examples of Credit Cards.

- **Prepaid Debit Cards:** These cards are frequently called as Prepaid Cards. You purchase a prepaid (debit) card, say for $5000 by <u>pre-paying</u> for it upfront. Then, when you make purchases against it, the available balance will be reduced electronically from the prepaid card. If you charge say $500 to buy a computer, the available balance will become 5000-500=$4500. When you try to charge more than the balance, your request will be denied. Note that since you pre-paid the debit card for $5000, you have incurred this cost – so even if you buy a $1 item, the cost you have already incurred is still $5000 – the remaining balance will become $4999. For purchases up to $5000, your cost is the $5000 that you already prepaid. This is an important concept that you need to remember. For your friend's birthday, you could give him a gift card for $25 which is actually a prepaid debit card for $25. You prepay $25 to purchase the debit card and your friend can use it for any number of purchases as long as the purchase amount does not exceed the balance.

- **Check/ATM Cards:** These are debit cards with the special feature that links them to a <u>bank checking account</u>. So, if you had $3000 in your bank checking account, you can charge up to $3000 in a single transaction to purchase something with this check/ATM (debit) card. You can keep on purchasing using the check/ATM card as long as you do not exceed the balance in your checking account. These cards are called as ATM cards as they are used to withdraw money from ATM machines.

- **Foreign Exchange:** When you go to a foreign country, you have to use the currency of that country. You exchange US Dollars for a foreign currency. Foreign exchange rates are posted on notice boards at airports and published in newspapers and the Internet. Given the exchange rate, you should know how to convert from one currency to another.

  Example: 1 USD=0.89 Euro – so, if you are in Italy and want to convert 1200 USD to Euros, you will get $1200 \; \cancel{\text{USD}} \cdot \frac{0.89 \; Euro}{\cancel{\text{USD}}} = 1068$ Euro.

  Example: 1 USD=63 Indian Rupees – so, if you are in India and want to buy a miniature Taj Mahal for Rs 5000, you will need $\cancel{\text{Rs}} \; 5000 \; \cdot \frac{1 \; USD}{\cancel{\text{Rs}} \; 63} = \text{USD } 79.36$.

- **Census and Surveys** – Review the lesson on Population and Sample.

- **Interest rate:** There are two types of interest - Simple interest and Compound interest. <u>Simple interest</u> is earned on the principal amount for a specified time period. If a bank offers a simple interest of r% in time t, then a Principal amount of P will earn an interest of $P \cdot r \cdot t$. The total amount after time t will be $P + P \cdot r \cdot t = P(1 + rt)$. **Example:** If the simple interest rate is 3% for 1 year, a deposit of $4000 will become $4000 \cdot (1 + 0.03 \cdot 1) = 4120$ after one year. Note that the formula $P(1 + rt)$ is linear.

  <u>Compound interest</u> is different from simple interest in that the amount earned in interest each year will also earn interest in subsequent years. The formula is $P(1 + r)^t$ where P is the principal amount, r is the interest rate, and t is the time duration. **Example:** If the compound interest rate is 3% per year, a deposit of $4000 will become $4000 \cdot (1 + 0.03)^3 = 4370.91$ after three years. Note that the formula $P(1 + r)^t$ is exponential.

- **Bytes and bits:** Computer memory is represented in Bits and Bytes. Every English character is normally 1 Byte. 1 Byte=8 bits. So, 2 Mega Bytes = 2 Mega $\cancel{\text{Byte}}$ · 8 bits/1 $\cancel{\text{Byte}}$ = 16 Mega bits. It is common to use capital B to represent Bytes and small b to represent bits. Note that Giga and Mega are represented in capital G and M respectively. You don't need to memorize this. Just be familiar with how calculations are made with bits and bytes.

- **File size:** Computer memory and file size are specified in Bytes. For example, a computer has a memory of 4 GB – this means it has 4 Giga Bytes of memory. G stands for Giga and M stands for Mega. Giga is 10^9 and Mega is 10^6. So, 4 GB = $4 \cdot 10^9$ Bytes. A PowerPoint file may be 2MB in size – so the file has $2 \cdot 10^6$ Bytes.

- **Internet data speed:** The speed at which data moves(transfers) in the internet is specified as Mega bits/second (**NOT** Mega Bytes/second). The internet data speed is typically 20 Mbits/s, where M stands for Mega(10^6). So, a file that is 2MB is 2M $\cancel{\text{Bytes}}$ · 8 bits/$\cancel{\text{Byte}}$ = 16 Mbits. At the rate of 20 Mbits/second; it will take 16 $\cancel{\text{Mbits}}$ / 20 $\cancel{\text{Mbits}}$/sec = 0.8 seconds to transfer.

  You can also set up a direct variation equation to find this. Review the lesson on Variation for more information on how to setup direct and indirect variations.
  20 Mbits   1 second
  16 Mbits x

This is direct variation; more bits transferred means more time; less bits transferred means less time; so $\frac{x}{1} = \frac{16}{20}$ $x = \frac{16}{20} \cdot 1 = 0.8$ seconds

Q4 What contexts are likely to be encountered in Extended Thinking Problems?

A4 That is not possible to predict, since math is pervasive in almost every context. What is possible however is to condition your mind to face a variety of contexts. The following are some popular contexts and some key words associated with them that you can familiarize yourself with, so that it becomes easy to digest them should you encounter them in ET-problems or in any other problem. You don't need to do extensive research on any of these keywords. Just keep your ears open to keywords in a variety of contexts so that they don't sound very strange when you face them in the test.

Context	Keywords
Social studies	population, immigration, emigration, net migration, population density, etc
Sports	miles per hour, marathon, meters, yards, innings, overtime, etc
Meteorology	atmosphere, pressure, temperature, humidity, wind speed, fahrenheit, celsius, etc
Physics	gravity, speed, motion, energy, angle of reflection, friction, electricity, etc
Chemistry	organic bond, thermal energy, pollution, carbon monoxide, sulphur, etc
Medicine	dosage, ounces, fluid ounces, milligrams, tablets per day, infections, etc
Nutrition	calories, fat content, grams, carbs, servings, etc
Manufacturing	fabrication, cost of goods, sale price, distribution, warehouse, inventory, etc
Transportation	buses, cars, trains, airplanes, miles, mileage, miles per gallon, etc
Environment	earthquake, richter scale, pollution, parts per million, tiger population, wildlife, bird population, crocodile population, etc
Finance	stocks, bonds, shares, portfolio, yield, loan, interest rate, etc
Government	federal and state income tax, jobs created, benefits, tax revenue, etc
Economics	gross domestic product (GDP), demand, supply, interest rate, percentage increase, unemployment level, etc
Business	profit and loss, cash flow, gross income, net income, assets, loans, etc
Accounting	credit, debit, taxes, credit card, debit card, deposit, withdraw, audit, etc

Q5 What Problem Solving Skills are essential for solving ET-problems?

A5 Various Problem Solving skills are described below with examples. Note that the examples below are focused on highlighting specific skills only. The ET-Problems are more challenging. One ET problem is discussed at the end of this review section followed by several ET problems in the practice section.

Diagramming the problem
Depending on the problem, you can draw diagrams to visualize the problem and arrive at a solution quickly.
- Use a tree diagram when the problem involves counting different ways to achieve a result.
- Use a Venn diagram when the problem involves information regards sets of data.

Example: Brian has 3 Red shirts, 2 Green Pants, and 1 Blue tie. In how many ways can he pick one set consisting of a shirt, a pant and a tie?
Solution: Draw a tree diagram as shown. Then, it is easy to figure out that there are $3 \cdot 2 \cdot 1 = 6$ ways to pick one set.

Example: In a class of 15 students, 10 speak English, and 8 speak Spanish. How many speak both English and Spanish.
Solution: Draw a Venn Diagram as shown. Let x be the number of students that speak both English and Spanish. So, $10 - x$ speak English only and $8 - x$ speak Spanish only. So, $10 - x + x + 8 - x = 15$;
$18 - x = 15$, $x = 3$ speak both English and Spanish.

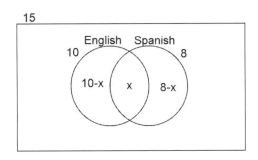

Making a Table
If the problem you are solving involves several events that happen at regular intervals and you need to sort them all out so that you know when all the events happen together, or when some specific set of events happen, then make a table showing the details of the events and then answer the questions.

Example: A pharmacy receives headache medicines every 5 days, fever medicines every 2 days, and allergy medicines every 4 days. If it received all the three medicines today, when will it receive all the medicines again?

Solution: This problem is best solved by spreading out the data in a table to sort out the details.

Day	0	1	2	3	4	5	6	7	8	9	10	11	12	13	14	15	16	17	18	19	20	21
Headache 5	X					X					X					X					X	
Fever 2	X		X		X		X		X		X		X		X		X		X		X	
Allergy 4	X				X				X				X				X				X	

Now, it is clear that all the medicines will be received again on the 20th day. You can also answer questions like when is the next day fever and allergy medicines will be received – that will be on the 4th day. Similarly, the headache and fever medicine will be received again on the 10th day. A table like this is hard to create in the space provided in the test. So, these types of problems are unlikely to appear in the test, but the problem solving skill using tables like this will come in handy. Moreover, you can build your mental strength when you solve a problem like this.

Making a List

If the problem you are solving is such that you need to count the possibilities of something, you can make an organized list and count, if it involves say three or four possibilities. If not, you can use the Permutation and Combination formulas.

Example: A special train will travel through stations A, B, and C and will stop in at least one station. How many possible trips can it make through these stations?

Solution 1: Make a list of possibilities for each possible stop scenario (1 stop, 2 stops, 3 stops).

# of stops =>	1	2	3
	A	A B	ABC
	B	B C	
	C	A C	

So there are $3 + 3 + 1 = 7$ trips that it can make through these stations, by making at least one stop.

Solution 2:

You can solve this problem using combination formula nCr. Review the lesson on Counting to understand how combination formula works.

Number of trips that stop in 1 station = 3C1 = 3 (3 possibilities, 1 stop)
Number of trips that stop in 2 stations = 3C2 = 3 (3 possibilities, 2 stops)
Number of trips that stop in 3 stations = 3C3 = 1 (3 possibilities, 3 stops)

Total = $3 + 3 + 1 = 7$.

Developing a model from data

- Observe a pattern in the given data or extract data from figures and text if you have to.
- Depending on the data available, develop an algebraic model (linear, exponential) or a model based on sequences (arithmetic and geometric). Review the lesson on Growth and Decay.

Arithmetic Sequence Model

Example: Paratroopers are dropped from a helicopter in the following pattern. First, 1 paratrooper is dropped, followed by 3 , 5, 7, and so on. On which drop will 99 paratroopers be dropped?

Solution: 1, 3, 5, 7   ... 99

Model is : term n = first-term $+(n-1)d$; where d is the difference

So, $99 = 1 + (n-1) \cdot 2$; solving for n, you get $n = 50$. So, 99 paratroopers will be dropped in the 50th drop.

Algebraic Model

Example: A car dealership initially has 2 cars – 1 red and 1 blue. Each day, it gets 3 red cars and 4 blue cars. After 15 days, what is the ratio of red cars to blue cars? What percentage of all the cars will be blue after 15 days?

Solution: Make a table to show how the red cars and blue cars grow over time (days) and identify a pattern. After n days, the number of red cars is $3n + 1$ and the number of blue cars is $4n + 1$. So, the total is $7n + 2$ and these models can be verified for different values.

Day	Red Cars	Model	Blue Cars	Model	Total Cars	Model
0	1	3·0+1	1	4·0+1	2	7·0+2
1	4	3·1+1	5	4·1+1	9	7·1+2
2	7	3·2+1	9	4·2+1	16	7·2+2
3	10	3·3+1	13	4·3+1	23	7·3+2
4	13	3·4+1	17	4·4+1	30	7·4+2
N		$3 \cdot n + 1$		$4 \cdot n + 1$		$7 \cdot n + 2$

Once a model is developed, it is easy to answer the questions, After 15 days, the number of red cars is $3 \cdot 15 + 1 = 46$ and the number of blue cars is $4 \cdot 15 + 1 = 61$. So the ratio is $\frac{46}{61}$. After 15 days, the total number of cars is $7(15) + 2 = 107$. So, $\frac{61}{107} \cdot 100 = 57\%$ of the total cars is blue after 15 days.

Guess and Check
When a problem is such that you need to test several combinations to arrive at a result, you can use the guess and check method.

Example: Marla wants to purchase a snack that costs 80 cents. What is the least number of coins she can use to pay for the snack if she has to use at least one quarter, one dime, and one nickel?
Solution: 1 Quarter 1 Dime 1 Nickel = 25+10+5 =40. You need 40 more cents and need to keep the number of coins to the minimum. Add one more dime and try – 2 Quarters 1 Dime 1 Nickel = 50+10+5=65. You are still 15 cents short. So, you cannot add a quarter since that will take the total to 65+25=90. So, add 1 Dime and 1 Nickel again – you now have 2 Quarters, 2 Dimes and 2 Nickels = 50+20+10 = 80 cents. So, by guessing and checking, you can arrive at a solution.

Identify a pattern
Observe the data carefully to see if you can identify a pattern connecting them. Patterns can follow an arithmetic sequence, a geometric sequence, or any other algebraic relationship (linear, exponential, or quadratic) could exist in the data.

Example: The number of birds visiting a marshland each week was observed as follows. If this pattern continues, how many birds will visit the marshland during the 8th week?

Week w	1	2	3	4
Birds b	10	20	30	40

Solution: The pattern here is birds $b = 10w$ - where w is the number of the week. So, during the 8th week, you will have $10 \cdot 8 = 80$ birds.

Example: A biologist performed some experiment with bacteria and noted the following results. If this growth continues, what will be the bacterial count on the 7th week?

Week w	1	2	3	4
Count c	200	400	800	1600

Solution: The pattern here is count $c = 100 \cdot 2^w$ where w is the number of the week. Note that this is an exponential pattern of growth of the form $y = a \cdot b^x$. Review the lesson on Growth and Decay for more information on exponential models.

Arithmetic Sequence: When something grows in such a way the terms have a constant difference, then the pattern/sequence is said to be arithmetic. If $a, a + d, a + 2d, ...$is the arithmetic sequence, then $a + (n-1)d$ is the nth term.

Example: The sequence 5,9,13,17... is an arithmetic sequence with a difference of 4. The 45th term in this sequence is 5+(45-1) · 4= 5 + 44 · 4= 5+176=181.

Geometric Sequence: When something grows in such a way that the successive terms have a constant ratio, then the pattern/sequence is said to be geometric. If $a, ar, ar^2, ...$is the geometric sequence, then $a \cdot r^{n-1}$ is the nth term.

Example: The sequence 2,4,8,16... is a geometric sequence with a ratio of $\frac{4}{2} = 2$. The 10th term in this sequence is $a \cdot r^{n-1} = 2 \cdot 2^{10-1} = 2 \cdot 2^9 = 2^{10} = 1024$.

Q6 How does an Extended Thinking Problem look like?

A6 The following problem was published by the College Board as a sample.

Problem: An international bank issues its Traveler Credit Cards worldwide. When a customer makes a purchase using a Traveler card in a currency different from the customer's home currency, the bank converts the purchase price at the daily foreign rate and then charges a 4% fee on the converted cost.

Part 1
Sara lives in the United States, but in on vacation in India. She used her Traveler card for a purchase that cost 602 rupees (Indian currency). The bank posted a charge of $9.88 to her account that included the 4% fee. What foreign exchange rate, in Indian rupees per one US dollar, did the bank use for Sara's charge? Round your answer to the nearest whole number.

Part 2
A bank in India sells a prepaid card worth 7500 rupees. Sara can buy the prepaid card using dollars at the daily exchange rate with no fee, but she will lose any money left unspent on the prepaid card. What is the least number of the 7500 rupees on the prepaid card Sara must spend for the prepaid card to be cheaper than charging all her purchases on the Traveler card? Round your answer to the nearest whole number of rupees.

FocusPrep Note: The first time you read the problem, you may be confused or overwhelmed by the amount of information about credit cards and prepaid cards. If you are not familiar with the way credit cards and debit cards work, this problem may be too difficult to comprehend. But, if you review the content in this lesson regarding how credit and debit cards work, you will see that this problem can be solved quickly.

Solution Part 1: Sara purchased something for 602 Indian Rupees. The bank charged her $9.88 including a 4% fee. What exchange rate, in Indian Rupees per 1 USD did the bank charge?

The bank converts the purchase price at the current exchange rate and then charges 4%

So, let 1USD= x Indian Rupees. So, the purchase for 602 Indian Rupees = $\frac{602\ Rupees}{\frac{x\ Rupees}{Dollar}} = \frac{602}{x}$ USD

After adding 4% fee to this purchase cost, the converted cost with fee is $\frac{602}{x} + 0.04 \cdot \frac{602}{x} = \frac{602}{x}(1.04)$. This is given to be $9.88.

So $\frac{602}{x}(1.04) = 9.88$

$x = \frac{(602 \cdot 1.04)}{9.88} = 63.37$

Since the question asks you to round to the nearest whole number, the exchange rate is 1 USD=63 Rupees.

Solution Part 2: Note that in this part, Sara is wanting to purchase a prepaid card for $7500. She has to decide up to what amount she can purchase using the traveler credit card for it to be cheaper than the prepaid card.

Thinking and dealing with one currency will help avoid errors in calculations. Remember that Sara is in India. If she wants to purchase something for USD x using the Traveler Credit Card, she will be charged USD $1.04x$ including the 4% fee. If she buys the Prepaid Card for Rs 7500, she would pay (7500 Rupees)/ ($\frac{63\ Rupees}{USD}$) = USD 119.05. So, she can make purchases up to USD 119.05 using this prepaid card and her cost will be 119.05 since she has to prepay this amount. Make a table like shown below to see how this works.

Purchase in USD	Traveler CreditCard 1.04 · Purchase Cost USD	Prepaid Card USD	
10	10.40	119.05	Credit card is cheaper than prepaid card Don't buy the prepaid card
25	26	119.05	Credit card is cheaper than prepaid card Don't buy the prepaid card
50	52	119.05	Credit card is cheaper than prepaid card Don't buy the prepaid card
x	$1.04\ x$	119.05	Credit card cost is equal to prepaid card's cost. For purchase above USD x, prepaid card will be cheaper.
118	122	119.05	Prepaid card is cheaper.

A few values are shown – say for USD 50 in converted cost, the cost using credit card is USD 52 and this is cheaper than the cost or purchasing this item using prepaid card which is 119.05. So, for some purchase that has converted cost of USD x, the cost using travelers credit card is $1.04x$ and this is going to be more than the cost of using the prepaid card of 119.05. In other words, for a purchase of USD x, the cost of charging it to the prepaid card will be cheaper than charging it to the travelers credit card. So, you can setup an equation to find this USD x. $1.04x >= 119.05$

$x \geq \frac{119.05}{1.04} = 114.47$ USD. So, for a purchase price of USD 114.47, the cost using traveler credit card is equal to the cost using a prepaid card. Convert this amount to Rupees – 114.47 USD · 63 Rs/USD=Rs 7211.61 and round it to a whole number – the answer is 7212. Making a table is a very useful problem solving skill as highlighted by this problem.

PROBLEM SOLVING AND DATA ANALYSIS

Lesson 14 — Extended Thinking — Practice

CALCULATOR SECTION

Jennifer plans to visit three cities in Australia and three cities in New Zealand. Her tour company charges are 600 AUD (Australian Dollars) to take her to three cities in Australia and 600 NZD (New Zealand Dollars) to take her to three cities in New Zealand. The Exchange Rate chart for today is shown below:

Country	1 USD
Australia	1.26 AUD
New Zealand	1.36 NZD
Singapore	1.34 SGD

1. What will be the total cost of Jennifer's trip in US Dollars if she were to pay for it today? (round to the nearest whole dollar)
GRID IN

2. Jennifer wants to book her ticket after 10 days, when the exchange rate will be different. If the exchange rate of New Zealand Dollars after 10 days drops by 20%, and she wants to keep the total cost of her trip the same as today's cost, by how much percentage should the exchange rate of Australian Dollars increase so that Jennifer can book her ticket? (round to the nearest whole percentage.)
GRID IN

CALCULATOR SECTION

Sabrina is a bank manager. She issues two credit cards to customers- Credit Card-1 and Credit Card-2. Both have a credit limit of $200. For purchases on Credit Card-1, the fee is 2% up to $100 and 2.5% above $100. For purchases on Credit Card-2, the fee is 2.5% up to $100 and 2% above $100.

3. If a person who has both credit cards gets a bill of $180 on both credit cards, what is the difference in the purchase amounts(in $) in the two cards? Round to the nearest hundredths place.
GRID IN

4. In which card will it be cheaper to buy a watch that costs $175? If Credit Card-1 is your answer, grid-in 1 as your answer; if Credit Card-2 is your answer, grid- in 2 as your answer.
GRID IN

CALCULATOR SECTION

Trevor went on an international trip to two foreign countries with a $5000 debit card. The first country that he visited had an exchange rate of 1 USD=60 local currency, and the second had an exchange rate of 1 USD=30 local currency. He spent some money in each country for food, shopping, travel, and other expenses.

5. If Trevor spent 10,000 local currencies in the second country and had $4000 left over in his debit card after the visit, what is the ratio of his expenses in the first country to that of his expenses in the second country?
GRID IN

6. After visiting the second country, Trevor decided to visit a third country with an exchange rate of 1 USD=20 local currency. He spent some money in this country as well and had a balance of $3000 after the visit. How much money, in thousands of local currency, did he spend in this country?
GRID IN

CALCULATOR SECTION

The Exchange rate today for Australian Dollar (AUD) is 1 USD=2.5 AUD. Christina is planning to visit Australia next month and has budgeted 5000 AUD for expenses there. She is afraid that the exchange rate will decrease next month when she is on vacation and hopes that her additional expenses due to this possible decrease does not exceed USD 200.

7. How low can the exchange rate for AUD go next month if Christina's additional expenses must not exceed USD 200? Round to the nearest hundredths place.
GRID IN

8. What will Christina's expense in USD next month be, if the exchange rate decreases as calculated in the previous question? (round to the nearest whole dollar)
GRID IN

CALCULATOR SECTION

Darren has two credit cards – one issued by Bank-1 and another issued by Bank-2. The one issued by Bank-1 has a fee of 7% on all purchases, whereas the one issued by Bank-2 has a fee of 4% on all purchases plus and additional fixed fee of $1 for all purchases.

9. If a purchase is made for $125 on both cards, how much more money is charged by the credit card issued by Bank-1 compared to the one issued by Bank-2? Round to the nearest hundredths place.
GRID IN

10. For what purchase amount does the credit card issued by Bank-1 become as expensive as the credit card issued by Bank-2? (round to the nearest whole dollar)
GRID IN

PROBLEM SOLVING AND DATA ANALYSIS

| Lesson 14 | Extended Thinking | Answers |

#	Explanation	Comments
1 917	Cost to Australia is 600 AUD – Exchange Rate is 1 USD= 1.26 AUD. You can set a direct proportion as follows : 1.26 AUD = 1 USD 600 AUD = x USD So, $\frac{x}{1} = \frac{600}{1.26}$; $x = 476.19$ USD Similarly, the cost to New Zealand is $\frac{600}{1.36} = 441.18$; Total cost =917.37. Nearest whole dollar is USD 917.	Note that the exchange rate of Singapore is given but there is nothing in the problem about Singapore. Learn to read the Exchange Rate for the appropriate country correctly. See lesson on variation to learn how to setup a direct variation ratio.
2 30	Note that the Exchange rates change every day and the problem says the chart is for today. Exchange rate for NZ drops by 20% - so the new exchange rate is 1 USD=1.36·0.8=1.09 NZD. The new cost to NZ is 600/1.09=550.46 USD. But she wants to keep the total cost of her trip the same as before – which is 917 USD, calculated in the first problem. So, 917=new cost in USD to AUS+ new cost in USD to NZ 917= new cost in USD to AUS+ 550.46 New cost to AUS (that she can pay)= 366.54 USD. The trip cost to AUS is 600 AUD – but since Jennifer can only pay USD 366.54 for the AUS trip, the new exchange rate, x, for AUS must be such that the USD value of the trip should be 366.54. So, $\frac{600}{x} = 366.54$. $x = \frac{600}{366.54} = 1.64$. The percentage increase is $\frac{1.64-1.26}{1.26} \cdot 100 = 30.15\%$	Exchange Rate for all countries is specified in terms of 1 USD. So, if the exchange rate increases, USD becomes stronger, and you pay less in USD for your purchases. If the exchange rate decreases, USD becomes weaker, and you pay more in USD. Remember that Exchange Rates change every day. Familiarize yourself with calculating the new cost based on new exchange rates and compare it to the old cost based on old exchange rates.
3 0.11	cc1 = credit card 1; cc2 = credit card 2 cc1=> 2% fee up to 100; 2.5% above 100 cc2=> 2.5% fee up to 100 and 2% above 100. Person gets a charge of $180 on both cards => charge on cc1 = charge on cc2 For a purchase amount of $100 on cc1, the charge would be 100(1.02)=102. Since the charge was 180, the purchase amount was more than 100. Let x, be the purchase using cc1. The charge for first $100 is 100(1.02)=102. The charge for the remaining amount	Review credit card basics in the lesson– you purchase items for some amount and the credit card company will bill you.

©GiftOfLogic http://www.GiftOfLogic.com

		that is more than $100 is $(x - 100) \cdot 1.025$. So $102 + (x - 100) \cdot 1.025 = 180$ $102 + 1.025x - 102.5 = 180$ $x = 176.09$ Similarly, for credit card 2, let y be the purchase amount; $1.025 \cdot 100 + (y - 100) \cdot 1.02 = 180$ $102.5 + 1.02y - 102 = 180$ $y = 175.98$ So, the difference in purchase amount=176.09-175.98=0.11= 11 cents.	
4	1	Cost of watch = $175 Using cc1, the cost is $100 \cdot 1.02 + 75 \cdot 1.025 = 178.88$ Using cc2, the cost is $100 \cdot 1.025 + 75 \cdot 1.02 = 179$ Since cc1 is cheaper by 12 cents, the answer is 1	
5	2	First country 1USD=60 local Second country 1USD=30 local Note that the name of the countries or the name of the currencies is not mentioned. p1 = purchases in first country in local currency p2= purchases in second country in local currency In terms of USD, the cost is p1/60 and p2/30 respectively. He had 4000 left in the debit card after visiting country2- this means he spent 5000-4000=USD 1000 in the first 2 countries. $\frac{p1}{60} + \frac{p2}{30} = 1000$ $\frac{p1 + 2p2}{60} = 1000$ $p1 + 2p2 = 60,000$ he spent 10,000 local currency in second country $p2 = 10,000$ So, $p1 = 60,000 - 2p2 = 60000 - 20000 = 40,000$ Since these values are in local currencies, we must convert them to USD to have a valid comparison: $$p1 = \frac{40000}{60} = \frac{2000}{3}$$ $$p2 = \frac{10000}{30} = \frac{1000}{3}$$ $$\frac{p1}{p2} = \frac{\frac{2000}{3}}{\frac{1000}{3}} = \frac{2000}{1000} = 2$$	Review how debit cards work; they are sometimes called as "prepaid cards" – as you make purchases with it, the balance will reduce. Remember to keep all numbers in the USD. Review the lesson for information on credit cards and debit cards.
6	20	He starts with USD 5000 and has USD 3000 after visiting the third country. 5000–first country–second country – third country=3000	In problems involving large amount of currencies, pay attention to whether the

	You already know that he had 4000 after visiting the second country; so 5000–first country–second country=4000; substituting this in the above equation, you get 4000–third country= 3000 Amount spent in the third country is 4000–3000=1000 USD; Note that the question asks for the answer in local currency. 1 USD=20 local currency in the third country; so 1000 USD=1000 · 20=20,000 local currencies. The answer is expected in thousands- so 20,000/1000=20 is the answer.	answer needs to be in actual USD or in hundreds or thousands of USD.
7 2.28	Note that exchange rates change and problems involving exchange rates will require you to calculate costs "now" and "later". Also, note that she has budgeted in a foreign currency - 5000 AUD. So, you will have to convert it to USD. Cost of her trip now is $\frac{5000}{2.5}$ USD Let x be the exchange rate next month; cost next month is $\frac{5000}{x}$; since the exchange rate is expected to decrease next month, $x < 2.5$ and so $\frac{5000}{x} > \frac{5000}{2.5}$; she hopes that her additional expenses due this rate decrease do not exceed USD 200. $\frac{5000}{x} - \frac{5000}{2.5} <= 200$ $5000\left(\frac{1}{x} - \frac{1}{2.5}\right) \leq 200$ $\left(\frac{1}{x} - \frac{1}{2.5}\right) \leq \frac{200}{5000} = 0.04$ $x \leq 2.272727$ So, the exchange rate must be at least 2.28 AUD (since we are rounding to the nearest hundredth place). Below that, her additional expenses will exceed USD 200	When people travel, they establish a budget – the most amount that they can spend. But as exchange rates change every day, their budget may or may not be sufficient to cover their expenses. That's why international travelers need to keep an eye on exchange rates every day. Remember that if exchange rate of a country decreases with respect to the USD, then you get less foreign currency and will have to pay more in USD. Learn to setup equalities and inequalities.
8 2193	If the exchange rate becomes 2.27, then her expense will be $\frac{5000}{2.28} = 2193$	
9 2.75	cc1- 7% fee cc2- 4% fee + $1 fixed fee for $125, cc1 = 125 · 1.07=133.75; cc2=125 · 1.04+1=131 The difference= 133.75-131=2.75	
10 33	Let x be the purchase amount for which cc1 = cc2 $1.07x = 1 + 1.04 x$ $1.07x - 1.04x = 1$ $0.03 x = 1$ $x = 33.33$ Rounding to nearest whole number, you get $x = 33$.	

CHAPTER 2 HEART OF ALGEBRA	
Lesson	**Title**
Lesson 15	Linear Equations
Lesson 16	System of Linear Equations
Lesson 17	Linear Inequalities
Lesson 18	System of Linear Inequalities
Lesson 19	Linear Models and Graphs
Lesson 20	Absolute Equalities and Inequalities

| Lesson 15 | HEART OF ALGEBRA
Linear Equations | Review |

FOCUSPREP CHECKLIST

- What is a Linear Equation?
- How do I solve a Linear Equation?
- Can I use PEMDAS to simplify a Linear Equation?
- Workout practice problems in Linear Equations

Q1 What is a Linear Equation?

A1 A Linear Equation of first degree is an equation where the exponent (or power) of the variable is 1. Linear equations can have one or more variables.

A Linear Equation with <u>one variable</u> is an equation typically of the form $ax + b = c$ where x is the variable and a, b, and c are constants and $a \neq 0$. Example: $3x + 5 = 30$.

A Linear equation can have more than one variable. For example, $x + y = 4$ is a linear equation with <u>two variables</u>. Linear equations with two variables are reviewed in the lesson on "Systems of Linear Equations".

Examples

$3x + 5 = 2$; $9x - 2 = 4x + 3$; $\frac{x}{5} = 2$; $2 - \frac{x}{5} = 8$; $\frac{x}{4} - \frac{x}{8} = 18$ are examples of linear equations with one variable.

Q2 What is a Linear Inequality?

A2 Linear Inequalities have $>, <, \geq, \leq$ signs. They do not have an $=$ sign. Example: $2x + 5 > 7$. Linear Inequalities are reviewed in a different lesson.

Q3 How do I solve a linear equation?

A3 Solving a Linear Equation means finding the value of the variable that will make the equation true. Depending on the problem, linear equations are solved by isolating the variable to one side of the equation, by performing operations on both sides of the equation, cross multiplying, and substituting. You can perform addition, subtraction, multiplication, and division operations on both sides of the equation in order to isolate the variable.

<u>Example (isolating by Addition)</u>:
$$x - 15 = 22$$
$$x - 15 + 15 = 22 + 15$$
$$x = 37$$

Example (isolating by Subtraction):
$$x + 2 = 6$$
$$x + 2 - 2 = 6 - 2$$
$$x = 4$$

Example (isolating by Multiplication):
$$\frac{x}{3} = 2 \quad \text{multiply by 3 on both sides to isolate } x$$
$$3 \cdot \frac{x}{3} = 2 \cdot 3$$
$$x = 6$$

Example (isolating by Multiplying by Inverse):
$$\frac{7x}{3} = \frac{21}{6} \quad \text{multiply by the inverse of } \frac{7}{3} \text{ on both sides}$$
$$\frac{3}{7} \cdot \frac{7x}{3} = \frac{3}{7} \cdot \frac{21}{6}$$
$$x = \frac{3}{2}$$

Example (isolating by Cross-Multiplication):
$$\frac{7x}{3} = \frac{21}{6} \quad \text{cross multiply to remove the denominators}$$
$$6 \cdot 7x = 21 \cdot 3$$
$$42x = 63; \quad \text{divide by 42 on both sides}$$
$$x = \frac{63}{42} = \frac{21}{14}$$

Example (isolating by Cross-Multiplication):
$$\frac{x-1}{3} = \frac{x+1}{4} \quad \text{cross multiply to remove denominators}$$
$$4(x-1) = 3(x+1) \quad \text{expand using distributive property}$$
$$4x - 4 = 3x + 3 \quad \text{isolate variable } x \text{ on one side}$$
$$4x - 3x = x = 3 + 4 = 7$$

Example (isolating by Division):
$$7x = 21 \quad \text{divide by 7 on both sides to isolate x}$$
$$\frac{7x}{7} = \frac{21}{7}; \quad x = 21$$

Q4 What is PEMDAS and why is it important while solving linear equations?

A4 When a linear equation has several terms, you can apply the PEMDAS rule to decide the order of operations. PEMDAS stands for: Parentheses, Exponents, Multiplication, Division, Addition, and Subtraction. You apply the rule from left to right of the expression.

Example: Solve for x:
$$3^2 \cdot (3 + 4x \div 2 - 1) = 18$$
$$9 \cdot \left(3 + \frac{4x}{2} - 1\right) = 18 \quad \text{within parenthesis do the division first}$$
$$9(3 + 2x - 1) = 18 \quad \text{process the parenthesis}$$
$$9(2 + 2x) = 18$$
$$2 + 2x = \frac{18}{9} = 2$$
$$2x = 2 - 2 = 0 \, ; \text{So, } x = 0$$

Example:

Solve for c : $5 \cdot (3 - 5c) = 25$; divide by 5 on both sides

$3 - 5c = \frac{25}{5} = 5$; isolate c on one side

$-5c = 5 - 3 = 2$

$c = \frac{2}{-5} = -\frac{2}{5}$

Q5 What does "In terms of" mean?

A5 When a problem asks you to "express y in terms of x", only y should be on the left hand side of the equation (ie, isolate y) ; x and all other constants must be on the right hand side of the equation.

Example: If $2x + y = 4$, then what is y in terms of x?
You want to isolate y, so, add $-2x$ to both sides

$2x + y = 4$

$-2x + 2x + y = -2x + 4;$

$y = -2x + 4$

Example: If $2x + 3y = 4$, express y in terms of x.
You want to isolate y, so add $-2x$ to both sides:

$$2x + 3y = 4$$
$$-2x + 2x + 3y = -2x + 4$$
$$3y = -2x + 4$$
$$y = \frac{-2x + 4}{3}$$
$$y = \frac{-2x}{3} + \frac{4}{3}$$

Q6 What if there are variables on both sides of the equation?

A6 When there are variables on both sides of the equation, bring the variables to the left hand side and move the constants to the right hand side of the equation.

Example:

Solve $2x + 4 = 7x + 9$

$2x - 7x = 9 - 4$ move terms with x to the left hand side and sum up

$-5x = 5$ divide both sides by -5 to isolate x

$-\frac{5x}{-5} = \frac{5}{-5}$; $x = -1$; arrive at the solution

Example:

Solve $3x + 6 = 7x + 9 - 2x$

$3x - 7x + 2x = 9 - 6$ move terms with x to the left hand side and sum up

$-2x = 3$ divide both sides by -2 to isolate x

$-\frac{2x}{-2} = \frac{3}{-2}$

$x = -\frac{3}{2}$; arrive at the solution

Q7 How do I solve word problems involving linear equalities?

A7 You may encounter word problems in which you will construct a linear equation and then solve it. Several problems in the practice section will help you to gain confidence in these types of problems.

HEART OF ALGEBRA

Lesson 15 — **Linear Equations** — **Practice**

NO CALCULATOR SECTION

1. If $3x + 5x - 2x = 1$, what is the value of x?

(A) $\frac{1}{8}$

(B) $\frac{1}{6}$

(C) $\frac{1}{4}$

(D) $\frac{1}{2}$

2. If $\frac{k}{3} = \frac{k+2}{4}$ then $k =$

(A) 3
(B) 4
(C) 6
(D) 12

3. The expression $-3(x + 6 \div 2) + 2^2 \cdot 3$ can be simplified as

(A) $-3(1 - x)$
(B) $-3(1 + x)$
(C) $3(1 - x)$
(D) $3(1 + x)$

4. If $\frac{3}{7}x + \frac{5}{7}x = 1$, what is the value of x?

(A) $\frac{8}{7}$

(B) $\frac{7}{8}$

(C) $\frac{1}{8}$

(D) $\frac{1}{35}$

NO CALCULATOR SECTION

5. For what value of x will the expression $3[x + (x - 3)] + 5x$ equal to 18?

(A) $\frac{9}{11}$

(B) $\frac{11}{27}$

(C) $\frac{27}{11}$

(D) $\frac{38}{11}$

6. Solve for x: $\frac{(x + 6 \div 2)}{16} = \frac{1}{2}$

(A) 5
(B) 8
(C) 16
(D) 32

7. If $\frac{z}{2} - \frac{z}{3} = 16$, then $z =$

(A) 6
(B) 32
(C) 48
(D) 96

NO CALCULATOR SECTION

8. A bee keeper has several bees inside a big jar. Due to a small hole in the jar, the bees escape at the rate of 3 bees per minute. If he initially had 1000 bees in the jar, after how many minutes will there be 400 bees in the jar?
(A) 100
(B) 200
(C) 300
(D) 400

9. Brian drove 3 hours at the speed of 60 miles/hr trying to reach his destination 350 miles away. If he drives the remaining distance at 85 miles/hr, how many more hours will he take to reach the destination?
(A) 1
(B) 2
(C) 3
(D) 4

10. 1000 is the result when 365 is subtracted from a number that is increased by 5 and then multiplied by 13. What is the number?
(A) 13
(B) 26
(C) 52
(D) 100

NO CALCULATOR SECTION

11. Brandi's bank balance initially was $1600, but she spent money at the rate of 20% of this amount every day. After how many days will she have a balance of $640 in her account?
(A) 10
(B) 20
(C) 30
(D) 40

12. John's salary includes a base salary of $1700 per month plus a commission of 20% of the monthly car sales, in dollars. If his salary in June was $8700, how much sales in dollars did he have in June?
(A) 25,000
(B) 35,000
(C) 70,000
(D) 75,000

13. Limousine rates are $50 flat rate plus an additional 30 cents for every mile. If Melissa paid $200 for a Limousine ride, how many miles did she travel?
GRID IN

CALCULATOR SECTION

14. A movie producer produces two movies, movie-1 and movie-2. He estimates the first day sales for movie-1 to be $3m + 300$ where m is the number of people who will watch movie-1 on the first day. He also estimates the first day sales for movie-2 to be $2n + 800$ where n is the number of people who will watch movie-2 on the first day. After the movies were released, the first day sales were the same for both movies and 350 people watched movie-2. How many people watched movie-1?
GRID IN

15. Joe purchases a phone plan that costs 30 dollars a month fixed charge plus 33 cents per text message. How much will Joe's monthly bill be if he sends 334 text messages in one month?
(A) $64.00
(B) $140.22
(C) $160.30
(D) $420.32

16. If $x\sqrt{3} + \sqrt{7} = \sqrt{9}$, then x is approximately equal to
(A) 0.20
(B) 0.42
(C) 1.42
(D) 1.68

CALCULATOR SECTION

17. For each of the first six months of a year, a pond gains 5 inches and for each of the last six months of the year, the pond loses six inches to evaporation. If the height of water in the pond after 3 years is 50 inches, how much water was there at the beginning of the first year?
GRID IN

18. The number of tigers left in the wild is declining at a constant rate. At the beginning of year 2001, there were 9000 tigers left. At the end of year 2010, there were 3500 tigers left. If this rate continues, how many years are left until the tigers population becomes zero? (round to the hundredths place)
GRID IN

HEART OF ALGEBRA

| Lesson 15 | Linear Equations | Answers |

#	Explanation	Comments
1 B	The variable x is on one side of the equation; sum up the variables and solve for x $3x + 5x - 2x = 1$; $6x = 1$ $x = \dfrac{1}{6}$	Note that all the problems in this lesson are one-variable linear equations.
2 C	The variable k is on both sides with a denominator; cross multiply and isolate k $\dfrac{k}{3} = \dfrac{k+2}{4}$ $4k = 3(k+2) = 3k + 6$; $4k - 3k = 6$; isolate k to one side $k = 6$ Verify the results $\dfrac{6}{3} = 2 = \dfrac{6+2}{4} = \dfrac{8}{4} = 2$	Verify your results by plugging it back into the equation.
3 C	Use PEMDAS, process the parenthesis first, within the parenthesis, process division first $-3(x + 6 \div 2) + 2^2 \cdot 3$ $-3(x + 3) + 2^2 \cdot 3$ $-3x - 9 + 2^2 \cdot 3$ $-3x - 9 + 4 \cdot 3$ $-3x - 9 + 12$ $-3x + 3$ $3(-x + 1)$ $3(1 - x)$	PEMDAS is critical to evaluating an expression correctly; get familiar with it.
4 B	$\dfrac{3}{7}x + \dfrac{5}{7}x = 1$ $x\left(\dfrac{3}{7} + \dfrac{5}{7}\right) = 1$; factor out the x that is common $x\left(\dfrac{8}{7}\right) = 1$ $x\dfrac{8}{7} \cdot \dfrac{7}{8} = 1 \cdot \dfrac{7}{8}$; multiply by reciprocal of $\dfrac{8}{7}$ to isolate x $x = \dfrac{7}{8}$	
5 C	$3(x + (x - 3)) + 5x = 18$ $3(x + x - 3) + 5x = 18$ $3(2x - 3) + 5x = 18$ $6x - 9 + 5x = 18$ $11x - 9 = 18$ $11x - 9 + 9 = 18 + 9 = 27$	Do not forget to add the 9 to both sides.

	$11x = 27$ $x = \dfrac{27}{11}$		
6 A	$\dfrac{(x + 6 \div 2)}{16} = \dfrac{1}{2}$ $\dfrac{(x+3)}{16} = \dfrac{1}{2}$; resolve the parenthesis first $2x + 6 = 16$; cross multiply $2x = 16 - 6 = 10$ $x = 5$	Resolve the parenthesis first.	
7 D	$\dfrac{z}{2} - \dfrac{z}{3} = 16$ $z\left(\dfrac{1}{2} - \dfrac{1}{3}\right) = 16$; separate the common factor $z \cdot \dfrac{3-2}{6} = 16$; simplify using LCM of the denominator. $z \cdot \dfrac{1}{6} = 16$ $z = 16 \cdot 6 = 96$; cross multiply to get z		
8 B	Initially he has 1000 bees; bees escape at the rate of 3 bees/minute; after some time there are 400 bees; Let m be the number of minutes for the bees in the jar to go from 1000 to 400. In this m minutes, $3m$ bees escape. Initial + net change = final Set the linear equation and solve for m; $1000 - 3m = 400$ $3m = 1000 - 400 = 600$ $m = 200$ minutes	Write the given facts and pause for a few seconds to get a clue about how to set up the equation. 1 minute → 3 bees escape m minutes → 3m bees escape remember that Initial + net change = final Net change can be positive or negative; be careful with the positive/negative sign.	
9 B	Total distance = 350 miles 3 hours @ 60 miles/hr = 180 miles Remaining distance is covered at 85 miles/hour Let t be the time taken to cover the remaining distance. Set up the linear equation. $180 + 85\,t = 350$ $85t = 350 - 180 = 170$ $t = 2$ hours	In some problems involving speed and distances, you may have to use the formula Speed= distance/time to set up the equation. Pay attention to the unit of time – seconds, minutes, or hours.	
10 D	$13(5 + x) - 365 = 1000$. $65 + 13x - 365 = 1000$ $13x - 300 = 1000$ $13x = 1300$ $x = 100$	This is a word problem involving linear equations; translate the words to math carefully. Review the lesson on Word Problems.	

11 C	Initial balance = 1600 Spent 20% **everyday** 20/100 · 1600=320 everyday Final balance = 640 Let d be the number of days for the balance to drop from 1600 to 640; in 1 day, she spends \$320, so in d days, she would have spent $320d$ dollars; set up the linear equation Initial – amount spent = final $1600 - 320d = 640$ $320d = 1600 - 640 = 960$ $d = \frac{960}{320} = 3$ days	In problems of this type, you will be asked to setup an equation connecting the initial amount and final amount. Note that the final amount may be more than or less than the initial amount depending on whether there is a net deposit or net withdrawal; set up the equation carefully.
12 B	Salary is base salary of 1700/month plus commission of 20% of sales June salary= 8700; how much sales? Let s be the sales for June Base salary + 20% of s = 8700 $1700 + 0.2s = 8700$ $0.2s = 8700 - 1700 = 7000$ $s = \frac{7000}{0.2} = \frac{70000}{2} = 35000$	Note that 20% of sales = $\frac{20}{100} \cdot s = 0.2\,s$; When dividing 7000/0.2, multiply numerator and denominator by 10 and then divide.
13 500	\$50 flat rate plus 30 cents per mile Melissa paid \$200 – how many miles? Set up the equation – convert dollars to cents $5000 + 30m = 20000$ $30m = 20000 - 5000 = 15000$ $m = \frac{15000}{30} = 500$ miles	Get familiar with problems involving a flat rate/ fixed charge plus a variable charge based on the miles traveled. Phone companies charge in a similar way; they will have fixed charges plus variable charges based on how long you speak.
14 400	Movie-1 first day sales=$3m + 300$ Movie-2 first day sales= $2n + 800$ First days sales is same for both movies; 350 watched movie-2 on day one. So $n=350$ $3m + 300 = 2n + 800$ $3m + 300 = 2 \cdot 350 + 800$ $3m + 300 = 700 + 800 = 1500$ $3m = 1500 - 300 = 1200$ $m = \frac{1200}{3} = 400$	In this problem, two linear equations are equated; even though there are two variables m and n, since n is given as 350, this problem becomes a one-variable linear equation problem. Though you can use a calculator for this problem, it is clearly not necessary.
15 B	30 dollars fixed charge Text – 33 cents/text; 334 text messages sent $30 + 0.33 \cdot 334 = 140.22$; Remember to convert cents to dollars.	In this problem, you should use the calculator to get results quickly.

16 A	$x\sqrt{3} + \sqrt{7} = \sqrt{9}$ $x\sqrt{3} = \sqrt{9} - \sqrt{7} = 3 - \sqrt{7}$ $x = \dfrac{3 - \sqrt{7}}{\sqrt{3}}$ $x = \dfrac{0.3542....}{\sqrt{3}}$ = approximately 0.20	Learn to calculate square roots and divide numbers by square roots. Note that the problem asks "x is approximately".
17 68	Let the water level at the beginning of the year be h inches. Pond gains 5 feet for 6 months and loses 6 feet for the next six months – so the net gain is $5 \cdot 6 - 6 \cdot 6 = -6$ inches/year. After 3 years, the height is 50 inches; so setup the equation as follows: beginning height + net change = final height $h + (-6 \text{ inches/year} \cdot 3 \text{years}) = 50$ $h - 18 = 50$ $h = 50 + 18 = 68$ inches	Think of this problem as initial + net change=final. Note that the net change is negative in this problem, but it could be positive in some other problem, depending on the data.
18 6.36	Note that data is given for years 2001 and 2010 and the question asks "how many years are left" – this means you need to count from year 2010. You need to find the rate at which tiger population is declining. Over 10 years, it declined by $3500 - 9000 = -5500$. This is a rate of $-\dfrac{5500}{10} = -500$/year. The problem states that the tiger population is declining at a constant rate and that this rate continues. The question is – how long will it take for the tiger population to go from 3500 to 0. Initial + net change=final $3500 - 550\,t = 0$ $550t = 3500$ $t = \dfrac{3500}{550} = 6.36$ years	Initial + net change=final Note the negative net change in this problem; be careful with the sign for net change – it can be positive or negative.

HEART OF ALGEBRA		
Lesson 16	System of Linear Equations	Review

> **FOCUSPREP CHECKLIST**
> - How does a System of linear equations look?
> - How do I solve a System of linear equations?
> - How many solutions can a system of linear equations have?
> - Workout practice problems in System of Linear Equations

Q1 What is a "system" of linear equations?

A1 A System of Linear Equations is a set of linear equations that can be solved together to find the values of the variables. A system can have 2 equations and 2 variables, 3 equation and 3 variables, etc.

Example: The following is a set of linear equations with two variables x and y.

$$x + y = 4$$
$$x - y = 2$$

Q2 How do I solve a system of linear equations involving two variables?

A2 A system of linear equations can be solved by using graphs, tables, or algebraically by substitution. The solution to a system with two variables is the ordered pair (x, y) that satisfies both equations of the system.

Q3 How do I solve a system of linear equations using tables?

A3 Create a table showing x and y values for both equations of the system. Then, see if there is one x value for which the y values of both equations are the same. This (x, y) pair is the solution to the system.

Example: Solve $x + y = 4$; $x - y = 2$

Prepare a table with different x values and y values from each of the two equations. Look for a x-value where the y values are the same. In this case, for $x = 3$, both equations have a y value of 1. So, the solution to the system of equations is $x = 3, y = 1$.

x	0	1	2	3	4
$y = 4 - x$	4	3	2	1	0
$y = x - 2$	-2	-1	0	1	2

Q4 How do I solve a system of linear equations by substitution?

A4 Substitution is the process of using one equation to get one variable in terms of the other, and then plugging this variable into the second equation as shown in the example below.

Example: Solve the system of equations:
$$x + 2 = y$$
$$2x = y$$

Write x in terms of y.
$$x = y - 2$$
$$2x = y$$

Now substitute x into the second equation.
$$2x = y$$
$$2(y - 2) = y \; ; \text{substitute } x$$
$$2y - 4 = y$$
$$2y - y = 4 \; ; \text{isolate } y$$
$$y = 4$$
$$\text{So, } x = y - 2 = 4 - 2 = 2$$
The solution to this system is $(x, y) = (2, 4)$

Q5 How do I solve a system of linear equations by elimination?

A5 You can solve for one variable by adding or subtracting the two equations together or by performing a multiplication or division operation on one or both equations. These equations can then be manipulated to get rid of one variable as shown in the example below.

Example: Solve the following system of linear equations.

$$2x + 3y = 4$$
$$2x + 6y = 7 \; ; \text{multiply by -1 on both sides}$$

$$2x + 3y = 4$$
$$-1 \cdot (2x + 6y) = -1 \cdot 7$$

$$2x + 3y = 4$$
$$-2x - 6y = -7$$

$$0 - 3y = -3 \; ; \text{add the corresponding terms}$$
$$-3y = -3 \; ; \text{divide by } -3 \text{ on both sides}$$
$$y = 1 \; ; \text{using } y = 1, \text{ find } x$$
$$2x + 6y = 7 \text{ substitute } y \text{ back into this equation to solve for x}$$
$$x = \frac{7 - 6y}{2} = \frac{7 - 6 \cdot 1}{2} = \frac{1}{2}$$

So, the solution to the system of equations is $x = \frac{1}{2}, y = 1$; Verify this by substituting these values back into the equations. $2x + 3y = 4$; $2\left(\frac{1}{2}\right) + 3 \cdot 1 = 1 + 3 = 4$. So the solution is correct.

Q6 How do I find the solution to a system of linear equations graphically?

A6 Each linear equation in the system can be expressed as $y = mx + b$ and therefore they are straight lines when plotted on a graph. The solution of the system is the point (x, y) in the graph where the two lines meet.

Q7 How many solutions can a system of linear equations have? How do I find this out?

A7 A system of linear equations can have no solution, one solution, or infinitely many solutions. You can find this algebraically or graphically. See the table below for a summary. It is easy to remember this.

No Solution: Example: $y = 2x - 7$ and $y = 2x + 5$
Algebraic: When you solve this system algebraically, you get $2x - 7 = 2x + 5$, $-7 = 5$. Since this is never true, this system has no solution.
Graphic: The slopes of the lines are the same but the intercepts are different. This means that they are parallel (the intercepts separate them) and so the system has no solution.

If the graphs of the equations have the same slope but different y intercept, then the graphs of these equations/lines are parallel lines that do not meet.

Only one solution: Example: $y = 2x - 7$ and $y = 3x + 5$
Algebraic: Substitute y from one equation into the other; $2x - 7 = 3x + 5$; $x = -12; y = 3 \cdot -12 + 5 = -31$. The solution is $(-12, 31)$.
Graphic: Slopes of these two lines are 2 and 3 respectively; since they are different, there is only one solution. If the graphs of the equations have different slopes, then they will intersect at one point only and the system will have only one solution.

Infinitely many solutions: Example: $y = 2x - 7$ and $2y = 4x - 14$.
Algebraic: When you solve this system algebraically, you get $y = 2x - 7$ and $y = \frac{4x-14}{2} = 2x - 7$; so, $2x - 7 = 2x - 7; 0 = 0$. Since 0=0 is true, this means both the equations are same – that is, they overlap and so have infinite solutions.

Graphic: If the graphs of the equations have the same slope and y intercept, then the graphs coincide with each other and the system has infinitely many solutions.

System of Linear Equations		
Different slopes	⨉	Only one solution
Same slope, different y intercept (parallel)	∥	No solution
Same slope and same y −intercept	—	Infinitely many solutions

HEART OF ALGEBRA

| Lesson 16 | System of Linear Equations | Practice |

NO CALCULATOR SECTION

1. Which of the following is the solution to the system shown below?

$$y = 3$$
$$3x + 2y = 0$$

(A) $(3, -2)$
(B) $(2, 3)$
(C) $(-3, 2)$
(D) $(-2, 3)$

2. Which of the following is the solution to the following system?

$$x - 4 = 3y$$
$$3x + 4y = 38$$

(A) $(10, 2)$
(B) $(2, 10)$
(C) $(-2, 10)$
(D) $(-10, 2)$

3. Given the linear equations $2(y + x) = 2.5$, and $x - y = 0.25$. which of the following ordered pairs satisfy the equation?
(A) $(1, 1)$
(B) $(0.5, 0.5)$
(C) $(0.75, 0.5)$
(D) $(0.25, 0.25)$

NO CALCULATOR SECTION

4. What value of c makes the following system have infinite solutions?

$$2x + 2y = 4$$
$$cx + 3y = 6$$

(A) 1
(B) 3
(C) 4
(D) 6

5 5 apples and 3 oranges cost 18 dollars. 7 apples and 4 oranges cost 25 dollars. What is the cost of 12 apples?
(A) 12
(B) 24
(C) 36
(D) 48

6 How many solutions does the following system have?

$$5x + 6y = 7$$
$$-5x - 6y = -7$$

(A) 0
(B) 1
(C) 2
(D) ∞

NO CALCULATOR SECTION

7. A team of 60 boys and girls are to be chosen for a singing competition with the condition that there should be twice as many girls as there are boys in the selection. If b boys and g girls were chosen, then the system of equations that models this scenario is
(A) $b = 50$, $g = 60$
(B) $b + g = 60$; $2g = b$
(C) $b + g = 60$; $2b = g$
(D) $b - g = 60$; $2b = g$

8. The two equations $y = 3x + 4$ and $y = 6x + 10$ have a solution in which of the following choices?
(A) $(-2, -4)$
(B) $(-2, -2)$
(C) $(-4, -2)$
(D) $(4, -2)$

9. $\frac{2}{3}$ cups of vanilla ice cream and $\frac{4}{3}$ cup of strawberry ice cream cost $10. $\frac{1}{3}$ cups of vanilla ice cream and $2\frac{2}{3}$ cups of strawberry ice cream cost $17. How much does one cup of vanilla ice cream cost?
(A) $1
(B) $2
(C) $3
(D) $6

NO CALCULATOR SECTION

10.
$$a + 3c = 4$$
$$3b + a = 7$$
$$3c + 3b = 9$$

Which of the following answer choices expresses the values of a, b and c as an ordered triplet (a, b, c) that satisfies all the three equations?
(A) (2,1,1)
(B) (1,2,1)
(C) (1,1,2)
(D) (2,1,2)

CALCULATOR SECTION

11. At a party store, 3 balloons and 4 hats cost $6.50. Also, 4 balloons and 3 hats cost $7.50. How much do 17 balloons and 10 hats cost?
GRID IN

CALCULATOR SECTION

12. A publisher sells two books – a Physics book and a Chemistry book. The Physics book weighs 2 lbs and the Chemistry book weighs 3 lbs. How many Physics books are there in a 150 lb box containing Physics and Chemistry books if there are six times as many physics books as there are chemistry books in it?
GRID IN

CALCULATOR SECTION

13. A department store sells two types of pillows- a soft one and a hard one. The soft pillow costs $5 each and the hard pillow costs $13 each. If the store sells a special bundle made up of 10 pillows for $66 per bundle, how many soft pillows are there in the bundle if the cost of the bundle is the cost of all the pillows that make up the bundle?
GRID IN

		HEART OF ALGEBRA	
Lesson 16		System of Linear Equations	Answers

#	Explanation	Comments
1 D	substitute $y = 3$ into the second equation. $$3x + 2(3) = 0$$ $$3x + 6 = 0$$ $$3x = -6$$ $$x = -2$$ So, the solution to the system is $(-2, 3)$	In this problem, y is given to be 3; if it is not given, then substitute x in one of the equations to find y.
2 A	Isolate x from one equation and substitute x into the second equation: $x - 4 = 3y$; so $x = 3y + 4$ $3(3y + 4) + 4y = 38$; substitute x from above $9y + 12 + 4y = 38$ $13y = 38 - 12$ $y = 2$ Plug $y = 2$ into the first equation: $x - 4 = 3(2)$; $so\ x = 4 + 6 = 10$ $x = 10$, $y = 2$; The solution is $(10, 2)$	From one equation, write one variable in terms of other and then substitute it into the other equation.
3 C	$2(y + x) = 2.5$. So, $(y + x) = 1.25$. The other equation is $x - y = 0.25$. Choice C satisfies both equations.	
4 B	For a system to have infinitely many solutions, the slope of the lines must be the same and the y-intercept must be the same; slope of a line of the form $y = mx + b$ is m. Convert the first equation into $y = mx + b$ format: $2x + 2y = 4$ $2y = -2x + 4$ $y = -x + 2$; so the slope is -1, and y-intercept is 2. Convert the second equation into $y = mx + b$ format $cx + 3y = 6$ $3y = -cx + 6$ $y = -\frac{c}{3}x + \frac{6}{2} = -\frac{c}{3}x + 2$; so the slope is $-\frac{c}{3}$ and intercept is 2. For the system to have infinite solutions, the slope and intercept must be the same. $$so, -\frac{c}{3} = -1; => c = 3$$	Review this lesson and learn when a system will have 1 solution, no solution, or infinite solutions. Remember that the solution for a 2-variable Linear system is an ordered pair (x, y) that satisfies the equations in the system.

5	C	Setting this up as a system, using a for apples and o for oranges gives: $5a + 3o = 18$ $7a + 4o = 25$ Eliminate a; LCM of 5 and 7 is 35. Multiply the first equation by 7 and the second equation by 5 so that the coefficient of a will sum up to 0 after subtraction, thereby eliminating it. $7(5a + 3o) = 7(18)$ $5(7a + 4o) = 5(25)$ $35a + 21o = 126$ $35a + 20o = 125$ Subtract the second equation from the first $o = 1$ Plug the o value back into the first equation: $5a + 3(1) = 18$ $5a = 15$ $a = 3$ 1 apple is $3, so, 12 apples cost is $36.	This is a classic system of linear equations problem that can be solved using the substitution and elimination methods discussed in this lesson. You can choose to eliminate either a or o. Remember to operate on both sides of the equation. After solving a system of linear equations, pay attention to the question – it may not ask you for the solution itself – it may ask you the sum or the product or the ratio of the variables involved.
6	D	$$5x + 6y = 7$$ $$-5x - 6y = -7$$ The equations are Adding up the equations, you get 0=0. Since this is true, the system has infinite solutions.	
7	C	Total of 60 boys and girls; so $b + g = 60$ Twice as many girls as boys; this can be confusing If you try $b = 2g$; when $g = 1, b = 2$ – there are twice as many boys as girls- so this is wrong; Try $g = 2b$, and plug $b = 1$, you get $g = 2$ – there are twice as many girls as boys; so, $b + g = 60$ and $g = 2b$ are the equations that define the system.	Note carefully that "twice as many girls as boys" translates to $g = 2b$. You don't have to memorize this word to math translation – just plug in $b = 1$ and see if it makes sense.
8	B	You can set the equations equal to each other as follows: $$3x + 4 = 6x + 10$$ Solving gives $3x = -6; x = -2$ Plug in the value of x to get y: $$y = 3(-2) + 4$$ $$y = -2$$ so, the solution of the system is $(-2, -2)$	

9 C	Set this up as a system, using v for vanilla and s for strawberry: $$\frac{2}{3}v + \frac{4}{3}s = 10$$ $$\frac{1}{3}v + \frac{8}{3}s = 17$$ Multiply the second equation by -2: $$\frac{2}{3}v + \frac{4}{3}s = 10$$ $$\frac{-2}{3}v + \frac{-16}{3}s = -34$$ Add the equations together: $$-\frac{12}{3}s = -24$$ $$4s = 24$$ $$s = 6.$$ Plug $s = 6$ into the first equation: $$\frac{2}{3}v + \frac{4}{3} \cdot 6 = 10$$ $$\frac{2}{3}v + 8 = 10$$ $$\frac{2}{3}v = 2$$ $$v = 3$$ One cup of vanilla ice cream costs $3.	
10 B	Notice that in this system of 3 variables and 3 equations, no two equations has the same set of two variables. To solve this system, you need to find two equations with the same two variables. You can start by subtracting the second equation from the first. $$3c + a = 4$$ $$3b + a = 7$$ $$3c - 3b = -3$$ You also have $3c + 3b = 9$. Using these two equations and adding them up, you get: $$3c - 3b = -3$$ $$3c + 3b = 9$$ $$6c = 6$$ $$c = 1$$ Plugging in $c = 1$ into the original equations, you get: $$a + 3 = 4;\ a = 1$$	You could also plug in the answer choices one by one into each equation.

©GiftOfLogic http://www.GiftOfLogic.com

	$1 + 3b = 7; b = 2$ Thus $(a, b, c) = (1,2,1)$	
11 30.5	$3b + 4h = 6.5$ $4b + 3h = 7.5$ Eliminate b by multiplying the first equation by 4 and the second by 3 and then subtracting the result. $12b + 16h = 26$ $12b + 9h = 22.5$ Subtracting the second equation from the first, you get $16h - 9h = 26 - 22.5$ $7h = 3.5$ $h = 0.5$; substitute this into the second equation to get b $b = \dfrac{7.5 - 3 \cdot 0.5}{4} = 1.5$ So, 17 balloons and 10 hats cost $17 \cdot 1.5 + 10 \cdot 0.5 = 30.5$	Use your calculator accurately.
12 60	Let there be p Physics and c Chemistry books Weight of these books = $2p + 3c$ These books make up the 150 lb box – so $2p + 3c = 150$ There are six times as many physics books as there are chemistry books – to set this up as an equation, try $p = 6c$ and plug $c = 1$ to verify; when $c = 1, p = 6$ – six times as many physics books as chemistry books. So the system is $2p + 3c = 150$ $p = 6c$ solve by substitution; $2(6c) + 3c = 150$ $12c + 3c = 150$; $15c = 150$ $c = 10$; so $p = 6c = 6 \cdot 10 = 60$	One equation involves weight of books and another involves the number of books. Setup the system of linear equations using this information.
13 8	Let there be s and h soft and hard pillows; bundle has 10 pillows, so $s + h = 10$; bundle costs \$66 and soft pillows cost \$5 and hard pillows cost \$13. $s + h = 10$ -first equation $5s + 13h = 66$ -second equation ---------------------- $5s + 5h = 50$ multiply first equation by 5 $5s + 13h = 66$ ---------------------- $8h = 66 - 50 = 16$ $h = \dfrac{16}{21} = 2$ So $h = 2$ and $s = 10 - h = 10 - 2 = 8$	In this problem, one equation involves the number of pillows in the bundle whereas another equation involves the cost of the pillows. Get used to solving these types of problems by constructing the system of linear equations.

| Lesson 17 | **HEART OF ALGEBRA** Linear Inequalities | Review |

FOCUSPREP CHECKLIST

- What is a Linear Inequality in one variable?
- How do I solve a Linear Inequality?
- When does the Linear Inequality reverse?
- Workout practice problems in Linear Inequalities

Q1 What is a Linear Inequality in one variable?

A1 A Linear Inequality is similar to a Linear Equality but the equal sign (=), is replaced with one of the inequality signs ($<, >, \leq, \geq$). The solution of an inequality falls within a range of values. Linear Inequalities can have one variable(reviewed in this lesson) or more than one variable (reviewed in the lesson on Systems of Linear Inequalities).

Example: $x > 5$, $x + 5 > 9$; $x - 8 > 23$; $22 + x < 99.53$; $30x + 500 \geq 700$ Note that the degree of a Linear inequality is 1. Inequalities such as $x^2 > 8$ are not linear inequalities. Pay very careful attention to the inequality signs. There is a big difference between $x > 3$ and $x \geq 3$.

Q2 How do I solve a linear inequality?

A2 Linear Inequalities are solved just like Linear equalities. You can perform addition, subtraction, multiplication, and division operations on both sides of an inequation.

Q3 When does the inequality sign reverse?

A3 When the inequality is multiplied or divided by a negative number, the inequality sign must be reversed. That is, $>$ will be come $<$, $>=$ will become $<=$ etc. Examples are presented below.

Example
Solve the inequality $-x < 3$

Solution: Convert $-x$ to $+x$ by multiplying by -1 on both sides $\quad -1 \cdot -x > -1 \cdot 3$; so, $x > -3$; multiplying by a negative number on both sides changes the inequality sign. So, the solution is $\{x | x > -3\}$.

Example
Solve the inequality: $-x + 3 > 9$

Solution:
$-x + 3 > 9$
$-x + 3 - 3 > 9 - 3$; eliminate 3 by adding -3 on both sides
$-x > 6$; $-1 \cdot x < -1 \cdot 6$
$x < -6$; Solution is $\{x | x - 6\}$.

Note that when you have an inequality like $a < -x < b$; when you multiply by -1 throughout, both signs get changed simultaneously. So, you get $-a > x > -b$ which can be rewritten as $-b < x < -a$.

HEART OF ALGEBRA
Lesson 17 — Linear Inequalities — Practice

NO CALCULATOR SECTION

1. The solution to the inequality

$$\frac{-3\pi x}{2} < \frac{3}{2} \text{ is}$$

(A) $x > -\frac{1}{\pi}$

(B) $x < -\frac{1}{\pi}$

(C) $x > \frac{\pi}{-1}$

(D) $x < \frac{\pi}{-1}$

NO CALCULATOR SECTION

3. Which of the following number lines represents the solution to the inequality $2x > 3$?

2. The average of one adult movie ticket ($a) and one child movie ticket ($c) is more than 100. Which equation best models this pricing?

(A) $\frac{a}{c} > 200$

(B) $a + c \leq 100$

(C) $a + c > 200$

(D) $a - c > 200$

4. Solve for x in $-3x + 8 \leq -2x + 4879$

(A) $x \geq -4871$

(B) $x \leq 4871$

(C) $x < 4897$

(D) $x = 4871$

CALCULATOR SECTION

5. Jean scores 97, 88, 56, 91, and 78 on her first five tests. She wants her average to be at least 80 after she takes her sixth test. What must her score x be on the sixth test to achieve her goal?

(A) $x > 480$

(B) $x < 70$

(C) $x \leq 480$

(D) $x \geq 70$

6. If b is a fraction such that $\frac{1}{4} \leq b \leq \frac{3}{4}$, which of the following is a true statement?
(A) $b \geq b^2 \geq b^{-1}$

(B) $b \leq b^2 \geq b^{-8}$

(C) $b \geq b^2 \geq b^{-1}$

(D) $b \geq b^2 \geq b^8$

CALCULATOR SECTION

7. Emily sells flowers. She wants to charge such that twice the cost of each bouquet (b) is at least 12 dollars and at most 52 dollars. Which inequality represents the pricing of a bouquet?
(A) $-12 \leq b > 52$
(B) $12 \leq b < 52$
(C) $6 \leq 2b \leq 26$
(D) $6 \leq b \leq 26$

8. Three times the number of polar bears (p) is more than twice the number of polar bears plus 45. Which of the following could possibly indicate the number of polar bears?
(A) 38
(B) 40
(C) 45
(D) 48

CALCULATOR SECTION

9. Which of the following points (x, y) satisfies the inequality $x < 3y - 7.5$?
(A) (10, 6)
(B) (7.5, 5)
(C) (5, 2)
(D) (-1, 1)

10. What is the smallest integer for which the following inequality $137 - 7x < -3$ holds true?
GRID IN

CALCULATOR SECTION

11. Pablo the gardener has 20 feet of fencing to enclose a rectangular garden. Which of the following inequalities represents the possible area A of the rectangular garden?
(A) $9 < A < 20$
(B) $10 \leq A \leq 25$
(C) $25 \leq A \leq 9$
(D) $9 \leq A \leq 25$

12. If $-350 \leq 15x + 25 < 650$, then which of the following CANNOT be a solution of this inequality?
(A) -25
(B) 35
(C) 41
(D) 45

HEART OF ALGEBRA

| Lesson 17 | Linear Inequalities | Answers |

#	Explanation	Comments
1 A	$\frac{-3\pi x}{2} < \frac{3}{2}$; multiply both sides by -2 ; $<$ becomes $>$ $3\pi x > -3$; divide by 3 on both sides $\pi x > -1$ $x > -\frac{1}{\pi}$; divide by π on both sides	Note carefully that the sign is reversed after multiplication by a negative number. If you don't reverse the sign, you will get a wrong answer!
2 C	The average of an adult ticket and a child ticket can be expressed as $\frac{a+c}{2}$. You know that this amount is more than 100, so $\frac{a+c}{2} > 100$. Multiply by 2 on both sides to get $a + c > 200$.	Keep a careful eye on the inequality sign. In this problem, you multiply both sides by a positive number and so the sign does NOT get reversed.
3 C	$2x > 3$; multiply by 2 on both sides $x > \frac{3}{2}$ This means that the number line will have an open circle and will consist of all values greater than 1.5.	An open circle at 1.5 means that the value of 1.5 is not included in the solution.
4 A	$-3x + 8 \leq -2x + 4879$ $-3x + 2x \leq 4879 - 8 = 4871$; isolate x to one side $-x \leq 4871$; multiply by -1 on both sides and reverse sign $x \geq -4871$	
5 D	Set up the inequality using her scores from all the six tests; at least 80 translates to $>= 80$ $\frac{97 + 88 + 56 + 91 + 78 + x}{6} \geq 80$ $410 + x \geq 480$ $x \geq 480 - 410 = 70$ $x \geq 70$	Inequalities can be setup in a variety of real life scenarios. This problem highlights one such scenario. Note that the solution indicates that she has to score at least 70 in her sixth test to average at least 80.
6 D	Use the fact that multiplying a fraction by itself will make the result smaller each time. Thus b will be greater than b^n where $n > 1$. Using this fact, you can conclude that the correct choice is choice D.	You can also plug in a value for b, say ¼ and test the inequalities. This may be an easy way to solve these kinds of problems. Number lines are very helpful to visualize abstract problems like this. In this problem, b^3, b^2, b appear in this order in the number line. Mark them on a number line to help you visualize quickly. So, $b \geq b^2 \geq b^3$

©GiftOfLogic http://www.GiftOfLogic.com

7 D	Since twice the cost of each bouquet costs at least 10 dollars, you know that $2b \geq 12$. Since twice the cost of each bouquet is at most 50 dollars, $2b \leq 52$. Combining these inequalities together, you get $12 \leq 2b \leq 52$; Dividing by 2 throughout, you get $6 \leq b \leq 26$.		Note $12 \leq 2b$ and $2b \geq 12$ both mean the same. Sometimes, like in this problem, you will need to combine inequalities.
8 D	"more than" translates to $>$ sign. $3p > 2p + 45$; pay attention to the $\geq$ sign. $3p - 2p > 45$ $p > 45$ Look for an answer choice that is more than 45. 48 in choice D is the correct answer		Note that the answer choices are such that only one falls in the solution range and others do not. Solutions to Inequality problems fall in a range of values.
9 A	Plugging in $x = 10$ and $y = 6$ from choice A, you get $10 < 18 - 7.5$, which holds to be true.		In problems like these, you will have to check each choice and see if the inequality holds true.
10 21	$137 - 7x < -3$; add -137 to both sides $-7x < -140$; divide by -7 and reverse sign $x > 20$; So, the smallest integer that will hold the inequality true is 21.		Reverse the sign of inequality if multiplying or dividing by a negative number.
11 D	Find the minimum and maximum values for the area of the garden keeping the perimeter to 20 ft. $2(l + w) = 20$ $l + w = 10$ Try combinations of l and w such that $l + w = 10$. When $l = 9$ and $w = 1$, $l + w = 10$, $A = lw = 9$. This is the smallest area. When $l = 5$ and $w = 5$, $l + w = 10$, $lw = 25$. This is the largest area possible. So, $9 \leq A \leq 25$.		
12 D	$-350 \leq 15x + 25 < 650$; subtract 25 throughout $-350 - 25 \leq 15x + 25 - 25 < 650 - 25$ $-375 \leq 15x < 625$; divide by 15 $-25 \leq x < 41.66$ $x = 45$ falls outside this range and CANNOT be a solution to this inequality.		Note that when you have an inequality like $a < x - k < b$, you have to add k in all three terms for the inequality to hold true. $a < x - k < b$ $a + k < x - k + k < b + k$ $a + k < x < b + k$

HEART OF ALGEBRA

| Lesson 18 | System of Linear Inequalities | Review |

FOCUSPREP CHECKLIST

- What is a System of Linear Inequalities?
- How do I solve a system of Linear Inequalities?
- Workout practice problems in System of Linear Inequalities

Q1 What is a System of Linear Inequalities?

A1 A System of Linear Inequalities is a set of two or more linear inequalities. The solution to the system lies in a region where all the inequalities hold true. For example, the two inequalities $y > x + 1$ and $y < -2x$ form a set of linear inequalities.

Q2 How is the solution region of a system of linear inequalities expressed?

A2 The solution is expressed as a shaded region formed by the overlapping of the regions that represent each of the inequalities. Since the solution is a region, it can have infinite points that satisfy the inequalities. It is also possible that there is no overlapping region in which case the system does not have any solution.

Q3 Can a system of linear inequalities have more than two equations?

A3 Yes. The system can have two, three, four, or more equations that bound the solution region.

Q4 How do I find out if a given answer choice is in the solution region of a system of linear inequalities?

A4 Plug the answer choice into each of the inequalities. A solution for a system of inequalities must satisfy all inequalities.

Q5 How do I solve a system of Linear Inequalities graphically?

A5 Each inequality in the system is graphed and the region that overlaps all the inequalities is the solution region.

Example: Which area of the graph shown indicates the solution to the system of linear inequalities defined as follows?

$y > x + 1$
$y < -2x$

Solution: Shade the areas defined by the inequalities – the intersecting area is the solution region for the system. In this set, the area above the line $y = x + 1$ is the solution region of the inequality $y > x + 1$ and the area below the line $y = -2x$ is the solution region of the inequality $y < -2x$. The intersecting regions are shown in a darker shade.

HEART OF ALGEBRA

Lesson 18 | System of Linear Inequalities | Practice

NO CALCULATOR SECTION

$x \leq 6$
$x > 4$
$y < x$
$y < 3$

1. For the system of inequalities shown above, one possible solution could be
- (A) (4,6)
- (B) (5,2)
- (C) (5,6)
- (D) (5,3)

$y \leq 3$
$y > -2$
$y < -x + 6$
$y \leq 3x + 5$

2. A system of inequalities is shown above. Which of the following is one possible solution for this system?
- (A) (0,1)
- (B) (0,4)
- (C) (5,1)
- (D) (5,3)

NO CALCULATOR SECTION

A manufacturing company pays interns according to the table below.

Hours Worked Per week	Pay Per Hour
≤ 20	$15/hr
> 20 and ≤ 40	$20/hr

3. Sara and Tara were the only two interns who worked during summer. Sara earned $15/hr and Tara earned $20/hr. If Sara worked s hours per week and Tara worked t hours per week, and the total budget for intern pay is $1600 per week, which of the following system of inequalities model their pay during one week of their internship?

(A) $15s + 20t < 1600$
$s > 0$
$s < 20$
$t > 20$
$t < 40$

(B) $15s + 20t \leq 1600$
$0 \leq s$
$s \leq 20$
$20 < t$
$t \leq 40$

(C) $15s + 20t \leq 1600$
$s > 0$
$s \leq 20$
$t > 20$
$t < 41$

(D) $15s + 20t \leq 1600$
$s > 0$
$s < 20$
$t > 20$
$t < 41$

CALCULATOR SECTION

4. Sanjay decides to apply to colleges in north and south of the country only but not those in east and west. He plans to apply to at most 10 colleges. The application fee for northern colleges is $100 each and that for southern colleges is $90 each. Which of the following pairs of northern and southern colleges can he apply to if his total application fee must be below $950?

(A) 5,10
(B) 5,5
(C) 6,5
(D) 4,5

5. At Sing&Dance, customers can rent singing and dancing rooms in increments of 1 minute with a minimum total of 30 minutes. The cost for renting the singing room is $10 per minute and the cost for renting the dancing room is $20 per minute. If the minimum total must be $500, then which of the following choices indicate a possible combination of singing and dancing minutes that can be rented?

(A) (15,15)
(B) (15,16)
(C) (15,17)
(D) (15,18)

NO CALCULATOR SECTION

6. A system of inequalities is shown below. Which regions marked in the graph represent the solution to the system?

$y < 3x$
$y \geq 3x - 5$

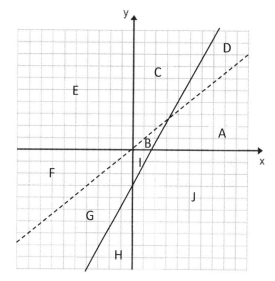

(A) B,I
(B) G,I
(C) B,G,I
(D) B

HEART OF ALGEBRA

| Lesson 18 | System of Linear Inequalities | Answers |

#	Explanation	Comments
1 B	$x \leq 6$; $x > 4$; $y < x$; $y < 3$ (5,2) satisfies all the inequalities $5 \leq 6$; $5 > 4$; $2 < 5$; $2 < 3$	A solution for a linear inequality must satisfy all the inequalities.
2 A	$y \leq 3$; $y > -2$; $y < -x + 6$; $y \leq 3x + 5$ (0,1) satisfies all inequalities $1 \leq 3$; $1 > -2, 1 < 6; 1 < 5$	
3 B	Sara worked s hours and earned $15/hour. Tara worked t hours and earned $20/hour. So, the total intern pay per week is $15s + 20t$; since the budget is 1600, $15s + 20t < 1600$. From the table, you can infer that since Sara earned $15/hour, she worked $\leq$ 20 hours; so $s \leq 20$. Similarly, Tara earned $20/hour, so she worked > 20 hours and less than or equal to 40 hours. So $t > 20$ and $t \leq 40$.	Check the inequations against the facts given; pay close attention to $>, \geq, <, \leq$ signs.
4 D	Let N be the number of colleges he applies to in the north and S be the number in the south. N+S≤10. Total cost of applications = $100N + 90S < 950$. So, the system of inequalities is : $N + S \leq 10$ $100N + 90S < 950$ Plug in the answer choices to see which one fits ALL inequalities; For $N = 4, S = 5$, you have $N + S = 9 \leq 10$ and $100 \cdot 4 + 90 \cdot 5 = 400 + 450 = 850 < 950$.	When plugging the answer choices to a system of inequalities, be careful not to mix up the first and second numbers in the ordered pair.
5 D	Let S be the number of minutes rented from the song room and D be the number of minutes rented from the dance room. Minimum total is 30 minutes – so $S + D \geq 30$ Minimum total cost of dancing = $10S + 20D \geq 500$. Plug in the choices – for $S = 15$ and $D = 18$, both inequalities are satisfied. $S + D = 15 + 18 = 33 > 30$ and $10 \cdot 15 + 20 \cdot 18 = 510 > 500$.	
6 C	Identify the lines corresponding to $y = 3x$ and $y = 3x - 5$. They both have positive slopes but one has a negative intercept and the other line passes thru the origin. Note the solution region for each inequality. For $y < 3x$, the solution region is G,H,B,A,I,J. For $y >= 3x - 5$, the solution region is G,F,E,B,C,I. The region common to both is G,B,I	The dotted line indicates that the solution does not fall on the line itself. When noting the solution region, go clockwise or anticlockwise, one quadrant at a time to avoid missing any region.

| Lesson 19 | HEART OF ALGEBRA
Linear Models and Graphs | Review |

FOCUSPREP CHECKLIST

- What is a Linear Model?
- How do I create a linear model – from a table, and from a graph?
- Workout practice problems in Linear Models and Graphs

Q1 What is a Linear model? How does it look?

A1 A Linear model is an algebraic equation that connects the dependent variable y and the independent variable x in such a way that when the data is graphed, the model is a straight line of the form $y = mx + b$ where m is the slope of the line and b is the y-intercept.

Examples:
$s = 5.85\ t$; where s = revenue for a movie, and t=number of tickets sold
$b = 0.03\ p + 200$; where b=bank balance, p is the principal amount

Q2 In a Linear model, what is the dependent variable and what is the independent variable?

A2 The dependent variable derives its value based on the values of the independent variable. It is the "y" variable in the model. The independent variable is plotted along the x-axis and the dependent variable is plotted along the y-axis.

Example:
In the linear relationship model, $s = 40\ t$; where s is the distance traveled by a car after driving for time t, s is the dependent variable and t is the independent variable. As time t increases, the distance traveled also increases linearly.

Q3 How do I create a Linear model?

A3 Depending on how the data is available, a Linear model can be created in different ways.

<u>Data is in a report/text format:</u> If the data is in a textual format, identify the independent and dependent variables, tabulate them in two rows, one for independent variable x and one for dependent variable y, and use trial and error of $\Delta y/\Delta x$ to see if there is a linear relationship of the form $y = mx + b$.

<u>Data is in a table:</u> If the data is already in a tabular form, identify the independent and dependent variables and use trial and error of $\Delta y/\Delta x$ to see if there is a linear relationship of the form $y = mx + b$.

<u>Data is in a graph:</u> If the data is in the form of a scatterplot, identify the independent and dependent variables, draw a line of best fit through the data, and use the slope intercept formula $y = mx + b$ to create the linear model.

HEART OF ALGEBRA
Lesson 19 — Linear Models and Graphs — Practice

NO CALCULATOR SECTION

S	N
1	200
2	180
3	160
4	140
5	120

Questions 1 and 2 refer to the table shown above.

1. Shoe sales at a store are shown in the table where S is the size of the shoe and N is the number of shoes sold at that size. Which one of the following choices models the number of shoes sold in terms of the size of shoes?

    (A) $N = -10S + 200$
    (B) $N = 10S + 220$
    (C) $N = -20S + 220$
    (D) $N = -20S + 200$

2. Using the data shown above, what is the best estimate of the number of shoes that will be sold for a shoe size of 10?

    (A) 0
    (B) 20
    (C) 40
    (D) 200

NO CALCULATOR SECTION

More rain means more grasshoppers. That was the conclusion made by Karla, the zoo keeper responsible for grasshoppers, after she recorded the growth in grasshopper population over time as shown below.

Year (Y)	2008	2010	2012	2014
Grasshopper count (C)	0	300	600	900

Questions 3 and 4 refer to the table shown above.

3. Which of the following equations can be used by Karla to model the grasshopper count (C) as a function of the time elapsed (t) in years since 2008?

    (A) $C = 300\,t$
    (B) $C = 300 + t$
    (C) $C = 150\,t$
    (D) $C = 150 - t$

4. Using the table above, what is the best estimate of the number of grasshoppers in the zoo in 2013?

    (A) 700
    (B) 750
    (C) 800
    (D) 900

NO CALCULATOR SECTION

Questions 5 to 7 refer to the graph above.

5. Jane visited her friend and then drove to the beach several hundred miles away from home. The graph above shows her location over time. Which of the models below describes her distance from home d at time t after she left for the beach?

(A) $d = 40 + t$
(B) $d = 40 + 40t$
(C) $d = 50 + 42.5t$
(D) $d = 50 - 40t$

6. Approximately how far was she from home after driving for 3.25 hours?

(A) 168 miles
(B) 178 miles
(C) 188 miles
(D) 288 miles

7. Which model describes Jane's distance from her friend's house?

(A) $d = 50 + 42.5t$
(B) $d = 50 - 40t$
(C) $d = 45t$
(D) $d = 42.5t$

NO CALCULATOR SECTION

8. An eagle sitting on top of a 50 foot tall building starts flying and gains altitude at a constant speed of 30 miles/hour. Which of the following graphs shows its altitude at time t after it starts flying?

(A)

(B)

(C)

(D)

NO CALCULATOR SECTION

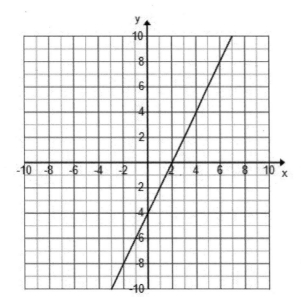

9. Which of the linear models below represents the graph shown above?

(A) $y = 2x + 4$
(B) $y = 2x - 4$
(C) $y = x - 4$
(D) $y = -x + 4$

10. The graphical relationship between gallons (g) and quarts (q) is shown above. Which of the choices below represents the algebraic relation between gallons and quarts?

(A) $g = 4q$
(B) $g = 2q$
(C) $q = 4g$
(D) $q = 2g$

NO CALCULATOR SECTION

11. The relation between the cost of olives per pound and the sale price of olive oil per gallon includes a surcharge of $5 as shown above. If the surcharge is increased by $2, which of the following graphs will show the modified price of olive oil per gallon?

NO CALCULATOR SECTION

12 If 1 mile (mi) is equal to 1760 yards (yd) and 1 yard (yd) is equal to 3 feet (ft) and 1 foot (ft) is equal to 12 inches (in) then, which of the following graphs represents the relation between miles and inches?

(A)

(B)

(C)

(D)

HEART OF ALGEBRA

| Lesson 19 | Linear Models and Graphs | Answers |

#	Explanation	Comments
1 C	Data is given in tabular form. Answer choices present several linear models. Take one choice and see if it models the data. Substitute s=1,2,3, etc., and see if the model gives the value of N correctly. The model $N = -20S + 220$ fits all the data points.	
2 B	Using the data in the table, the model that best fits this data was found to be $N = -20S + 220$; So, for a shoe size of 10, $S = 10, N = -20 \cdot 10 + 220 = -200 + 220 = 20$	Models can be used to estimate future values.
3 C	Note that the relationship expected is the elapsed time in years since 2008 – so, create another independent variable t which has a value of 0 when data collection began- that is t=0 in 2008, t=2 in 2010,etc. | Year Y	2008	2010	2012	2014
---	---	---	---	---
Elapsed Time t	0	2	4	6
Grasshopper count C	0	300	600	900 | Every 2 years, the grasshopper count C increases by 300 – so per year growth is 300/2=150. C=150 t is the linear model that fits the data.	
4 B	In year 2013, t=5, that is, 2013 would be 2013-2008=5 years since the data collection began. So C=150 · 5=750 grasshoppers.	Be careful while plugging in the value of the independent variable. In this problem, it was indexed from 2008 with a different variable- t.
5 C	Note that the graph is given and you are asked to pick a model. The graph is linear. So, it can be modeled using the slope intercept formula $y = mx + b$, where b is the y-intercept. It is clear from the graph that the y-intercept is 50. So, the model will be, partially, $y = mx + 50$. So, it has to be choices C or D. To find m, the slope, pick any two points and find Δy/Δx. For example, pick (1,92.5) and (2,135). Δy/Δx=(135-92.5)/(2-1)=42.5/1=42.5. So, the linear model is $d = 42.5t + 50$	Note that the value of d at $t = 0$ is 50, as labeled in the graph.
6 C	After 3.25 hours, she was 42.5·3.25+50=188.12=188	
7 D	Note that this question is about her distance from her friend's house – not her distance from home. At t=0, she was at her friend's house and then her distance is described by the graph with a slope of 42.5 and a y-intercept of 0. The model for this is $d = 42.5t$	In this problem, the model's point of reference has changed from her home to her friend's home. So, the y-intercept is 0.

8 A	This problem describes the model in verbal format. It says an eagle is at top of a 50 feet building. So, this is its starting height. Then it gains altitude at the rate of 30 miles/hour. So its altitude at any time is $50 + 30t$ or $30t + 50$. This corresponds to a line that has a y-intercept of 50 and that has a slope of 30. Choice A and D are the only choices that have a y-intercept of 50. To eliminate one of these choices, you have to find which graph has a slope of 30. Choice A has a $\Delta y / \Delta x$ of 30 since each data point is 30 more than the previous one. Choice D has a $\Delta y / \Delta x$ of 20.	Read the graph carefully. To calculate slope of a line, pick any 2 points, and calculate $\Delta y / \Delta x$.
9 B	Note that the graph is a straight line – so the algebraic model is $y = mx + b$; The line has an intercept of -4 and answers B and C have an y-intercept of -4. So, you need to look at the slope. Pick 2 points on the line (2,0) and (4,4). The slope is $\Delta y / \Delta x =$ (4-0)/(4-2)=2. So, the equation of the model is $y = 2x - 4$.	Pay attention to the labels in the x and y axes. The major units increase by 2 on both axes.
10 C	Note carefully that g is on the x-axis and q is on the y-axis. For $g = 1, q = 4,$ for $g = 2, q = 8$ – for every 1 gallon, the quarts increases 4 times. So $q = 4g$ describes the graph correctly.	
11 B	The surcharge was initially $5 and it increased by $2 to $7. So, the y-intercept must be shifted up to 7. But the slope of the graph must still be the same since only the surcharge has increased. Choice B shows an y-intercept of 7 and the same slope of 5.	
12 A	1 mile=1760 yards · 3 feet/yard · 12 inches/ feet = 63360 inches. Since the graph is in 100,000 units, 1 mile= 63360/100000=0.6336.	Read the graph carefully and note the units on the title.

HEART OF ALGEBRA

Lesson 20 | Absolute Equalities and Inequalities | Review

FOCUSPREP CHECKLIST

- What is the Absolute value of a number?
- How do I solve an Absolute equality problem?
- How do I solve an Absolute inequality problem?
- Workout practice problems in absolute equalities and inequalities.

Q1 What is the absolute value of a number?

A1 The absolute value of a number x is represented as $|x|$ and is defined as follows:
$|x| = x$ when $x > 0$
$\quad\ -x$ when $x < 0$

Example:
$|3| = 3;\ |-4| = 4;\ |4 - 7| = |-3| = 3;\ |7 - 4| = |3| = 3$
Note that $|x - y| = |y - x|$ for any two numbers x and y.

Q2 What is an absolute equality? How do I solve it?

A2 An absolute equality is an equality involving an absolute variable. You can solve an absolute equality for the variable by using the fact that if $|x| = k$, then $x = +k$ or $x = -k$. Thinking of numbers as being placed in a number line will help in visualizing and solving problems involving absolute numbers.

Example: Solve for x: $|x| = 43$
Solution $\{x | x = -43\ or\ x = 43\}$.

Example: Solve for x: $|x + 3| = 43$
Solution: $x + 3 = -43\ or\ x + 3 = 43$
If $x + 3 = -43$, then $x = -46$; If $x + 3 = 43$, then $x = 40$.
So the solution to $|x + 3| = 43$ is $x = -46$ or $x = 40$. Substitute and verify.

Q3 What is an Absolute value Inequality? How do I solve it?

A3 The absolute value inequality is an inequality involving an absolute variable.

$|x| \leq k$ implies that $-k \leq x \leq k$

$|x| \geq k$ implies that $x \leq -k\ or\ x \geq k$

Examples
$|x| < 3$ implies that $-3 < x < 3$

$|x - 4| \leq 3$ implies $-3 \leq x - 4 \leq 3;\ -3 + 4 \leq x \leq 3 + 4$; so the solution is $1 \leq x \leq 7$

$|x - 4| > 3$, so $x - 4 > 3\ or\ x - 4 < -3$; so the solution is $x > 7$ or $x < 1$

HEART OF ALGEBRA

Lesson 20 | Absolute Equalities and Inequalities | Practice

NO CALCULATOR SECTION

1. If $|4m + 8| = 40$, then which of the following is one possible solution?
   - (A) -8
   - (B) 12
   - (C) -12
   - (D) 14

2. If $|3v - 4| = 20$ then one possible value of v is:
   - (A) $-\frac{3}{16}$
   - (B) -8
   - (C) $\frac{3}{16}$
   - (D) None of the above

3. If $|3x + 4| = 3$, then which of the following is one possible solution?
   - (A) $+\frac{7}{3}$
   - (B) -8
   - (C) $-\frac{1}{3}$
   - (D) No Solution

NO CALCULATOR SECTION

4. How many integer solutions does the inequality $\frac{|3x+6|}{3} < 5$ have?
   - (A) 0
   - (B) 8
   - (C) 9
   - (D) 11

5. Which of the following is not a solution of the inequality $\left|\frac{2x+4}{6}\right| \leq 12$?
   - (A) -40
   - (B) -38
   - (C) 16
   - (D) 34

NO CALCULATOR SECTION

6. Mondays' high temperature is $x°$. Tuesday's high temperature is $y°$. The high temperature on Wednesday is the absolute difference between Monday's and Tuesday's high temperatures. Which of the following represents the temperature on Wednesday?

(A) $|y - x|$
(B) $|xy|$
(C) $|x + y|$
(D) None

7. If $|2x + 3| < -|2x + 5|$, what is a possible value for x?

(A) -2
(B) -1.5
(C) 2
(D) No solution

NO CALCULATOR SECTION

8. How many points of intersection do the graphs of $y = |2x - 3|$ and $y = 15$ have?

(A) 0
(B) 1
(C) 2
(D) No Solution

9. The Mariana trench has a depth of 11 kilometers below sea level. Mount Kilimanjaro has a height of 6 kilometers above sea level. What is the absolute difference between the two heights?

GRID IN

10. What value of x satisfies both absolute equations shown below?

$$|4x - 6| = 4$$
$$|8x + 3| = 7$$

GRID IN

HEART OF ALGEBRA		
Lesson 20	Absolute Equalities and Inequalities	Answers

#	Explanation	Comments
1 C	$4m + 8 = 40$, or $4m + 8 = -40$. $m = \frac{32}{4} = 8$ or $m = -\frac{48}{4} = -12$.	Note that only one solution will be in the choices.
2 D	$3v - 4 = 20$, or $3v - 4 = -20$. $v = 8$ or $v = -\frac{16}{3}$. Since neither of these answers are choices, the answer is none of the above.	The solution does not always have to appear in the choices.
3 C	$\|3x + 4\| = 3$ $3x + 4 = 3$, or $3x + 4 = -3$ $x = -\frac{1}{3}$ or $x = -\frac{7}{3}$.	Remember that if $\|x\| = k$ then $x = -k$ or k
4 C	$\frac{\|3x+6\|}{3} < 5$ $\|3x + 6\| < 15$ $-15 < 3x + 6 < 15$ add -6 to all terms $-21 < 3x < 9$; divide by 3 throughout $-7 < x < 3$ The possible values of x are $-6, -5, -4, -3, -2, -1, 0, 1, 2$, a total of nine possibilities. Remember that 0 is an integer and must be counted.	Simplify the inequality. Remember that if $\|x\| \leq k$ then $x \geq -k$ or $x \leq k$. Remember that less than signs are not inclusive. That is, if $x < 3$, then $x = 3$ is not valid.
5 A	$-12 \leq \frac{2x+4}{6} \leq 12$. Multiply by 6 throughout $-72 \leq 2x + 4 \leq 72$; subtract 4 throughout $-76 \leq 2x \leq 68$; divide by 2 throughout $-38 \leq x \leq 34$. -40 does not satisfy the range of values of for x.	Note that the question has a <u>not</u> in it.
6 A	The difference in temperatures between Monday and Tuesday is $\|x - y\|$. This is not an answer choice. Note that $\|x - y\| = \|y - x\|$, since the difference is absolute.	Remember that $\|x - y\| = \|y - x\|$. For example $\|4-6\|=\|6-4\|=2$
7 D	Pause and think for a second before proceeding. The absolute value $\|2x + 3\|$ is always positive, and $-\|2x + 5\|$ is always negative. Since a positive number cannot be less than a negative number, the inequality does not have a solution.	Lookout for tricky problems; positive values are always greater than negative values.
8 C	When two graphs intersect, their values are the same at the point of intersection. So, you can set the equation $\|2x - 3\| = 15$. You know that solving this absolute equality will give us 2 solutions. $2x - 3 = +15$ giving $x = 9$ and $2x - 3 = -15$ giving $x = -6$.. At $x = 9$ and $x = -6, y = \|2x - 3\| = 15$ and this graph intersects with $y = 15$ at	

		these two points.	
9	17	Since one is a depth and the other is a height, you need to sign the numbers correctly before calculating the difference. Measurements above the ground are positive and below the ground are negative. Mariana trench has a height of -11, Mount Kilimanjaro has a height of +6. The absolute value $|11 - (-6)| = 17$.	Depth is negative.
10	$\frac{1}{2}$	Solve the first equation first $|4x - 6| = 4$ $4x - 6 = 4 \ or \ 4x - 6 = -4$ $x = \frac{5}{2}$ or $x = \frac{1}{2}$. Plugging $x = \frac{5}{2}$ into the second equation gives $\left|8 \cdot \frac{5}{2} + 3\right| = 9 <> 7$. This means that $x = \frac{5}{2}$ is not a solution. Plugging $x = \frac{1}{2}$ into the second equation gives $\left|8 \cdot \frac{1}{2} + 3\right| = 7$. This means that $x = \frac{1}{2}$ satisfies both equations and therefore is a solution.	This problem is an example of a system of absolute equalities in one variable. Solve one equation and check which one of the two solutions will fit the second equation.

CHAPTER 3 PASSPORT TO ADVANCED MATH	
Lesson	**Title**
Lesson 21	Polynomials and Quadratic Equations
Lesson 22	Linear- Quadratic Systems
Lesson 23	Functions and Transformations
Lesson 24	Radicals and Fractional Exponents

PASSPORT TO ADVANCED MATH
Lesson 21 | Polynomials and Quadratic Equations | Review

FOCUSPREP CHECKLIST

- How do I add, subtract, multiply, and divide polynomial expressions?
- How do I factorize polynomial expressions?
- How do I solve polynomial equations?
- How do I complete the square to solve quadratic equations?
- Workout practice problems in Polynomials and Quadratic equations

Q1 What is a Polynomial?

A1 A Polynomial is an expression of one or more terms. If there is only one term, it is a monomial. If it has two terms, it is called a binomial. If it has three terms, it is called a trinomial. It can have any number of terms.

Examples:

Monomial: x, $2x$, $-4xy$, x^2 – these polynomials have only one term
Binomials: $x^2 + 3x$, $xy + 4$, $x^3 - 3$ – these polynomials have two terms
Trinomials: $2x^9 + 3x^5 + 2x^2$, $x^4 - x^2 + x$ – these polynomials have three terms

Q2 What is the degree of a polynomial?

A2 The degree of a term is the sum of the exponents of all variables in the term. The degree of a polynomial is the degree of the term with the highest degree. To find the degree of a polynomial, first find the degree of all the terms. The highest degree you have is the degree of the polynomial.

Example: $2x^{11} + 3x^2 + 1$ The first term has a degree of 11, the second term has a degree of 2 and the third term has a degree of 0. The highest degree is 11. So this polynomial has a degree of 11.

Example: $2x^2y^2 + 3xy + 1$ The first term has a degree of 4 (2 + 2), the second term has a degree of 2 (1 + 1) and the third term has a degree of 0. The highest degree is 4. So, this polynomial has a degree of 4.

Q3 What are polynomials used for?

A3 Polynomials are used to model a variety of scenarios in the real world. Linear and Quadratic functions are special types of polynomial functions that are used to model physical, chemical, biological, and economic observations, to name a few. For example, the value of a property can be modeled with a quadratic polynomial. The altitude gained by an aircraft can be modeled with a linear polynomial. Using data gathered in experiments, you can model the relationship between dependent and independent variables using polynomial functions.

Q4 What operations can I do on a polynomial?

A4 You can add, subtract, multiply, or divide polynomials.

Add Polynomials: Add two polynomials by adding the like terms. For example, a term that has x^2 term must be added to another term that also has x^2.

Example:
$$(2x^3 + 2x^2 + 2x) + (3x^3 + 5x^2 + 3x + 1)$$
$$= 2x^3 + 3x^3 + 2x^2 + 5x^2 + 2x + 3x + 1 \text{ ; gather like terms and add them}$$
$$= 5x^3 + 7x^2 + 5x + 1$$

You can also place the polynomials one below the other and line up the like terms and add them up.

Subtract Polynomials: Subtracting polynomials is similar to subtracting two numbers – just remember to negate the second polynomial.

Example:
$$(2x^3 + 2x^2 + 2x) - (3x^3 + 3x^2 + 3x + 1)$$
$$= 2x^3 + 2x^2 + 2x - 3x^3 - 3x^2 - 3x - 1 \text{ ; negate the second polynomial}$$
$$= 2x^3 - 3x^3 + 2x^2 - 3x^2 + 2x - 3x - 1 \text{ ; gather like terms}$$
$$= -x^3 - x^2 - x - 1 \text{ ; add like terms}$$

Multiply Polynomials: Use distributive property of multiplication ; $a(b + c) = ab + ac$

Example: (multiply a monomial(one term) and trinomial(three terms))
$$2x(x^5 + 3x^4 + 2x);$$
$$= 2x \cdot x^5 + 2x \cdot 3x^4 + 2x \cdot 2x \text{ ; use } a(b + c + d) = ab + ac + ad$$
$$= 2x^6 + 6x^5 + 4x^2 \text{ ; simplify}$$

Example: (multiply a binomial and another binomial)
Use the FOIL method (First, Outer, Inner, Last) to multiply the two binomials.
$$(2x + 4)(x + 3)$$
$$= 2x \cdot x + 2x \cdot 3 + 4 \cdot x + 4 \cdot 3 \text{ ;use FOIL method}$$
$$= 2x^2 + 6x + 4x + 12 \text{ ; simplify}$$
$$= 2x^2 + 10x + 12 \text{ ; add like terms}$$

Divide Polynomials: (divide a polynomial by a monomial). Divide each term of the polynomial by the denominator separately as shown:

Example:
$$\frac{16x^4 + 4x^2 + 8}{4}$$
$$= \frac{16x^4}{4} + \frac{4x^2}{4} + \frac{8}{4}$$
$$= 4x^4 + x^2 + 2$$

Example: (divide a polynomial by another polynomial)

There are two ways to divide a polynomial by another polynomial: Factoring and Long Division.

<u>Divide two polynomials by factoring:</u>   Factor normally, and then cancel out the numerator and denominator as shown below: Factoring is discussed in detail later in this lesson.

Example: (division by factoring)

$$\frac{x^2+9x+14}{x+7} \text{ ; factor the numerator}$$

$$= \frac{(x+2)\cancel{(x+7)}}{\cancel{(x+7)}}$$

$$= (x+2)$$

Example: (division by long division – no remainder)

$$x+7 \overline{\smash{\big)}\, x^2 + 9x + 14}$$

$$\begin{array}{r} x + 2 \\ x+7 \overline{\smash{\big)}\, x^2 + 9x + 14} \\ -(x^2 + 7x) \\ \hline 0 + 2x + 14 \\ 2x + 14 \\ \hline 0 \end{array}$$

When the polynomial cannot be divided into the divisor anymore, the extra part is left as the remainder.

Example: (Division by long division – with remainder)

$$\begin{array}{r} x^2 - 2x + 4 \\ 3x+1 \overline{\smash{\big)}\, 3x^3 - 5x^2 + 10x - 6} \\ -(3x^3 + x^2) \\ \hline -6x^2 + 10x - 6 \\ -(-6x^2 - 2x) \\ \hline 12x - 6 \\ -(12x + 4) \\ \hline -10 \end{array}$$

In this case, the answer to the division is $x^2 - 2x + 4 - \frac{10}{3x+1}$. This is similar to how division works with real numbers. For example, when you divide 7 by 4, you get a quotient of 1 and a remainder of 3. You can write this as $\frac{7}{4} = 1 + \frac{3}{4}$. The result of the above polynomial division is also written in this way.

Q5 What does <u>factoring</u> a polynomial mean? Why do I need to factorize a polynomial?
A5 When you say that 9 and 4 are factors of 36, you know that 9·4=36. Factoring a polynomial is also similar in meaning. Factoring a polynomial is the process of breaking down the polynomial into other polynomials(factors) such the product of the factors is equal to the original polynomial.

Factoring a polynomial is useful when finding the zeros of a polynomial function and while solving polynomial equations. Zeros of a function is covered in the lesson on Functions.

Q6 What are some special factorizations to remember?
A6 Remembering the following formulas will help you in factoring the polynomials quickly. See the examples column to learn how they are used.

Special Factorizations	Examples
$a^2 + b^2 + 2ab = (a+b)^2$ Perfect Square Formula	$x^2 + 4x + 4 = (x+2)^2$
$a^2 + b^2 - 2ab = (a-b)^2$ Perfect Square Formula	$x^2 - 6x + 9 = (x-3)^2$
$a^2 - b^2 = (a+b)(a-b)$ Difference of Squares Formula	$x^2 - 81 = (x+9)(x-9)$
$(a^3 - b^3) = (a-b)(a^2 + ab + b^2)$ Cubic Formula	$x^3 - 27 = (x-3)(x^2 + 6x + 9)$
$(a^3 + b^3) = (a+b)(a^2 - ab + b^2)$ Cubic Formula	$x^3 + 27 = (x+3)(x^2 - 6x + 9)$

Q7 How do I factor a polynomial?
A7 There are a several methods available to factor polynomials. Be familiar with all the methods since some factoring problems can be tricky. Note that these methods apply to factoring any type of polynomial-binomials, trinomials, quadratics etc. As you solve problems, these methods will come naturally to you. Polynomials in SAT are not difficult to factorize, but you have to be careful to handle all the terms correctly. Always remember the special factorizations listed above.

Method 1: <u>Factoring using GCF</u>: If the terms of a polynomial has factors that appear to be common, then use the GCF(Greatest Common Factor) and extract out the common factors. This method can be used as part of other methods. GCF has been reviewed in a different lesson.

Example: Factor $4x^3 - 2x^2$
The GCF OF 2 and 4 is 2 and the GCF of x^2 and x^3 is x^2. So, factor out $2x^2$.
$4x^3 - 2x^2$
$= 2x^2(2x - 1)$

Method 2: <u>Factoring by Grouping</u>: Often, all the terms may not contain a common factor, but a pair of terms may. In that case, group the terms in pairs and factor out the common factors using GCF method.

Example: Factor $x^3 + x^2 - x - 1$
Solution: All the terms do not contain a common factor other than 1. So, try the grouping method. Pause a few seconds to observe if a pair of terms can be factored out and which terms would best form the pair.

$x^3 + x^2 - x - 1$
$= (x^3 + x^2) - x - 1$; group the terms that have a common factor
$= x^2(x + 1) - 1(x + 1)$; $x + 1$ is the common factor
$= (x + 1)(x^2 - 1) = (x + 1)(x + 1)(x - 1)$; use the difference of squares factorization

Method 3A Factoring $x^2 + bx + c$ by Reverse FOIL method:
If you have a quadratic expression $ax^2 + bx + c$, where the coefficient of $x^2 = a = 1$, then find two numbers p and q such that their product is c and their sum is b. If you can find p and q, then $(x + p)(x + q)$ are the factors of the quadratic.

Example: Factorize (or, what are the factors of) $x^2 - 4x + 3$

Solution: GCF method will not work since there is no common factor in all the three terms. Grouping method will not work since you have only 3 terms and you need 4 terms to group. Using Reverse FOIL method, you have to find two numbers p and q such that $p.q = 3$ and $p + q = -4$. If $p = -1$ and $q = -3$, then $pq = 3$ and $p + q = -4$. So $x - 1$ and $x - 3$ are factors. So, $x^2 - 4x + 3 = (x - 1)(x - 3)$. You can expand using FOIL to check whether $(x - 1)(x - 3)$ adds up to $x^2 - 4x + 3$.

Method 3B Factoring $x^2 + bx + c$ by Reverse FOIL method:
Since it is possible to make mistakes while writing the factors correctly as $x + p$ and $x + q$ when p and q are negative, you can follow an alternative method shown below.

$x^2 - 4x + 3$
Find p, q such that $pq = 3, p + q = -4$. Try $p = -3$ and $q = -1$; now, rewrite the polynomial using p and q.

$x^2 - 4x + 3$
$= x^2 - 3x - x + 3$; rewrite using p and q to sum up to coefficient of x
$= x(x - 3) - 1(x - 3)$; group and factor out the GCF;
$= (x - 3)(x - 1)$; $(x - 3)$ is common to both terms

Method 4 Factoring $ax^2 + bx + c$, $a \neq 1$ by Reverse FOIL method: If you have a quadratic expression $ax^2 + bx + c$ where the coefficient of x^2 is a, and $a \neq 1$, then find two numbers p and q such that their product is $a \cdot c$ and their sum is b. Then, rewrite the expression in terms of p and q and group the terms and factorize.

Example: Factor $2x^2 + 11x + 12$
Solution: GCF method will not work since there is no common factor in all the three terms. Grouping method will not work since you have only 3 terms and you need 4 terms to group. So, try the FOIL method with $a \neq 1$. Using FOIL method, you have to find two numbers p and q such that $p.q = a.c = 2 \cdot 12 = 24$ and and $p + q = b = 11$. If $p = 8$ and $q = 3$, then $pq = 24$ and $p + q = 11$.

$2x^2 + 11x + 12$
$= 2x^2 + 8x + 3x + 12$; rewrite using p and q; $2x$ and 3 are common factors
$= 2x(x + 4) + 3(x + 4)$; $(x + 4)$ is the common factor
$= (x + 4)(2x + 3)$

Method 5: Using special factorizations: While factorizing some polynomials, it may be easier to use the special factorization formulas discussed earlier to factorize.

Example: Factorize $4x^2 - 4x + 1$

Solution: Pause to observe the terms for a few seconds. You can observe that the first term is $(2x)^2$ and the last term is 1^2. The perfect square formula is $a^2 + b^2 - 2ab = (a-b)^2$. So, you can factorize $4x^2 - 4x + 1$ as $(2x)^2 - 2 \cdot 2x + 1^2 = (2x - 1)^2$.

Example: Factorize $27x^3 - 8y^3$

Solution: Pause to observe the terms for a few seconds. You can observe that the terms are in the forms of $a^3 - b^3$. Notice that his polynomial has two variables x and y. Use the special factorization formula for cubes.

$27x^3 - 8y^3$
$=(3x)^3 - (2y)^3$; 27 and 8 are perfect cubes, and the expression is in the cubic form of $a^3 - b^3$
$= (3x - 2y)(9x^2 + 6xy + 4y^2)$ – use the special factorization formula for cubes

Q8 What is the Factor Theorem? When is it useful?

A8 The factor theorem states that for any polynomial $P(x)$, $(x - a)$ is a factor if and only if $P(a) = 0$. This theorem does not give you all the factors of a polynomial. It only tells you under what condition $(x - a)$ will be a factor.

Example: Is $(x - 4)$ a factor of $x^2 - 16$?

Solution: The value of the polynomial when $x = 4$ is $4^2 - 16 = 16 - 16 = 0$; So, according to Factor theorem, you can conclude that $x - 4$ will be a factor.

Q9 How is polynomial factoring helpful in simplifying rational expressions?

A9 Rational expressions are of the form $\frac{a}{b}$, where a and b are polynomial expressions and b is not 0. To simplify, factorize and cancel out common factors in numerator and denominator.

Example: Simplify $\frac{x+1}{x^2-1}$

Solution:

$$\frac{x+1}{x^2-1}$$

$$= \frac{\cancel{x+1}}{(\cancel{x+1})(x-1)} \text{ ; use difference of squares to factorize the denominator}$$

$$= \frac{1}{(x-1)}$$

Example: Simplify $\frac{x^2+y^2+2xy}{x^2-y^2}$

Solution:

$$= \frac{(x+y)^2}{(x+y)(x-y)} \text{ ; factorize using perfect square formula, and difference of squares}$$

$$= \frac{(x+y) \cdot (x+y)}{(x+y)(x-y)} = \frac{x+y}{x-y}$$

Q10 How do I solve a polynomial/quadratic equation?

A10 Use one or more of the following methods to solve a polynomial/quadratic equation.
Isolate the variable and constants and set the equation to 0.
Factorize and solve for the variable.
Take square root or cube root on both sides of the equation if required.
Use special factorizations if required.
Use the completing the square method explained below if applicable for the problem at hand.

Example Solve for x in $x^2 - 5x + 4 = 18$
$x^2 - 5x + 4 = 18$;
$x^2 - 5x + 4 - 18 = 0$;
$x^2 - 5x - 14 = 0$; find p and q such that $pq = -14$, and $p + q = -5$; try $p = -7$, $q = 2$
$x^2 - 7x + 2x - 14 = 0$; rewrite using p and q
$x(x - 7) + 2(x - 7) = 0$
$(x - 7)(x + 2) = 0$
$x - 7 = 0$ and $x + 2 = 0$
$x = 7$ and $x = -2$
Verify by substituting in the equation; when $x = 7$, $7^2 - 5 \cdot 7 + 4 = 18$; when $x = -2, (-2)^2 - 5 \cdot -2 + 4 = 18$.
So, the solutions are $x = -2$ and $x = 7$

Example Solve $(x - 3)^2 = 16$
$(x - 3) = \pm\sqrt{16} = \pm 4$; take square root on both sides
$x = 3 \pm 4$; $3 + 4 = 7$ or $3 - 4 = -1$

Example Solve $(x - 3)^3 = 27$
$(x - 3) = \sqrt[3]{27} = 3$; note that $\sqrt[3]{27} <> -3$; it is only $+ 3$
$x = 3 + 3 = 6$

Q11 How do I complete the square to solve a quadratic equation?

A11 While solving polynomial equations, if you have to factorize $x^2 + bx$ but don't have the remaining term, you can add $\left(\frac{b}{2}\right)^2$ and complete the square. This is called the "completing the square" method.

Example: Solve for x: $4x^2 + 16x = 0$
Solution: Pause to observe the terms for a few seconds. Observe the GCF of 4 in both terms. Factor it out and observe further.

$4x^2 + 16x = 0$
$4(x^2 + 4x) = 0$ factor out 4 from both terms; $x^2 + 4x$ is missing one term that will make it a square
$x^2 + 4x = 0$ divide by 4 on both sides
$(x^2 + 4x + 4 - 4) = 0$; to complete the square, add $\left(\frac{b}{2}\right)^2$ where b=4 ; so add $\left(\frac{4}{2}\right)^2 =4$ and subtract 4
$(x + 2)^2 - 4 = 0$; use the perfect square formula
$(x + 2)^2 = 4$
$x + 2 = \pm\sqrt{4}$; take square root on both sides
$x = -2 \pm 2$; $x = -2 + 2 = 0$ and $-2 - 2 = -4$
Verify the results: when $x = 0$ $4 \cdot 0^2 + 16 \cdot 0 = 0$; when $x = -4, (-4)^2 + 16(-4) = 64 - 64 = 0$

PASSPORT TO ADVANCED MATH
Lesson 21 | Polynomials and Quadratic Equations | Practice

NO CALCULATOR SECTION

1. Which of the following can be a solution to the quadratic equation below?
$$x^2 - 81 = 0$$
(A) -12
(B) -10
(C) -9
(D) -3

2. The sum of the solutions of $(x-2)^2 = 16$ is
(A) -12
(B) -10
(C) -8
(D) 4

3. If $x^2 + 8x = 0$, then which of the following is true?
I $x = 0$
II $x = 8$
III $x = -8$

(A) I only
(B) II only
(C) I and III
(D) II and III

4. If $z^2 - 4z = 21$, the product of the solutions is
(A) -28
(B) -24
(C) -21
(D) -15

NO CALCULATOR SECTION

5. The largest solution to $(x+4)^2 = (x+4)$ is
(A) -3
(B) -2
(C) 3
(D) 12

6. If $p^2 - 2^2 = 8 \cdot (p+2)$, then $p=$
(A) 2
(B) 8
(C) 10
(D) 12

7. The solution to $(x+2)^2 - (x-2)^2 = 88$ is
(A) less than 11
(B) equal to 11
(C) greater than 11
(D) cannot be determined

8. If $(m+5)(3m-21) = 0$ then $m =$
(A) -5 and -7
(B) 5 and -7
(C) -5 and 7
(D) 5 and 7

9. If $(z-p)^2 = 36$, then z could be
(A) p
(B) $p+6$
(C) $6p$
(D) $\frac{6}{p}$

NO CALCULATOR SECTION

10. If $x^3 + y^3 = 2a(x^3 - y^3)$ then $\frac{x^3}{y^3} =$

(A) $\frac{2a+1}{1-2a}$

(B) $\frac{2a-1}{2a+1}$

(C) $\frac{2a+1}{2a-1}$

(D) $\frac{2a+1}{1-2a}$

11. If $\frac{9x^2}{3x+1} = \frac{1}{3x+1} + A$, what is A in terms of x?

(A) $2x + 1$

(B) $3x + 1$

(C) $2x - 1$

(D) $3x - 1$

NO CALCULATOR SECTION

12. $\frac{100x^3y^3 - 50x^2y^2}{25xy} =$

(A) $\frac{2xy}{2xy-1}$

(B) $\frac{2xy}{xy-1}$

(C) $2xy(2xy - 1)$

(D) $2xy(2xy + 1)$

13. If $\frac{1}{x} + a = \frac{1}{y}$ then what is x in terms of y?

(A) $\frac{y}{1+ay}$

(B) $\frac{y}{1-ay}$

(C) $\frac{1+ay}{y}$

(D) $\frac{1-ay}{y}$

NO CALCULATOR SECTION

14. The factors of $x^2 + 8x + 12$ are
(A) $(x + 6)$ and $(x - 2)$
(B) $(x - 6)$ and $(x - 2)$
(C) $(x - 6)$ and $(x + 2)$
(D) $(x + 6)$ and $(x + 2)$

15. The factors of $x^2 + x - 12$ are
(A) $(x + 4)$ and $(x - 3)$
(B) $(x + 4)$ and $(x + 3)$
(C) $(x - 4)$ and $(x - 3)$
(D) $(x - 6)$ and $(x + 2)$

16. The factors of $x^2 - 8x - 20$ are
(A) $(x + 2)$ and $(x + 10)$
(B) $(x - 2)$ and $(x - 10)$
(C) $(x + 2)$ and $(x - 10)$
(D) $(x - 2)$ and $(x + 10)$

NO CALCULATOR SECTION

17. The factors of $-4p^2 - 16p + 9$ are
(A) $(2p - 1)$ and $(2p + 9)$
(B) $-(2p - 1)$ and $(2p + 9)$
(C) $(2p - 9)$ and $(2p - 1)$
(D) $-(p - 1)$ and $(p + 1)$

18. After using the completing the square method, $x^2 + 16x$ can be simplified as
(A) $(x + 8)^2 - 8$
(B) $(x + 8)^2 + 8$
(C) $(x + 8)^2 + 64$
(D) $(x + 8)^2 - 64$

19. After using the completing the square method, $4x^2 - 16x$ can be simplified as
(A) $4(x - 2)^2 - 4$
(B) $(x - 2)^2 + 16$
(C) $4(x - 2)^2 + 16$
(D) $4((x - 2)^2 - 4)$

NO CALCULATOR SECTION

20. The area of a rectangle is given by the expression: $x^2 + 9x + 18$. What is the perimeter of the rectangle?

(A) $x + 9$
(B) $2x + 9$
(C) $4x + 9$
(D) $4x + 18$

21. The length of a rectangle of l is three times its width w. If the length is increased by 5 units and width is increased by 2 units, the area of a rectangle is given by which of the following expression?

(A) $3w^2 + 11w + 10$
(B) $3w^2 - 11w + 10$
(C) $11w^2 + 3w + 10$
(D) $11w^2 - 3w - 10$

NO CALCULATOR SECTION

22. When $3x^2 + 4x + 1$ is divided by $3x + 1$, the remainder is

(A) $x + 1$
(B) 0
(C) $2x + 1$
(D) $2x - 1$

PASSPORT TO ADVANCED MATH
Lesson 21 | Polynomials and Quadratic Equations | Answers

#	Explanation	Comments
1 C	$x^2 - 81 = 0$ $x^2 = 81$ $x = \sqrt{81} = \pm 9$ Since only 9 is in the answer choice, C is the correct answer	
2 D	$(x-2)^2 = 16$ $(x-2) = \sqrt{16} = \pm 4$ $x = 2 \pm 4 = 6 \text{ or } -2$ Sum of the solutions $= 6 + (-2) = 6 - 2 = 4$	Note that the question asks for the sum of the solutions.
3 C	$x^2 + 8x = 0$ In this expression, $x^2 + 8x$ appears like it is missing a term to complete the square $x^2 + 8x + 16 - 16 = 0$ $(x+4)^2 - 16 = 0$ $(x+4)^2 = 16$ $(x+4) = \sqrt{16} = \pm 4$ $x = -4 \pm 4$ $x = 0 \text{ or } -8$ Choice C indicates these 2 solutions	Completing the square is an important method for solving quadratic equations.
4 C	$z^2 - 4z = 21$ $z^2 - 4z - 21 = 0$; find p, q such that $pq = -21$ and $p + q = -4$; try $p = -7$ and $q = 3$ $z^2 - 7z + 3z - 21 = 0$ $z(z - 7) + 3(z - 7) = 0$ $(z - 7)(z + 3) = 0$ $z - 7 = 0$; or $z + 3 = 0$ $z = 7$ or $z = -3$ Product of the solutions is $7 \cdot -3 = -21$	Note that the quadratic variable is z; it does not have to be x all the time.
5 A	$(x+4)^2 = (x+4)$ $x^2 + 8x + 16 = x + 4$ $x^2 + 8x + 16 - x - 4 = 0$ $x^2 + 7x + 12 = 0$ $x^2 + 4x + 3x + 12 = 0$ $x(x + 4) + 3(x + 4) = 0$ $(x + 4)(x + 3) = 0$ $x = -4, \text{ or } x = -3$; verify these by substituting The larger of these is -3.	
6 C	$p^2 - 2^2 = 8 \cdot (p + 2)$ $p^2 - 4 = 8p + 16$ $p^2 - 4 - 8p - 16 = 0$ $p^2 - 8p - 20 = 0$	

	$p^2 - 10p + 2p - 20 = 0$ $p(p - 10) + 2(p - 10) = 0$ $(p - 10)(p + 2) = 0$ $so, p = 10 \text{ or } p = -2$ Choice C is equal to 10 and is the correct answer.	
7 B	$(x + 2)^2 - (x - 2)^2 = 88$ $x^2 + 4x + 4 - (x^2 - 4x + 4) = 88$ $x^2 + 4x + 4 - x^2 + 4x - 4 = 88$ $8x = 88$ $x = 11$	
8 C	$(m + 5)(3m - 21) = 0$; so either or both is 0 $(m + 5) = 0 \quad m = -5$ $3m - 21 = 0; \quad m = 7$	Use zero product rule – if $a \cdot b = 0$ then $a = 0$ or $b = 0$ or both $= 0$.
9 B	$(z - p)^2 = 36$ $z - p = \pm 6$ $z = p \pm 6$ $z = p + 6 \text{ or } p - 6$	If you see only one solution of the quadratic in the answer choices, pick that answer choice.
10 C	$x^3 + y^3 = 2a(x^3 - y^3)$ $x^3 + y^3 = 2ax^3 - 2ay^3$ $x^3 - 2ax^3 = -y^3 - 2ay^3$ $x^3(1 - 2a) = -y^3(1 + 2a)$ $\dfrac{x^3}{y^3} = \dfrac{-1(1 + 2a)}{(1 - 2a)} = \dfrac{2a + 1}{2a - 1}$	This is a problem involving simplifying an algebraic fraction; isolate the variables and simplify Do not be intimidated by the problem; pause for a second to see patterns and then proceed.
11 D	$\dfrac{9x^2}{3x + 1} = \dfrac{1}{3x + 1} + A$ Notice that the denominator is the same, A can be written in terms of x and simplified $A = \dfrac{9x^2}{3x + 1} - \dfrac{1}{3x + 1}$ $A = \dfrac{(3x)^2 - 1^2}{3x + 1} = \dfrac{\cancel{(3x + 1)}(3x - 1)}{\cancel{(3x + 1)}} = 3x - 1$	Isolate A and then use the difference of square formula to simplify this rational expression.
12 C	$\dfrac{100x^3y^3 - 50x^2y^2}{25xy}$ $= \dfrac{50x^2y^2(2xy - 1)}{25xy}$ $= 2xy(2xy - 1)$	Factor out the GCF from the two terms in the numerator.

13 B	$\frac{1}{x} + a = \frac{1}{y}$ $\frac{1}{x} = \frac{1}{y} - a = \frac{1-ay}{y}$ $x = \frac{y}{1-ay}$	
14 D	Several choices are given for the factors of $x^2 + 8x + 12$. So, without factorizing, you can evaluate the answer choices. In choice D, $6 \cdot 2 = c = 12$ and $6 + 2 = b = 8$, so it is the correct answer.	Remember that for a quadratic $x^2 + bx + c$, $(x+p)$ and $(x+q)$ are factors if $pq = c$ and $p + q = b$.
15 A	$x^2 + x - 12$ Find p, q such that $pq = -12$ and $p + q = 1$, then $(x+p)(x+q)$ are factors. Choice A shows $p = 4$ and $q = -3$, $pq = -12$ and $p + q = 1$	
16 C	$x^2 - 8x - 20$ Find p, q such that $pq = -20$ and $p + q = -8$, then $(x+p)(x+q)$ are factors. Choice C shows $p = 2$ and $q = -10$, $pq = -20$ and $p + q = -8$	
17 B	$-4p^2 - 16p + 9$ $= -1(4p^2 + 16p - 9)$ Find p, q such that $pq = 4 \cdot -9 = -36$ and $p + q = 16$. Try $p = 18$ and $q = -2$. $= -1(4p^2 + 18p - 2p - 9)$ $= -1(\,(2p(2p+9) - 1(2p+9))$ $= -1\,(2p+9)(2p-1)$	Remember that for a quadratic $ax^2 + bx + c$, find p and q such that $pq = ac$ and $p + q = b$. Then write out the expression using p and q and factorize; a little tedious process but if you take care of the positive and negative signs, you can find the answer confidently.
18 D	$x^2 + 16x$ $x^2 + 16x + 64 - 64$; add $\left(\frac{16}{2}\right)^2$ to complete the square $(x+8)^2 - 64$	Review the completing the square question in the review section; add $\left(\frac{b}{2}\right)^2 = \left(\frac{16}{2}\right)^2$.
19 D	$4x^2 - 16x$ $= 4(x^2 - 4x)$ $= 4(x^2 - 4x + 4 - 4);$ $= 4((x-2)^2 - 4);$	Choice A looks similar to choice D but is different. Choice D has an extra parenthesis.
20 D	Area of rectangle is given as $x^2 + 9x + 18$ You know that the area of a rectangle $A = l.w$. So, the length and width are factors of the area. Factorize $x^2 + 9x + 18$ $= x^2 + 6x + 3x + 18$ $= (x+6)(x+3)$	

		So, the sides of the rectangle are $(x+6)$ and $(x+3)$ Perimeter of rectangle= $2(l+w) = 2(x+6+x+3) = 2(2x+9) = 4x+18$.	
21	A	$l = 3w$ $new\ area\ =\ (l+5)\ (w+2)$ $=\ (3w+5)(w+2)$ $=\ 3w^2 + 6w + 5w + 10$ $=\ 3w^2 + 11w + 10$	
22	B	Do the long division $$\begin{array}{r} x+1 \\ 3x+1\overline{\smash{)}3x^2+4x+1} \\ -(3x^2+x) \\ \hline 0+3x+1 \\ -(3x+1) \\ \hline 0 \end{array}$$	

PASSPORT TO ADVANCED MATH

Lesson 22 | **Linear Quadratic Systems** | **Review**

FOCUSPREP CHECKLIST

- What is a Linear Quadratic System?
- How do I solve a Linear Quadratic System?
- How many solutions can a Linear Quadratic System have?
- Workout practice problems in Linear Quadratic Systems

Q1 What is a Linear Quadratic System?

A1 A Linear Quadratic system contains two functions - a linear function and a quadratic function.

Example:

$$y = x^2 + 6x + 10$$
$$y = 3x - 6$$

The graph of this system will have a parabola corresponding to the quadratic function and a straight line corresponding to the linear function. The functions may intersect each other at two points (2 solutions) or at one point (one solution) or may not intersect at all (no solution).

At the points of intersection, the values of both functions are the same.

Examples:

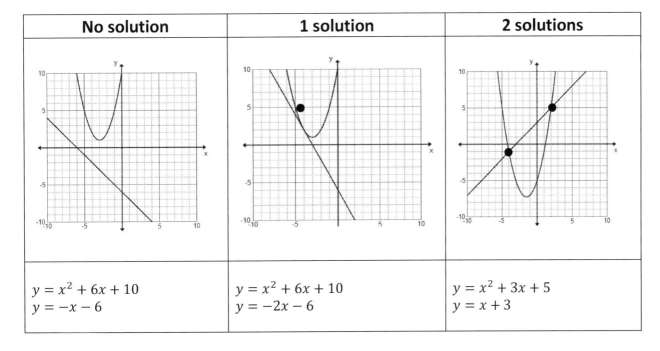

No solution	1 solution	2 solutions
$y = x^2 + 6x + 10$ $y = -x - 6$	$y = x^2 + 6x + 10$ $y = -2x - 6$	$y = x^2 + 3x + 5$ $y = x + 3$

Q2 How do I solve a Linear Quadratic System? How many solutions can be there?

A2 The system can be solved algebraically by equating the two functions and finding the solution. Remember that you may end up with 1 solution, 2 solutions, or no solution.

Example (2 Solutions) : Solve the system of linear and quadratic equations.
$$y = -4x - 3$$
$$y = x^2$$

Equate the two functions: $-4x - 3 = x^2$
Write in standard form: $x^2 + 4x + 3 = 0$
$(x + 3)(x + 1) = 0$; factorize
so, $x = -3, x = -1$
when $x = -3, y = (-3)^2 = 9$; when $x = -1, y = (-1)^2 = 1$
So the solutions are $(-3, 9), (-1, 1)$. There are 2 solutions.

Example (1 solution): Solve the system of linear and quadratic equations.
$$y = x^2 + 6x + 10$$
$$y = -2x - 6$$
Equate the functions, and simplify:
$x^2 + 6x + 10 = -2x - 6$
$x^2 + 6x + 2x + 10 + 6 = 0$
$x^2 + 8x + 16 = 0$; find p and q such that $pq = 16$ and $p + q = 8$; try
$x^2 + 4x + 4x + 16 = 0$
$x(x + 4) + 4(x + 4) = 0$; factorize
$(x + 4)^2 = 0$
$(x + 4) = 0$, so $x = -4$
when $x = -4, y = -2 \cdot -4 - 6 = 8 - 6 = 2$

This system of linear-quadratic has only one solution at $(-4,2)$. If you draw both functions, you will see that they intersect at only one point $(-4,2)$.

Example: A graph of quadratic function $g(t) = -t^2 + 4t$ intercepts the graph of linear function $h(t) = -t + 4$ at which of the following points?
    (A) (1,3) and (2,0)
    (B) (2,3) and (3,0)
    (C) (1,3) and (4,0)
    (D) (2,3) and (4,0)

Solution: When they meet, both functions have the same value. Equate the functions and solve for t.
$-t^2 + 4t = -t + 4$
$t^2 - 5t + 4 = 0$; find p and q such that $pq = 4$ and $p + q = -5$; try $p = -4$ and $q = -1$
$t^2 - 4t - t + 4 = 0$;
$t(t - 4) - 1(t - 4) = 0$;
$(t - 4)(t - 1) = 0$
$t = 1$ and $t = 4$
when $t = 1$ $h(t) = 3$ and when $t = 4$ $h(t) = 0$;
So, the functions intercept each other at $(1,3)$ and $(4,0)$. The correct answer is (C).

PASSPORT TO ADVANCED MATH

Lesson 22 | Linear Quadratic Systems | Practice

NO CALCULATOR SECTION

1. The solution to the system below that lies in the first quadrant of the Cartesian coordinate system is

$$y = x^2 - 6$$
$$y = x + 6$$

(A) $(4, -10)$
(B) $(-4, 10)$
(C) $(4, 10)$
(D) $(-3, 3)$

2. The distance between the solutions to the following system in the Cartesian plane is

$$y = x^2 - 6$$
$$y = x + 6$$

(A) 7
(B) $\sqrt{2}$
(C) $7\sqrt{2}$
(D) $7\sqrt{7}$

NO CALCULATOR ECTION

3. The solution to the system below that lies in the third quadrant is

$$y = x^2 - 3$$
$$y = x - 1$$

(A) $(-1, 2)$
(B) $(-1, -2)$
(C) $(2, 1)$
(D) $(-2, -1)$

4. A stone is thrown from the ground along a parabolic path defined by the function $y = -x^2 + 4x$. The stone hits the tip of a vertical pole that is 4 feet tall at the vertex of its path. How far is the pole from the point where the stone was thrown?

(A) 1
(B) 2
(C) 4
(D) 16

NO CALCULATOR SECTION

CALCULATOR SECTION

5. The system of functions shown above has a solution at
(A) $(-2, 4.5)$
(B) $(1.5, 2.1)$
(C) $(4, 0.9)$
(D) $(0, 0)$

7. A circus clown walks down a straight rope from a point 9 feet above the ground as shown. At the same time, a trapeze artist swings down a parabolic path shown. After crossing the trapeze artist for the first time at 9 feet, approximately how far does the clown walk down the rope before meeting the trapeze artist again?
(A) 3
(B) 5
(C) 6
(D) 7

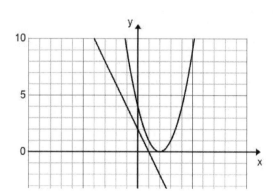

6. How many solutions does the linear quadratic system graphed above have?
(A) 0
(B) 1
(C) 2
(D) 3

PASSPORT TO ADVANCED MATH

Lesson 22 — Linear Quadratic Systems — Answers

#	Explanation	Comments
1 C	$x^2 - 6 = x + 6$ $x^2 - 6 - x - 6 = 0$ $x^2 - x - 12 = 0$; find p and q such that $pq = -12$ and $p + q = -1$; try $p = -4, q = 3$; rewrite the equation with p and q $x^2 - 4x + 3x - 12 = 0$ $x(x - 4) + 3(x - 4) = 0$ $(x - 4)(x + 3) = 0$ $x - 4 = 0$ or $x + 3 = 0$ $x = 4$ or $x = -3$ The question asks which solution is in the first quadrant; when $x = 4, y = 4 + 6 = 10$. So, $(4,10)$ is the solution in the first quadrant.	Observe first that this is a Linear Quadratic System, one function is quadratic and another is linear. To find the solution to this system, equate them and solve for x and then find y.
2 C	$x^2 - 6 = x + 6$ $x^2 - 6 - x - 6 = 0$ $x^2 - x - 12 = 0$; find p and q such that $pq = -12$ and $p + q = -1$; try $p = -4, q = 3$; rewrite the equation with p and q. $x^2 - 4x + 3x - 12 = 0$ $x(x - 4) + 3(x - 4) = 0$ $(x - 4)(x + 3) = 0$ $x - 4 = 0$ or $x + 3 = 0$ $x = 4$ or $x = -3$ when $x = 4$ $y = 4 + 6 = 10$ when $x = -3$ $y = -3 + 6 = 3$ The solutions are $(4,10)$ and $(-3,3)$ The distance between these points= $\sqrt{(3 - 10)^2 + (-3 - 4)^2} = \sqrt{49 + 49} = \sqrt{(2 \cdot 49)} = 7\sqrt{2}$	This is a linear quadratic system; the question asks for the distance between the solutions; find the solutions first and then find the distance.
3 B	$x^2 - 3 = x - 1$ $x^2 - 3 - x + 1 = 0$ $x^2 - x - 2 = 0$; find p and q such that $pq = -2$ and $p + q = -1$; try $p = -2, q = 1$; rewrite the equation with p and q $x^2 - 2x + x - 2 = 0$ $x(x - 2) + 1(x - 2) = 0$ $(x - 2)(x + 1) = 0$ $x - 2 = 0$ or $x + 1 = 0$ $x = 2$ or $x = -1$ when $x = 2$ $y = 2 - 1 = 1$ when $x = -1$ $y = -1 - 1 = -2$ The solutions are $(2,1)$ and $(-1,-2)$.	Remember that in the third quadrant, both x and y are negative.

©GiftOfLogic http://www.GiftOfLogic.com

4	B	The stone takes a parabolic path which opens downward, since the coefficient of x^2 is -1. The path of the stone intersects the tip of the pole that is 4 feet tall. This can be represented as $y = 4$. Together, you have a linear quadratic system. $y = -x^2 + 4x$ $y = 4$ Equate them and solve for x. $-x^2 + 4x = 4$ $x^2 - 4x = -4$ $x^2 - 4x + 4 = 0$ $x^2 - 2x - 2x + 4 = 0$ $x(x - 2) - 2(x - 2) = 0$ $(x - 2)(x - 2) = 0$ $(x - 2) = 0; x = 2, y = 4$ The stone touches the pole at $x = 2$.	Read the given facts carefully; one equation is given but only a hint is given for the other equation. The hint is that the stone hits the tip of the pole that is 4 feet tall. Draw a small sketch as shown below to figure out that you need the other function $y = 4$ to solve this system.
5	B	Note that the solution to the system is at the point where all the functions of the system meet. This is at point (1.5, 2.1) in the first quadrant.	At the solution point, all the functions must have the same value. Note that there are two quadratics and one linear function in this system.
6	A	For a linear quadratic system to have a solution, the line and the quadratic must meet. From the graph, there is no point of intersection; so there is no solution	
7	D	The first point where they meet is $(1, 9)$. The second point of meeting is $(6,4)$. The distance that the clown walked down the rope is $\sqrt{(4-9)^2 + (6-1)^2} = \sqrt{25 + 25} = 7.07$ ft. This is approximately equal to 7 feet.	Select the points from the graph; note that the question asks "approximately how far", thereby giving you a clue to round your answer. Use the distance formula and your calculator to find the square root.

| Lesson 23 | PASSPORT TO ADVANCED MATH / Functions and Transformations | Review |

FOCUSPREP CHECKLIST

- What are the algebraic forms of linear, quadratic, exponential, and cubic functions?
- What are the graphical forms of linear, quadratic, exponential, and cubic functions?
- How do I find the Zeros of a function?
- What is a Composite function $(fog)(x)$?
- How do I to find $f(g(x))$ algebraically and from a graph?
- What happens to a function when it is transformed (Translated, Reflected, Stretched, and Compressed) ?
- Workout practice problems in functions and transformations

Q1 What is a Function? What are they used for?

A1 A Function is an algebraic expression that models the relation between a dependent variable and an independent variable. Functions are used to make estimates, to find out maximum and minimum values and other properties of the variables that are modeled. The independent variable is plotted on the x axis and dependent variable is plotted on the y axis. The general form of a function is represented as $y = f(x)$.

Q2 What is the domain and range of a function?

A2 The domain of a function is a set of all values for which it is defined. The range is the set of all y-values that correspond to the x-values.

Q3 What are the different types of functions? How do they look?

A3 There are several types of functions – linear functions, quadratic functions, exponential functions, cubic functions, etc. Their graph and their algebraic expressions are shown in the table below.

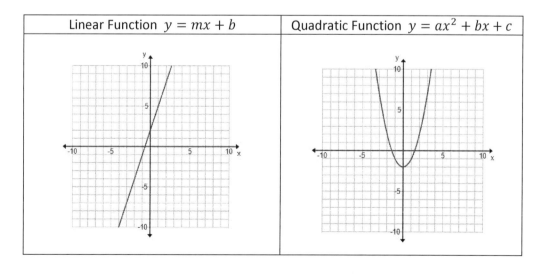

| Linear Function $y = mx + b$ | Quadratic Function $y = ax^2 + bx + c$ |

Exponential Function $y = ab^x$	Cubic Function $y = x^3$
	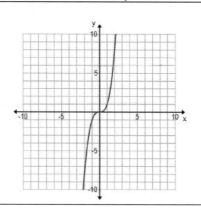

Q4 What are the important things to remember about linear, quadratic, exponential and cubic functions?

A4 The table below summarizes the important facts about linear, quadratic, exponential and cubic functions.

Linear Function $y = mx + b$	Quadratic Function $y = ax^2 + bx + c$
slope-intercept formula: $y = mx + b$ where m is the slope and b is the y-intercept. slope =$m= \frac{y2-y1}{x2-x1}$ where $(x1, y1)$ and $(x2, y2)$ are two points on the line. point slope formula: $y - y1 = m(x - x1)$ At the y-intercept, $x = 0$; when $x = 0, y = b$ At x-intercept, $y = 0$: when $y = 0, x = -\frac{b}{m}$ **Examples:** $y = 4x + 5$; $y = 8.5x + 33.67$	Quadratic graphs take the form of a parabola. **Standard form** is $y = ax^2 + bx + c$ Axis of symmetry: $x = -\frac{b}{2a}$ Vertex of parabola : $(-\frac{b}{2a}, f(-\frac{b}{2a}))$ If $a > 0$ the parabola opens upward, the minimum point is at $(-\frac{b}{2a}, f\left(-\frac{b}{2a}\right))$ If $a < 0$ the parabola opens downward, the maximum point is at $(-\frac{b}{2a}, f(-\frac{b}{2a}))$ y-intercept = c **Vertex form** is $y = a(x - h)^2 + k$ Vertex is at (h, k) Axis of symmetry: $x = h$ y-intercept: find by substituting $x = 0$ If $a > 0$, parabola opens upward and has minimum point (minima) at the vertex (h, k).

Exponential Function $y = ab^x$	
	If $a < 0$, parabola opens downward and has maximum point (maxima) at the vertex (h, k). **Examples:** Standard form: $y = 3x^2 - 2x + 4$; Vertex form: $y = (x - 4)^2 + 5$
Exponential Function $y = ab^x$	**Cubic Function** $y = x^3$
$y = ab^x$ When $b > 1$ then it is exponential growth. When $0 < b < 1$ then it is exponential decay. Another detailed form of exponential function: Exponential Growth: $y = a(1 + r)^t$; where a=initial value, r=percentage rate of growth, t=time period of growth Exponential Decay: $y = a(1 - r)^t$; where a=initial value, r=percentage rate of decay, t=time period of growth **Examples:** $y = 1.5 \cdot 2^t$ $y = 0.7^x$	steeper than quadratic function the ends of the function go in opposite directions. **Examples:** $y = x^3$ $y = 2x^3 + 3x^2 - 77$

Q5 What does Zeros or Roots of a function mean?

A5 The Zeros or Roots of a function $f(x)$ are the x-values where the function has a value of 0. In graphical sense, the zeros are the intercepts on the x-axis. If a function intercepts the x-axis at more than one point, those points are called Zeros of the function. A function has one or more zeros or no zeros.
For example, the quadratic function $x^2 - 1$ has $(x + 1)$ and $(x - 1)$ as factors. To find the Zeros of the function, set it to 0, since its value at the x-intercept is 0. So $(x + 1) \cdot (x - 1) = 0$. So, by the zero product rule, you have $x + 1 = 0 \Rightarrow x = -1$ and $x - 1 = 0 \Rightarrow x = 1$. There are 2 zeros for this function. The figure below shows the graph of this function. Notice that the zeros of the function are the x intercepts at -1 and $+1$. At these zeros, the function has a value of 0.

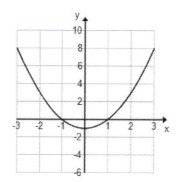

Q6 How do I find the zeros/roots of function? How many zeros (or roots) does a function have?
A6 To find the zeros/roots of a function, follow these steps:
      Step 1: set the function to 0
      Step 2: solve for x, factorize if necessary

Linear Functions: Since linear functions of the type $y = mx + b$ are graphed as straight lines, they have only one zero/root.
  Example: What are the roots of $f(x) = 2x + 3$?
  Solution: Set the function to 0: $2x + 3 = 0$; $x = -\frac{3}{2}$;

Quadratic functions $f(x) = ax^2 + bx + c$ can have
      2 Distinct Real solutions - function intercepts the x axis at two different points
      1 Real solution - function intercepts the x axis at one point only
      2 Distinct complex number solutions of the form $a + bi$ – function does not intercept the x-axis

You can find the roots of a quadratic function by setting it to 0, and factoring it. You can also use the following quadratic formula:

$$x = \frac{-b \pm \sqrt{b^2 - 4ac}}{2a}$$

Depending on the value of the discriminant $\sqrt{b^2 - 4ac}$ as shown in the table below, there can be 1 or 2 real solutions or 2 complex solutions.

$b^2 - 4ac > 0$	2 distinct real solutions	$\frac{-b+\sqrt{b^2-4ac}}{2a}$; $\frac{-b-\sqrt{b^2-4ac}}{2a}$
$b^2 - 4ac = 0$	1 real solution	$-\frac{b}{2a}$
$b^2 - 4ac < 0$	2 distinct complex number solutions	$-\frac{b}{2a} + i\frac{1}{2a}\sqrt{b^2 - 4ac}$; $-\frac{b}{2a} - i\frac{1}{2a}\sqrt{b^2 - 4ac}$

Example: What are the roots of $f(x) = x^2 - 4x + 3$?
Solution:
$x^2 - 4x + 3 = 0$; Set the function to 0:
$x^2 - 3x - x + 3 = 0$
$x(x - 3) - 1(x - 3) = 0$
$(x - 3)(x - 1) = 0$
$(x = 3) = 0$ and $(x - 1) = 0$
$x = 3$ and $x = 1$ are the roots of the equation.

Q7 What are the parts of a parabola (quadratic function)?

A7 Note carefully, the maxima, minima, vertex, axis of symmetry, and the roots/zeros. Parabolas that open upward have minima at their vertex and parabolas that open downwards have maxima at their vertex.

Q8 What operations can be performed on functions?

A8 Functions can be added, subtracted, multiplied, and divided similar to the way these operations are performed on polynomial expressions.

Example:

If $f(x) = x^2 + 2x + 2$; $g(x) = 3x + 4$, then the following operations can be performed on these functions.

Addition: $(f + g)(x) = f(x) + g(x) = x^2 + 2x + 2 + 3x + 4 = x^2 + 5x + 6$

Subtraction: $(f - g)(x) = f(x) - g(x) = x^2 + 2x + 2 - 3x - 4 = x^2 - x - 2$

Multiplication: $(fg)(x) = f(x)g(x) = (x^2 + 2x + 2)(3x + 4) = 3x^3 + 10x^2 + 8$

Division: $\left(\frac{f}{g}\right)(x) = \frac{f(x)}{g(x)} = \frac{x^2+2x+2}{3x+4} = \frac{(x+1)^2}{3x+4}$

Q9 How do I find the Zeros of a function from a graph?

A9 Zeros of a function $f(x)$ are the x-values where $f(x) = 0$. If you have the graph of the function, then you can find the Zeros of the function by reading its x-intercepts from the graph.

Q10 How do I find all the points where a function has the same value?

A10 To find all the points where a function has the same value, say k, draw a horizontal line y=k and note the x-value points where this line intercepts the function.

Example: At what values of x does the function shown below have a value of 7?

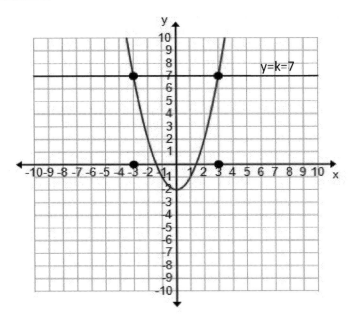

(A) -1 and 1
(B) -2 and 2
(C) -3 and 3
(D) -4 and 4

Solution: Draw a line of y=7 and note the two intercepts – the x values of these points are -3 and +3.

Example: For the function shown in the graph, what are the zeros of the function?

Solution: The Zeros are where the function has a value of 0. These are points where the function intercepts the x-axis. From the graph, the zeros are $x = -1.5$ and $x = 1.5$.

Q11 What is a **composite** function? How is it defined?
A11 A composite function is a function obtained by "composing" two functions. If you have two functions $f(x)$ and $g(x)$, the composite function is $f(g(x))$. Evaluate the inner function first and then the outer function. Another notation for composite function is $(f \circ g)(x) - pronouced$ "fog" of x.

Example: Let $f(x) = x^2$ and $g(x) = x + 1$. What is the value of composite function $f(g(x))$? What is the value of $g(f(x))$?

Solution: $f(g(x)) = f(x + 1)$; evaluate the inner function first, $g(x) = x + 1$

$= (x + 1)^2$; since $f(x) = x^2, f(x + 1) = (x + 1)^2$

So, the composite function $f(g(x)) = (x + 1)^2$

$g(f(x)) = g(x^2)$; evaluate the inner function first, $f(x) = x^2$

$= x^2 + 1$; since $g(x) = x + 1$, $g(x^2) = x^2 + 1$

So, the composite function $g(f(x)) = x^2 + 1$

Example: In the functions $f(x)$ and $g(x)$, evaluate $f(g(2))$ and $g(f(2))$.

Solution: $f(g(2)) = f(2 + 1) = f(3) = 3^2 = 9$

$g(f(2)) = g(2^2) = g(4) = 4 + 1 = 5$

Q12 What happens when a function/graph is moved horizontally or vertically? Stretched or Compressed horizontally or vertically? Reflected over its x-axis or y-axis?

A12 When a function/graph is **transformed** as described in the question, all the points in the graph get moved to new positions and a new graph/function is created. For example if you move the graph of $f(x)$ by 2 units to the right, you have a new graph and the new function corresponding to this graph is $f(x - 2)$. Similarly, you get new functions for other types of transformations. More details are given in the answers to the following questions. Transformations include Translation, Reflection, Stretch, and Compression.

Remember that a function has an algebraic form and a graphical form. When you transform this function, you get a new function with a new algebraic form and a new graph.

Q13 What happens when a graph/function is **translated** (moved) horizontally or vertically?

A13 The table below shows the new function that will be created due to translation.

The graph of $f(x)$ is moved horizontally to the right by k units.	$f(x)$ becomes $f(x - k)$
The graph of $f(x)$ is moved horizontally to the left by k units.	$f(x)$ becomes $f(x + k)$
The graph of $f(x)$ is moved vertically up by k units.	$f(x)$ becomes $f(x) + k$
The graph of $f(x)$ is moved vertically down by k units.	$f(x)$ becomes $f(x) - k$
Examples in graphical form are shown below. The function can be in linear or quadratic or in any other form.	

$f(x)$	$f(x)$ becomes $f(x-4)$ due to translation to right by 4 units
When function $f(x)$ is moved to the right by 4 units, you get $f(x-4)$; notice that the vertex has moved 4 points to the right.	
$f(x)$	$f(x)$ becomes $f(x+4)$ due to translation to left by 4 units
When function $f(x)$ is moved to the left by 4 units, you get $f(x+4)$	
$f(x)$	$f(x)+4$ is translation upward
When function $f(x)$ is moved up by 4 units, you get $f(x)+4$ Note that this is NOT $f(x+4)$	

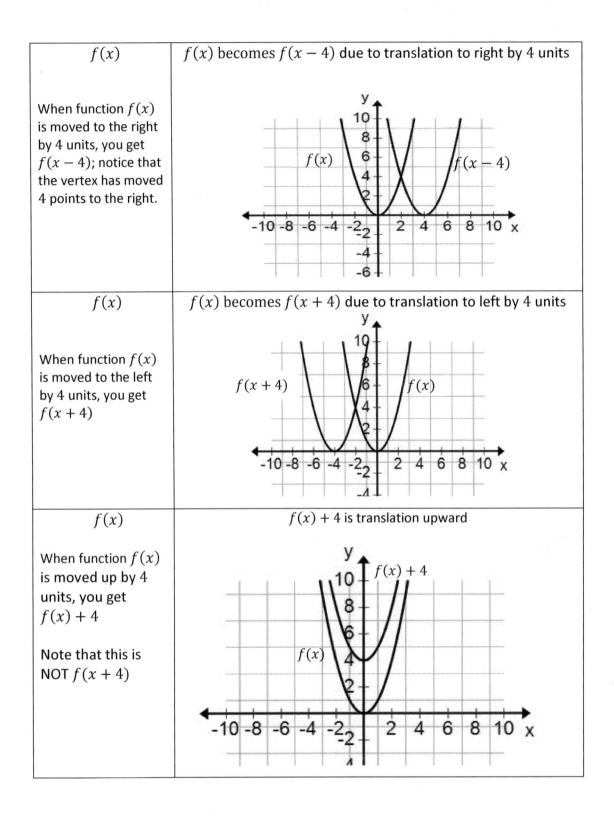

| $f(x)$ When function $f(x)$ is moved down by 4 units, you get $f(x) - 4$. Note that this is NOT $f(x-4)$ | $f(x-4)$ is translation downward |

Q14 What happens when a function is reflected over the x-axis or y-axis?

A14 The table below shows the new function that will be created due to reflection.

The graph of $f(x)$ is reflected over the x-axis	$f(x)$ becomes $-f(x)$
The graph of $f(x)$ is reflected over the y-axis.	$f(x)$ becomes $f(-x)$
Examples in graphical form are shown below. The function can be in linear or quadratic or in any other form.	

Function $f(x)$ is reflected over the x-axis.	$-f(x)$ is reflection of $f(x)$ over x-axis
When a function is reflected over the x axis, all y values become negative y values. So, $f(x)$ becomes $-f(x)$	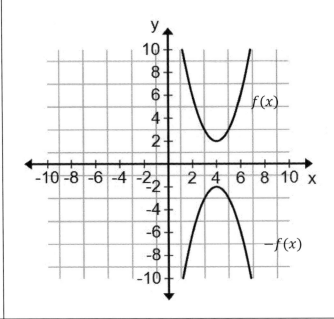
Function $f(x)$ is reflected over the y-axis	$f(-x)$ is reflection of $f(x)$ over y-axis
When a function is reflected over the y axis, all x values become negative x values. So, $f(x)$ becomes $f(-x)$	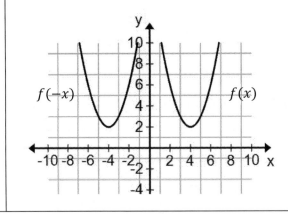

Q15 What happens when a function is **stretched or compressed horizontally or vertically**?

A15 The table below shows the new function that will be created due to stretching and compression.

Horizontal Stretch/Compression General Formula: $f(x)$ becomes $f\left(\dfrac{1}{b}x\right)$	$b > 1$ Horizontal Stretch $0 < b < 1$ Horizontal compression
Vertical Stretch/Compression General Formula: $f(x)$ becomes $bf(x)$	$b > 1$ Vertical Stretch $0 < b < 1$ Vertical Compression
Examples in graphical form are shown below. The function can be in linear or quadratic or in any other form.	

Function $f(x)$ is **horizontally stretched/compressed** by a factor of b	Horizontal Stretch $f\left(\frac{1}{b}x\right), b > 1$
General formula for horizontal stretch/ compression: $f(x)$ becomes $f(\frac{1}{b}x)$ $b > 1$ is stretch $0 < b < 1$ is compression	$f\left(\frac{1}{3}x\right)$ is a horizontal stretch by a factor of 3. 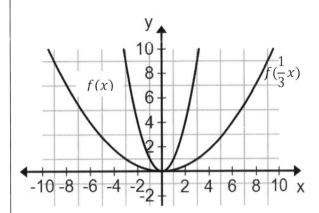
Example: $f(\frac{1}{3}x)$ is horizontal stretch; $b = 3$ $f(3x)$ is horizontal compression; $b = \frac{1}{3}$	Horizontal Compression $f\left(\frac{1}{b}x\right), 0 < b < 1$ $f(3x)$ is a horizontal compression by a factor of $\frac{1}{3}$. 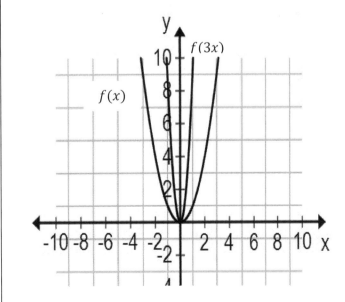

Function $f(x)$ is **vertically stretched/compressed** by a factor of b.	Vertical Stretch
General formula for vertical stretch/compression	$f(x)$ is vertically stretched to $3f(x)$ by a factor of 3
$f(x)$ becomes $bf(x)$	
$b > 1$ is stretch	Vertical Compression
$0 < b < 1$ is compression	$f(x)$ is vertically compressed to $\frac{1}{3}f(x)$ by a factor of $\frac{1}{3}$ 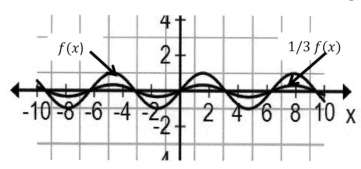

Q16 What happens when a function has more than one transformation – move to the right 5 units and then move down 2 units?

A16 When there are several transformations, apply each transformation <u>one at a time</u>. In this case, $f(x)$ moves to the right 5 units and becomes $f(x-5)$ and then moves down 2 units and becomes $f(x-5) - 2$.

Q17 What kind of problems may appear in SAT regarding functions and transformation of functions?

A17 A few problems and their solutions are presented below. The practice section contains more.

Example: Let $f(x) = x^2 + 2x$. Let $g(x)$ be the function obtained after translating $f(x)$ by 7 units to the left. What is $g(4)$? **Solution:** $g(x) = f(x)$ translated 7 units to the left. So, $g(x) = f(x+7) = (x+7)^2 + 2(x+7)$. So, $g(4) = (4+7)^2 + 2(4+7) = 121 + 22 = 143$.

Example: Let $f(x) = x^2 + 2x$. Let $g(x)$ be the function obtained after translating $f(x)$ 7 units to the left. What is $f(g(4))$? **Solution:** $g(x) = f(x)$ translated 7 units to the left $= f(x+7) = (x+7)^2 + 2(x+7)$. So, $g(4) = (4+7)^2 + 2(4+7) = 121 + 22 = 143$. Now, $f(g(4)) = f(143) = 143^2 + 2 \cdot 143 = 20735$.

Example: Let $f(x - 2) = 3x - 5$. What is $f(x)$ and what is $f(4)$? **Solution:** Note that you are given $f(x-2)$ but not $f(x)$. Rewrite it in terms of $(x-2)$ as $f(x-2) = 3(x-2) + 6 - 5 = 3(x-2) + 1$. Since, $3(x-2)$ introduces a -6, you have to cancel it with a $+6$. $f(x-2) = 3(x-2) + 1$ is the same as $f(x) = 3x + 1$. So, $f(4) = 3 \cdot 4 + 1 = 13$. Another method is $f(4) = f(6-2) = 3 \cdot 6 - 5 = 13$.

Example Two functions are shown in the graph below. What is $g(f(2))$?

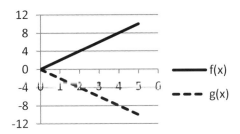

Solution: From the graph, $f(2) = 4$ and so $g(f(2)) = g(4) = -8$

Example: When a function $V(t) = -16t^3 + 21t^2 + 3t - 5$ is stretched horizontally by a factor of 3, what is the value of the new function at t=1?

Solution: $V(t) = -16t^3 + 21t^2 + 3t - 5$. When a function is stretched, the new function is $V(\frac{1}{3}t)$

$V(t) = -16t^3 + 21t^2 + 3t - 5$

$V(\frac{1}{3}t) = -16(\frac{1}{3}t)^3 + 21(\frac{1}{3}t)^2 + 3(\frac{1}{3}t) - 5$

$= -\frac{16}{27}t^3 + \frac{21}{9}t^2 + t - 5$

$= -\frac{16}{27}t^3 + \frac{7}{3}t^2 + t - 5$

At t=1, the value is $-\frac{16}{27} + \frac{7}{3} - 5 = -3.26$.

Example If the graph of the function shown below is written in the form of $a(x - h)^2 + k$, then $a =$?

Solution: From the graph, the vertex of the parabola is $(h, k) = (1,1)$. The vertex form of the parabolic function is $y = a(x - h)^2 + k$. Substituting h and k, you get $y = a(x - 1)^2 + 1$. Pick any point on the parabola – say (2,3). This point must satisfy the function. So, $3 = a(2 - 1)^2 + 1$, giving $a = 3 - 1 = 2$.

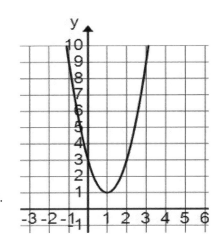

Example Express the quadratic $y = 2x^2 - 4x + 3$ in vertex form.
Solution:
The vertex form is $y = a(x - h)^2 + k$
$y = 2x^2 - 4x + 3$
$y = 2(x^2 - 2x) + 3$;
$y = 2(x^2 - 2x + 1) + 3 - 2$; complete the square by adding 2 and subtracting 2
$y = 2(x - 1)^2 + 1$; this is in vertex form $a(x - h)^2 + k$

Know how to convert a quadratic in standard form to vertex form and vice versa. To convert from the vertex form to standard form, expand the terms inside the square.

PASSPORT TO ADVANCED MATH

Lesson 23 — Functions and Transformations — Practice

NO CALCULATOR SECTION

1. The table below shows the values of functions $f(x)$ and $g(x)$. What is the value of $f(2) \cdot f(g(2))$?

x	1	2	3	4	5
$f(x)$	1	3	5	7	9
$g(x)$	2	4	8	16	32

(A) 3
(B) 8
(C) 15
(D) 21

2. The table shows the values of functions $f(x)$ and $g(x)$.

x	1	2	3	4	5
$f(x)$	2	3	4	5	6
$g(x)$	6	9	12	15	18

$g(x) =$

(A) $f(x)$
(B) $f(x^2)$
(C) $3f(x)$
(D) $f(3x)$

NO CALCULATOR SECTION

3. If $f(x) = x^2 - 2$ and $g(x) = 2x^2 + 5$ then $(f - g)(x) =$

(A) $-x^2 + 3$
(B) $-x^2 - 7$
(C) $-x^2 - 3$
(D) $-x^2 + 7$

4. If $f(x) = 1 + \frac{1}{x}$ and $g(x) = 1 - \frac{1}{x}$ then what is $(fg)(2)$?

(A) $\frac{1}{4}$

(B) $\frac{1}{2}$

(C) $\frac{3}{5}$

(D) $\frac{3}{4}$

5. If $f(x) = x^2$ and $g(x) = x^4$ then $\left(\frac{f}{g}\right)(3) =$

(A) $\frac{1}{10}$

(B) $\frac{1}{9}$

(C) 3

(D) 9

NO CALCULATOR SECTION

6. If $f(x) = x^2$ and $g(x) = x + 5$ then what is $g(f(x))$?

(A) $(x + 5)^2$
(B) $x^2 + 5$
(C) $x^2 + x + 5$
(D) $x^3 + 5x$

7. If $f(x) = x^2$ and $g(x) = \frac{1}{x^2}$ then what is $g(f(x))$?

(A) $\frac{1}{x}$

(B) $\frac{1}{x^2}$

(C) $\frac{1}{x^4}$

(D) $\frac{1}{x^3}$

8. If $f(x) = 2^{x-5}$ and $f(b) = 8^3$ then $b =$

(A) 9
(B) 14
(C) 23
(D) 25

NO CALCULATOR SECTION

9. If $f(x) = \sqrt{2x}$ and $g(x) = \frac{1}{\sqrt{3x}}$ then $f(x^2)g(x^2) =$

(A) $\frac{2}{3}$

(B) $\sqrt{\frac{2}{3}}$

(C) $\frac{3}{2}$

(D) $\sqrt{\frac{3}{2}}$

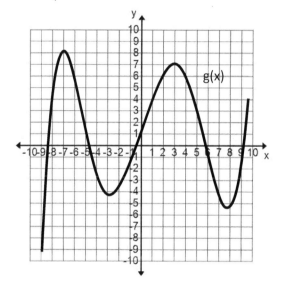

Questions 10-12 relate to the graph shown above.

10. If $g(-7) - g(2) =$

(A) -7
(B) 0
(C) 2
(D) 9

11. The number of turning points in the graph is

(A) 1
(B) 2
(C) 3
(D) 4

NO CALCULATOR SECTION

12. $h(x)$ is a graph (not shown) obtained by moving $g(x) = x - 3$ to the right by 4 units. What is $h(4)$?

(A) -3
(B) -2
(C) 0
(D) 3

13. If $g(x)$ is a function obtained by moving the function $f(x) = 3x + 5$ by 4 units to the right, then what is $g(6)$?

(A) 11
(B) 27
(C) 30
(D) 33

14. If $g(x)$ is a function obtained by moving the function $f(x) = -2x - 1$ by 2 units to the left, then $f(2) \cdot g(2) =$

(A) 5
(B) 9
(C) 25
(D) 45

15. If $g(x)$ is a function obtained by shifting the function $f(x) = 2x^2 - 3$ by 5 units down, what is $g(x)$?

(A) $g(x) = 2x^2 - 3$
(B) $g(x) = 2x^2 - 2$
(C) $g(x) = 2x^2 - 8$
(D) $g(x) = 2x^2 - 15$

NO CALCULATOR SECTION

16. If $g(x)$ is a function obtained by shifting the function $f(x) = \sqrt{3x + 5}$ by 4 units to the right, then what is $g(6)$?

(A) $\sqrt{11}$
(B) $\sqrt{17}$
(C) $\sqrt{35}$
(D) $\sqrt{39}$

17. If $h(x)$ is a function obtained by moving the function $f(x) = 5x^2 + 12$ to the right by 4 units, and then moving 3 units vertically down, then what is $h(2)$?

(A) 10
(B) 15
(C) 20
(D) 29

NO CALCULATOR SECTION

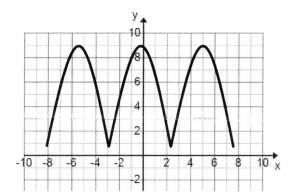

18. The line $y = 4$ intercepts the function shown at how many points?
(A) 3
(B) 4
(C) 5
(D) 6

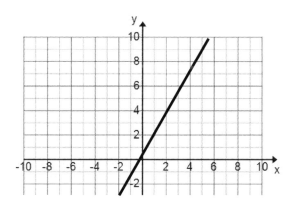

19. The slope of the line shown above, after it is reflected over the y-axis is
(A) -3
(B) -2
(C) 1
(D) 2

NO CALCULATOR SECTION

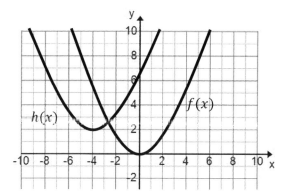

20. The graph of $f(x)$ is shifted to coincide with the graph of $h(x)$. Which of the following is true?
(A) $h(x) = f(x - 4) + 2$
(B) $h(x) = f(x + 4) - 2$
(C) $h(x) = f(x + 4) + 2$
(D) $h(x) = f(x - 4) - 2$

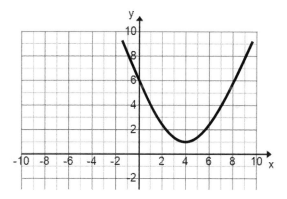

21. If the parabola shown above is moved to the left by 6 units and moved up 4 units, the vertex will be at
(A) $(-4, 5)$
(B) $(-2, -5)$
(C) $(-2, 5)$
(D) $(4, -5)$

NO CALCULATOR SECTION

22. If a function $p(x) = 8x^2 + 24$ is stretched horizontally by a factor of 2, the resulting function will be
(A) $h(x) = 4x^2 + 12$
(B) $h(x) = 2x^2 + 12$
(C) $h(x) = 2x^2 - 24$
(D) $h(x) = 2x^2 + 24$

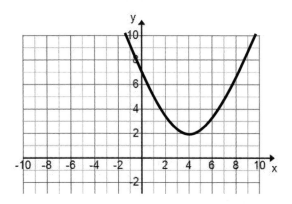

23. If the graph shown above is reflected over the x-axis, the maxima will be intercepted by

(A) $x = 2$
(B) $y = 2$
(C) $y = -2$
(D) $x = -4$

24.

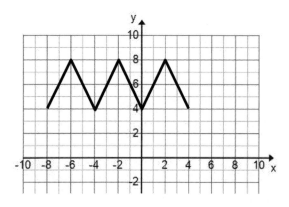

NO CALCULATOR SECTION

If the graph of $f(x)$ shown is transformed to $f(x - 2) + 2$, then which of the graphs below shows the transformation?

(A)

(B)

(C)

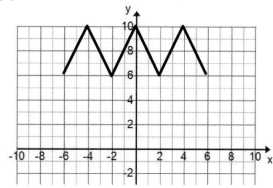

CALCULATOR SECTION

25. A manufactuing company makes wheels for automobiles. The monthly sales revenue of wheels can be modeled as $200\,t^2 + 50t$, where t is the month of the year (January=1, December=12). The monthly cost of manufacturing the wheels can be modeled as $125\,t^2 + 20t$. If the tax on the profits is 20%, which of the following functions can be used to model the tax paid each month?
  (A) $75t^2 - 30t$
  (B) $75t^2 + 30t$
  (C) $15t^2 - 6t$
  (D) $15t^2 + 6t$

26. The polynomial function that can be used to model the number of items sold at a store is $N(t) = 16t^3 - 2t^2 + 13$, where t is the month (Jan=1, Dec=12). The average price of the items each month and can be modeled as $P(t) = 2t + 4$. The function $R(t)$ that can be used to model the revenue from these items is
  (A) $R(t) = 32t^3 + 60t^2 - 8t + 52$
  (B) $R(t) = 32t^4 + 60t^3 - 8t^2 + 26t + 52$
  (C) $R(t) = 32t^4 + 60t^3 - 8t^2 + 26t$
  (D) $R(t) = 32t^4 + 8t^2 + 26t + 52$

CALCULATOR SECTION

$x + 2$

?

Questions 27 and 28 refer to the above figure.

27. The area of a rectangular carpet can be modeled as $x^2 - 2x - 8$, where x is a portion of one side that has a length of $x + 2$. What is the length of the other side?
  (A) $x - 4$
  (B) $x + 4$
  (C) $x - 2$
  (D) $x + 2$

28. If $x = 16$, what is the perimeter of the carpet?
  (A) 30
  (B) 38
  (C) 56
  (D) 60

PASSPORT TO ADVANCED MATH
Lesson 23 — Functions and Transformations — Answers

#	Explanation	Comments
1 D	$f(2) = 3$ $f(g(2)) = f(4) = 7$ So $f(2) \cdot f(g(2)) = 3 \cdot 7 = 21$	Get the function values carefully from the table. For $f(g(2))$, get the value of the inner function $g(2)$ first and then $f(g(2))$.
2 C	It is clear from the table that $g(x)$ values are 3 times the values of $f(x)$. So, $g(x) = 3\, f(x)$.	Note that when $f(x)$ becomes $3f(x)$, the graph of $f(x)$ is vertically compressed by a factor of 3.
3 B	$f(x) = x^2 - 2$ and $g(x) = 2x^2 + 5$ $(f - g)(x) = f(x) - g(x) = x^2 - 2 - (2x^2 + 5)$ $= -x^2 - 7$	Functions can be added, subtracted, multiplied, and divided. Be careful with the negative signs.
4 D	$f(x) = 1 + \frac{1}{x}$ and $g(x) = 1 - \frac{1}{x}$ $(fg)(2) = f(2) \cdot g(2) = \left(1 + \frac{1}{2}\right)\left(1 - \frac{1}{2}\right) = \frac{3}{2} \cdot \frac{1}{2} = \frac{3}{4}$	Note that the notation $(fg)(2)$ is not the same as $f(g(2))$.
5 B	$f(x) = x^2$ and $g(x) = x^4$ $\left(\frac{f}{g}\right)(3) = \frac{f(3)}{g(3)} = \frac{3^2}{3^4} = \frac{1}{3^2} = \frac{1}{9}$	
6 B	$f(x) = x^2$ and $g(x) = x + 5$ $g(f(x)) = g(x^2) = x^2 + 5$	Evaluate the inner function first.
7 C	$f(x) = x^2$ and $g(x) = \frac{1}{x^2}$ $g(f(x)) = g(x^2) = \frac{1}{(x^2)^2} = \frac{1}{x^4}$	Use the power formula $(a^m)^n = a^{mn}$.
8 B	$f(x) = 2^{x-5}$ and $f(b) = 8^3$ $f(b) = 2^{b-5} = 8^3 = (2^3)^3 = 2^9$ So, $b - 5 = 9, b = 14$	
9 B	$f(x) = \sqrt{2x}$ and $g(x) = \frac{1}{\sqrt{3x}}$ $f(x^2) = \sqrt{2x^2} = x\sqrt{2}$ $g(x^2) = \frac{1}{\sqrt{3x^2}} = \frac{1}{x\sqrt{3}}$ $f(x^2)g(x^2) = \sqrt{2x} \cdot \frac{1}{\sqrt{3x}} = \frac{\sqrt{2}}{\sqrt{3}} = \sqrt{\frac{2}{3}}$	
10 C	$g(-7) - g(2) = ?$. Reading from the graph, $g(-7) = 8$ and $g(2) = 6$. So, $8 - 6 = 2$.	
11 D	There are 4 turning points, where the graph turns at its vertices.	Turning point is where the slope is 0.
12 A	$g(x) = x - 3$ When this function is moved to the right by 4 units, the	When $f(x)$ is moved right by k units, the new function is $f(x - k)$.

©GiftOfLogic http://www.GiftOfLogic.com

	new function is $g(x-4) = x - 4 - 3 = x - 7$. So, $h(x) = x - 7$. $h(4) = 4 - 7 = -3$	Refer to the review section to learn about the translation of functions.
13 A	$g(x) = f(x-4) = 3(x-4) + 5 = 3x - 7$ $g(6) = 3 \cdot 6 - 7 = 11$	
14 D	$f(x) = -2x - 1$, move 2 units to the left $g(x) = f(x+2) = -2(x+2) - 1 = -2x - 5$ $f(2) = -4 - 1 = -5 \quad g(2) = -4 - 5 = -9$ $f(2)g(2) = -5 \cdot -9 = 45$	
15 C	$f(x) = 2x^2 - 3$ shifting down $f(x)$ by 5 units gives $f(x) - 5$ $g(x) = f(x) - 5 = 2x^2 - 3 - 5 = 2x^2 - 8$	
16 A	$f(x) = \sqrt{3x+5}$ $g(x) = \sqrt{3(x-4)+5} = \sqrt{3x - 12 + 5}$ $g(x) = \sqrt{3x - 7}$ $g(6) = \sqrt{3 \cdot 6 - 7} = \sqrt{11}$	
17 D	$f(x) = 5x^2 + 12$ after shifting to right by 4 units, $f(x)$ becomes $f(x-4) = g(x) = 5(x-4)^2 + 12$ After shifting 3 units down, $g(x)$ becomes $g(x) - 3 =$ $h(x) = 5(x-4)^2 + 12 - 3 = 5(x-4)^2 + 9$ $h(2) = 5(2-4)^2 + 9 = 29$	shift to the right by 4 and then shift down by 3; process these two transformation separately, one at a time.
18 D	Draw a line y=4 and count the number of intercepts of the line with the function. There are 6 intercepts.	
19 B	Pick 2 points on the line, (0,0) and (2,4) Calculate the slope = $\frac{(y2-y1)}{(x2-x1)} = \frac{4-0}{2-0} = 2$ Equation of line is $y = 2x + 0$ since the y intercept is 0 Equation of reflected line is $y = f(-x) = -2x = mx + b$; So, the slope of the reflected line is -2.	Find the equation of the line using its slope and y-intercept. Then use the fact that if a function $f(x)$ is reflected over the y axis, it becomes $f(-x)$.
20 C	Observe the vertex of $f(x)$. If $f(x)$ is shifted to coincide with $h(x)$, then it has to be moved 4 units to the left and 2 units up. Consider these transformations one at a time. Shifting to the left by 4 units makes $f(x) = f(x + 4)$. Shifting it up again makes it $f(x + 4) + 2$.	Focus on one point or the vertex and see what the transformation steps are. Then process each transformation one at a time.
21 C	Vertex now is at (4,1) Move left by 6 units takes the vertex to (4-6,1)=(-2,1) Moving it up by 4 units takes the vertex to (-2,1+4)=(-2,5)	Evaluate one move at a time to avoid mistakes.
22 D	$p(x) = 8x^2 + 24$ Horizontal stretch by a factor of 2 $p(x)$ will become $p\left(\frac{1}{2}x\right) = 8\left(\frac{x}{2}\right)^2 + 24 = \frac{8x^2}{4} + 24$ $= 2x^2 + 24$	Horizontal stretch formula $f(x)$ becomes $f(\frac{1}{b}x)$, $b > 1$ is horizontal stretch.
23 C	The vertex is originally at (4,2). After reflection over the x axis, the vertex will be at $(4, -2)$. So, a line $y = -2$ will intercept the parabola at it new vertex.	

24 C	$f(x)$ is transformed to $f(x-2)+2$ This means the $f(x)$ was shifted right 2 units and then shifted up 2 units. Pick one point and trace its transformation. The leftmost tip is at $(-8,4)$. After shifting 2 units right and 2 units up, it should be at $(-8+2, 4+2) = (-6,6)$	
25 D	Sales revenue=$200\,t^2 + 50t$ Cost of manufacturing=$125\,t^2 + 20t$ Tax on profit =20% Profit=sales-cost=$200\,t^2 + 50t - (125\,t^2 + 20t)$ $= 200\,t^2 - 125t^2 + 50t - 20t$ $= 75\,t^2 + 30\,t$ Tax = $\frac{20}{100} \cdot$ profit $= 0.2(75\,t^2 + 30t) = 15t^2 + 6t$	Polynomial functions can be subtracted, and operated upon like numbers. This question tests your ability to apply the concept of polynomial operations to a real world problem.
26 B	Items sold each month= $N(t) = 16t^3 - 2t^2 + 13$ Price of items each month= $P(t) = 2t + 4$. Revenue= $N(t) \cdot P(t)=$ $(16t^3 - 2t^2 + 13) \cdot (2t + 4)$ $= 32\,t^4 + 64\,t^3 - 4t^3 - 8t^2 + 26\,t + 52$ $= 32\,t^4 + 60t^3 - 8t^2 + 26\,t + 52$	
27 A	Since $l \cdot w$=area, $(x+2) \cdot w = x^2 - 2x - 8$ You can find w by long division. $$\begin{array}{r} x - 4 \\ x+2\overline{\smash{\big)}\,x^2 - 2x - 8} \\ \underline{-(x^2 + 2x)} \\ 0 - 4x - 8 \\ \underline{-4x - 8} \\ 0 \end{array}$$ Another way is to factorize $x^2 - 2x - 8$ Find p, q such that $pq = -8, p + q = -2$; try $p = -4\ q = 2$ $x^2 - 2x - 8$ $= x^2 - 4x + 2x - 8$ $= x(x-4) + 2(x-4)$ $= (x-4)(x+2)$	Long division is covered in the lesson on Polynomials and Quadratic Equations.
28 D	From the previous question, you know that $x - 4$ and $x + 2$ are the sides of the rectangle. So, the perimeter is $2(l+w) = 2(x-4+x-2) = 2(2x-2) = 4x - 4$. When $x = 16$, the perimeter= $4 \cdot 16 - 4 = 60$ units.	This problem extends your thinking from the previous problem.

PASSPORT TO ADVANCED MATH

Lesson 24 | **Radicals and Fractional Exponents** | **Review**

FOCUSPREP CHECKLIST

- What is a Radical?
- How do I solve a radical equation?
- What is an extraneous solution?
- How do I simplify an expression with fractional exponents?
- Workout practice problems in Radicals

Q1 What is a Radical? What is a Radical Expression?

A1 A radical is represented as $\sqrt[n]{x}$. x is the radicand, n is the index of the radical. $\sqrt[n]{x}$ is called the nth root of x. If n is not specified, it is assumed to be 2. A radical can be a square root, cube root, etc. Note that $\sqrt[n]{x} = x^{\frac{1}{n}}$.

A Radical expression is an expression with one or more terms inside the radical, including terms with variables. **Examples:** $\sqrt{x}$, $\sqrt[3]{x-5}$, $\sqrt{4-x}$, $\frac{1}{\sqrt{9-t}}$.

Q2 How do I simplify a radical expression?

A2 The table below shows the properties of radicals that can be used to simplify a radical expression. Radicals can be added and subtracted, multiplied and divided.

$\sqrt[n]{p} = p^{\frac{1}{n}}$ $\frac{1}{\sqrt[n]{p}} = \frac{1}{p^{\frac{1}{n}}} = p^{-\frac{1}{n}}$	$\sqrt[n]{p^n} = (p^n)^{\frac{1}{n}} = p$	$\sqrt[2]{-1} = i$ (see lesson on Complex Numbers) $\sqrt[3]{-1} = -1$ because $-1 \cdot -1 \cdot -1 = -1$
$\sqrt[n]{pq} = \sqrt[n]{p} \cdot \sqrt[n]{q}$ $(pq)^{\frac{1}{n}} = p^{\frac{1}{n}} q^{\frac{1}{n}}$	$\sqrt[n]{\frac{p}{q}} = \frac{\sqrt[n]{p}}{\sqrt[n]{q}}$	$(3 + \sqrt{7})(3 - \sqrt{7}) = 3^2 - (\sqrt{7})^2$ $= 9 - 7 = 2.$

Q3 Is $\sqrt{x}$ the same as $x^{\frac{1}{2}}$? What is the formula for cube root and n-th root?

A3 The general formula to convert a radical sign to a fractional exponent is $\sqrt[n]{x} = x^{\frac{1}{n}}$. So, $\sqrt[2]{x} = x^{\frac{1}{2}}$, $\sqrt[5]{x} = x^{\frac{1}{5}}$, and so on. As a special case $\sqrt[2]{x}$ is written as $\sqrt{x}$ without the 2.

Examples: Simplify the following radicals.

$\sqrt[3]{27} = \sqrt[3]{3^3} = (3^3)^{\frac{1}{3}} = 3^{3 \cdot \frac{1}{3}} = 3^1 = 3$

$\sqrt[3]{27b^3c^6} = \sqrt[3]{3^3 b^3 c^6} = (3^3 b^3 c^6)^{\frac{1}{3}} = 3bc^2$

$\sqrt[3]{-8c^4} = \sqrt[3]{-2^3 c^3 c} = -2c\sqrt[3]{c}$; cube root of -1 is -1

$3\sqrt[3]{a} + 4\sqrt[3]{a} = 7\sqrt[3]{a}$; add like radicals

$3\sqrt[3]{a} + 4\sqrt[3]{b}$; cannot be added since the radicands are not identical

$3\sqrt[3]{a} + 4\sqrt[3]{ab}$; cannot be added since the radicands are not identical

$3\sqrt[3]{a} - \sqrt[3]{a} = 2\sqrt[3]{a}$; subtract like radicals

$3\sqrt[3]{a} \cdot 4\sqrt[3]{b} = 12\sqrt[3]{ab}$; multiplication property of radical

$3\sqrt[3]{a}(4\sqrt[3]{b} + 2\sqrt[3]{c}) = 12\sqrt[3]{ab} + 6 \cdot \sqrt[3]{ac}$; distributive property $a(b+c) = ab + ac$

$(3 + \sqrt{4})(3 - \sqrt{4}) = 3^2 - (\sqrt{4})^2 = 9 - 4 = 5$; difference of squares $(a+b)(a-b) = a^2 - b^2$

$(3 + \sqrt{5})(2 - \sqrt{7}) = 3 \cdot 2 - 3\sqrt{7} + 2\sqrt{5} - \sqrt{5} \cdot \sqrt{7} = 6 - 3\sqrt{7} + 2\sqrt{5} - \sqrt{35}$; use FOIL to simplify

$\frac{\sqrt{5}}{\sqrt{7}} = \frac{\sqrt{5}}{\sqrt{7}} \cdot \frac{\sqrt{7}}{\sqrt{7}} = \frac{\sqrt{35}}{7}$; multiply both numerator and denominator by the denominator and simplify

$\frac{(3+\sqrt{5})}{(2-\sqrt{7})} = \frac{(3+\sqrt{5})}{(2-\sqrt{7})} \cdot \frac{(2+\sqrt{7})}{(2+\sqrt{7})} = \frac{(6+3\sqrt{7}+2\sqrt{5}+\sqrt{35})}{(4-7)} = -\frac{1}{3} \cdot (6 + 3\sqrt{7} + 2\sqrt{5} + \sqrt{35})$; remove the radical from the denominator, use FOIL to expand the numerator, use difference of squares in the denominator.

Q4 What is a Radical Equation?
A4 When a radical expression is part of an equation, then it is called a radical equation.
Examples: $\sqrt{x} = 16$; $\sqrt[3]{x - 5} = 2$ are radical equations.

Q5 Is $\sqrt{x}$ positive or negative?
A5 While every positive number has two square roots, one positive and one negative, the square root symbol $\sqrt{}$ refers to the **positive** square root only. This is very important to remember while solving radical equations.

Examples
* $\sqrt{4} = +2$ only, it is not -2 ; $\sqrt{}$ by definition, refers to the positive square root only
* If $x^2 = 81$, then $x = \pm\sqrt{81} = \pm 9$ (+9 and -9). Note the $\pm$ sign.
* $\sqrt{9 + 7} = \sqrt{16} = +4$ only; $\sqrt{16}$ is not -4.
* The equation, $\sqrt{x} = -8$, where x is positive does not have any solution, since the $\sqrt{}$ of a positive number cannot be negative. If you solve this equation by squaring both sides, you get $x = 64$, but when

you plug it back into the original equation, you get $\sqrt{64} = +8 <> -8$. Remember that the radical $\sqrt{}$ refers to the positive square root only.

* Note that the equation $x^2 = 9$ has two solutions. Applying the square root on both sides, you get $\sqrt{x^2} = x = \pm\sqrt{9} = +3$ and -3.

* If you are applying the $\sqrt{}$ radical on a number, include the $\pm$ sign. If you are only evaluating the radical expression $\sqrt{}$, then remember that $\sqrt{}$ is defined for a positive number and the result of evaluating a $\sqrt{}$ is a positive number.

Q6 How do I solve a Radical Equation?

A6 If the radical is a square root, then square both sides of the equation to get rid of the radical and simplify. If it is a cube root, raise both sides to the power of 3 and simplify. Apply the rules of rational exponents as required and solve for the variable. Then, verify if the solution is valid by plugging it into the original equation. If the solution satisfies the original equation, only then it is a valid solution. If the solution does not satisfy the original equation, then it is NOT a valid solution. It is an <u>extraneous solution.</u>

Example: Solve for : $\sqrt{x} = 6$;

$\sqrt{x} = 6$;

$(\sqrt{x})^2 = 6^2$; square both sides

$x = 36$; check: $\sqrt{36} = 6$ valid solution

Example: $\sqrt[3]{x-5} = 2$

$(x-5)^{\frac{1}{3}} = 2$; write the radical in exponential form

$(x-5)^{\frac{1}{3} \cdot 3} = 2^3$; cube both sides to remove the exponent

$(x-5) = 8$

$x = 13$

Check $\sqrt[3]{13-5} = \sqrt[3]{8} = 2$ ok

Example: $\sqrt[5]{x} = 3$

$x^{\frac{1}{5}} = 3$

$\left(x^{\frac{1}{5}}\right)^5 = 3^5$; raise both sides to the fifth power

$x = 3^5$; check $\sqrt[5]{3^5} = 3$

Q7 How do I find if a solution is an <u>extraneous solution</u>?

A7 When solving a radical equation, you may end up with solutions that do not hold true when you plug them back into the original equation. These solutions are called **extraneous solutions** and must be discarded.

Not all radical equations have a valid solution. After you arrive at a solution, you must verify it by plugging it back into the radical equation. Only after the solution is verified, it is a valid solution. This is because of the fact that during the simplification process (by squaring or cubing both sides), you end up with a new equation, whose solution may or may not be valid for the original radical equation that you started with.

In summary, verify your result against the original radical equation to decide if it is a valid solution or an **extraneous** solution. A valid solution will yield equal values on both sides of the equation. An extraneous solution will not.

Example: Solve $\sqrt{x-3} + 6 = 5$
$\sqrt{x-3} = 5 - 6 = -1$; isolate the radical to one side
$(\sqrt{x-3})^2 = (-1)^2$; square both sides
$x - 3 = 1$
$x = 3 + 1 = 4$
Check the solution: $\sqrt{4-3} + 6 = 5; 1 + 6 = 7 \neq 5$; Note that $\sqrt{4-3} = +1$ only, not -1.
So, $x = 4$ is not a solution to the radical equation. It is an **extraneous solution** that popped up during the solution finding process but it does not check out when plugged into the original radical equation.

Example: Solve $\sqrt{x+7} = x + 5$
$(x + 7) = (x + 5)^2$; square both sides to remove the radical
$x + 7 = x^2 + 10x + 25$
$x^2 + 9x + 18 = 0$
$x^2 + 6x + 3x + 18 = 0$
$x(x + 6) + 3(x + 6) = 0$
$(x + 6)(x + 3) = 0$
$x = -6$ and $x = -3$
Verify the solutions:
when $x = -6, \sqrt{x+7} = \sqrt{-6+7} = 1$ and $x + 5 = -6 + 5 = -1$. So, $x = -6$ is not a solution.
when $x = -3, \sqrt{x+7} = \sqrt{-3+7} = 2$ and $x + 5 = -3 + 5 = 2$. So, $x = -3$ is a solution.
The **extraneous solution** is $x = -6$ and this is discarded. The **only solution** is $x = -3$.

Q8 What is a Rational exponent? How do I simplify rational exponents?

A8 A Rational exponent (fractional exponent) takes the form of $x^{\frac{m}{n}}$; $n \neq 0$. For example, $x^{\frac{1}{2}}, x^{\frac{5}{7}}$ are rational exponents. Rational exponents can also take the form of $a^{x/3}$ where the variable is in the exponent. Rational exponents follow the same rules as integer exponents.

Formula	Examples
$x^m x^n = x^{m+n}$	$2^{\frac{2}{3}} 2^{\frac{1}{3}} = 2^{\left(\frac{2}{3}+\frac{1}{3}\right)} = 2^1 = 2$
$\dfrac{x^m}{x^n} = x^{m-n}$	$\dfrac{5^{\frac{2}{3}}}{5^{\frac{1}{3}}} = 5^{(2/3 - 1/3)} = 5^{\frac{1}{3}}$
$x^{\frac{m}{n}} = (x^m)^{1/n} = (x^{1/n})^m$	$8^{\frac{2}{3}} = (8^2)^{\frac{1}{3}} = \left(8^{\frac{1}{3}}\right)^2 = 2^2 = 4$ $8^{\frac{x}{3}} = (2^3)^{\frac{x}{3}} = 2^{\frac{3x}{3}} = (2^x)^{\frac{2}{3}}$

$x^0 = 1$	$9 \cdot 15^0 = 9 \cdot 1 = 9$
$x^{-1} = \dfrac{1}{x}$	$\left(\dfrac{2}{3}\right)^{-1} = \dfrac{1}{\frac{2}{3}} = \dfrac{3}{2}$
$x^{-m} = \dfrac{1}{x^m}$	$8^{-\frac{1}{3}} = (2^3)^{-\frac{1}{3}} = 2^{3 \cdot -\frac{1}{3}} = 2^{-1} = \dfrac{1}{2}$

Examples:

* $\sqrt[5]{2^5} = (2^5)^{\frac{1}{5}} = 2^{5 \cdot \frac{1}{5}} = 2^1 = 2$
* $27^{-\frac{2}{3}} = ((27)^{\frac{1}{3}})^{-2} = \left(3^{3 \cdot \frac{1}{3}}\right)^{-2} = 3^{-2} = \dfrac{1}{3^2} = \dfrac{1}{9}$
* If $8 = 2^{4x}$ find x. $8 = 2^3 = 2^{4x}$ So, since the base is eth same, exponents will be the same.
$3 = 4x => x = \dfrac{4}{3}$

Q9 How are radical equations used in real life?

A9 Radical equations appear frequently in Physics, Chemistry, and Biology. The following example shows how they may appear in a real life situation.

Example: A metallurgist found that the time T it takes in seconds to heat a circular metallic plate of radius R inches to a temperature of 120 degrees Fahrenheit is given by the following equation:
$R = \dfrac{3\pi}{\sqrt{T}}$. How long does it take to heat a circular plate of radius 5 inches to 120 degrees Fahrenheit?

Solution: Notice that the equation is a radical equation. Rearrange to get T to the numerator.
$\sqrt{T} = \dfrac{3\pi}{R}$
$(\sqrt{T})^2 = \left(\dfrac{3\pi}{R}\right)^2$; square both sides
$T = \left(\dfrac{3\pi}{R}\right)^2 = \dfrac{9\pi^2}{R^2}$
So, $T = \dfrac{9\pi^2}{R^2}$
For a circular plate of radius=5 inches, the time to heat is= $\dfrac{9\pi^2}{5^2} = 3.55$ seconds.

PASSPORT TO ADVANCED MATH

Lesson 24 — Radicals and Fractional Exponents — Practice

NO CALCULATOR SECTION

1. If $\sqrt{x+1} = \sqrt{2x-5}$ then $x =$
   (A) 2
   (B) 4
   (C) 6
   (D) 7

2. If $a = 1$, and $b = -1$, then $\sqrt{a^2 + b^2 + 2ab} =$
   (A) 0
   (B) 1
   (C) 2
   (D) 4

3. If $8^2 \, 8^3 \, 8^x = 2^y$, what is x in terms of y?
   (A) $y + 3$
   (B) $\dfrac{y+15}{3}$
   (C) $\dfrac{y-15}{3}$
   (D) $y - 15$

4. If $\dfrac{1}{\sqrt{x-2}} = 5$, and $x > 2$, then $x =$
   (A) $\dfrac{25}{50}$
   (B) $\dfrac{25}{40}$
   (C) $\dfrac{50}{25}$
   (D) $\dfrac{51}{25}$

NO CALCULATOR SECTION

5. If $\sqrt{2^2 \cdot x} = 16$, then $x =$
   (A) 4
   (B) 16
   (C) 32
   (D) 64

6. What is the absolute value of the extraneous solution of x in the equation $x + 1 = \sqrt{5 - x}$.
   GRID IN

7. If $\sqrt{2^{-3z}} = 8$, then $z =$
   (A) -3
   (B) -2
   (C) 2
   (D) 3

8. If $\sqrt{3} \, \sqrt{bc} = d$, what is b in terms of d and c?
   (A) $\dfrac{d}{c}$
   (B) $\dfrac{d^2}{3c}$
   (C) $\dfrac{c^2}{3d}$
   (D) $\dfrac{d}{2c}$

NO CALCULATOR SECTION

9. If $\sqrt{(k-1)a} = \sqrt{2a}$ then $k =$
(A) 0
(B) 1
(C) 2
(D) 3

10. If $\frac{1}{(a+\sqrt{5})(a-\sqrt{5})} = \frac{1}{20}$, then a could be
(A) -6
(B) -5
(C) 1
(D) 6

11. If $\frac{100^{-p}}{100^{-q}} = 10^2$, then $p - q$ is
(A) -3
(B) 0
(C) -1
(D) 1

12. If $p^2 p^{-x} = p^4$ and $q^{-2}q^y = q^6$, then $x + y =$
(A) -2
(B) 4
(C) 6
(D) 10

NO CALCULATOR SECTION

13. If $2^{-1}\, 2^0\, 2^1 = 2^z$, then $z =$
(A) 0
(B) 1
(C) 2
(D) 3

14. If $\sqrt[3]{a^6 b^{15}} = b^3$, then $a^2 b^2 =$
(A) $\frac{1}{2}$
(B) $\frac{1}{3}$
(C) $\frac{1}{4}$
(D) 1

15. If $a^{-\frac{5}{2}} = 2^5$, then $a =$
(A) $\frac{1}{8}$
(B) $\frac{1}{4}$
(C) $\frac{1}{2}$
(D) 1

CALCULATOR SECTION

16. In Physics, the motion of a falling object is given by the formula $s = ut + \frac{1}{2}gt^2$, where s is the distance traveled in time t, u is the initial velocity in m/s, and g is the gravitational constant of $9.8 \ m/s^2$. If the initial velocity of an object is 0 m/s, how many seconds will it take for an object to fall a distance of 500 meters?
(A) 6.10
(B) 10.10
(C) 20.20
(D) 102.04

CALCULATOR SECTION

17. When an object is in motion, its velocity v is related to its kinetic energy E, and its mass m, by the formula $v = \sqrt{\frac{2E}{m}}$. If the velocity of an object of mass $m2$ is twice the velocity of an object of mass $m1$, and the kinetic energy of both objects are the same, then what is the ratio of $\frac{m1}{m2}$?
GRID IN

PASSPORT TO ADVANCED MATH

Lesson 24 | Radicals and Fractional Exponents | Answers

#	Explanation	Comments
1 C	$\sqrt{x+1} = \sqrt{2x-5}$ $x + 1 = 2x - 5$; square both sides $x - 2x = -5 - 1$ $-x = -6$ $x = 6$; verify the solution in the original equation $\sqrt{6+1} = \sqrt{7} = \sqrt{2 \cdot 6 - 5} = \sqrt{7}$	Be careful with negative signs.
2 A	$a = 1$, and $b = -1$ $\sqrt{a^2 + b^2 + 2ab} =$ $\sqrt{1 + (-1)^2 + 2 \cdot 1 \cdot (-1)}$ $\sqrt{1 + 1 - 2} = \sqrt{0} = 0$	
3 C	$8^2 \, 8^3 \, 8^x = 2^y$ $2^{3 \cdot 2} \, 2^{3 \cdot 3} \, 2^{3x} = 2^y$ $2^6 \, 2^9 \, 2^{3x} = 2^y$ $2^{15+3x} = 2^y$ $15 + 3x = y$ $x = \dfrac{y - 15}{3}$	Use the property of exponents $a^m a^n = a^{m+n}$.
4 D	$\dfrac{1}{\sqrt{x-2}} = 5$ $\dfrac{1}{x-2} = 5^2 = 25$; square both sides $x - 2 = \dfrac{1}{25}$ $x = 2 + \dfrac{1}{25} = \dfrac{51}{25}$	
5 D	$\sqrt{2^2 \cdot x} = 16$ $2^2 x = 16^2 = 256$ $4x = 256$; $x = \dfrac{256}{4} = 64$	
6 4	$x + 1 = \sqrt{5 - x}$ $(x + 1)^2 = 5 - x$ $x^2 + 2x + 1 = 5 - x$ $x^2 + 3x - 4 = 0$ $x^2 + 4x - x - 4 = 0$ $x(x + 4) - 1(x + 4) = 0$ $(x + 4)(x - 1) = 0$	Note that the extraneous solution is $x = -4$, but the question asks for the absolute value of the extraneous solution. So $|-4| = 4$.

		$x = -4$ and $x = 1$ Verify the solutions; If $x = -4, x + 1 = -4 + 1 = -3 =$ $\sqrt{5 - (-4)} = \sqrt{9} = 3$ invalid $-$ extraneous If $x = 1, x + 1 = 1 + 1 = 2 = \sqrt{5 - 1} = \sqrt{4}$ $= 2$ valid	Remember that $\sqrt{9} = +3$, by definition. It is not -3. Review the lesson to understand this. If you assumed that $\sqrt{9} = -3$, then $x = -4$ would appear to be a valid solution, but that is incorrect.
7	B	$\sqrt{2^{-3z}} = 8$ $2^{-3z} = 8^2 = (2^3)^2 = 2^6$;squaring both sides $-3z = 6$ $z = -2$	
8	B	$\sqrt{3}\sqrt{bc} = d$ $\sqrt{3bc} = d$ $3bc = d^2$ $b = \dfrac{d^2}{3c}$	use $\sqrt{p}\sqrt{q} = \sqrt{pq}$ you can simplify directly as well by squaring the first step itself $\sqrt{3}\sqrt{bc} = d$; square each term $3bc = d^2$ $b = \dfrac{d^2}{3c}$
9	D	$\sqrt{(k-1)a} = \sqrt{2a}$; squaring both sides $(k-1)a = 2a$ $k - 1 = 2$ $k = 3$	
10	B	$\dfrac{1}{(a+\sqrt{5})(a-\sqrt{5})} = \dfrac{1}{20}$ $(a+\sqrt{5})(a-\sqrt{5}) = 20$ $a^2 - (\sqrt{5})^2 = 20$ $a^2 - 5 = 20$ $a^2 = 25$ $a = \pm\sqrt{25} = \pm 5$	Observe the equation for a few seconds; you can take the reciprocal of both sides; also use the difference of squares formula. Note that when $a^2 = 25$, then $a = \pm\sqrt{25}$. The $\pm$ sign is important, since the negative sign brings in $-\sqrt{25}$ as the solution in addition to $+\sqrt{25}$. If you wrote $a = \sqrt{25}$, that would include only $+5$ as the solution which is incorrect. Note that while a could be $+5$ or -5, only -5 is available in the answer choices.
11	C	$\dfrac{100^{-p}}{100^{-q}} = 10^2$ $\dfrac{(10^2)^{-p}}{(10^2)^{-q}} = 10^2$	

	$\dfrac{10^{-2p}}{10^{-2q}} = 10^{2q-2p} = 10^2$ $2q - 2p = 2(q - p) = 2$ $q - p = 1$ Multiply by -1 on both sides, you get $p - q = -1$.	
12 C	$p^2 p^{-x} = p^4$ $p^{2-x} = p^4$ $2 - x = 4$ $x = 2 - 4 = -2$ $q^{-2} q^y = q^6$ $q^{y-2} = q^6$ $y - 2 = 6; y = 8$ so, $x + y = -2 + 8 = 6$	Pause and observe the equations; from one equation you can get x, and from the other equation you can get y; the question simply asks you the sum of x and y. Pausing and observing the problem for a few seconds is an effective time saving strategy to attack a problem.
13 A	$2^{-1}\, 2^0\, 2^1 = 2^z$, $2^{-1+0+1} = 2^0 = 2^z$ so, $z = 0$	0 is a valid exponent.
14 D	$\sqrt[3]{a^6 b^{15}} = b^3$, $(a^6 b^{15})^{\tfrac{1}{3}} = b^3$ $a^{\tfrac{6}{3}} b^{\tfrac{15}{3}} = b^3$ $a^2 b^5 = b^3$; $\dfrac{a^2 b^5}{b^3} = 1$ $a^2 b^2 = 1$	Use properties of exponents to simplify.
15 B	$a^{-\tfrac{5}{2}} = 2^5$ $\left(a^{-\tfrac{1}{2}}\right)^5 = 2^5$ $a^{-\tfrac{1}{2}} = 2$; $a^{-\tfrac{1}{2} \cdot -2} = 2^{-2}$; make the exponent=1 by multiplying by -2 $a^1 = 2^{-2} = \dfrac{1}{2^2} = \dfrac{1}{4}$	Manipulate the exponents to get the required exponent; if you have $a^{-\tfrac{1}{2}}$ and want to get a^1, multiply the exponent by -2, $a^{-\tfrac{1}{2} \cdot -2} = a^1$.
16 B	The question asks for time it takes for an object to fall 500 meters, but the equation is for the distance. So, rearrange the equation to express t in terms of other variables. $s = ut + \dfrac{1}{2} g t^2$	Rearrange the equation and then use your calculator to get the results.

	$s = 0 \cdot t + \frac{1}{2}gt^2$ $t = \sqrt{\frac{2s}{g}}$ Plug in $s = 500$ and $g = 9.8$ to get $t = 10.10$.	
17 4	Though strange looking, this problem is easy to solve; there are 2 objects, of mass $m1$ and $m2$. Let $v1$ and $v2$ be their velocities. Their kinetic energies are the same. $v1 = \sqrt{\frac{2E}{m1}}; \quad v2 = \sqrt{\frac{2E}{m2}}$ $v2 = 2v1$ - given fact So, $\sqrt{\frac{2E}{m2}} = 2\sqrt{\frac{2E}{m1}}$; square both sides $\frac{2E}{m2} = 4\frac{2E}{m1}$; don't forget to square the 2 Therefore, $\frac{m1}{m2} = 4$	Set up the equation and review the question to see what is asked. Then, isolate the variables and simplify to answer the question.

CHAPTER 4 ADDITIONAL TOPICS IN MATHEMATICS	
Lesson	**Title**
Lesson 25	Lines and Angles
Lesson 26	Triangles
Lesson 27	Pythagorean Theorem
Lesson 28	Circles
Lesson 29	Polygons
Lesson 30	Volume of Solids
Lesson 31	Complex Numbers
Lesson 32	Trigonometry
Lesson 33	Radians

ADDITIONAL TOPICS IN MATHEMATICS

Lesson 25 — Lines and Angles — Review

> **FOCUSPREP CHECKLIST**
> - How are angles classified?
> - What are complementary and supplementary angles?
> - What is a transversal? What is a vertical angle?
> - What are the line related formulas in the coordinate plane?
> - Workout practice problems in Lines and Angles

Q1 What is an angle and how are angles classified?

A1 An angle is the space created between two intersecting rays. They are classified as follows.

Acute Angle		Acute angles are angles that are greater than 0 degrees and less than 90 degrees.
Right Angle		Right angles are angles that are exactly 90 degrees.
Obtuse Angle		Obtuse angles are angles that are greater than 90 degrees and less than 180 degrees.
Straight Angle		A straight angle is an angle of exactly 180 degrees.

©GiftOfLogic http://www.GiftOfLogic.com

Q2 When are two angles complementary or supplementary?

A2 Complementary angles are two angles that add up to 90 degrees. Supplementary angles are two angles that add up to 180 degrees.

Supplementary   Complementary

 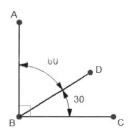

Q3 What are Vertical angles?

A3 Vertical angles are opposite angles created by two intersecting lines. Vertical angles are always equal. **Example**: In the diagram below, the two angles represented as x° and y° are vertical angles.

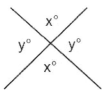

Q4 What is a Transversal and how does it affect parallel lines?

A4 When a line cuts through two coplanar lines, it is called a Transversal. When the coplanar lines are parallel as shown below, the angles formed have relationships as described.

Corresponding angles: Angles that lie on the same side of the transversal and also on the same side of lines AB and CD. Corresponding angles are equal. For example ∠EGA = ∠EHC. ∠EGB = ∠EHD.
Alternate interior angles: Interior non-adjacent angles that are on opposite sides of the transversal. Alternate interior angles are equal. For example ∠AGF = ∠EHD. ∠BGF = ∠EHC
Alternate exterior angles: Exterior non-adjacent angles that are on opposite sides of the transversal. They are equal. ∠EGA = ∠DHF. ∠EGB = ∠CHF.
Same side interior angles: Interior angles that are on the same side of the transversal. They are not equal. ∠AGF <> CHE.

Q5 What are the line related formulas in the coordinate plane?

A5 The general formula of a line is $y = mx + b$ where m is the slope and b is the y-intercept. The slope of a line (m) is calculated using two points $(x1, y1)$ and $(x2, y2)$ that are on the line using the formula $m = \frac{y2-y1}{x2-x1}$. If you know the slope m and one point $(x1, y1)$ on the line, you can use the point-slope formula to find the equation of the line: $y - y1 = m(x - x1)$. If two lines are parallel, then they have the same slope but different y-intercepts. If two lines with slopes $m1$ and $m2$ are perpendicular, then the product of their slopes is -1; that is, $m1 \cdot m2 = -1$.

ADDITIONAL TOPICS IN MATHEMATICS

Lesson 25 — Lines and Angles — Practice

NO CALCULATOR SECTION

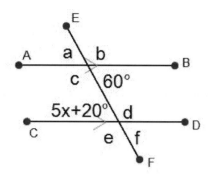

1. In the figure above, what is the value of $x + f$?
    (A) 60
    (B) 65
    (C) 68
    (D) 120

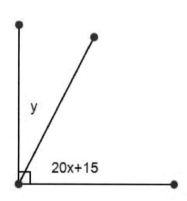

2. In the figure above, what is the value of angle y in terms of x?
    (A) $-20x + 75$
    (B) $-20x - 75$
    (C) $20x + 75$
    (D) $20x - 75$

NO CALCULATOR SECTION

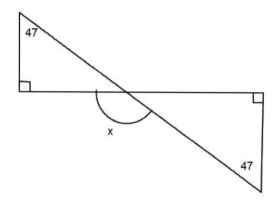

3. In the diagram above, what is the value of x?
    (A) 47
    (B) 94
    (C) 137
    (D) 180

4. In the diagram below, what is the value of angle z?
    (A) 25
    (B) 50
    (C) 65
    (D) 90

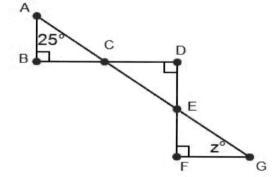

NO CALCULATOR SECTION

5. The equation of the line that is parallel to the line $y = -5x + 21$ could be
(A) $y = -21x + 5$
(B) $y = -5x - 25$
(C) $y = -3x - 21$
(D) $y = 5x - 21$

6. The y-intercept of the line that passes through the point (6,3) and is parallel to the line $y = 3x + 2$ is
(A) −15
(B) −2
(C) 2
(D) 15

7. The lines $y = 3x + 2$ and $2y = 6x + 4$ are
(A) Parallel since they have the same slope
(B) Perpendicular since they have the same slope
(C) Parallel since they have the same slope and same y-intercepts
(D) Not parallel since they have the same slope and same y-intercepts

NO CALCULATOR SECTION

8. A line perpendicular to the line $y = -5x + 21$ could be
(A) $y = -\frac{1}{5}(x - 1)$
(B) $y = \frac{1}{5}(x - 1)$
(C) $y = \frac{1}{5}(2x - 1)$
(D) $y = 5x - 21$

9. The y-intercept of the line that passes through the point (6,3) and is perpendicular to the line $y = 3x + 2$ is
(A) −5
(B) −2
(C) 5
(D) 6

10. The lines $y = 3x + 2$ and $y = -\frac{1}{3}x + 2$ are
(A) Parallel since the product of their slopes is -1
(B) Perpendicular since the product of their slopes is -1
(C) Parallel since they have the same y-intercepts
(D) Perpendicular since they have the same y-intercepts

ADDITIONAL TOPICS IN MATHEMATICS

Lesson 25 — Lines and Angles — Answers

#	Explanation	Comments
1 C	$\angle a$ and $60°$ are vertical angles – so $\angle a = 60°$. $\angle a$ and $5x + 20$ are corresponding angles and so they are equal. $5x + 20 = 60$. So, $x = 8$. Since $\angle a$ and $\angle f$ are opposite exterior angles, they are equal – so $\angle f = \angle a = 60°$. So, $x + f = 8 + 60 == 68°$	Parallel lines- corresponding and vertical angles.
2 A	$\angle y$ and $\angle 20x + 15$ are complementary. So $y + 20x + 15 = 90$. $y + 20x = 75$. $y = -20x + 75$.	The sum of two complementary angles is 90.
3 C	The third angle of the triangle is $180 - 90 - 47 = 43°$. Since the straight angle is $180°$, $x + 43 = 180$; $x = 180 - 43 = 137°$.	A straight angle is 180 degrees.
4 C	$\angle BAC = 25°$. Since $\triangle ABC$ is a right triangle, $\angle ACB = 90 - 25 = 65°$. Using vertical angles, $\angle DCE = 65°$ as well. This means that $\angle DEC = 180 - 90 - 65 = 25°$ and so $\angle FEG = 25°$. Since $\triangle EFG$ is also a right triangle, $\angle z = 180 - 90 - 25 = 65°$.	
5 B	The slope of $y = -5x + 21$ is -5. The line parallel to this line must have the same slope and must have a different y-intercept other than 21. $y = -5x - 25$ satisfies this condition. Note the "could be" in the question. There can be any number of lines parallel to $y = -5x + 21$ as long as the slope is the same and y-intercept is different.	Parallel lines must have the same slope but different y-intercept
6 A	The slope of the line $y = 3x + 2$ is 3. The slope of the line parallel to this line must also be 3. Since the parallel line passes through (6,3), using the point slope formula, you get $y - 3 = 3(x - 6)$ which simplifies to $y = 3x - 15$.	
7 D	One of the lines $2y = 6x + 4$ can be simplified as $y = 3x + 2$. This is the same as the other line. So, they are not parallel since they have same slope and the same y-intercept.	
8 B	The line perpendicular to $y = -5x + 21$ must have a slope of $-\frac{1}{m}$, where m is the slope of this line (=−5). So, the slope of the perpendicular line is $-\frac{1}{-5} = +\frac{1}{5}$. Only choice B has an equation with this slope. Note the "could be" in the question. There can be any number of perpendiculars, each with a slope of $\frac{1}{5}$ but with a different y-intercept. In choice C, the slope is $\frac{2}{5}$, not $\frac{1}{5}$.	If the slope of a line is m, the slope of its perpendicular is $-\frac{1}{m}$.
9 C	The slope of $y = 3x + 2$ is 3. The slope of its perpendicular is $-\frac{1}{3}$. It is given that this perpendicular line passes through (6,3). So, since you know the slope and the coordinates of a point, use the point slope formula. $y - y1 = m(x - x1)$; $y - 3 = -\frac{1}{3}(x - 6)$; bring this to the form of $y = mx + b$ $y = -\frac{1}{3}x + 2 + 3$; $y = \frac{1}{3}x + 5$. So, the y-intercept is 5.	When you know the slope and a point, use the point slope formula.
10 B	Just glancing the equations of the two lines indicates that the slope of one line m1 is 3 and the slope of the other line m2 is $-\frac{1}{3}$. So, $m1 \cdot m2 = -1$.	

©GiftOfLogic   http://www.GiftOfLogic.com

ADDITIONAL TOPICS IN MATHEMATICS

| Lesson 26 | Triangles | Review |

> **FOCUSPREP CHECKLIST**
> - How do I identify congruent and similar triangles?
> - What are the special properties of an equilateral triangle?
> - What is a triangle inequality?
> - Workout practice problems in Triangles

Q1 What are the different types of triangles?

A1 Triangles are classified as shown below.

Type	Remarks	Example
Acute triangle	All three angles are less than 90°	50°, 60°, 70°
Obtuse triangle	Has one angle greater than 90° and less than 180°	30°, 40°, 100°
Right triangle	Has one angle equal to 90°	30°, 60°, 90°
Equilateral triangle	All three sides are congruent	5,5,5 side lengths
Isosceles triangle	Two sides are congruent	3,5,5 side lengths
Scalene triangle	No congruent sides	10,11,12 side lengths

Q2 What is a special condition of right triangles?

A2 Right triangles can contain similar triangles inside them as shown below:

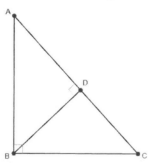

In the picture above, triangle ADB is similar to triangle ABC. Using this information you get:

$$\frac{AD}{AB} = \frac{AB}{AC} = \frac{BD}{BC}$$

Special properties of right triangles that have 30-60-90 or 45-45-90 angles are discussed in the lesson on Pythagorean theorem.

Q3 What are some special properties of equilateral triangles?

A3 An equilateral triangle has three equal sides and three equal angles of 60 degrees. The area of an equilateral triangle can be calculated with one side length as shown below:

©GiftOfLogic http://www.GiftOfLogic.com

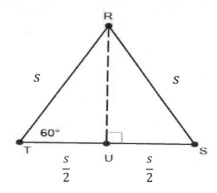

Drop a perpendicular line to side TS from R. This creates two congruent triangles using the SAS rule. So U bisects side TS.

Using the special rules of 30-60-90 triangles, RU equals $\sqrt{s^2 - \left(\frac{s}{2}\right)^2} = \frac{s\sqrt{3}}{2}$. Using this height, you find that the area of the equilateral triangle is $\frac{1}{2} \cdot s \cdot \frac{s\sqrt{3}}{2} = \frac{s^2\sqrt{3}}{4}$.

Q4 What are some special properties of an isosceles triangle?

A4 An isosceles triangle has two sides that are congruent(equal) and the angles opposite to the equal sides are also equal. The side that is not congruent to the other sides is the base. The altitude drawn to the base will bisect the base and it also bisects the vertex angle.

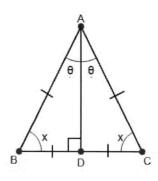

In the figure shown, triangle ABC is isosceles because it has two congruent sides AB and AC. So, AB=AC. Since the angles opposite to the congruent sides are equal, $\angle ACB = \angle ABC$. AD is an altitude drawn to the base BC. AD bisects the base. So, BD=DC. AD also bisects the vertex angle. So, ∠BAD=∠CAD.

The area of the isosceles triangle is $\frac{1}{2} \cdot b \cdot h = \frac{1}{2} \cdot BC \cdot AD$, where the height AD can be calculated using the Pythagorean theorem using AB and BD, where $BD = \frac{BC}{2}$.

Q5 What is Triangle Inequality and how is it used?

A5 The triangle inequality states that when the lengths of the two shorter sides of a triangle are added together, they must be greater than the longest side. This provides a constraint for the side lengths of a triangle. If $a, b,$ and c are the three side lengths of a triangle, and $a < b < c$, then $a + b > c$.

Triangle inequality is used to determine if three given lengths can form the sides of a triangle.
Examples:
Triangle with sides 6,7,7 satisfies the triangle inequality since $6 + 7 > 7$
Triangle with sides 4,3,5 satisfies the triangle inequality since $3 + 4 > 5$
Triangle with sides (6,8,13) satisfies the triangle inequality since $6 + 8 > 13$
Triangle with sides 1,2,3 does not satisfy the triangle inequality since $1 + 2 = 3$
Triangle with sides 1,3,5 does not satisfy the triangle inequality since $1 + 3 < 3$

Q6 What does Congruent mean and how can I determine if two triangles are congruent?

A6 Congruent means that two triangles have the exact same side lengths and angles. There are five ways to determine if two given triangles are congruent, as listed below.

SSS-Side, Side, Side		Two triangles are congruent when all three sides have the same lengths.
ASA-Angle Side Angle		Two triangles are congruent when two angles and the side in between are the same.
SAS-Side Angle Side		Two triangles are congruent when two sides and the angle in between are the same.
AAS-Angle Angle Side		Two triangles are congruent when two angles and a non-included side are the same.
HL-Hypotenuse Leg		Two triangles are congruent if the hypotenuse and one leg are of the same length.

Q7 What is Triangle similarity and how do I determine if two triangles are similar?

A7 Triangles are similar if they are of the same shape, but are of different sizes:

AA-Angle Angle	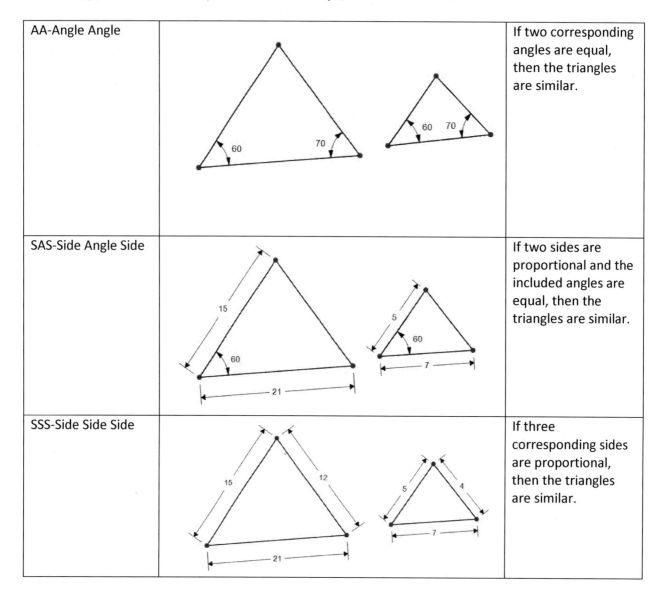	If two corresponding angles are equal, then the triangles are similar.
SAS-Side Angle Side		If two sides are proportional and the included angles are equal, then the triangles are similar.
SSS-Side Side Side		If three corresponding sides are proportional, then the triangles are similar.

ADDITIONAL TOPICS IN MATHEMATICS

Lesson 26 — Triangles — Practice

NO CALCULATOR SECTION

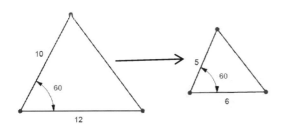

1. By what rule and scale factor are the triangles similar?

    (A) AA, 2
    (B) AA, 0.5
    (C) SAS, 2
    (D) SAS, 0.5

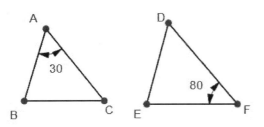

2. If triangle ABC is similar to triangle DEF, what is the measure of angle ABC?

    (A) 30
    (B) 50
    (C) 70
    (D) 80

NO CALCULATOR SECTION

3. In the figure shown, $\overline{BD}$ bisects side $\overline{AC}$. The triangles that are congruent are

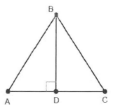

   (A) ABD and CAD
   (B) ABC and ADC
   (C) ABD and ABC
   (D) DBA and DBC

4. In the figure above, what value of x makes the two triangles congruent?

    (A) 40
    (B) 50
    (C) 60
    (D) 70

NO CALCULATOR SECTION

5. What side length of an equilateral triangle gives it an area of $25\sqrt{3}$?
GRID IN

6. If the two shorter sides of a triangle are 5 and 6, what is the greatest possible integer value of the third side?
GRID IN

CALCULATOR SECTION

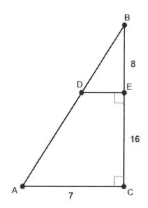

7. Based on the figure above, which of the following is closest to the value of DE?
- (A) 2.33
- (B) 3.50
- (C) 7
- (D) 12.5

CALCULATOR SECTION

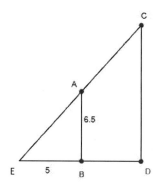

8. A man, represented by line AB, is $6\frac{1}{2}$ feet tall. The man's shadow, EB, is 5 feet long. A tree, represented by line CD, is three times taller than the man. Based on this information, what is the distance (BD) between the man and the tree?
- (A) 2.5
- (B) 5
- (C) 10
- (D) 15

9. Can a triangle have side lengths of 8, 12, and 20?
- (A) Yes
- (B) No
- (C) Sometimes
- (D) Insufficient Information

CALCULATOR SECTION

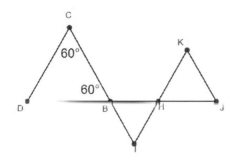

10. In the figure above, DJ has a length of 1200. If the three triangles shown are similar, what is the sum of their perimeters?

(A) 1200
(B) 2400
(C) 3600
(D) $3600\sqrt{2}$

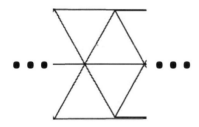

11. Tiles shaped like equilateral triangles are put together as shown above. Each triangle has a side length of 1 foot. To the nearest tenths, how many triangular tiles are needed for 100 square feet of tiling?

(A) 230.9
(B) 231.0
(C) 231.9
(D) 239.0

CALCULATOR SECTION

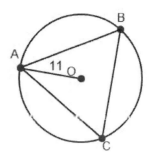

12. An equilateral triangle is inscribed in a circle with a radius of 11. What is the area of the triangle?

A) $\frac{121\sqrt{3}}{4}$

B) $\frac{363\sqrt{3}}{4}$

C) $121\sqrt{3}$

D) $242\sqrt{3}$

13. As shown in the diagram, a hexagon is broken into 15 smaller equilateral triangles and a large equilateral triangle with a side length of 12. What is the area of the hexagon?

A) $70\sqrt{3}$
B) $72\sqrt{3}$
C) $96\sqrt{3}$
D) $108\sqrt{3}$

CALCULATOR SECTION

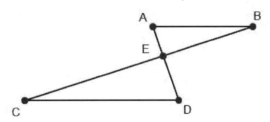

14. Which of the following postulates prove that the two triangles shown above are congruent?

  I. ASA
  II. SAS
  III. AAS

A) I and II only
B) II and III only
C) I and III only
D) I, II and III only

15. In the diagram shown above, AE has a length of 3. AD has a length of 9. AB and CD are parallel. What is the ratio of the area of triangle CED to triangle AEB?
GRID IN

CALCULATOR SECTION

16. A 10 feet long string is cut into 3 pieces and the pieces are arranged to form an isosceles triangle. How many distinct isosceles triangles can be created assuming that the pieces are of integral length?
GRID IN

	ADDITIONAL TOPICS IN MATHEMATICS	
Lesson 26	Triangles	Answers

#	Explanation	Comments
1 D	The side lengths are being multiplied by 0.5, therefore 0.5 is the scale factor. You are given a side, angle, and side. This means that the triangles are similar by the SAS rule.	Identify SAS triangles and scale factor.
2 C	If the two triangles are similar, then they have the same angle measures by the AA rule. This means angle ACB is 80 degrees. Solving for the third angle gives $180 - (30 + 80) = 70$ degrees.	AA similarity.
3 D	Since BD bisects side AC, AD=DC. Since angle BDA is 90, angle BDC is also 90 degrees. You also know that BD=BD. Using these facts, you conclude that triangle DBA is congruent to triangle DBC.	SAS Similarity.
4 B	Congruent triangles have equal angles. This means that the value of x is $180 - (60 + 70) = 50$.	Congruent triangles have the same angles.
5 10	The area of an equilateral triangle is $\frac{s^2\sqrt{3}}{4}$. Setting this equal to $25\sqrt{3}$ gives: $\frac{s^2\sqrt{3}}{4} = 25\sqrt{3}$, $s^2 = 100$, $s = 10$.	Refer to equilateral triangle formula.
6 10	If the two shortest sides of a triangle are 5 and 6, the longest side will be the largest integer less than 11, which is 10.	Triangle Inequality.
7 A	You can see that triangle BDE is similar to triangle BAC. You can set up the ratio for DE as: $\frac{DE}{8} = \frac{7}{24}$. $DE = \frac{56}{24} = 2.33$	$BC = BE + EC$
8 C	Triangle ABE is similar to triangle CDE with a scale factor of three. Since the tree is three times taller than the man, the tree's shadow is also three times taller than the man. This means that the distance from the end of the man's shadow, ED, to the tree is $3 \cdot 5 = 15$. It follows that BD is 10 since $ED - 5 = 10$.	
9 B	If a triangle has side lengths of 8, 12, and 20, then the sum of the two shorter legs equals the third leg, giving 20=20, which does not satisfy the triangle inequality.	Review triangle inequality.
10 C	The three triangles are equilateral. The sum of the perimeters of the three triangles is three times the sum of their respective side lengths. Therefore, the perimeter of the triangles is $3 \cdot 1200 = 3600$.	
11 A	The area of one triangle is $\frac{s^2\sqrt{3}}{4} = \frac{1^2\sqrt{3}}{4} = \frac{\sqrt{3}}{4}$. For 100 square feet, $\frac{100}{\frac{\sqrt{3}}{4}} \cong 230.9$	Practice using your calculator with square roots.

12	B	Drop a perpendicular from center O to the midpoint of AC at F. Since ABC is equilateral, ∠OAF=30° and OAF is a 30-60-90 triangle. So, the sides OF, AF, and AO are in the ratio $1:\sqrt{3}:2$. Since OA=11, OF=$\frac{11}{2}$ and AF = $\frac{11}{2} \cdot \sqrt{3}$. So, the side length AC of the triangle ABC = $s = 2 \cdot AF = 11\sqrt{3}$. Therefore, the area of the equilateral triangle is $\frac{s^2\sqrt{3}}{4} = \frac{121 \cdot 3 \cdot \sqrt{3}}{4} = \frac{363\sqrt{3}}{4}$.	Know how to use the Pythagorean ratios quickly. Review the lesson on Pythagorean theorem. Practice calculating the area of an equilateral triangle of side *s* quickly.
13	C	The 15 smaller equilateral triangles have a side length of 4. Each small triangle has an area of $4\sqrt{3}$, a total of $60\sqrt{3}$. The area of the larger triangle is $36\sqrt{3}$. $36\sqrt{3} + 60\sqrt{3} = 96\sqrt{3}$.	
14	D	The triangles can be proven to be congruent by ASA, SAS, and AAS rules.	
15	4	AE=3 and ED=6. Also, since AB and CD are parallel, $\angle ABE = \angle ECD$ and $\angle EAB = \angle ECD$. This means that triangles ABE and ECD are similar by AA similarity. This means that the side lengths of the larger triangle are twice the smaller triangle. Hence, the area of the larger triangle is $2^2 = 4$ times the area of the smaller triangle.	Compare areas of triangles based on side lengths.
16	2	The possible cases are (1,1,8)(2,2,6)(3,3,4)(4,4,2). Out of these, only (3,3,4) and (4,4,2) satisfy the triangle inequality (sum of two shorter sides must be greater than the third side).	

Lesson 27	ADDITIONAL TOPICS IN MATHEMATICS	
	Pythagorean Theorem	Review

FOCUSPREP CHECKLIST

- What is the Pythagorean theorem?
- What are special Pythagorean ratios?
- What is a Pythagorean Triple?
- Workout practice problems in Pythagorean Theorem

Q1 What is the formula for the Pythagorean theorem?

A1 The Pythagorean theorem is defined as $a^2 + b^2 = c^2$, where a and b are the legs of the right triangle and c is the hypotenuse.

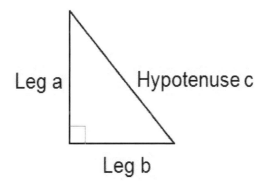

Example: Given legs 3 and 4, what is the hypotenuse of the right triangle shown below?

Solution: Using the Pythagorean theorem, you get $3^2 + 4^2 = x^2 \to 25 = x^2 \to x = 5$

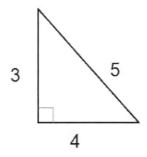

©GiftOfLogic http://www.GiftOfLogic.com

Q2 What are some special Pythagorean ratios?

A2 Pythagorean ratios are $1:1:\sqrt{2}$ for a 45-45-90 triangle and $1:\sqrt{3}:2$ for a 30-60-90 triangle. In the 45-45-90 triangle shown below, $\frac{AB}{AC} = \frac{1}{\sqrt{2}}, \frac{BC}{AC} = \frac{1}{\sqrt{2}}, \frac{AB}{BC} = \frac{1}{1}$. In the 30-60-90 triangle shown below, $\frac{EF}{FD} = \frac{1}{2}, \frac{ED}{FD} = \frac{\sqrt{3}}{2}, \frac{ED}{EF} = \frac{\sqrt{3}}{1}$.

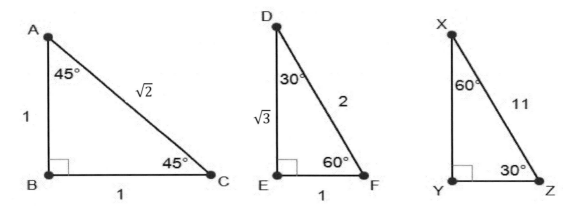

Example 1:

In triangle X,Y,Z shown above, what are the lengths of $\overline{XY}$ and $\overline{YZ}$?

Solution: Using the Pythagorean ratio of $1:\sqrt{3}:2$ for 30-60-90 triangle, $\frac{XY}{11} = \frac{1}{2}$; so $XY = \frac{11}{2}$. $\frac{YZ}{11} = \frac{\sqrt{3}}{2}$; so $YZ = \frac{11}{2}\sqrt{3}$. Remember that the side opposite to 30° is 1 and the side adjacent to 30° is $\sqrt{3}$ in the Pythagorean ratio.

Example 2:

Given a 45-45-90 triangle with side lengths $2y, 2y$, and z, what is z in terms of y?

Solution: Using the Pythagorean ratio of $1:1:\sqrt{2}$ for 45-45-90 triangle, you can observe that two sides of lengths $2y$, and $2y$ are in the ratio of 1:1. So, the third side will be $\sqrt{2}$ times the other side. So, $z = 2y \cdot \sqrt{2}$.

Q3 What is a Pythagorean Triple?

A3 If $a^2 + b^2 = c^2$, then a, b, c is a Pythagorean Triple.

If a, b, c is a Pythagorean Triple, then ka, kb, kc, where k is a constant, is also a Pythagorean Triple.

Example: If 3,4,5 is a Pythagorean triple, then what is another triple?

Solution: Since 3,4,5 is a Triple, then $3k, 4k, 5k$ is also a Triple.

Let $k = 2$, this gives that 6,8,10 is also a Pythagorean Triple. Let $k = 3$, this gives that 9,12,15 is also a Pythagorean Triple.

ADDITIONAL TOPICS IN MATHEMATICS

Lesson 27 — Pythagorean Theorem — Practice

NO CALCULATOR SECTION

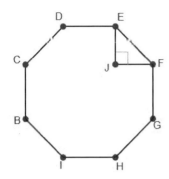

1. In the diagram above, octagon $BCDEFGHI$ has a side length of $2\sqrt{2}$. What is the length of $\overline{EJ}$?
(A) 2
(B) $2\sqrt{2}$
(C) 4
(D) $4\sqrt{2}$

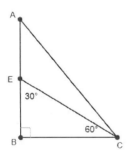

2. In the diagram above, E is the midpoint of $\overline{AB}$. Furthermore, $\overline{AE}$ has length $\sqrt{3}$. What is the area of triangle EBC?

(A) $\dfrac{\sqrt{3}}{2}$

(B) $\dfrac{2}{\sqrt{3}}$

(C) $\dfrac{3\sqrt{3}}{2}$

(D) $\dfrac{3\sqrt{3}}{4}$

NO CALCULATOR SECTION

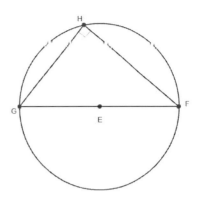

3. In the diagram above, GF is the diameter of circle E. If the legs of triangle FGH are 6 and 8, which inequality represents the value of the diameter d?
(A) $-8 \leq d \leq -6$
(B) $6 \leq d < 10$
(C) $8 \leq d \leq 12$
(D) $6 \leq d \leq 8$

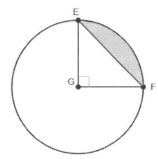

4. In the diagram above, angle EGF is 45°. The radius of the circle has a length of 10. What is the area of the shaded region? (answer in terms of π)
(A) $25\pi - 50$

(B) $25 - 12.5\pi$

(C) $50 - 25\pi$

(D) $\dfrac{100-50\pi}{4}$

NO CALCULATOR SECTION

5. A ladder with length $15\sqrt{2}$ is placed against a brick wall at a 45 degree angle. How far away is the base of the ladder from the wall?
(A) 6
(B) 8
(C) 12
(D) 15

6. A right triangle with side lengths 5, 12, and 13 is enlarged by a scale factor of 3. What is the length of the new hypotenuse?
(A) 15
(B) 26
(C) 36
(D) 39

7. Pam walks north 2.5 miles, then east 6 miles, then north 2.5 miles again, then east 6 miles again. How far away is Pam from her starting position?
(A) 5
(B) 7.5
(C) 12
(D) 13

NO CALCULATOR SECTION

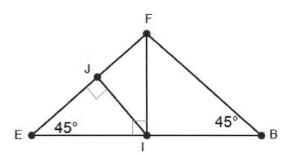

8. In the figure above, $\overline{FB}$ has length 5. What is the length of JI?
(A) 2.5
(B) 5
(C) 5.2
(D) $5\sqrt{2}$

9. A right triangle has side lengths of $x + 7$, 8, and 10. Which of the following is a possible value of x?
(A) -1
(B) 1
(C) 6
(D) 8

CALCULATOR SECTION

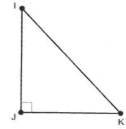

10. Triangle IJK is a right triangle. Leg $\overline{IJ}$ has a length of $\frac{\sqrt{3}}{2}$. Leg JK has a length of $\frac{\sqrt{8}}{3}$. Which of the following is the closest to the length of the hypotenuse?
(A) 0.71
(B) 0.74
(C) 0.91
(D) 1.28

NO CALCULATOR SECTION

11. The sides of a right triangle are x, 7, and 8. How many different possible values are there for x?
(A) 1
(B) 2
(C) 3
(D) 4

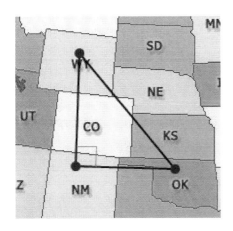

12. Enrique takes a bus from his home in New Mexico to Oklahoma, then to Wyoming, then back home to New Mexico. He notices that his route is in the shape of 45-45-90 triangle. He also knows that the distance from New Mexico to Oklahoma is 600 miles. How much distance did the bus travel in total?
(A) $1200\sqrt{2}$
(B) 1800
(C) $600 + 1200\sqrt{2}$
(D) $1200 + 600\sqrt{2}$

NO CALCULATOR SECTION

13. In a 100 yard by 120 yard field, Peyton runs along the bolded line, from the top left corner of the field to the center line. Then he runs to the bottom right corner. Eli runs along the dashed line, from the bottom left corner to the center line, then to the bottom right corner. How many more yards did Eli run than Peyton?
(A) 40
(B) 60
(C) 80
(D) 100

14. If side DE has a length of 1, what is the length of side GF?

(A) $2\sqrt{2}$

(B) $\dfrac{2\sqrt{6}}{3}$

(C) $\dfrac{3\sqrt{2}}{6}$

(D) $\sqrt{2}$

NO CALCULATOR SECTION

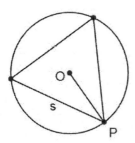

15. An equilateral triangle is inscribed in a circle as shown in the diagram above. The side length of the triangle is s. If the radius OP of the circle can be expressed in the form $\frac{s}{3}\sqrt{a}$ then what is the value of a?
GRID IN

NO CALCULATOR SECTION

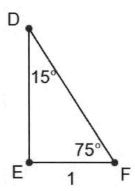

16. In the figure shown above, the base of the triangle has a length of 1. If the length of side DE can be expressed in the form $b + \sqrt{c}$ then what is the sum $b + c$?
GRID IN

ADDITIONAL TOPICS IN MATHEMATICS

Lesson 27 — Pythagorean Theorem — Answers

#	Explanation	Comments
1 A	Since EJF is a 45-45-90 right triangle, you can set the ratio as $x:x:2\sqrt{2}$, giving that $x=2$	Use the 45:45:90 right triangle ratio.
2 A	Since E is the midpoint of AB, then $AE=EB$, using the ratio $1x:x\sqrt{3}:2x$, you get $x:\sqrt{3}:2x$, giving that triangle EBC has legs of lengths 1 and $\sqrt{3}$. The area of this triangle is $\frac{1}{2}\sqrt{3}\cdot 1.=\frac{\sqrt{3}}{2}$.	Use midpoint of triangle and 30:60:90 triangle ratio.
3 C	FGH is a right triangle. The diameter of circle E is congruent to the hypotenuse of the right triangle. Using this fact and the Pythagorean theorem, you get that $6^2+8^2=10^2$. This means that the diameter, d, has a length of 10. The only inequality that contains 10 is $8 \le d \le 12$.	Be alert – 6,8,10 form a Pythagorean triple. The sides are multiples of 3,4,5 which is a Pythagorean triple.
4 A	To find the area of the shaded region, you need to find the area of the quarter circle and subtract the right triangle from it. Since the radius of the circle is 10, the area of the quarter circle is 25π. The two legs of the triangle are both 10 since EFG is a 45-45-90 triangle. Hence, the area of the triangle is $\frac{10\cdot 10}{2}=50$. Subtracting gives $25\pi-50$.	Area of sector minus area of triangle.
5 D	The ladder is the hypotenuse of a 45-45-90 triangle. This means that the sides are in the ratio $x:x:x\sqrt{2}$. You are given that $15\sqrt{2}=x\sqrt{2}$, implying that $x=15$.	45:45:90 triangle.
6 D	Increasing by a scale factor means that each side length is multiplied by a scale factor. In this case, $5\cdot 3=15$, $12\cdot 3=36$, and $13\cdot 3=39$. Checking with the Pythagorean theorem gives $15^2+36^2=39^2$. $225+1296=1521$, which holds true.	Scale factor means each side is multiplied by the same number.
7 D	This diagram shows Pam's route. The dashed line DH represents the value that you are trying to calculate. You can use the larger right triangle with legs 5 and 12 to calculate Pam's distance from her starting point. This can be written as $5^2+12^2=x^2$, solving gives that $x=13$.	Directions and right triangles.

8 A	[Figure: Triangle with vertex F at top, E at bottom-left, B at bottom-right, I at bottom middle, J on segment EF. Angles at E and B are 45°, right angles at J and I.]	Use 45-45-90 right triangle ratios.
	FB=5. Using the 45-45-90 triangle ratio on $\triangle FIB$ gives→ $FI:IB:5$. So, $5 = FI\sqrt{2}$. Therefore, $FI = \frac{5}{\sqrt{2}} = \frac{5\sqrt{2}}{2}$. Since FIE is a 45-45-90 right triangle, $EI = \frac{5\sqrt{2}}{2}$. Using the 45-45-90 triangle ratio on $\triangle JIE$ gives→ $JI:EJ: \frac{5\sqrt{2}}{2}$. $JI = \frac{5\sqrt{2}}{2\sqrt{2}} = 2.5$	
9 A	Solution 1: Pythagorean Theorem
$$(x+7)^2 + 8^2 = 10^2$$
$$x^2 + 14x + 49 + 64 = 100$$
$$x^2 + 14x + 13 = 0$$
$$(x+1)(x+13) = 0$$
$$x = -1 \text{ or } x = -13$$

Since a side length $x + 7$ cannot be a negative number, the answer cannot be -13. For $x = -1, x + 7 = 6$ is positive and is the answer.

Solution 2: Pythagorean Triple

If you look at the last two given side lengths, you can see a part of the Pythagorean triple 6,8,10. You want the first side length to be 6, so you get $x + 7 = 6, x = -1$. | Use the Pythagorean Theorem or Pythagorean Triples. |
| 10 D | Using the Pythagorean Theorem, you can write the equation:
$$\left(\frac{\sqrt{3}}{2}\right)^2 + \left(\frac{\sqrt{8}}{3}\right)^2 = hypotenuse^2$$
Squaring both fractions gives:
$$\left(\frac{3}{4}\right) + \left(\frac{8}{9}\right) = hypotenuse^2$$
Adding the fractions gives
$$\frac{59}{36} = hypotenuse^2$$
Taking the square root of both sides gives | Use the calculator correctly to get the square root. |

	$$\sqrt{\frac{59}{36}} = hypotenuse$$ Using a calculator, you get $$hypotenuse = 1.28$$	
11 B	There are two possible cases, x can either be a leg of the triangle or x can be the hypotenuse itself. Since the problem does not ask to find the actual values for x, so there are two different possible values for x.	Find possible locations of x.
12 D	Find the perimeter of a 45-45-90 triangle with a leg of length 600. Using the 45-45-90 ratio, the side lengths of the triangle are 600, 600 and $600\sqrt{2}$. The sum of these side lengths is $1200 + 600\sqrt{2}$.	Use 45:45:90 right triangle ratio.
13 C	Calculate Peyton's distance and Eli's distance separately first. Peyton runs the first diagonal that has length 130 yards. Peyton's last stretch is half the sideline, which means it has a length of 50. In total Peyton ran 180 yards. Eli ran two times the diagonal, which had a length of 130 yards. This means Eli ran 260 yards. Subtracting the two distances gives $260 - 180 = 80$ yards.	Use Pythagorean triple 5-12-13.
14 A	Using the 30-60-90 triangle ratios $(1:\sqrt{3}:2)$, you get that DF=2. Using the 45-45-90 triangle ratio $(1:1:\sqrt{2})$ on ΔGDF gives that x has a length of $2\sqrt{2}$.	Review the ratios for 30-60-90 and 45-45-90 triangles and know how the ratios work.
15 3	Drawing a line from D shows that is perpendicular to side GF. This results in a 30-60-90 triangle. Since H bisects side GF, the length of side HF is $\frac{s}{2}$. Using the 30-60-90 triangle ratio gives that side DH has length $\frac{s\sqrt{3}}{6}$ and that DF has a length of $\frac{s\sqrt{3}}{6} \cdot 2 = s\sqrt{3}$. Since DF is also the radius of the original circle, you have $\frac{s}{3}\sqrt{3} = \frac{s}{3}\sqrt{a}$, giving $a = 3$.	Split the equilateral triangle into a 30:60:90 triangle.

©GiftOfLogic http://www.GiftOfLogic.com

16	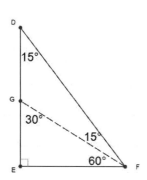 Drawing an extra line from F to side DE makes a 30-60-90 triangle and an isosceles triangle. Since EF has length one, using the 30-60-90 triangle ratio, gives that side GE has a length of $\sqrt{3}$ and GF has a length of 2. Since triangle DGF is isosceles, DG also has a length of 2. Finally, DG+GE can be expressed as $2 + \sqrt{3}$, which is in the form $b + \sqrt{c}$, so $b = 2, c = 3$, giving $b + c = 2 + 3 = 5$.	Split 15:75:90 triangle into 30:60:90 triangle by drawing an extra (auxiliary) line.
5		

ADDITIONAL TOPICS IN MATHEMATICS

Lesson 28 — Circles — Review

> **FOCUSPREP CHECKLIST**
> - How do I identify chords, arcs, and sectors of circles?
> - How do I find the angle of an arc, and the area of a sector?
> - What is the equation of a circle?
> - Workout practice problems in Circles.

Q1 What is the definition of a circle?

A1 A circle is a set of points equidistant from one center point. Circles contain many parts, such as a radius, diameter, chords, angles, arcs, and sectors. Circles can also be graphed on a coordinate plane.

Q2 What is the area and circumference of a circle?

A2 For a circle with radius of r units, the area is πr^2 square units and the circumference is $2\pi r$ units.

Q3 What is a chord of a circle? What is the tangent of a circle?

A3 A chord is a line segment connecting any two points on the circumference of the circle. AB is a chord. The diameter is the largest chord. A tangent is a line that intersects the circle at only one point. Line m is a tangent to the circle at point D. The tangent is perpendicular to the radius at the point of tangency. OD is a radius that is perpendicular to the tangent m at D.

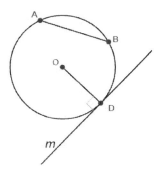

Q4 How does an arc of a circle relate to its angle?

A4 An arc of a circle is a portion of its circumference. The measure of an arc is the measure of its central angle.

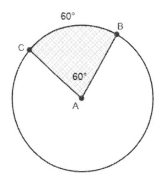

Example: In the figure shown, the measure of the arc BC is 60°, which is the same as its central angle.

©GiftOfLogic http://www.GiftOfLogic.com

Q5 How do I calculate the length of an arc?

A5 The circumference of a circle subtends 360°. If the measure of an arc is $x°$, then the length of the arc is $\frac{x}{360}$ of the circumference = $\frac{x}{360} \cdot 2\pi r$

Example:
If the radius of a circle is 10, what is the length of a 90° arc on the circumference?
The arc has a length that is $\frac{90}{360} = \frac{1}{4}$ of the circumference. The circumference has a length of $2\pi \cdot 10 = 20\pi$. So, the length of the arc is $\frac{20\pi}{4} = 5\pi$.

Q6 What is a sector of a circle and how do I find its area?

A6 A sector is the part of a circle enclosed by two radii and the arc intercepted by them. The area or the sector is $\frac{\pi r^2}{360} \cdot x$, where x is the interior angle of the arc. You can setup a direct proportion ratio to derive this formula.

$$360° \quad \pi r^2$$
$$x° \quad A$$

Set direct ratio $\frac{x}{360} = \frac{?}{\pi r^2}$

$A = \frac{\pi r^2}{360} \cdot x$

Example: In the circle below, what is the area of the sector shown?
Solution: The central angle is 120°. The circle has a radius of 12, with an area of $\pi \cdot 12^2 = 144\pi$.
Set up the direct proportion:
360°   144 π
120°   x

$$\frac{120}{360} = \frac{x}{144\pi}$$

$3x = 144\pi$
$x = \frac{144\pi}{3} = 48\pi$

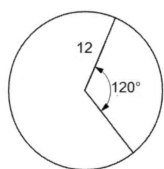

Q7 What is the equation of a circle?

A7 The equation of a circle is $(x - h)^2 + (y - k)^2 = r^2$, where h and k are the coordinates of the center of the circle and r is the length of the radius.

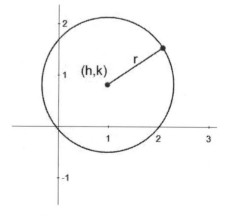

Q8 What is the distance from the center of a circle to the origin?

A8 Using the Pythagorean formula, $d = \sqrt{h^2 + k^2}$, where d is the distance and (h, k) is the center of the circle. Note that d is not the radius of the circle.

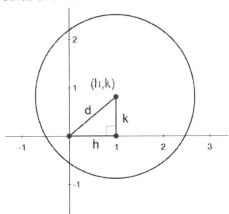

Q9 What if a circle is inscribed in a polygon?

A9 If a circle is inscribed, it's radius is perpendicular to the sides of the polygon at the point of contact as shown in the example below. This fact can be used to find the area of the circle or the area of the region between the circle and polygon.

Example: Circle O has a radius of 5 and is inscribed inside square EBCD. What is the area of the shaded region?

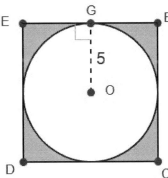

Solution: The circle has an area of $\pi \cdot 5^2 = 25\pi$. ED has a length of twice the radius = $2 \cdot 5 = 10$. Therefore the square has an area of $10 \cdot 10 = 100$. The shaded region is the difference between the area of the square and the circle, $100 - 25\pi$.

ADDITIONAL TOPICS IN MATHEMATICS

Lesson 28 — Circles — Practice

NO CALCULATOR SECTION

1. A circle has a circumference of 12π. What is the area of this circle?

   (A) 36π
   (B) 49π
   (C) 64π
   (D) 144π

2. Chord BC has the same length as the radius of Circle A. If chord BC has a length of 6, what is the area of triangle ABC?

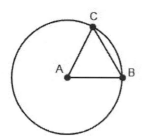

   (A) $3\sqrt{3}$
   (B) $9\sqrt{3}$
   (C) $12\sqrt{3}$
   (D) $16\sqrt{3}$

NO CALCULATOR SECTION

3. In the figure below, triangle ABC is isosceles, with angle ABC being 40 degrees. Based on this information, how many degrees is arc BC?

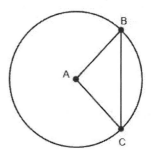

   (A) 20°
   (B) 40°
   (C) 80°
   (D) 100°

4. The sector of a circle shown below has a central angle of 45 degrees and an area of 8π. What is the radius of the circle from?

   (A) 2
   (B) 4
   (C) 8
   (D) 16

NO CALCULATOR SECTION

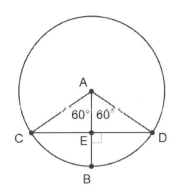

5. Based on the diagram above, if chord CD has a length of 10, what is the length of AB?

(A) 10

(B) $\frac{10\sqrt{3}}{3}$

(C) $5\sqrt{3}$

(D) $\frac{10\sqrt{2}}{3}$

6. A regular twelve sided polygon is inscribed in a circle. What is the angle x of the arc, created by the two radii shown above?

(A) 30
(B) 36
(C) 60
(D) 150

NO CALCULATOR SECTION

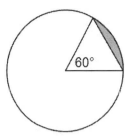

7. In the diagram shown above, what is the area of the shaded region if the radius of the circle is 6?

(A) $9\sqrt{3} + 6\pi$
(B) 6π
(C) $9\sqrt{3}$
(D) $6\pi - 9\sqrt{3}$

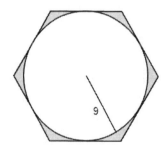

8. In the figure above, a circle is inscribed in a regular hexagon. The circle has a radius of 9. What is the area of the shaded region?

(A) $27\sqrt{3} - 81\pi$
(B) $54\sqrt{3} - 81\pi$
(C) $162\sqrt{3} - 81\pi$
(D) $162\sqrt{3} + 81\pi$

NO CALCULATOR SECTION

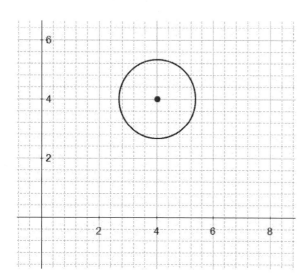

9. The equation of the circle shown above can be expressed as $(x - h)^2 + (y - k)^2 = r^2$. What is the sum of h and k?
GRID IN

10. What value of h in the equation $(x - h)^2 + y^2 = r^2$ makes the positive distance from the point (h, k) to the origin exactly 8?
GRID IN

NO CALCULATOR SECTION

11.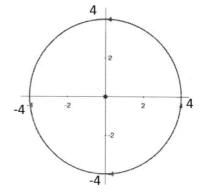

Which of the following is the equation of the circle shown above?
 (A) $x^2 + (y - 1)^2 = 4$
 (B) $x^2 + y^2 = 4$
 (C) $x^2 + y^2 = 16$
 (D) $(x - 1)^2 + y^2 = 16$

12. A city that is laid out in the form of a circle is divided into 5 different sectors. The ratio of the central angles is 3:4:7:8:18. What is the sum of the angles of the smallest sector and the largest sector of the city?
 (A) 21
 (B) 84
 (C) 162
 (D) 189

13. The circular wheel shown below has a radius of 5. What is the sum of the circumference and the 5 radii of the wheel?

 (A) $25 - 10\pi$
 (B) $25 + 10\pi$
 (C) 25π
 (D) 35π

NO CALCULATOR SECTION

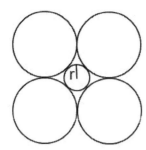

14. In the figure above, all circles are tangent to each other. The larger circles have a radius of 1. If the radius r of the smaller circle in the center is expressed as $-a + \sqrt{b}$ then what is the product of a and b?
GRID IN

15. After the interior angle of circle is divided into n equal parts, each sector has a value of $\frac{360}{n}$. How many values of n less than 10 make the angle of each sector an integer?
GRID IN

NO CALCULATOR SECTION

16. If a circle with its origin at $(0,0)$ passes through the point $(-4,0)$, then which one of the following points is on the circumference of the circle?

(A) $(-4,1)$
(B) $(0,5)$
(C) $(-1, \sqrt{15})$
(D) $(2, \sqrt{14})$

17. If the endpoints of a chord of circle are $(1,4)$ and $(5,4)$, then which one of the following is the coordinate of the midpoint of the chord?

(A) $(0,0)$
(B) $(3,4)$
(C) $(4,4)$
(D) $(-3,4)$

ADDITIONAL TOPICS IN MATHEMATICS

Lesson 28 — Circles — Answers

#	Explanation	Comments
1 A	$2\pi r = 12\pi$, $r = 6$, $\pi(6)^2 = 36\pi$	
2 B	Triangle ABC is equilateral since the three side lengths are the same. Height=$\sqrt{36-9} = \sqrt{27} = 3\sqrt{3}$. Area=$\frac{1}{2} \cdot 6 \cdot 3\sqrt{3} = 9\sqrt{3}$.	Equilateral triangle in a circle.
3 D	Triangle ABC is isosceles since AB=AC. Angles ABC and ACB are both 40 degrees, and angle BAC is 100 degrees. Therefore arc BC is 100 degrees.	Isosceles triangle in a circle.
4 C	The central angle of the sector is 45°. This represents $\frac{45}{360} = \frac{1}{8}$ of the area of the circle. The area of the sector is given as 8π. So, $8\pi = \frac{\pi r^2}{8}$. $64\pi = r^2$. So, $r = \sqrt{64} = 8$.	
5 B	You can use the 30-60-90 triangles created when triangle ACD is divided into two. This gives CD=5, AE=$\frac{5\sqrt{3}}{3}$, and AC=$\frac{10\sqrt{3}}{3}$. AB is a radius of the circle and has the same value as AC.	30-60-90 triangles.
6 C	The 12-gon divides the circle into 12 pieces, each having 30 degrees. Since the angle shown contains two of these pieces, $30 \cdot 2 = 60$ degrees.	
7 D	The area of the shaded region is the area of the equilateral triangle subtracted from the area of the sector. The area of the sector is $\frac{36\pi}{6} = 6\pi$. The area of the equilateral triangle is $\frac{6^2\sqrt{3}}{4} = \frac{36\sqrt{3}}{4} = 9\sqrt{3}$. Subtracting, you get $6\pi - 9\sqrt{3}$.	Subtract the area of the equilateral triangle from the area of the sector.
8 C	As shown in the diagram, the area of the hexagon can be found using equilateral triangles. Using the 30-60-90 triangle ratio, sides $\frac{x}{2} : 9 : x$ are in the ratio of $1:\sqrt{3}: 2$, where x is the side length of the equilateral triangle. So, $\frac{x}{2}\sqrt{3} = 9$. $x = \frac{18}{\sqrt{3}} = 18\frac{\sqrt{3}}{3} = 6\sqrt{3}$. Using the formula for the area of an equilateral triangle, the area of $\frac{1}{6}$ th of the hexagon is $\frac{x^2\sqrt{3}}{4} = 6^2 \cdot 3 \cdot \frac{\sqrt{3}}{4} = 27\sqrt{3}$. The area of the hexagon is $6 \cdot 27\sqrt{3} = 162\sqrt{3}$. The area of the circle is $\pi \cdot 9^2 = 81\pi$. So, the area of the shaded region is $162\sqrt{3} - 81\pi$.	Use the properties of circles inscribed in regular polygons. Learn to apply the 30-60-90 ratio to the problem. Understand why $\frac{x}{2}\sqrt{3} = 9$.
9 8	The center of the circle is (h,k), which is $(4,4)$. The equation of this circle is $(x-4)^2 + (y-4)^2 = r^2$. You are asked $h+k = 8$.	Find the center of the circle from the graph.

©GiftOfLogic http://www.GiftOfLogic.com

10	8	Based on the equation given, $k=0$, which means that h is on the x axis. The two points that are 8 units away from the origin on the x axis are 8 and -8. The positive distance is 8.	
11	C	The center of the circle is $(0,0)$. The radius of the circle is 4. The equation of this circle is $(x-0)^2 + (y-0)^2 = 4^2$, $x^2 + y^2 = 16$.	
12	D	The 5 angles can be represented as $3x, 4x, 7x, 8x,$ and $18x$. The sum of these angles is 360, so $3x + 4x + 7x + 8x + 18x = 360$, $40x = 360$, $x = 9$. The smallest angle is 27 and the largest is 162. The sum is 27+162=189.	
13	B	The circumference = $2\pi \cdot 5 = 10\pi$. 5 times the radius = $5 \cdot 5 = 25$. The sum is $25 + 10\pi$.	
14	2	Using the above figure, triangle MLB is a 45-45-90 triangle with a Pythagorean ratio of $1:1:\sqrt{2}$. This means $MB = \sqrt{2}\ LB = 2\sqrt{2}$. Hence, $MB = 2\sqrt{2} = 1 + r + r + 1 = 2r + 2$, therefore $2r = -2 + 2\sqrt{2}$, $r = -1 + \sqrt{2} = -a + \sqrt{b}$. This means $a = 1, b = 2$. Therefore, product ab equals $1 \cdot 2 = 2$.	Create a right triangle using the radii of the circles. Learn to apply the 45-45-90 ratio to the problem. Understand why MB = $\sqrt{2}\ LB$.
15	8	For $\frac{360}{n}$ to be an integer, n must be a factor of 360 and less than 10. The factors of 360 less than 10 are: 1,2,3,4,5,6,8, and 9. This is a total of 8 values.	Find factors of 360 that are less than 10.
16	C	Since the circle has its origin at $(0,0)$ and passes through $(-4,0)$, its radius has a length of 4 units. So, any other point on the circle must satisfy the equation $x^2 + y^2 = r^2 = 4^2 = 16$. Of the choices given, only choice C $(-1, \sqrt{15})$ satisfies the equation. $(-1)^2 + (\sqrt{15})^2 = 1 + 15 = 16$.	The equation of the circle is $x^2 + y^2 = r^2$.
17	B	The chord is a straight line with ends having coordinates of $(1,4)$ and $(5,4)$. So, the midpoint of the chord is $\frac{1+5}{2}, \frac{4+4}{2} = 3,4$.	If $(x1, y1)$ and $(x2, y2)$ are two points in the Cartesian coordinate system, then the midpoint of the line connecting them is $(\frac{x1+x2}{2}, \frac{y1+y2}{2})$. The distance between the points is $\sqrt{(x2-x1)^2 + (y2-y1)^2}$

ADDITIONAL TOPICS IN MATHEMATICS

Lesson 29 — Polygons — Review

FOCUSPREP CHECKLIST

- How do I find angles and lengths in polygons?
- How do I Identify similar polygons?
- What are the different types of quadrilaterals?
- How do I find the perimeter and area of polygons?
- Workout practice problems in Polygons

Q1 What is a Polygon?

A1 A polygon is a closed two dimensional shape with straight sides. This includes triangles, squares, pentagons, hexagons, etc. It does not include circles, ovals, or other curved surfaces.

Q2 What is the difference between a regular and an irregular polygon?

A2 The sides and interior angles of a regular polygon are equal. An irregular polygon can have sides or angles of different values.

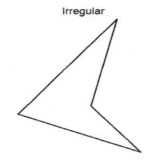

Q3 How is the sum of the interior angles of a polygon determined?

A3 The formula $S = (n-2) \cdot 180$ is the sum of the interior angles of a polygon where n is the number of sides.

Example: A quadrilateral has 4 sides. Therefore $180 \cdot (4-2) = 360$ is the sum of the four angles of this polygon.

Polygon	Number of Sides	Sum of Interior Angles
Triangle	3	180
Quadrilateral	4	360
Pentagon	5	540
Hexagon	6	720
n-gon	n	$(n-2) \cdot 180$

Q4 What is an Apothem?

A4 The apothem of a regular polygon is a line from the center of the polygon to the midpoint of one of the sides.

Q5 How is the area of a regular polygon calculated?

A5 The area of a regular polygon is calculated using the formula $A = \frac{apothem \cdot perimeter}{2}$.

Example:

In this hexagon, the perimeter is $5 \cdot 6 = 30$ and the apothem is 3. Hence the area is $\frac{3 \cdot 30}{2} = 45$. If the side of the hexagon is s, then its perimeter is $6s$ and its apothem, using Pythagorean theorem is $\sqrt{s^2 - \left(\frac{s}{2}\right)^2} = \frac{\sqrt{3}\,s}{2}$ and the area is $6s \cdot \frac{\sqrt{3}\,s}{2} = 3\sqrt{3}\,s^2$. Learn to derive this formula quickly.

Q6 When are two polygons similar?

A6 Two polygons are similar if the ratios of their corresponding sides are equal and their corresponding interior angles are equal. In other words, they have to be of the same shape but can be of different size. In the following polygons, all the sides the sides are in ratio of $\frac{15}{7.5} = 2 = \frac{14}{7}$ and all the interior angles are the same. So, these two polygons are similar.

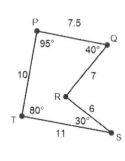

Q7 What are some special types of quadrilaterals?

A7 The table below summarizes the different types of quadrilaterals.

Quadrilaterals	Diagram	Properties
Square		4 equal sides and angles. Perimeter=$4s$ Area= s^2
Rectangle		4 right angles, 2 pairs of equal sides Perimeter= $2L + 2W$ Area= $L \cdot W$
Rhombus		4 equal sides, different angle values Area=product of diagonals divided by 2 = $\frac{d_1 \cdot d_2}{2}$.
Parallelogram		2 sets of parallel sides. Note that a rhombus is a type of parallelogram. Area= $b \cdot h$
Trapezoid		One pair of parallel sides. Area= $\frac{1}{2} \cdot h \cdot (b1 + b2)$

ADDITIONAL TOPICS IN MATHEMATICS

Lesson 29 — Polygons — Practice

NO CALCULATOR SECTION

1. What is the measure of one of the interior angles of a regular pentagon?
   - (A) 90
   - (B) 108
   - (C) 154
   - (D) 180

2. Quadraliteral A has four equal sides. Quadrilateral B also has four equal sides. Are the two figures similar?
   - (A) They are always similar
   - (B) They are sometimes similar
   - (C) They are never similar
   - (D) Cannot be determined

3. If the area of a regular pentagon with a side length of 10 is 50, what is its apothem?
   - (A) 1
   - (B) 2
   - (C) 5
   - (D) 10

NO CALCULATOR SECTION

4. If the following octagon is regular, what is the measure of angle IAD?

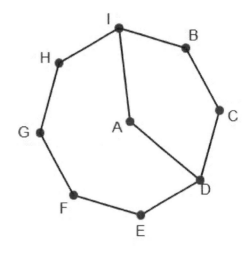

   - (A) 45°
   - (B) 120°
   - (C) 135°
   - (D) 150°

5. A regular octagon is inscribed in a square with a side length of 10. What is the side length of the octagon?

   - (A) $10 - 5\sqrt{2}$
   - (B) $10 + 5\sqrt{2}$
   - (C) $5 - 2\sqrt{2}$
   - (D) $10 - 2\sqrt{2}$

NO CALCULATOR SECTION

6. Which of the following quadrilaterals always have perpendicular diagonals?

I. Squares
II. Rhombi
III. Trapezoids

(A) I and II
(B) I and III
(C) II and III
(D) I, II, and III

7. What is the scale factor from polygon A to polygon B, assuming that they are similar?

(A) $\frac{1}{9}$
(B) $\frac{1}{4}$
(C) 4
(D) 9

8. If the dotted lines represent heights of the trapezoid and CD has a length of 34, what is the length of AB?

(A) 5
(B) 12
(C) 20
(D) 34

NO CALCULATOR SECTION

9. What is the difference between the sum of the interior angles of a polygon with 12 sides and a polygon with 4 sides?

(A) 1080
(B) 1440
(C) 1620
(D) 1800

10. An object has rotational symmetry if it can be rotated on its center point and look the same. How many of the following triangles have rotational symmetry?

(A) 1
(B) 2
(C) 3
(D) 4

11. A polygon has reflectional symmetry when it can be folded in half and both halves are mirror images of each other. How many of the following polygons have reflectional symmetry?

(A) 1
(B) 2
(C) 3
(D) 4

NO CALCULATOR SECTION

12. How many diagonals does a pentagon have?
GRID IN

13. How many regions are formed after all the diagonals of a regular pentagon are drawn?
GRID IN

CALCULATOR SECTION

14. An equilateral triangle is inscribed in a regular hexagon as shown in the diagram below. What is the angle measure of x in degrees?

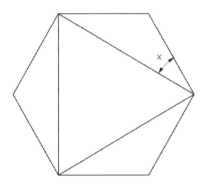

(A) 15
(B) 30
(C) 60
(D) 120

CALCULATOR SECTION

15. Rectangle ABCD is divided into square pieces of different sizes. What is the least number of squares needed to divide the rectangle?

(A) 1
(B) 3
(C) 12
(D) 72

16. What is the area of a rhombus that has two equal diagonals of length 10?
GRID IN

17. In the rectangle shown, AB has a length of 4, EC has a length of 3, and BC has a length of 1. What is the area of triangle BFC? Express your answer to the nearest hundredths place. (Hint: Use a coordinate system)

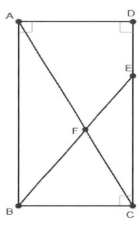

ADDITIONAL TOPICS IN MATHEMATICS

Lesson 29	Polygons	Answers

#	Explanation	Comments
1 B	The sum of the interior angles of a pentagon is 540°. So, $\frac{540}{5} = 108$ degrees.	
2 B	The polygons can sometimes be similar if they have proportional side lengths and angles. The polygons are not always similar since they can have different angles or side lengths.	Refer to quadrilateral chart.
3 B	$\frac{1}{2} \cdot apothem \cdot 50 = 50, apothem = 2$.	Use the Apothem formula.
4 C	If a circle is circumscribed about the octagon, the circle will be divided into 8 parts, each with an angle of 45 degrees. Since IAD contains three of those parts, the angle has a measure of 135 degrees.	
5 A	As shown in the diagram above, the length of the side of a square can be represented as $2s + s\sqrt{2} = 10$, $s(2 + \sqrt{2}) = 10$, $s = \frac{10}{(2+\sqrt{2})} \cdot \frac{2-\sqrt{2}}{2-\sqrt{2}}$ $s = 10 - 5\sqrt{2}$	Use 45-45-90 special triangle ratio.
6 A	The diagonals of squares and rhombi are always perpendicular. A trapezoid can have perpendicular diagonals, but not always.	Refer to quadrilateral chart.
7 B	The ratio of the side lengths is $\frac{36}{144} = \frac{1}{4}$.	Use proportional side lengths of similar polygons.
8 C	To find AB, you need to find the third leg of the two right triangles created by the heights. One leg has a length of 9, the other leg has a length of 5. $34 - 5 - 9 = 20$.	Use Pythagorean theorem in quadrilaterals.
9 B	A polygon with 12 sides has a sum of $10 \cdot 180 = 1800$ degrees. A quadrilateral has 360 degrees. $1800 - 360 = 1440$.	Sum of interior angles.
10 A	Only the second triangle can be rotated about its center and still maintain the same figure.	Rotational symmetry.
11 C	The first, third, and fourth polygon can be folded in half and be symmetric.	Reflectional symmetry.
12 5	Draw the diagonals and count 5 diagonals	

©GiftOfLogic http://www.GiftOfLogic.com

13 11	As shown in the diagram above, the pentagon is split into 11 regions.		
14 B	One angle of a hexagon is 120 degrees. One angle of an equilateral triangle is 60 degrees. Thus: $2x + 60 = 120$, $x = 30$.	Use angles of regular equilateral triangle and regular hexagons.	
15 B	The largest square that fits into the rectangle is 8×8. After this a 4×8 rectangle remains. This smaller rectangle can be split into two 4×4 squares. A total of 3 squares are needed to divide the rectangle.		
16 50	The diagonals split the rhombus into four right triangles, each with two legs of 5. So, $4 \cdot \frac{1}{2} \cdot 5 \cdot 5 = 50$.	Area of a rhombus.	
17 0.86	If the point B is $(0,0)$, then the equation of line AC is $y = -4x + 4$ and the equation of line BE is $y = 3x$. Solving the equation gives: $$y = -4x + 4$$ $$y = 3x$$ $$-4x + 4 = 3x$$ $$4 = 7x$$ $$x = \frac{7}{4}$$ Plugging the value of x back into the original equation gives: $$y = 3 \cdot \frac{4}{7} = \frac{12}{7}$$ Their intersection, point F, is $(\frac{4}{7}, \frac{12}{7})$. This means the height of triangle BFC is $\frac{12}{7}$. The area of triangle BFC is $\frac{1}{2} \cdot 1 \cdot \frac{12}{7} = \frac{12}{14} = 0.86$	Use a coordinate system to find lengths.	

	ADDITIONAL TOPICS IN MATHEMATICS	
Lesson 30	Volume of Solids	Review

> **FOCUSPREP CHECKLIST**
> - How do I calculate the surface area and volume of solids?
> - How do I find the length of the diagonal of a cube?
> - Workout practice problems in Volume of Solids

Q1 What is a solid figure?

A1 Solid figures are three dimensional shapes that have height, length, and depth. These figures enclose a volume which can be calculated using the side lengths, or areas of the faces.

Q2 How do I calculate the surface are and volume of a solid figure?

A2

Solid	Figure	Volume Formula	Surface Area
Cube		$V = s \cdot s \cdot s = s^3$	$6s^2$
Rectangular Prism		$V = l \cdot d \cdot h$	$2(lw + lh + wh)$
Cylinder		$V = \pi r^2 \cdot h$	$2\pi r^2 + 2\pi r h$

©GiftOfLogic http://www.GiftOfLogic.com

Cone		$V = \frac{1}{3} \cdot \pi r^2 \cdot h$	$S = \pi r l + \pi r^2$
Sphere		$V = \frac{4}{3} \cdot \pi \cdot r^3$	$S = 4\pi r^2$
Pyramids		$V = \frac{1}{3} \cdot l \cdot h \cdot w$	$S = 2lw + w^2$
Regular Prisms		$V = B \cdot h$, B is the area of the base	$S = PBh + 2B$, P is the perimeter of the base

Q3 What is a lateral surface area?

A3 This is the surface area not including the bases.

Q4 How do I calculate the lateral side length, l, of a cone or pyramid?

A4 Using the Pythagorean Theorem, values can be found as shown below:

Example:

$l = \sqrt{12^2 + 5^2} = 13$

©GiftOfLogic http://www.GiftOfLogic.com

Q5 How do I calculate the volume of a solid that is missing a piece inside?

A5 To calculate the volume of this new solid, subtract the volume of the missing piece from the volume of the solid.

Example: If a cylinder with a radius of 5 and a height of 10 is taken out of a cylinder of radius 10 and a height of 5, what is the volume of the new solid?

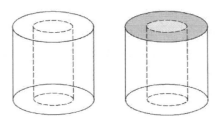

Answer: The volume of the original cylinder is $\pi \cdot 10^2 \cdot 5 = 500\pi$, using the volume of a cylinder formula. The volume of the smaller cylinder is $\pi \cdot 5^2 \cdot 10 = 250\pi$. To find the volume of the new figure, you subtract the volumes, giving $500\pi - 250\pi = 250\pi$.

Q6 How do I find the length of a diagonal of a cube?

A6 The Pythagorean Theorem is manipulated to find the length of the diagonal.

Example: If the volume of this cube is $1000\ ft^3$, what is the length of AF?

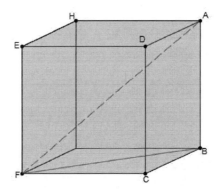

To find the length of the interior diagonal, you first must find the length of BF. You know that the side length of the cube is 10 since $\sqrt[3]{1000} = 10$. Using the Pythagorean theorem, $FC^2 + CB^2 = BF^2$, $10^2 + 10^2 = BF^2$, $BF^2 = 200$, $BF = 10\sqrt{2}$. Now, using right triangle ABF, you can apply the Pythagorean theorem a second time. This gives $10^2 + \left(10\sqrt{2}\right)^2 = AF^2$. This simplifies to $100 + 200 = AF^2$, $AF = \sqrt{300} = 10\sqrt{3}$.

This method for finding interior diagonals can be applied to rectangular prisms as well.

ADDITIONAL TOPICS IN MATHEMATICS
Lesson 30 — Volume of Solids — Practice

NO CALCULATOR SECTION

1. The volume of Cube A is 27 times the volume of Cube B. What is the ratio of the side length of Cube A to the side length of Cube B?
   (A) 1
   (B) 3
   (C) 9
   (D) 27

2. A sphere with a radius of r is inscribed in a cylinder that also has a radius of r. What is the ratio of the volume of the cylinder to the volume of the sphere?
   (A) $\frac{2}{3}$
   (B) $\frac{\sqrt{3}}{2}$
   (C) $\frac{3}{2}$
   (D) $\frac{\sqrt{2}}{3}$

3. Two cubes with side lengths of 5 are placed adjacently as shown in the diagram below. What is the length of the interior diagonal of the newly formed rectangular prism?

   (A) 5
   (B) $5\sqrt{5}$
   (C) $5\sqrt{6}$
   (D) $6\sqrt{5}$

CALCULATOR SECTION

4. A regular hexagonal prism with a volume of $60\sqrt{3}$ has a height of 10. What is the side length of the base?

   (A) 2
   (B) 3
   (C) $\sqrt{3}$
   (D) $2\sqrt{2}$

5. An octahedron is created by attaching two square pyramids together by their bases. The height of each pyramid is 6 and the base length of each pyramid is 6. What is the volume of the octahedron?

   (A) 108
   (B) 144
   (C) $136\sqrt{2}$
   (D) 216

6. Three faces of a cube have a combined surface area of 147. What is the volume of the cube?
   GRID IN

CALCULATOR SECTION

7. 100 wooden cutting boards with dimensions of 1 inch by 10 inches by 8 inches are manufactured every hour. One cubic inch of wood costs $0.33. What is the value of all the cutting boards that could be made in eight hours?

(A) $21,120
(B) $22,114
(C) $26,004
(D) $26,400

8. The side lengths of a rectangular prism are consecutive integers. The surface area of the prism is 94. Which of the following could be a possible volume of the solid?

(A) 54
(B) 60
(C) 72
(D) 84

9. A thick wooden pencil is made by attaching a cylinder with a radius of $\frac{1}{4}$ and a height of 6 to a cone of radius $\frac{1}{4}$ and a height of 1. What is the volume of the pencil?

(A) $\frac{19\pi}{48}$

(B) $\frac{48\pi}{19}$

(C) $\frac{7\pi}{8}$

(D) $\frac{8\pi}{7}$

CALCULATOR SECTION

10. In cells where the surface area is greater than the volume, diffusion occurs quickly. In cells where the surface area is less than the volume, diffusion takes longer. Cell A is in the shape of a cube and has a side length of 3. Cell B is also in the shape of a cube and has a side length of 9. Which cell will diffuse faster?

(A) Cell A
(B) Cell B
(C) Neither
(D) Cannot Be determined

11. A test tube is created by attaching a hemisphere to a cylinder. The hemisphere has a radius of 2 and the cylinder has a radius of 2 and a height of 6. What is the volume of the test tube?

(A) $\frac{3}{104\pi}$

(B) $\frac{3\pi}{88}$

(C) $\frac{88\pi}{3}$

(D) $\frac{104\pi}{3}$

CALCULATOR SECTION

12. A cylinder with a radius of 5 is carved out of a hexagonal prism with a height of 10 and a side length of 10. What is the volume of the remaining solid?

(A) $1250\sqrt{3} - 250\pi$
(B) $1500\sqrt{3} - 250\pi$
(C) $1500\sqrt{2} - 250\pi$
(D) $1250\sqrt{3} + 250\pi$

13. As shown in the diagram below, a cone with a height of 8 inches and a radius of 6 inches is cut halfway at a height of 4 inches. The cut off cone has a radius of 3 inches. What is the volume of the new solid that is left over?

(A) 60π
(B) 72π
(C) 84π
(D) 96π

14. The following net is folded into a cylinder with a radius of 4 and a volume of 128π. What is the value of h?

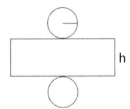

(A) $2\sqrt{2}$
(B) 8
(C) 16
(D) 32

CALCULATOR SECTION

15. A portion of a cookie tin is manufactured in octagonal prisms as shown. The height of the tin is 8 inches and the side lengths of the octagonal faces are 3 inches. What is the lateral surface area of the cookie tin?

(A) 96
(B) 192
(C) 384
(D) 576

16. Ice cream at the Pi Creamery is sold in cubic inches. A standard cone consists of a spherical scoop of ice cream with a radius of 3 inches and a cone with a radius of 1 inch and a height of 3 inches. π cubic inches of cone costs $3.50, and π cubic inches of ice cream costs $0.50. What is the cost of one ice cream?
GRID IN

17. A cube is inscribed in a sphere so that the vertices of the cube touch the surface of the sphere. The volume of the cube is 8. If the volume of the sphere can be expressed as $a\pi\sqrt{b}$ then what is the sum of a and b?
GRID IN

ADDITIONAL TOPICS IN MATHEMATICS

Lesson 30 — Volume of Solids — Answers

#	Explanation	Comments
1 B	A cube with a volume of 27 has a side length of 3. A cube with a volume of 1 has a side length of 1. The ratio is $\frac{3}{1} = 3$.	Use ratio of volumes of two solid figures.
2 C	A sphere with a radius r has a volume of $\frac{4}{3}\pi r^3$. The cylinder has a radius of r and a height of $2r$. The volume of the cylinder is $2\pi r^3$. $\frac{2\pi r^3}{\frac{4}{3}\pi r^3} = \frac{3}{2}$	Use volume of cylinder and sphere formulas.
3 C	The length of the diagonal is the same as a rectangular prism with dimensions of $5 \times 5 \times 10$, which is $5\sqrt{6}$.	Find the diagonal of the rectangular prism.
4 A	$B \cdot 10 = 60\sqrt{3}$, The area of the base is $6\sqrt{3}$. $\frac{6s^2\sqrt{3}}{4} = 6\sqrt{3}$, $s = 2$	Use area of hexagon formula.
5 B	The area of one pyramid is $\frac{1}{3} \cdot 36 \cdot 6 = 72$. The volume of two pyramids is $72 \cdot 2 = 144$.	Split the octahedron into two pyramids to calculate volume. Refer to volume of Pyramids formula.
6 343	If three faces have an area of 147, six faces have an area of 296. $\frac{294}{6} = 49$. $\sqrt{49} = 7$. The side length of the cube is 7. The volume is $7^3 = 343$.	
7 A	One board has a volume of 80 in^3, so the cost of each board is $80 \cdot 0.33 = \$26.40$. 100 boards cost $\$2,640$. Eight hours of boards costs $\$2640 \cdot 8 = \$21,120$.	
8 B	The surface area of the prism is $2(lw + lh + wh) = 94$, $lw + lh + wh = 47$. Using guess and check, you find that $l = 3, w = 4, h = 5$. The volume is $3 \cdot 4 \cdot 5 = 60$.	The fastest method to solve this problem is to Guess and Check.
9 A	The volume of the cone is $\frac{1}{12}\pi$ and the volume of the cylinder is $\frac{6}{16}\pi$. The sum is $\frac{19}{48}\pi$.	Calculate volumes of solids with fractional lengths.
10 A	Cell A has a volume of 27 and a surface area of 54, the surface area is greater than the volume. In Cell A, diffusion occurs quickly.	
11 C	The hemisphere has a volume of $\frac{1}{2} \cdot \frac{4}{3} \cdot \pi \cdot 2^3 = \frac{32}{6}\pi$. The cylinder has a volume of $\pi \cdot 2^2 \cdot 6 = 24\pi$. The sum is $\frac{32}{6}\pi + 24\pi = \frac{176}{6}\pi = \frac{88}{3}\pi$.	The volume of a hemisphere is half the volume of a sphere.
12 B	The volume of the cylinder is 250π. The area of the base of the hexagonal prism is $3s^2\frac{\sqrt{3}}{2} = 3 \cdot 10^2 \cdot \frac{\sqrt{3}}{2} = 150\sqrt{3}$. The volume of the hexagonal prism is $150\sqrt{3} \cdot 10 = 1500\sqrt{3}$. The difference is $1500\sqrt{3} - 250\pi$	Area of a hexagon is $\frac{3s^2\sqrt{3}}{2}$, where s is the side length. Review the lesson on polygons.
13 C	The volume of the whole cone is 96π. The area of the smaller cone is	Truncated cone.

©GiftOfLogic http://www.GiftOfLogic.com

14 B	12π. The difference is 84π. $\pi \cdot 4^2 \cdot h = 16\pi h = 128\pi, h = \frac{128}{16} = 8.$	A net is a pattern that can be cut and folded into a solid shape.
15 B	The area of one rectangular face is $3 \cdot 8 = 24$. There are eight bases, so $8 \cdot 24 = 192$.	Lateral surface area.
16 21.50	The volume of the spherical ice cream is $\frac{4}{3} \cdot \pi \cdot 3^3 = \frac{4}{3} \cdot \pi \cdot 27 = 36\pi$ cubic inches. The volume of the cone is $\frac{1}{3} \cdot \pi \cdot 1^2 \cdot 3 = \pi$ cubic inches. Since π cubic inches of cone costs \$3.50, the cost of the cone is \$3.50. Since π cubic inches of ice cream costs \$0.50, 36π cubic inches of ice cream costs $36 \cdot 0.5 = \$18$. Total is $\$18 + \$3.50 = \$21.50$.	Review this lesson for volume of spheres and cones.
17 7	The diameter of the sphere is the same as the diagonal of the cube. The diagonal of the cube, which has a side length of 2, is $2\sqrt{3}$ (review the lesson to find out why). The radius of the sphere is half the diagonal= $\frac{2\sqrt{3}}{2} = \sqrt{3}$. The volume of the sphere is $\frac{4}{3}\pi r^3 = \frac{4}{3}\pi \left(\sqrt{3}\right)^3 = 4\pi\sqrt{3}$. So, equating $4\pi\sqrt{3} = a\pi\sqrt{3}$, you get, and $b = 3$. So $a + b = 4 + 3 = 7$.	Interior diagonals and spheres.

ADDITIONAL TOPICS IN MATHEMATICS

Lesson 31 — Complex Numbers — Review

FOCUSPREP CHECKLIST

- What are the parts of a complex number?
- How do I add, subtract, multiply, and divide complex numbers?
- What is a conjugate of a complex number?
- How do I simplify expressions involving square root of negative numbers?
- Workout practice problems in Complex numbers

Q1 What are complex numbers? Are they different from real numbers?

A1 A Complex number is made of two numbers – a real number and an imaginary number. A complex number is represented in the form of $a + bi$ where a is the real part, b is the imaginary part and i is the imaginary unit. $i = \sqrt{-1}$. Note that $i^2 = \sqrt{-1} \cdot \sqrt{-1} = -1$.

Examples: $2 + 3i, 2 - 3i, -2 + 3i, -2 - 3i, -20.5 + 50.6i, -\frac{3}{4} + \frac{59}{65}i, -44i$.

Q2 Why do we need complex numbers? Where are they used?

A2 Complex numbers are used to describe properties of various phenomena that occur in the field of physics. They are also used mathematics to describe unique situations that occur where solutions involve calculating the square root of negative numbers. For example, if the solution of an equation is $\sqrt{-3}$, then since the square root of a negative number is not defined, mathematicians define an imaginary number i to be equal to $\sqrt{-1}$ and thus $\sqrt{-3}$ becomes $\sqrt{-1 \cdot 3} = \sqrt{-1} \cdot \sqrt{3} = i\sqrt{3}$. Another example where complex numbers are useful is when a quadratic equation does not have any roots – that is, it does not intercept the x-axis. In that case, the roots are said to be imaginary and are represented in the form of $a + bi$.

Q3 Can you add, subtract, multiply, and divide complex numbers?

A3 Yes. See examples below. Always remember to isolate the real and imaginary parts and that $i = \sqrt{-1}$ and $i^2 = -1$.

Adding Complex Numbers
When adding two complex numbers, add their real and imaginary parts separately.
$z1 = a + bi$
$z2 = c + di$
$z1 + z2 = (a + c) + (b + d)i$

Example:
Let $z1 = 3 + 4i$; $z2 = 5 - 6i$
$z1 + z2 = 3 + 4i + 5 - 6i = 3 + 5 + 4i - 6i = 8 + (4 - 6)i = 8 - 2i$

Subtracting Complex Numbers
When subtracting two complex numbers, subtract their real and imaginary parts separately.
$z1 = a + bi$
$z2 = c + di$
$z1 - z2 = (a + bi) - (c + di)$
$= a + bi - c - di$
$= (a - c) + i(b - d)$

Example:
Let $z1 = 3 + 4i;\ z2 = 5 - 6i$
$z1 - z2 = 3 + 4i - (5 - 6i) = 3 + 4i - 5 + 6i = 3 - 5 + i(4 + 6) = -2 + 10i$

Multiplying Complex Numbers
When multiplying complex numbers, use the FOIL (First, Outer, Inner, Last) method, and remember that $i^2 = -1$.

$z1 = a + bi$
$z2 = c + di$

$z1 \cdot z2 = (a + bi) \cdot (c + di)$
$= ac + adi + bci + bdi^2$; using $i^2 = -1$ and combining the real and imaginary terms, you get
$z1 \cdot z2 = (ac - bd) + i(ad + bc)$

Example:
Let $z1 = 3 + 4i;\ z2 = 5 - 6i$
$z1 \cdot z2 = (3 + 4i) \cdot (5 - 6i)$
$= 3 \cdot 5 - 3 \cdot 6i + 4i \cdot 5 - 4i \cdot 6i$
$= 15 - 18i + 20i - 24\, i^2$
$= 15 + 24 + i(-18 + 20)$
$= 39 + 2i$

Q4 What is a Conjugate of a complex number?   Where is it used?

A4 The conjugate of a complex number is another complex number with the same real part but a sign-changed imaginary part. The conjugate of $a + bi$ is $a - bi$ and the conjugate of $a - bi$ is $a + bi$. The conjugate is also referred to as the complex conjugate.

Example: The conjugate of $2 + 3i$ is $2 - 3i$, and the conjugate of $-11 + 16i$ is $-11 - 16i$.

When you multiply a complex number with its conjugate, you get
$(a + bi) \cdot (a - bi) = a^2 - abi + bai - b^2 i^2 = a^2 + b^2$, since $i^2 = -1$.

The conjugate of a complex number is used to divide two complex numbers.

Dividing Complex Numbers
When dividing complex numbers, multiply the numerator and denominator by the conjugate of the denominator, so that you can convert the denominator from a complex number to a real number.

$z1 = a + bi$
$z2 = c + di$

$$\frac{z1}{z2} = \frac{a+bi}{c+di} = \frac{a+bi}{c+di} \cdot \frac{c-di}{c-di} = \frac{ac-adi+bci-bd\,i^2}{c^2+d^2} = \frac{(ac+bd)+i(bc-ad)}{c^2+d^2} = \frac{(ac+bd)}{c^2+d^2} + \frac{(bc-ad)\,i}{c^2+d^2}$$

Note the real and imaginary parts of the complex number.

Example:
Let $z1 = 3 + 4i;\ z2 = 5 - 6i$

$$\frac{z1}{z2} = \frac{3+4i}{5-6i} = \frac{3+4i}{5-6i} \cdot \frac{5+6i}{5+6i} = \frac{3\cdot5+3\cdot6i+4i\cdot5+4i\cdot6i}{5^2+6^2} = \frac{(15-24)+i(18+20)}{61} = \frac{-9}{61} + \frac{38\,i}{61}$$

Q5 How do I simplify a square root of a negative number?
A5 Use the fact that $i = \sqrt{-1}$ and $i^2 = \sqrt{-1} \cdot \sqrt{-1} = -1$ to simplify any expression involving square root of negative numbers.

Examples:
$\sqrt{-25} = \sqrt{-1 \cdot 25} = \sqrt{-1} \cdot \sqrt{25} = i.5 = 5i$

$4\sqrt{-25} = 4\sqrt{-1 \cdot 25} = 4\sqrt{-1} \cdot \sqrt{25} = 4 \cdot i \cdot 5 = 20i$

$-3\sqrt{-25} = -3\sqrt{-1 \cdot 25} = -3\sqrt{-1} \cdot \sqrt{25} = -3i.5 = -15i$

$\sqrt{-18} = \sqrt{-1 \cdot 18} = \sqrt{-1} \cdot \sqrt{18} = \sqrt{-1} \cdot \sqrt{9 \cdot 2} \quad i\sqrt{9}.\sqrt{2} = 3i\sqrt{2}$

$-\frac{2}{3}\sqrt{-27} = -\frac{2}{3} \cdot \sqrt{-1 \cdot 27} = -\frac{2}{3} \cdot \sqrt{-1} \cdot \sqrt{27} = -\frac{2}{3} \cdot i \cdot \sqrt{9 \cdot 3} = -\frac{2}{3} \cdot i \cdot 3.\sqrt{3} = -2i\sqrt{3}$

Q6 When are two complex numbers equal?
A6 Two complex numbers are equal when their real parts are equal and their imaginary parts are equal.
Example: Solve for x and y in the equation: $7x + 8i = 21 - 5yi$.
Solution: Note that this is an equation involving two complex numbers $7x + 8i$ and $21 - 5yi$.
$7x + 8i = 21 - 5yi$.
The real parts have to be equal. So $7x = 21 \Rightarrow x = \frac{21}{7} = 3$
The imaginary parts have to be equal. So $8 = -5y \Rightarrow y = -\frac{8}{5}$
So, for $x = 3$ and $y = -\frac{8}{5}$, the complex equality holds true.

Q7 What is the absolute value of a complex number?
A7 The absolute value of a complex number $z = a + bi$ is written as $|z|$ and is equal to $\sqrt{a^2 + b^2}$.
Example: If $z = -4 - 3i$, then $|z| = \sqrt{(-4)^2 + (-3)^2} = 5$.

ADDITIONAL TOPICS IN MATHEMATICS

Lesson 31 — Complex Numbers — Practice

NO CALCULATOR SECTION

1. $\sqrt{-121}$ can be simplified to which one of the following?

   (A) 11
   (B) −11
   (C) −11i
   (D) 11i

2. $-2\sqrt{-49}$ can be simplified to which one of the following?

   (A) −14
   (B) 14i
   (C) 7i
   (D) −14i

3. The expression $-\frac{4}{5}\sqrt{-25}$ can be simplified as

   (A) 4i
   (B) −4i
   (C) 5i
   (D) −5i

NO CALCULATOR SECTION

4. The sum of two complex numbers $4 + 6i$ and $7 - 8i$ is equal to which one of the following?

   (A) $11 - 2i$
   (B) $11 + 14i$
   (C) $11 - 8i$
   (D) $11 + 8i$

5. If complex number $7 + 4i$ is subtracted from complex number $8 - 3i$, the result is

   (A) $7 - i$
   (B) $7 + i$
   (C) $1 - 7i$
   (D) $4 - 7i$

6. The product of two complex numbers $9 + 4i$ and $6 - 2i$ is equal to which of the following complex numbers?

   (A) $54 - 8i$
   (B) $2 + 62i$
   (C) $62 + 6i$
   (D) $7 + 4i$

NO CALCULATOR SECTION

7. The conjugate of $-\frac{2}{3} + \frac{4}{5}i$ is

(A) $\frac{2}{3} + \frac{4}{5}i$
(B) $\frac{2}{3} - \frac{4}{5}i$
(C) $-\frac{2}{3} + \frac{4}{5}i$
(D) $-\frac{2}{3} - \frac{4}{5}i$

8. When $6 - 7i$ is multiplied by its conjugate, the result is

(A) -13
(B) -85
(C) 13
(D) 85

9. If $10 + 8i = 10 + 2ai$ then a equals

(A) 1
(B) 2
(C) 3
(D) 4

NO CALCULATOR SECTION

10. If $10x + 8i = 100 + 8i$ then x equals

(A) 8
(B) 9
(C) 10
(D) 11

11. When $9 + 4i$ is divided by $6 - 2i$, the resulting complex number is

(A) $\frac{23}{20} + \frac{21}{20}i$
(B) $42 + 46i$
(C) $\frac{23}{20} - \frac{21}{20}$
(D) $42 - 46i$

12. If $-3x + 9yi = 15 + 27i$, then the values of x and y are

(A) (-5,-3)
(B) (-5,3)
(C) (5,-3)
(D) (5,3)

NO CALCULATOR SECTION

13. If $x^2 + 81 = 0$, then x is

   (A) 0
   (B) 9
   (C) −9
   (D) 9i

14. If $\frac{x^2}{4} + 3 = 0$, then x is

   (A) $2\sqrt{3i}$
   (B) $2i\sqrt{3}$
   (C) $3\sqrt{2i}$
   (D) $2\sqrt{3}$

15. $(3i)^{-2} =$

   (A) $-\frac{1}{9}$

   (B) $-\frac{1}{3}$

   (C) $\frac{1}{9}$

   (D) $\frac{1}{3}$

CALCULATOR SECTION

16. $\frac{2+1.5i}{2-1.5i} =$

   (A) $1+0.75i$
   (B) $0.28 + 0.75i$
   (C) $0.28 + 0.96i$
   (D) $0.96 + 0.28i$

17. The product of $(5 + 5i) \cdot (5 - 6i)$ can be expressed in the form $a + bi$. What is the sum $a + b$?
   GRID IN

18. The imaginary part of the product of $(3 + 5i) \cdot (3 - 5i)$ is equal to
   GRID IN

ADDITIONAL TOPICS IN MATHEMATICS
Lesson 31 — Complex Numbers — Answers

#	Explanation	Comments
1 D	$\sqrt{-121} = \sqrt{-1}\sqrt{121} = 11i$	$\sqrt{-1} = i$
2 D	$-2\sqrt{-49} = -2\sqrt{-1 \cdot 49} = -2 \cdot \sqrt{-1} \cdot \sqrt{49} = -14i$	$\sqrt{-1} = i$
3 B	$-\frac{4}{5}\sqrt{-25} = -\frac{4}{5} \cdot 5i = -4i$	
4 A	$4 + 6i + 7 - 8i = 4 + 7 + 6i - 8i = 11 - 2i$	Add the real and imaginary parts separately.
5 C	$8 - 3i - (7 + 4i) = 8 - 3i - 7 - 4i = 1 - 7i$	
6 C	$(9 + 4i)(6 - 2i) = 54 - 18i + 24i + 8 = 62 + 6i$	Use FOIL to expand.
7 D	Conjugate of $-\frac{2}{3} + \frac{4}{5} = -\frac{2}{3} - \frac{4}{5}i$	Change sign of the imaginary part.
8 D	$(6 - 7i) \cdot (6 + 7i) = 36 + 49 = 85$	$(a + bi) \cdot (a - bi) = a^2 + b^2$
9 D	$10 + 8i = 10 + 2ai$ $8 = 2a$, so $a = 4$	Two complex numbers are equal when their real and imaginary parts are equal.
10 C	$10x + 8i = 100 + 8i$ $10x = 100$, so $x = 10$	Equate real parts to get x.
11 A	$\frac{9+4i}{6-2i} \cdot \frac{6+2i}{6+2i} = \frac{46+42i}{40} = \frac{46}{40} + \frac{42}{40i} = \frac{23}{20} + \frac{21}{20}i$	Multiply by conjugate of denominator and simplify.
12 B	$-3x + 9yi = 15 + 27i$ $-3x = 15$, so $x = -5$ $9y = 27$, so $y = 3$	Equate real and imaginary parts.
13 D	$x^2 + 81$ $x = \sqrt{-81} = \sqrt{-1} \cdot \sqrt{81} = \pm 9i$ $9i$ is the only correct answer choice.	$\sqrt{-1} = i$;
14 B	$\frac{x^2}{4} + 3 = 0$; multiply by 4 throughout $x^2 + 12 = 0$ $x^2 = -12$ $x = \sqrt{-12} = \sqrt{4 \cdot -3} = \pm 2\sqrt{-3} = \pm 2\sqrt{-1}\sqrt{3} = \pm 2i\sqrt{3}$ Only $2i\sqrt{3}$ is available in the answer choices.	Answer choice A has i inside the square root- it should be outside as in choice B.
15 A	$(3i)^{-2}$ $= 1/(3i)^2$ $= \frac{1}{9i^2} = = \frac{1}{9 \cdot -1} = = \frac{1}{-9} = -\frac{1}{9}$	Use $x^{-m} = \frac{1}{x^m}$ to simplify.
16 C	$\frac{2+1.5i}{2-1.5i}$ $= \frac{2+1.5i}{2-1.5i} \cdot \frac{2+1.5i}{2+1.5i} = \frac{4+2.25i^2+6i}{4+2.25} = \frac{1.75+6i}{6.25} = \frac{1.75}{6.25} + \frac{6}{6.25}i$ $= 0.28 + 0.96i$	Since answer choices are in decimals, use your calculator to multiply and divide the decimals.
17 50	$(5 + 5i) \cdot (5 - 6i) = 25 - 30i + 25i + 30 = 55 - 5i$ Sum of a and b $= 55 + (-5) = 50$	Note that you need to sum up the real and imaginary parts.
18 0	$(3 + 5i) \cdot (3 - 5i) = 3^2 - (5i)^2 = 9 - (25i^2)$ $= 9 - (-25) = 34$	$34 = 34 + 0i$ has an imaginary part $= 0$.

ADDITIONAL TOPICS IN MATHEMATICS

Lesson 32 | **Trigonometry** | **Review**

FOCUSPREP CHECKLIST

- How the trigonometric are functions sin, cos, and tan defined?
- When do I use the inverse trigonometric functions $\sin^{-1}$, $\cos^{-1}$, $\tan^{-1}$?
- What does Add Sugar To Coffee mean?
- What are the sin, cos, and tan values of angles in a special right triangle?
- Workout practice problems in Trigonometry

Q1 What is Trigonometry and what is it used for?

A1 Trigonometry is a branch of Mathematics that deals with angles and distances. It can be used to find the side lengths of a triangle, height of clock towers, and the angle at which a package must be dropped from an airplane to reach its target, etc.

Q2 What are the Trigonometric functions?

A2 The basic trigonometric functions are sine, cosine, and tangent, normally referred to as sin, cos, and tan respectively. For the right angled triangle shown, they are defined as follows. Remember these along with the Pythagorean theorem. Note that all angles in this lesson are measured in degrees.

$\sin \theta = \dfrac{opposite\ side}{hypotenuse} = \dfrac{a}{c}$

$\cos \theta = \dfrac{adjacent\ side}{hypotenuse} = \dfrac{b}{c}$

$\tan \theta = \dfrac{opposite\ side}{adjacent\ side} = \dfrac{a}{b}$

Pythagorean: $a^2 + b^2 = c^2$

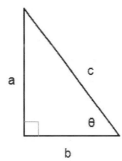

Q3 What are the special right triangles and their trigonometric functions?

A3 Special right triangles are 30°-60°-90° triangle and 45°-45°-90° triangle. Remember the sin and cos values as they are very important to solve problems.

Special Triangles	Figure	Trigonometric functions	
30°-60°-90°	(triangle with 60° at top, 30° at bottom right, legs 1 and √3, hypotenuse 2)	$\sin 30° = \frac{1}{2}$ $\cos 30° = \frac{\sqrt{3}}{2}$ $\tan 30° = \frac{\sin 30°}{\cos 30°} = \frac{1}{\sqrt{3}} = \frac{\sqrt{3}}{3}$	$\sin 60° = \frac{\sqrt{3}}{2}$ $\cos 60° = \frac{1}{2}$ $\tan 60° = \sqrt{3}$
45°-45°-90°	(triangle with 45° angles, legs 1 and 1, hypotenuse √2)	$\sin 45° = = \frac{1}{\sqrt{2}} = \frac{\sqrt{2}}{2}$ $\cos 45° = = \frac{1}{\sqrt{2}} = \frac{\sqrt{2}}{2}$ $\tan 45° = \frac{\sin 45°}{\cos 45°} = 1$	
Note: sin 45° and cos 45° are the same ($= \frac{\sqrt{2}}{2}$) and so $\tan 45° = \frac{\sin 45°}{\cos 45°} = 1$. $\sin 30° = \cos 60° = \frac{1}{2}$; $\cos 30° = \sin 60° = \frac{\sqrt{3}}{2}$ sin 0°= 0, cos 0° = 1, tan 0°=0/1=0 ; sin 90° = 1, cos 90° = 0; tan 90°=1/0=undefined			

Q4 What are $\sin^{-1}$, $\cos^{-1}$, $\tan^{-1}$? When are these used? How do I calculate these?

A4 $\sin^{-1}$, $\cos^{-1}$, $\tan^{-1}$ are called <u>inverse</u> trigonometric functions. They are used to find the angle if you know the ratio of the sides. You can find them using your calculator. It is easy to understand these with some examples.

Example: sin 30° =0.5. So, $\sin^{-1} 0.5 = 30°$. Conversely, if $\sin^{-1} 0.5 = 30°$ then sin 30° = 0.5

Example: If sin θ=0.6, what is θ?
Solution: sin θ=0.6, so θ =$\sin^{-1} 0.6 = 36.86°$ using your calculator.

Example: cos 30°=0.86. So, $\cos^{-1} 0.86 = 30°$.

Example: If cos θ=0.4, what is θ?
Solution: θ=$\cos^{-1} 0.4 = 66.42°$ using your calculator.

Example: tan 60° = 1.732. So, tan^{-1} 1.732 = 60°.

Example: If tan θ=1.5, what is θ?
Solution: θ= tan^{-1} 1.5 = 56.30° using your calculator.

In summary, if you know the ratio of the sides of a triangle, then you can use the inverse trigonometric functions sin^{-1}, cos^{-1}, tan^{-1} to calculate the angle. If you know the opposite side & hypotenuse, then use sin^{-1}. If you know the adjacent side & hypotenuse, then use cos^{-1}. If you know the opposite side & adjacent side, the use tan^{-1}.

Q5 How are trigonometric functions used to calculate the side lengths of a right triangle?

A5 Example: In the triangle shown, what is the length of the hypotenuse?
Solution: As you can see, you cannot apply the Pythagorean theorem since one side length is not known. This is where trigonometry is helpful. You know that sin θ= opposite side/hypotenuse. You also know that sin 30°=$\frac{1}{2}$.

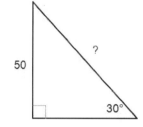

So sin 30= $\frac{1}{2}$=opposite/hypotenuse= 50/hypotenuse.
Cross multiplying, you get hypotenuse = 50 · 2=100

Q6 How are the inverse trigonometric functions used to calculate the angles of a right triangle?

A6

Example: In the triangle shown, what is the angle θ?
Solution: You know the adjacent side and hypotenuse.
So cos θ= adjacent side/hypotenuse=$\frac{50}{90} = \frac{5}{9}$
So, θ = cos$^{-1}\frac{5}{9}$ = 56.25°

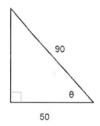

Q7 What is an angle of elevation? What is an angle of depression?

A7 If you are standing on the ground and look at the top a building, the angle at which you look at the top of a building is the angle of elevation. If you stood on the top of a building and looked down on an object, then the angle at which you look down is the angle of depression. Their value is the same but you should know the meaning of these angles.

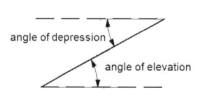

Q8 What do I need to know to solve problems in trigonometry?

A8 Review this lesson on Trigonometry. Remember the trigonometric ratios of special angles. Know how to use your calculator to find values of trigonometric functions and inverse trigonometric functions.

Example: From the point on ground where it was launched, a balloon ascends at an angle of 30°. What is its elevation from the ground after it has drifted 300 feet away horizontally from the launching point?

Solution:
Draw the figure as shown. You know the adjacent side and the angle and you need to find the opposite side. Applying the tan trig function, tan 30° = oppo/adja = height/300. So, the height of the balloon is 300 · tan 30° = 300 · 0.58 = 174 ft using your calculator.

Example: From the top of a 50 feet tall building where it was launched, a balloon has drifted 300 feet away horizontally and can be seen at an angle of elevation of 30 degrees. How high is the balloon from the ground?

Solution:
Applying the trigonometric function, tan 30 = height/300. This height is measured from the top of the building. tan 30 using calculator is 0.58. So, the height of the balloon is 300 · tan 30 = 174 ft. But note that the balloon was launched from the building that is 50 ft tall. So, the elevation of the balloon from the ground is 50 + 174 = 224 ft. Be careful not to miss any detail mentioned in the problem.

Q9 Are angles positive or negative?

A9 By convention, if the angle is measured in the anticlockwise direction, it is positive. If the angle is measured in the clockwise direction, it is negative. This is true whether the angle is measured in degrees or radians. Radians are reviewed in a separate lesson.

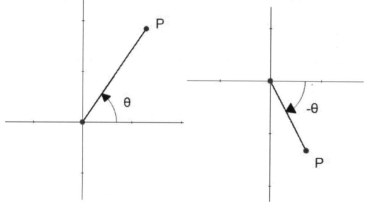

Q10 What are Initial side, Terminal side, and Standard position?

A10 These relate to how an angle is measured. If you think that an angle is formed by rotating a ray about its vertex, then the initial position of the ray is the <u>initial side</u> and the final position of the ray is the <u>terminal side</u>. If the initial side coincides with the positive x-axis, then the angle is said to be in <u>standard position</u>. For example, the statement "the terminal side of the angle θ in standard position passes through the point $(-4,5)$" implies that the angle is formed by the positive x-axis ray and the ray passing through the point $(-4,5)$.

Q11 What is a Unit circle?

A11 A unit circle is a circle of radius 1 unit. It is used to determine the values and signs (+ or −) of trigonometric functions. For a point P with coordinates (x, y) on the unit circle, using Pythagorean theorem, $x^2 + y^2 = 1$. Also, $\cos \theta = x$ and $\sin \theta = y$; $x^2 + y^2 = \sin^2 \theta + \cos^2 \theta = 1$

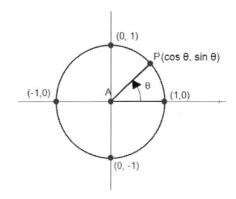

Q12 What is a Reference angle?

A12 A reference angle is the angle formed by the terminal point with the x axis (positive x-axis or negative x-axis). It is used to calculate the value of trigonometric functions (sin, cos, tan) when the angle is greater than 90° or when it is less than 0°. In that case, to calculate the trig functions, the reference angle can be used instead of the original angle. In the figure shown, the radius of unit length is rotated anticlockwise by an angle θ=110° and the terminal point P falls in Quadrant II. The reference angle is equal to 180-θ =180° − 110° =70°. Reference angles do not have a sign attached to them. They are neither positive nor negative.

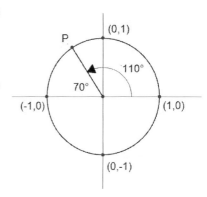

Example: In each of the examples below, find the reference angle.
Remember that the reference angle is the angle formed by the terminal point with the x-axis. The drawing for 110° is shown above.
Reference angle of 60°   Answer: 60°
Reference angle of 110° Answer: 70° (180-110)
Reference angle of 240° Answer: 60° (240-180)
Reference angle of 325° Answer: 35° (360-325)

Q13 How do I find sin, cos, tan of an angle that is greater than 90 or less than 0 using Reference Angles and without using a calculator?

A13
Step 1: Find the quadrant where the terminal point falls.
Step 2) Find the reference angle
Step 3) Find the sin,cos,or tan of the reference angle
Step 4) Change the sign using **ASTC** (described below).

To remember the quadrant where sin,cos, and tan is positive, it is normal practice to remember the acronym **ASTC** or the catch phrases: **A**dd **S**ugar **T**o **C**offee or **A**ll **S**tudents **T**ake **C**hemistry Or **A**ll **S**ilver **T**ea **C**ups. The first letters of these phrases are A,S,T,C – they correspond to which quadrants the corresponding trig functions are positive. The table below and the figure show this clearly.

Quadrant I	All trigs (sin,cos,tan) are positive
Quadrant II	Sin is positive
Quadrant II	Tan is positive
Quadrant IV	Cos is positive

```
   Sugar      |      Add

   sin +    II | I    all trigs +
           ----+----
            III| IV
   To         |       Coffee

   tan +      |       cos +
```

©GiftOfLogic   http://www.GiftOfLogic.com

Example: Find sin 210°
Solution:
Step 1: Terminal point falls in 3rd quadrant (since 2nd quadrant goes up to 180° only)
Step 2: Reference angle = 30° (210-180)
Step 3: sin 210° = sin 30°=$\frac{1}{2}$
Step 4: Change the sign– in 3rd quadrant, only tan is positive, so sin is negative; so sin 210°=$-\frac{1}{2}$

Example: Find sin 420°
Solution:
Step 1: The angle is more than 360° — so, the angle is the same as 420° − 360° = 60°. This angle falls in 1st quadrant.
Step 2: The reference angle is also 60°. In Quadrant I, the angle and its reference angle are the same.
Step 3: Using the reference angle, sin 420° = sin 60° =$\frac{\sqrt{3}}{2}$ (remember trig values for 30°, 45°, 60°)
Step 4: Change the sign: In quadrant I, all trigs are positive. So sin 420° = $\frac{\sqrt{3}}{2}$.

Example: Find sin (-120°)
Solution:
Step 1: Note that the angle is in negative, so it is measured clockwise. The angle falls in the third quadrant going clockwise.
Step 2: The terminal point is 30° beyond the negative y-axis – and makes a 60° with the x axis. So, the reference angle is 60°.
Step 3: Using the reference angle, sin (-120°) = sin 60°=$\frac{\sqrt{3}}{2}$
Step 4: using ASTC, sin is negative in the third quadrant; so sin -120° = $-\frac{\sqrt{3}}{2}$

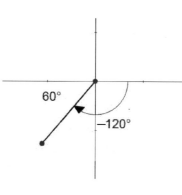

Example: Find sin 3660°
Solution:
Step 1: The angle is more than 360° – find how much more than 360° ; $3660 = 10 \cdot 360 + 60$; So, the terminal point will be at 60°. This angle falls in 1st quadrant.
Step 2: The reference angle is also 60° in Quadrant I.
Step 3: Using the reference angle, sin 3660° = sin 60° =$\frac{\sqrt{3}}{2}$
Step 4: Change sign: In quadrant I, all trigs are positive. So sin 3660° = $\frac{\sqrt{3}}{2}$

Q14 What are some other types of trigonometric problems?
A14 You can expect problems that test your understanding of ASTC.
Example: Point (-4,5) lies in the terminal side of an angle in standard position. What is the cosine of this angle?
Solution:
The point (-4,5) lies in Quadrant II. If you draw a figure as shown, you can see that cos θ is the cos of its reference angle= $\frac{adja}{hypo} = \frac{4}{\sqrt{41}}$, where hypotenuse= $\sqrt{5^2 + 4^2} = \sqrt{41}$. Using ASTC, cos is negative in Quadrant II. So, cos θ= $-\frac{4}{\sqrt{41}}$.

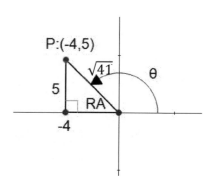

Example: If angle θ is such that tan θ > 0 and sin θ < 0, in which quadrant does θ lie in?
   A) Quadrant I   B) Quadrant II   C) Quadrant III   D) Quadrant IV

Solution: Using ASTC, you know that tan is positive in Quadrant III and sin is negative in quadrant III. So, θ lies in Quadrant III.

Example: If $\sin \theta = -\frac{2}{\sqrt{51}}$ and tan θ > 0 then what is cos θ?

Solution:
tan θ is positive and sin θ is negative— so the angle is in the 3rd quadrant. Since sin θ = oppo/hypo, draw a triangle in 3rd quadrant with −2 as opposite side and hypotenuse as $\sqrt{51}$. Now, you can find the adjacent side of the triangle;

$x^2 + (-2)^2 = (\sqrt{51})^2$
$x^2 + 4 = 51$
$x = \pm\sqrt{47}$

Since θ is in the 3rd Quadrant, cos θ is negative (using ASTC). For cos θ to be negative, x has to be negative. So, $x = -\sqrt{47}$. $\cos \theta = -\frac{\sqrt{47}}{\sqrt{51}} = -\sqrt{\frac{47}{51}}$.

Q15 What are some additional trigonometric formulas and tips?

A15 You have to remember the following formulas and tips. These are true for angles in degrees or radians. Radians are covered in a separate lesson. Remember that angles are positive when measured counterclockwise and negative when measure clockwise.

$\sin(-\theta) = -\sin \theta$
$\cos(-\theta) = \cos \theta$
$\tan(-\theta) = \frac{\sin(-\theta)}{\cos(-\theta)} = \frac{-\sin(\theta)}{\cos(\theta)} = -\tan \theta$
$\sin(90 - \theta) = \cos \theta$
$\cos(90 - \theta) = \sin \theta$
$\tan(90 - \theta) = \frac{\sin(90 - \theta)}{\cos(90 - \theta)} = \frac{\cos(\theta)}{\sin(\theta)} = \frac{1}{\tan(\theta)}$

$\sin^2 \theta = \sin \theta \cdot \sin \theta$
$\sin^2 \theta$ is not equal to $\sin(2\theta)$
$\frac{\sin^2 \theta}{\cos^2 \theta} = \tan^2 \theta$

$\sin^2 \theta + \cos^2 \theta = 1$

If sin θ=0.5, then $\sin^2 \theta = \sin \theta \cdot \sin \theta = 0.5 \cdot 0.5 = 0.25$
If sin θ=0.5, then $\theta = \sin^{-1} 0.5 = 30°$ and $\sin 2\theta = \sin 60°$
If $\theta = 30°$, then $\sin 2\theta = \sin 60° = \frac{\sqrt{3}}{2}$.

ADDITIONAL TOPICS IN MATHEMATICS

Lesson 32 — Trigonometry — Practice

NO CALCULATOR SECTION

1. In the triangle shown below, sin θ + cos θ is which one of the following

   (A) 1
   (B) $\frac{1+\sqrt{3}}{2}$
   (C) $1+\frac{\sqrt{3}}{2}$
   (D) $\frac{\sqrt{3}}{2} - 1$

2. In the triangle shown below, tan θ is which one of the following ratios?

   (A) $\frac{3}{5}$
   (B) $\frac{3}{4}$
   (C) $\frac{4}{3}$
   (D) $\frac{1}{2}$

3. In the triangle shown below, what is the value of x?

   (A) 100
   (B) $100\sqrt{2}$
   (C) $50\sqrt{2}$
   (D) $\frac{\sqrt{2}}{100}$

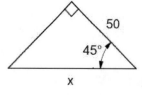

NO CALCULATOR SECTION

4. In the triangle shown below, the ratio of sin θ to cos θ is which one of the following?

   (A) $\frac{1}{\sqrt{3}}$
   (B) 1
   (C) $\sqrt{2}$
   (D) $\sqrt{3}$

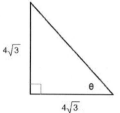

5. A ladder rests on a wall at an angle of 42° as shown below. The lower end of the ladder is 6 feet from the wall. What is the measure of h, the upper end of the ladder from the bottom of the wall?

   (A) 6 tan 42°
   (B) $\frac{6}{\tan 42°}$
   (C) 6 sin 42°
   (D) 6 cos 42°

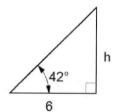

6. Two trees AB and CD are 2 feet apart as shown. The shorter tree is 5 feet from point O. The top of both trees have an angle of elevation of 30° from point O. What is the difference in height between the trees?

   (A) 2 tan 30°
   (B) 3 tan 30°
   (C) 5 tan 30°
   (D) 7 tan 30°

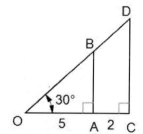

©GiftOfLogic http://www.GiftOfLogic.com

CALCULATOR SECTION

7. In the triangle shown below, what is the value of θ in degrees?

(A) 37.50°
(B) 20.55°
(C) 22.02°
(D) 67.98°

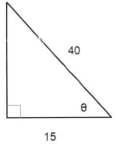

8. What is the product of sin 60° and cos 30°?

(A) $\frac{3}{4}$

(B) $\frac{3}{2}$

(C) $\frac{\sqrt{3}}{2}$

(D) 1

9 What is the radius of the circle in the figure shown?

(A) 5.38
(B) 13.74
(C) 14.70
(D) 16.88

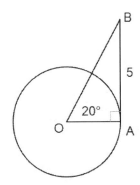

CALCULATOR SECTION

10. In the triangle shown below, what is the measure of the angle θ in degrees?

GRID IN

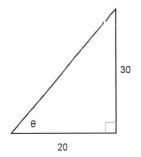

11. In the triangle shown below, what is the value of cos θ ?

GRID IN

12. Two buildings, one 50 feet tall and another 100 feet tall are 25 feet apart as shown. What is the angle of elevation θ of the top of the 100 feet tall building?

(A) 30°
(B) 60°
(C) 33.43°
(D) 63.43°

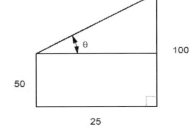

©GiftOfLogic http://www.GiftOfLogic.com

CALCULATOR SECTION

13. An airplane currently is at point A, 500 feet away from point X, and makes a 45° angle of elevation from X as shown. After some time, the airplane moves horizontally to point B, 500 feet from point A. What angle of elevation θ does the airplane now make from X?
 GRID IN

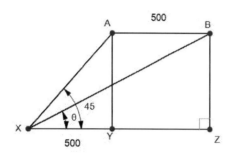

14. A dog was spotted at point Y from the top of a 15 feet tall building at an angle of depression of 45° as shown. After some time, the same dog was spotted at point X at an angle of depression of 71°. How much distance did the dog walk toward the building? (round your answer to the hundredths)
 GRID IN

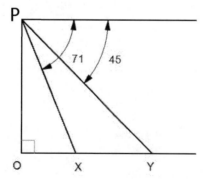

CALCULATOR SECTION

15. From a survey instrument that is 4 feet above the ground, a tip of a clock tower can be seen at an angle of elevation of 30°. If the clock tower is 200 feet from the survey instrument, what is the height of the clock tower to the nearest foot? (figure is not to scale)
 GRID IN

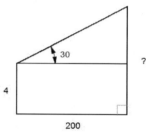

16. In the triangle shown, what is cos θ ?
 GRID IN

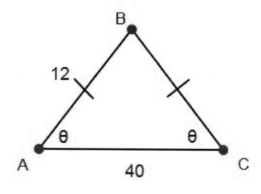

©GiftOfLogic http://www.GiftOfLogic.com

ADDITIONAL TOPICS IN MATHEMATICS

Lesson 32 — Trigonometry — **Answers**

#	Explanation	Comments
1 B	$\sin \theta =$ oppo/hypo; apply Pythagorean rule hypo $= \sqrt{\left(4^2 + \left(4\sqrt{3}\right)^2\right)} = \sqrt{16 + 16 \cdot 3} = \sqrt{64} = 8$ $\sin \theta =$ oppo/hypo $= \frac{4}{8} = \frac{1}{2}$ $\cos \theta =$ adja/hypo $= \frac{4\sqrt{3}}{8} = \frac{\sqrt{3}}{2}$ so, $\sin \theta + \cos \theta = \frac{1}{2} + \frac{\sqrt{3}}{2} = \frac{1+\sqrt{3}}{2}$	Be careful not choose choice C as the answer.
2 B	$\tan \theta =$ oppo/adjacent; opposite side can be found by Pythagorean rule $= \sqrt{50^2 - 40^2} = \sqrt{900} = 30$ $\tan \theta =$ oppo/adja $= \frac{30}{40} = \frac{3}{4}$	
3 C	You know one angle and its adjacent side, you have to find x, the hypotenuse $\cos 45 = \frac{\sqrt{2}}{2} =$ adja /hypo $= \frac{50}{x}$ cross multiplying, $\sqrt{2}\, x = 100$, so $x = \frac{100}{\sqrt{2}} = 100\frac{\sqrt{2}}{2} = 50\sqrt{2}$	other answer choices are there to trick you in case you get the definition of $\cos \theta$ wrong
4 B	observe the question for a few seconds before you start solving; the question asks for $\sin \theta / \cos \theta$; this is the same as $\tan \theta =$ oppo/adja $= \frac{4\sqrt{3}}{4\sqrt{3}} = 1$	Do not waste time calculating the hypotenuse
5 A	$\tan 42° =$ h/6; so h = 6 tan 42°	$\tan \theta =$ opposite/adjacent
6 A	Let b=height of big tree and s=height of small tree $\tan 30 = \frac{b}{7}$, so $b = 7 \tan 30°$ $\tan 30 = \frac{s}{5}$, so $s = 5 \tan 30°$ the difference in height between the trees is 7 tan 30 - 5 tan 30 = 2 tan 30°	pause for a few seconds and notice the two right triangles, one with the small tree as one side and another with the big tree as one side. Then, apply the tan trig function.
7 D	the adjacent side and hypotenuse are given so, $\cos \theta =$ adja/hypo = 15/40 = 3/8 = 0.375 using calculator, $\theta = \cos^{-1} 0.375 = 67.98°$	make sure the calculator is set to mode=Degrees. The calculator should NOT be set to Radians. Learn to calculate inverse trig function $\cos^{-1}$. Review the Calculator lesson.
8 A	$\sin 60° = \frac{\sqrt{3}}{2}$ and $\cos 30° = \frac{\sqrt{3}}{2}$; so the product is $\frac{\sqrt{3}}{2} \cdot \frac{\sqrt{3}}{2} = \frac{3}{4}$	memorize the sin, cos, tan values for 30, 45 and 60 degrees.
9 B	$\tan 20° = \frac{oppo}{adja} = \frac{5}{r}$ $r \tan 20° = 5$ $r = \frac{5}{\tan 20} = 13.74$	do not round off tan 20° and then do 5/tan20°; use the calculator to find 5/tan 20° in one shot.

©GiftOfLogic http://www.GiftOfLogic.com

10 56.3	$\tan\theta = \frac{30}{20} = 1.5, \theta = \tan^{-1} 1.5 = 56.31°$	Use your calculator to find $\tan^{-1} 1.5$
11 0.59	You know the adjacent and opposite sides, so you can find $\tan\theta =$ oppo/adja$=\frac{22}{16}$=1.375, so $\theta = \tan^{-1} 1.375 = 53.97°$; so $\cos\theta = \cos 53.97° = 0.59$	In this problem, see how $\cos\theta$ is calculated without finding the hypotenuse and saving valuable time.
12 D	Note that the angle of elevation in this problem is marked for you as being measured from the top of the 50 ft tall building. $\tan\theta = \frac{oppo}{adja} = \frac{100-50}{25} = 2, \theta = \tan^{-1} 2 = 63.43°$	Review the meaning of angle of elevation.
13 26.6	You need to find θ; you know $XZ = 500 + 500 = 1000$ $$\tan\theta = \frac{BZ}{XZ} = \frac{BZ}{1000}$$ To find BZ, use the fact that $BZ = AY$. You know that $\tan 45 = \frac{AY}{500}$ So, $AY = 500 \tan 45° = 500 \cdot 1 = 500$. So, $\tan\theta = \frac{BZ}{1000} = \frac{AY}{1000} = \frac{500}{1000} = 0.5$ $\theta = \tan^{-1} 0.5 = 26.56°$	Review the meaning of angle of depression.
14 9.84	Draw the figure and use the fact that opposite interior angles are equal to mark the 45° and 71° angles. You need to find YX. $\tan 45 = \frac{oppo}{adja} = \frac{15}{OY}; OY = \frac{15}{\tan 45} = \frac{15}{1} = 15$ $\tan 71 = \frac{oppo}{adja} = \frac{15}{OX}; OX = \frac{15}{\tan 71} = 5.16$ note that the question asks how much distance the dog walked toward the building; that distance is $YX = OY - OX = 15 - 5.16 = 9.84$ ft.	Notice that the question asks how far the dog walked toward the building YX – not how far the dog is away from the building XO. Drawing the figure correctly is important to solve the problem.
15 119	Note that the angle of elevation is measured in this problem from the survey instrument that is 4 ft above the ground. Let h be the height of the clock tower; from the figure, you get $\tan 30 = \frac{oppo}{adja} = \frac{h-4}{200}; h - 4 = 200 \tan 30° = 115.47$ ft $h = 4 + 115.47 = 119.47$ ft = 119 after rounding.	Be careful to account for the height of the instrument.

| 16 1.67 | Since the triangle is isosceles, drop a perpendicular to the side that is 40 ft long – this will bisect the side to two segments of 20 ft each.
In triangle ADB, $\cos \theta = \dfrac{\text{adja}}{\text{hypo}} = \dfrac{AD}{AB} = \dfrac{20}{12} = 1.67$
 | Sometimes you have to draw lines or drop a perpendicular to create right triangles so that you can apply the trig functions. |

ADDITIONAL TOPICS IN MATHEMATICS

Lesson 33 — Radians — Review

> **FOCUSPREP CHECKLIST**
> - What is a Radian?
> - How do I convert Radians to Degrees and Degrees to Radians?
> - How do I calculate trigonometric functions using Radians?
> - How do I calculate arc lengths using radians ($s = r\theta$)?
> - Workout practice problems in Radians

Q1 What is a Radian? Why do we need it?

A1 While a Degree is normally used to measure angles, a Radian is another way to measure an angle. Radians are used to measure angles in several science and engineering problems. It is easy to measure certain things with radians instead of degrees. For example, objects that revolve around a central point have angular velocity that is best measured with the help of radians. Radians are also used to specify a point in the Polar Coordinate system.

Q2 How is 1 Radian defined?

A2 1 Radian is the measure of the central angle inscribed by an arc of length r which lies on the circumference of a circle of radius r. If the radius is say 50 feet, then an arc length of 50 feet will subtend an angle of 1 radian. If the radius is 1000 feet, then an arc length of 1000 feet will subtend an angle of 1 radian.

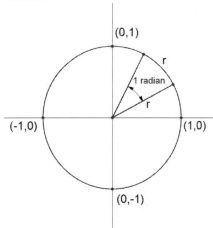

Q3 How do I convert Radians to Degrees and Degrees to Radians?

A3 Just as there are 360° in one full circle, there are 2π radians in one full circle. So, 2π radians = 360°. It follows that π radians = 180°. The normal convention is to remember that π radian corresponds to 180° instead of remembering that 2π radians = 360°. Using the fact that π radians = 180°, you can set up a direct proportion to calculate any conversion between degrees and radians and vice versa.

Example: Convert 210° to radians.

$180° = \pi$ radians
$210° = \frac{\pi}{180} \cdot 210 = \frac{7\pi}{6}$ radians

Example: Convert $\frac{\pi}{4}$ radians to degrees

π radians $= 180°$
$\frac{\pi}{4}$ radians $= \frac{180}{4} = 45°$

Example: Convert $-60°$ to radians.
When the angle is negative, retain the sign and do the conversion as usual.

$180° = \pi$ radians
$-60° = \frac{\pi}{180} \cdot -60° = -\frac{\pi}{3}$ radians

Note that angle measurements, whether in Degrees or in Radians, are positive if measured in counterclockwise direction and negative if measured in clockwise direction.

Q4 How do I find the length of the arc, if I know the radius and central angle?
A4 The formula is $s = r \cdot \theta$ where r is the radius and θ is the central angle in <u>radians.</u>
Remembering this formula is important. However, if you forget it, it is easy to derive this formula from the definition of a radian as follows.
<u>Derive s=r θ from the definition of a radian</u>
1 radian is the angle inscribed by an arc of length r (lying on a circle of radius r)
1 radian => arc of length r
θ radians => $\frac{r}{1} \cdot \theta = r \cdot \theta$
So, θ radians will intercept an arc of length $r \cdot \theta$.

Example: What is the length of the arc intercepted by a central angle of $\frac{\pi}{6}$ radians if the radius of the circle is 15 ft?
Solution: $s = r\theta = 15 \cdot \frac{\pi}{6} = 7.85$ ft. Note that you must enter 3.14 for π in your calculator.

Q5 What is the formula for the arc length and area of a <u>sector</u> of radius r and angle θ, where θ is in <u>radians and degrees</u>?
A5 Remember that there are 2π radians or 360 degrees in a full circle that has an area of πr^2 and a circumference of $2\pi r$. Use this fact to derive the formulas.

Arc length of a sector of θ radians	Area of a sector of θ radians
2π radians => $2\pi r$	2π radians => πr^2
θ radians => $\frac{2\pi r}{2\pi} \cdot \theta = r \cdot \theta$	θ radians => $\frac{\pi r^2}{2\pi} \cdot \theta = \frac{1}{2} r^2 \cdot \theta$
Arc length of a sector of θ degrees	Area of a sector of θ degrees
360 degrees => $2\pi r$	360 degrees => πr^2
θ degrees => $\frac{2\pi r}{360} \cdot \theta$	θ degrees => $\frac{\pi r^2}{360} \cdot \theta$

A few problems involving radians are shown below with solutions.

Example: Find $\cos\left(\frac{2\pi}{3}\right)$ (No Calculator)

Solution: Step 1: Note that the angle is in radians. Convert the angle to degrees. Since $\pi = 180°$, $\frac{2\pi}{3} = 2 \cdot \frac{180}{3} = 120°$. This angle falls in the second quadrant. You convert the angle to degrees since it is easy to work with degrees.

Step 2: The reference angle in second quadrant is 180°-θ = 180°-120°=60°.

Step 3: $\cos(120°) = \cos(60°) = \frac{1}{2}$

Step 4: cos is negative in the second quadrant; so $\cos(120°) = -\frac{1}{2}$. So, $\cos\left(\frac{2\pi}{3}\right) = -\frac{1}{2}$.

Example: A line from the origin to a point P makes an angle of $\frac{\pi}{8}$ with the x-axis. This point is reflected over the origin. What is the cosine of the angle made with the x-axis by the line from the origin to the reflected point?

Solution1: (not using Reference angle) (Calculator)

Step 1: Note that the angle is in radians. $\frac{\pi}{8}$ is less than $\frac{\pi}{2}$ and so the point falls in the first quadrant.

Step 2: The reflection of this point over the origin will place it in the Quadrant III. The angle of this reflected point= $\frac{\pi}{8} + \pi = \frac{9\pi}{8}$. Note that this angle is measured counterclockwise.

Step 3: Using your calculator, set the mode to Radians and calculate $\cos(\frac{9\pi}{8})$. Remember to key 3.14 for π. So $\cos(\frac{9\pi}{8}) = \cos\left(9 \cdot \frac{3.14}{8}\right) = \cos(3.5325) = -0.92$

Solution2: (using Reference Angle) (Calculator)

Step 1: Note that the angle is in radians. $\frac{\pi}{8}$ falls in the first quadrant.

Step 2: The reflection of this point over the origin will place it in the Quadrant III. The reference angle in the third quadrant is the angle this point makes with the x-axis which is also $\frac{\pi}{8}$. Remember that the reference angle does not have a sign attached to it.

Step 3: cosine of this reflected point in the 3rd quadrant is the cosine of the reference angle = $\cos(\frac{\pi}{8}) = 0.92$. Make sure to set the mode in the calculator to Radians.

Step 4: Using ASTC, attach the positive or negative sign. The reflected point is in the 3rd quadrant where cosine is negative. So, the cosine of the reflected point is -0.92.

Example: A line from the origin to a point P makes an angle of $\frac{\pi}{8}$ with the x-axis. This point is reflected over the x-axis. What is the cosine of the angle made with the x-axis by the line from the origin to the reflected point? Use your calculator.

Solution: Step 1: Note that the angle is in radians. $\frac{\pi}{8}$ falls in the first quadrant.

Step 2: The reflection of this point over the x-axis will place it in the Quadrant IV. The reference angle of this reflected point= $\frac{\pi}{8}$. Step 3: $\cos(\frac{\pi}{8}) = 0.92$. Step 4: cosine is positive in Quadrant IV (ASTC). So, the cosine of the reflected point is $+0.92$

Example: If the length of an arc with an angle of $\frac{\pi}{5}$ radians is 9π, what is the radius of the arc?

Solution: Since $s = r\theta$, substituting the values of s and θ gives => $9\pi = r \cdot \frac{\pi}{5}$

So, $r = 9\pi \cdot \frac{5}{\pi} = 45$

ADDITIONAL TOPICS IN MATHEMATICS

Lesson 33 — Radians — Practice

CALCULATOR SECTION

1. 135° converted to radians is

   (A) $\frac{\pi}{3}$

   (B) $\frac{3\pi}{4}$

   (C) $\frac{\pi}{2}$

   (D) $\frac{\pi}{6}$

2. $\frac{4\pi}{9}$ converted to degrees is

   (A) 30°
   (B) 60°
   (C) 80°
   (D) 90°

3. $\frac{2\pi}{9}$ lies in which quadrant?

   (A) I
   (B) II
   (C) III
   (D) IV

CALCULATOR SECTION

4. The sin trigonometric function is positive in which quadrant?

   (A) I and II
   (B) I and III
   (C) I and IV
   (D) II and III

5. The reference angle of $\frac{3\pi}{4}$ is

   (A) $\frac{\pi}{8}$
   (B) $\frac{\pi}{4}$
   (C) $\frac{\pi}{2}$
   (D) π

6. $4 \cdot \sin\left(\frac{\pi}{4}\right)$ is

   (A) 0.71
   (B) 0.95
   (C) 1.85
   (D) 2.84

CALCULATOR SECTION

7. A wheel of diameter 19 inches rotates 30° in 1 minute. How much distance does it cover in 1 hour?

    (A) 99.48
    (B) 298.45
    (C) 496.90
    (D) 598.45

8. A house fly sits on the circumference of a wheel of radius 20 inches that rotates 50 revolutions every minute. How many inches does the fly travel in 10 minutes?

    (A) 31,400
    (B) 32,000
    (C) 62,400
    (D) 62,800

CALCULATOR SECTION

9. The radius of Earth is 3959 miles. What is the angle measure in radians that would intercept an arc of length 9645 miles on the circumference of the earth? (round to hundredths).
GRID IN

10. A pendulum of a clock swings from one end to another and covers a distance of 22 inches while describing an angle of 80°. What is the length of the pendulum? (round to tenths).
GRID IN

ADDITIONAL TOPICS IN MATHEMATICS

| Lesson 33 | Radians | Answers |

#	Explanation	Comments
1 B	$180° = \pi$ radians $135° = \dfrac{\pi}{180} \cdot 135 = \dfrac{3}{4}\pi$	memorize $180° = \pi$ radians
2 C	$\dfrac{4\pi}{9} = 4 \cdot \dfrac{180}{9} = 4 \cdot 20 = 80°$	Substitute 180° instead of π radians.
3 A	$\dfrac{2\pi}{9} = 2 \cdot \dfrac{180}{9} = 40°$, this is in the Quadrant I	
4 A	Remember the catch phrase: **A**dd **S**ugar **T**o **C**offee – In first and second quadrants, sin is positive. Other phrases to remember are **A**ll **S**tations **T**o **C**entral **A**ll **S**tudents **T**ake **C**hemistry **A**ll **S**ilver **T**ea **C**ups	Remember one of these phrases to help you know in which quadrants the trig functions are positive.
5 B	$\dfrac{3\pi}{4}$ is $3 \cdot \dfrac{180}{4} = 135°$ - this falls in 2nd quadrant. The reference angle is $\pi - \dfrac{3\pi}{4} = \dfrac{\pi}{4}$.	Reference angle is reviewed in the Trigonometry lesson.
6 D	$4 \cdot \sin\left(\dfrac{\pi}{4}\right) = 4 \cdot 0.71 = 2.84$	Remember to set your calculator to Radian mode and use 3.14 for π.
7 B	Formula is $s = r\theta$ (θ is in radians) $\theta = 30°$ $180° = \pi$ radians $30° = \dfrac{\pi}{180} \cdot 30 = \dfrac{\pi}{6}$ radians $s = \dfrac{19}{2} \cdot \dfrac{\pi}{6}$ in 1 minute In 1 hour=60 minutes, $s = \dfrac{19}{2} \cdot \dfrac{\pi}{6} \cdot 60 = 298.45$ inches	This example shows the use of radians to calculate distance covered by a revolving wheel. Applications like this are common in Physics.
8 D	In 1 revolution, the fly covers 2π radians 50 revolutions => $50 \cdot 2\pi = 100\pi$ radians 1 minute => 100π radians 10 minutes => 1000π radians $s = r\theta$ (θ in radians) $\theta = 1000\pi$ $s = 20 \cdot 1000\pi = 62{,}800$ inches	Note that one rotation is 2π radians and the wheel rotates a total of 1000π radians.
9 2.43	$s = r\theta$ $9645 = 3959\theta$ $\theta = \dfrac{9645}{3959} = 2.44$ radians	Note that the answer is in radians.
10 15.8	$180° = \pi$ radians; $80° = \dfrac{\pi}{180} \cdot 80 = 1.396$ radians $s = r\theta$ $22 = r \cdot 1.396$ $r = \dfrac{22}{1.396} = 15.75$ ft = 15.8 ft when rounding to tenths.	Note carefully that the angle is in degrees and must be converted to radians before using it in the formula.

©GiftOfLogic   http://www.GiftOfLogic.com

APPENDIX	
Lesson	**Title**
Lesson 34	Calculator
Lesson 35	Blueprint Problems-1

	APPENDIX	
Lesson 34	Calculator	Review

> **FOCUSPREP CHECKLIST**
>
> - Which calculator models can I use?
> - Can I use a calculator for any problem?
> - Do I need to use a calculator?
> - Workout practice problems using the Calculator

Q1 What calculator models are allowed on the new PSAT 10 and SAT?

A1 Graphing and Scientific calculators are allowed. Visit https://sat.collegeboard.org/register/calculator-policy for a list of all approved calculators. The TI-84 Plus is the calculator that is most used. TI-83 calculators and Casio FX-9750 calculators are commonly used as well. Make sure you calculator has new batteries before you take the test.

Q2 Can I use a calculator for any problem?

A2 No. The new PSAT 10 and SAT exams have two sections that are clearly marked as CALCULATOR and NO CALCULATOR.

Q3 Do I need to use a calculator while solving problems in the CALCULATOR SECTION?

A3 Simple calculations in the CALCULATOR section can be made without a calculator. For example, if you have to find $2 \cdot 3 + 6$, you don't need to use a calculator. But, for more complex calculations, it may be advantageous to use a calculator to save time. For example, you can calculate $2.25 \cdot 15$ quickly and accurately using the calculator rather than multiplying it yourself and possibly making a mistake.

Q4 How do I practice using my calculator?

A4 Consider each row in the following table and use your calculator to find the result. Keystroke hints are provided for each problem along with a screenshot. In addition, use your calculator every day and get familiar with various functions. The keystrokes shown below are from a **TI-84 Plus** calculator. If you use a different calculator, it may have different keystrokes and screens. Get familiar with the keystrokes for your calculator.

©GiftOfLogic http://www.GiftOfLogic.com

	APPENDIX	
Lesson 34	Calculator	Practice & Answers

Problem	Keystrokes	Screen/Answer
$\dfrac{(3-2)^2}{5+5}$	Use parentheses in the correct places using PEMDAS rules.	`(3-2)²/(5+5)` `.1`
Average of 10,13,45,57,92	Place numbers in parentheses before dividing.	`(10+13+45+57+92)/5` `43.4`
Weighted average: $\dfrac{35 \cdot 55 + 25 \cdot 65 + 25 \cdot 75}{85}$	Place numbers within parentheses before dividing.	`(35*55+25*65+25*75)/85` `63.82352941`

Standard Deviation of 6,5,4,7,6
 	
Questions in SAT do not require you to calculate standard deviations, but it will be helpful to know how to use your calculator to find it.
	STAT, 1, 6, enter, 5, enter, 4, enter, 7, enter, 6, enter, STAT, CALC, 1, enter	`1-Var Stats`
		`x̄=5.6`
		`Σx=28`
		`Σx²=162`
		`Sx=1.140175425`
		`σx=1.019803903`
		`↓n=5`
		
		Note that σx refers to the population standard deviation (n=5) and Sx refers to the sample standard deviation (n=4).

$\sqrt{45}$ in decimals	2nd, x^2, 45)	`√(45)` `6.708203932`
$\sqrt{4^2 + 3^2}$	2nd, x^2, 4, x^2, +, 3, x^2)	`√(4²+3²)` `5`

©GiftOfLogic http://www.GiftOfLogic.com

$\sqrt{(4-6)^2 + (5-2)^2}$ in decimals	2nd, x^2, (4-6), x^2, +, (5-2), x^2)	`√(((4-6)²+(5-2)²)` `           3.605551275`
8% of 20	8% = 0.08 $0.08 \cdot 20 = 1.6$	`0.08*20` `              1.6`
$\dfrac{7.05 - 3.02}{4}$	Remember to include parentheses.	`(7.05-3.02)/4` `           1.0075`
$\dfrac{60 \cdot 6 + 62 \cdot 9}{6 + 9}$	Remember to include parentheses.	`(60*6+62*9)/(6+9)` `             61.2`

Percentage increase from 200 to 300	Second number minus first number, divided by first number.
	
	Multiply result by 100 to get the percentage.
		`(300-200)/200`
		`              .5`
		`Ans*100`
		`               50`

Percentage decrease from 300 to 100	Second number minus first number, divided by first number.
	
	Multiply result by 100 to get the percentage. Answer will be negative since there is a decrease in percentage.
		`(100-300)/300`
		`      -.6666666667`
		`Ans*100`
		`       -66.66666667`

©GiftOfLogic   http://www.GiftOfLogic.com

$\pi \cdot 4^2$	2nd, ^, x4, x^2	π*4² 50.26548246	
$2\pi \cdot 4 \cdot 12$	2, 2nd, ^, x4, x12	2π*4*12 301.5928947	
$180 - (32 + 47)$	Key parentheses.	180-(32+47) 101	
$\frac{1}{2} \cdot 4 \cdot 12$	Key parentheses for fractions.	(1/2)*4*12 24	
$3^2 \cdot 2^5$	3, x^2, x2, ^, 5	3²*2^5 288	
$300 \cdot 1.05^{10}$	Use caret for exponents.	30*1.05^10 48.8668388	
$400(1 - 0.02)^8$	Parentheses and exponent caret.	40(1-0.02)^8 34.0305209	
$1200 \cdot 0.04 \cdot 12$		1200*0.04*12 576	

Calculate x $$\frac{x}{3} = \frac{20}{15}$$	cross multiply. $15x = 60$ $x = \frac{60}{15}$	`60/15` `             4`
$\frac{20}{3} \cdot \frac{6}{5} \cdot \frac{1}{4}$	Enter parentheses for all fractions.	`(20/3)*(6/5)*(1/4)` `             2`
$121 \cdot \frac{\sqrt{3}}{4}$	Parentheses with square root.	`121*(√(3)/4)` `   52.39453693`
$200 \cdot 24^{\frac{1}{3}}$	Place the exponent within parentheses	`200*24^(1/3)` `    576.8998281`

$5!$	5, MATH, PRB, 4	`MATH NUM CPX PRB`
		`1:rand`
		`2:nPr`
		`3:nCr`
		`4:!`
		`5:randInt(`
		`6:randNorm(`
		`7:randBin(`
		
		`5!`
		`           120`

$5! \cdot 6!$	5, MATH, PRB, 4, x6, MATH, PRB, 4	`5!*6!` `         86400`

$(2+3) \cdot \dfrac{4}{5} \cdot (19-3)$	Three sets of parentheses.	`(2+3)(4/5)(19-3)` `                64`
$\dfrac{\frac{1}{3}}{\frac{4}{9}}$ in decimals	Parentheses for both fractions.	`(1/3)/(4/9)` `          .75`
$\dfrac{\frac{1}{3}}{2}$ In decimals	Fraction in parenthesis.	`(1/3)/2` `    .1666666667`

$\dfrac{11827}{31134} \cdot 100$		`(11827/31134)*10`
		`0`
		`      37.98740926`

$\dfrac{36}{96} \cdot 100$		`(36/96)*100` `          37.5`

Permutation 10P3	10, MATH, PRB, 2, 3	`MATH NUM CPX PRB`
		`1:rand`
		`2:nPr`
		`3:nCr`
		`4:!`
		`5:randInt(`
		`6:randNorm(`
		`7:randBin(`
		
		`10 nPr 3`
		`           720`

Combination 10C2	10, MATH, PRB, 3, 2	10 nCr 2 45
From Degree mode, switch to Radian mode From Radian mode, switch to Degree mode	Mode, Radian Mode, Degree	NORMAL SCI ENG FLOAT 0 1 2 3 4 5 6 7 8 9 **RADIAN** **DEGREE** FUNC PAR POL SEQ CONNECTED DOT SEQUENTIAL SIMUL REAL a+bi re^θi FULL HORIZ G-T SET CLOCK 01/07/01 11:37AM
$\sin 35°$	Mode, Degree, sin(35)	sin(35) .5735764364
$\cos 42°$	Mode, Degree, cos(42)	cos(42) .7431448255
$\sin^{-1} 0.6$	Mode, Degree, 2nd, $\sin^{-1}(0.6)$	sin⁻¹(0.6) 36.86989765
$\tan^{-1} 0.5$	Mode, Degree, 2nd, $\tan^{-1}(0.5)$	tan⁻¹(0.5) 26.56505118
If $r = 20$ and $\theta = \frac{\pi}{3}$ radians then calculate s where $s = r \cdot \theta$	20, 2nd, ^, /3	20π/3 20.94395102

APPENDIX

| Lesson 35 | Blueprint Problems-1 | Review |

> **FOCUSPREP CHECKLIST**
> - What kinds of problems are there in Blueprint Problems-1?
> - How do I solve Blueprint Problems-1?
> - Workout practice problems in Blueprint Problems-1

Q1 What kinds of problems are there in Blueprint Problems-1? How do I solve them?

A1 This lesson is intended to give you additional practice opportunity in solving problems **similar** to the ones found in the blueprint published by the College Board. It is highly recommended that you review and solve all the practice problems in all the lessons in this workbook before you solve the problems in this lesson.

Note carefully that sample problems in the blueprint are a **very small percentage** of the entire syllabus and are **NOT** guaranteed to appear in the actual test. You must review and workout the practice problems in all the lessons to prepare well for the PSAT 10 & SAT.

Q2 Can I solve the blueprint problems first before reviewing the other lessons?

A2 You may try some, but there are topics that are new to PSAT 10 and SAT. It is recommended that you finish all the lessons before trying to attempt the blueprint problems. You need to be well oriented and have a comprehensive understanding of all the topics to be able to solve the blueprint problems.

| Lesson 35 | APPENDIX
Blueprint Problems-1 | Practice |

CALCULATOR SECTION

1. Joe eats at a restaurant once every night. His bill before a tax of 8.25% is $25.00. He also leaves a tip of 15% on his meal before tax. Approximately how much money does Joe spend at this restaurant every month, considering a month has 31 days?

(A) $964.33
(B) $964.39
(C) $964.75
(D) $964.78

NO CALCULATOR SECTION

2. A new electric hybrid car has a gas mileage of 45 miles per gallon. The car has a gas tank that holds 16 gallons of gas. The car with a half-full tank is driven at 90 miles an hour. Which of the following functions f models the amount of gas remaining in the tank after t hours?

(A) $f(t) = 8 - 2t$
(B) $f(t) = 8 + 2t$
(C) $f(t) = 16 - t$
(D) $f(t) = 16 - 2t$

NO CALCULATOR SECTION

3. If $-\frac{10}{3} < -4x + 3 < \frac{11}{3}$, which of the following is an integral solution for x?

(A) 0
(B) 2
(C) 3
(D) 4

NO CALCULATOR SECTION

4. The equation $\frac{4(z+3)}{2} = \frac{3(z-3)}{7}$ can be represented as the fraction $-\frac{a}{11}$. What is the value of a?

(A) 7
(B) 11
(C) 28
(D) 51

NO CALCULATOR SECTION

5. $3x + 2y = 6$
$7x + 4y = 9$

Based on the system of equations above, what is the value of the product xy?

(A) $-\frac{45}{2}$
(B) $-\frac{9}{2}$
(C) -3
(C) $\frac{15}{2}$

NO CALCULATOR SECTION

6. If $\frac{1}{5}x + \frac{1}{6}y = 31$, then what is the value of $6x + 5y$?

(A) 155
(B) 186
(C) 930
(D) 992

NO CALCULATOR SECTION

7. The amount of dimes and nickels in Janie's purse is a multiple of 5. The value of the dimes and nickels is $7.50. Which of the following systems of equations could model this relationship?

(A) $d + n = 15$
$10d + 5n = 7.50.$

(B) $d + n = 25$
$10d + 5n = 750.$

(C) $d + n = 10$
$5d + 10n = 75.0.$

(D) $d + n = 17$
$10d + 5n = 750.$

NO CALCULATOR

8. If k is a positive constant not equal to 1, which of the following could be a graph of $y + x = k(x - y)$ in the xy-plane?

(A)

(B)

(C)

(D)

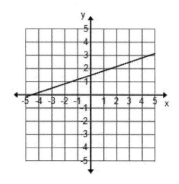

NO CALCULATOR SECTION

9.

$$\frac{1}{2}x - \frac{1}{4}y = 5$$

$$14x - by = 140.$$

In the system of linear equations above, b is a constant. If the system has infinite solutions, what is the value of b?

(A) 5
(B) 7
(C) 28
(D) 56

CALCULATOR SECTION

10. The height of an airplane is increasing at a linear rate. Ten minutes after takeoff, the plane is 1,225 feet above sea level. Twenty-five minutes after takeoff, the plane is 15,570 feet above sea level. Which of the following is the value of the constant rate at which the plane's height is increasing per minute?
   (A) 956.334
   (B) 965.334
   (C) 8338.334
   (D) 14,345

NO CALCULATOR SECTION

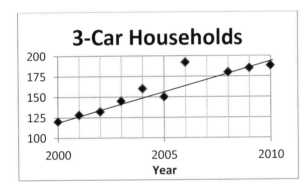

11. The scatterplot above shows the increase in households with 3 cars from 2000 to 2015 in a small community. Based on the line of best fit shown, which of the following values is closest to the average yearly increase in the number of households with 3 cars?

   (A) 5
   (B) 7
   (C) 11
   (D) 15

CALCULATOR SECTION

12. One Gigabyte is 1024 Megabytes. A DVD can hold 4.7 Gigabytes of data. A floppy disc can hold 1.44 Megabytes of data. If the data from x floppy discs can be fit into one DVD, what is the value of x?
   (A) 3342
   (B) 3343
   (C) 3555
   (D) 3558

CALCULATOR SECTION

Questions 13 and 14 refer to the table below:

In a historical town of Alexandria, the number of voters increased each year as shown in the table below:

Year	Age	Number of Voters
594 AD	18-30	7520
	31-45	10000
	46-51	11530
	52-65	1500
595 AD	18-30	8900
	31-45	9500
	46-51	9800
	52-65	1800
596 AD	18-30	15800
	31-45	10000
	46-51	11690
	52-65	2000

13. Which age group had the greatest increase in voters between 594 AD and 596 AD?

   (A) 18-30
   (B) 31-45
   (C) 46-51
   (D) 52-65

345
©GiftOfLogic   http://www.GiftOfLogic.com

CALCULATOR SECTION

14. If the population percentage of 46-65 year olds in 597 AD is 10% less than the population percentage of this group in 596 AD, then approximately what percent would that be?
  (A) 25%
  (B) 35%
  (C) 40%
  (D) 45%

NO CALCULATOR SECTION

15. If the two roots of $6x^2 + 6x = 12$ are r_1 and r_2, what is the product $r_1 \cdot r_2$?

  (A) -2
  (B) -1
  (C) 1
  (D) 2

NO CALCULATOR SECTION

16. The function $f(x) = ax^3 + ax^2 + ax + c$ passes through the points $(0,4)$ and $(-1,2)$. What is the value of $a + c$?
  (A) 2
  (B) 4
  (C) 6
  (D) 8

NO CALCULATOR SECTION

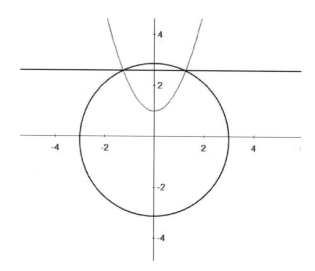

17. The graphs of a system of equations – a parabola, a straight line, and a circle are shown in the figure above. How many solutions does the system have?
  (A) 0
  (B) 1
  (C) 2
  (D) 3

NO CALCULATOR SECTION

18. If the solution to $\frac{\sqrt{2}}{x+\sqrt{2}} - \frac{\sqrt{2}}{x-\sqrt{2}} = 3$ is positive, what is the value of x?

  (A) $\frac{\sqrt{6}}{3}$

  (B) $\frac{3\sqrt{6}}{2}$

  (C) $\frac{3}{\sqrt{6}}$

  (D) $\frac{\sqrt{2}}{3}$

NO CALCULATOR SECTION

19. Bob can paint a fence three times faster than Joe. When working together, they can paint a fence in 5 hours. If x represents the time in hours taken by Joe to paint one fence, which equation below indicates how much of the fence Bob and Joe can paint together in one hour?

(A) $\frac{1}{x} + \frac{3}{x} = \frac{1}{5}$

(B) $\frac{x}{1} + \frac{x}{3} = 5$

(C) $3x + x = 5$

(D) $\frac{1}{x} + \frac{x}{3} = \frac{1}{5}$

CALCULATOR SECTION

The New Express Bank issues its Credit Cards worldwide. When a customer makes a purchase using these Credit Cards in a foreign currency, the bank converts the purchase price at the daily foreign rate and then charges a 5% fee on the converted cost.

20. Marla lives in USA, and is currently on vacation in Shanghai, China. For a purchase that she made in Shanghai for 75 Yuans, the bank posted a charge of $12.42 to her account, including the 5% fee. What Foreign Exchange Rate in (Chinese Yuan per US dollar) was used to calculate Marla's purchase? Round your answer to the nearest hundredths.
GRID IN

21. A bank in China sells a debit card worth 2000 Yuans. Charges to the debit card incur no additional fee on top of the purchases. Marla wants to know the minimum amount of purchase she can make using the Debit Card so that it is cheaper than the Credit card. Round your answer to the nearest whole number of Yuans.
GRID IN

CALCULATOR SECTION

$$x^2 + y^2 = 185$$
$$x = -6y$$

22. If (x, y) is a solution to the system of equations shown above, then $y^2 =$
(A) 3
(B) 4
(C) 5
(D) 6

NO CALCULATOR SECTION

23. If $\frac{9x^2}{3x+1} = \frac{1}{3x+1} + B$, B in terms of x is?

(A) $3x + 1$
(B) $3x - 1$
(C) $2x + 1$
(D) $2x - 1$

CALCULATOR SECTION

24. A cylinder with a radius of 5 cm is carved out of a hexagonal prism with a height of 10 cm and a side length of 10 cm. If the density of this cylinder is 3.2 grams/cubic cm, what is the mass of the cylinder, to the nearest whole gram? (figure not drawn to scale)
GRID IN

NO CALCULATOR SECTION

CALCULATOR SECTION

25. In the figure above, a semicircle of radius r has a chord $\overline{CD}$ that is parallel to diameter $\overline{AB}$ and is $\frac{1}{4}$ of $\overline{AB}$. What is distance between chords $\overline{AB}$ and $\overline{CD}$ in terms of r ?

(A) $\sqrt{15}\, r$

(B) $\frac{\sqrt{15}}{4} r$

(C) $\frac{\sqrt{15}}{2} r$

(D) $\sqrt{15}\, r$

NO CALCULATOR SECTION

26. If $\cos x = -p$ where the radian measure of angle x is such that $\pi < x < \frac{3\pi}{2}$ and $\cos y = p$, then y can be which one of the following?

A) $\pi - x$
B) $x + \frac{\pi}{2}$
C) $x + 2\pi$
D) $x - 2\pi$

APPENDIX

Lesson 35 — **Blueprint Problems-1** — **Answers**

#	Explanation	Comments
1 D	The cost of one night of food is $\$25.00 \cdot 1.15 \cdot 1.0825 = 31.12 \cdot 31 = 964.78$.	Round in the last step, not the intermediate steps, to ensure accuracy.
2 A	The car starts off with 8 gallons of gas. Each hour, it loses 2 gallons of gas. This is represented by $8 - 2t$.	
3 A	Subtracting three from all sides gives: $-\frac{19}{3} < -4x < \frac{2}{3}$. Dividing the three sides by -4, flipping the signs, gives: $\frac{19}{12} < x < -\frac{1}{6}$. The only answer choice that satisfies this condition is 0.	Flip signs when dividing or multiplying by a negative.
4 D	$28(z+3) = 6(z-3)$ $28z + 84 = 6z - 18$ $22z = -102$ $z = -\frac{102}{22}$ $z = -\frac{51}{11}$	Review the lesson on Linear Equalities.
5 A	Solve the system of linear equations: $3x + 2y = 6$ $7x + 4y = 9$ Multiply the first equation by 2 throughout. $6x + 4y = 12$ $7x + 4y = 9$ Subtract the first equation from the second. $x = -3, y = \frac{9-7x}{4} = \frac{9+21}{4} = \frac{30}{4} = \frac{15}{2}$. The product is $-3 \cdot \frac{15}{2} = -\frac{45}{2}$.	Review the lesson on System of Linear Equations.
6 C	Multiply the whole equation by LCM of 5 and 6 (30) : $6x + 5y = 30 \cdot 31 = 930$	Simplify the expression using LCM.
7 B	You are given that $d + n = $ a multiple of 5. Furthermore, when expressed in cents, $10d + 5n = 750$. The only system which satisfies this is system B.	Review the lesson on System of Linear Equations.
8 B	$y + x = k(x - y)$ $y + x = kx - ky$ $y + ky = kx - x$ $y(1 + k) = x(k - 1)$ $y = \frac{k-1}{k+1} x$ so when x=0, y=0 ; this means the line has to grow through the origin; only choice B shows a line thru the origin.	

©GiftOfLogic http://www.GiftOfLogic.com

9	B	Multiplying the first equation by 28 gives: $$14x - 7y = 140$$ $$14x - by = 140$$ Since the system has infinite solutions, the equations/lines are the same. So, $b = 7$.	Since the system has infinite solutions, make the equations have the same coefficients.
10	A	The two points of the plane are (10,1225) and (25,15570). The rate at which the height is increasing per minute is $\frac{15570-1125}{25-10} = 956.334$ feet/minute	Review the lesson on Linear Models.
11	B	2001- 125 households 2008 – 175 households Average = $\frac{175-125}{7} = \frac{50}{7} = 7$ approximately	Review the lesson on Scatterplots.
12	A	A DVD can hold $1024 \cdot 4.7$ megabytes, which is 4812.8. $\frac{4812.8}{1.44} = 3342.222$. Since only full discs can be fit, the largest whole number less than 3342.222 is 3342.	Review the lesson on Unit Conversions.
13	A	The number of voters from 18 to 30 nearly doubled between 594 and 596, a higher increase than the other three age groups.	Review the lesson on Graphs and Tables.
14	B	The voter percentage of 46-65 year olds in 596 AD is (11690+2000)/39490=34.67%. The voter percentage of this group in 597 AD is 10% less. So it is 34.67-10=24.67%= approximately 25%.	Review the lesson on Graphs and Tables.
15	A	Dividing the equation by 6 gives: $x^2 + x - 2 = 0$. Factoring gives $(x-1)(x+2) = 0$. The roots are 1 and -2. The product of the roots is $1 \cdot -2 = -2$.	Solve for the roots of quadratic. Review the lesson on Polynomials and Quadratic Equations.
16	C	Plugging in the given points gives two equations: $f(0) = c, 4 = c$ $f(-1) = -a + a - a + c, 2 = -a + c$ Substituting for c gives: $2 = -a + 4, a = 2$. $a + c = 2 + 4 = 6$.	
17	C	Solutions to the system are points where all three equations intersect. This occurs at two coordinates only.	Find the solutions from graphs of equations.
18	A	Use the common denominator and simplify. $$\frac{\sqrt{2} \cdot (x - \sqrt{2})}{x^2 - 2} - \frac{\sqrt{2} \cdot (x + \sqrt{2})}{x^2 - 2} = 3$$ $$\frac{x\sqrt{2} - 2}{x^2 - 2} - \frac{x\sqrt{2} + 2}{x^2 - 2} = 3$$ $$-\frac{4}{x^2 - 2} = 3$$ $$-4 = 3x^2 - 6$$ $$3x^2 + 0x - 2 = 0$$	Use $(a+b)(a-b)=(a^2 - b^2)$

	$$x^2 = \frac{2}{3}$$ $$x = \sqrt{\frac{2}{3}} = \frac{\sqrt{2}}{\sqrt{3}}\frac{\sqrt{3}}{\sqrt{3}} = \frac{\sqrt{6}}{3}$$	
19 A	It takes x hours for Joe to paint 1 fence. So, Joe paints at the rate of $\frac{1}{x}$ fence/hr. Bob paints three times faster than Joe, so Bob paints at a rate of $\frac{3}{x}$ fence/hr. When they work together, it takes them 5 hours to paint a fence, so the combined rate is 1/5 fence/hr. So, rate at which Bob paints + rate at which Joe paints= rate at which both paint. $\frac{1}{x} + \frac{3}{x} = \frac{1}{5}$.	Review the lesson on Rates.
20 6.34	Marla purchased something for 75 Yuans. The bank charged her $12.42 including a 5% fee. What exchange rate, Chinese Yuan per 1 USD did the bank charge? The bank converts the purchase price at the current exchange rate and then charges 4%. So let 1USD= x Chinese Yuans So, 75 Yuans = $\frac{75\ Yuans}{x\frac{Yuans}{Dollar}} = \frac{75}{x}$ USD After adding 5% fee to this purchase cost, the converted cost with fee is $\frac{75}{x} + 0.05 \cdot \frac{75}{x} = \frac{75}{x}(1.05)$. This is given to be $12.42. So $\frac{75}{x}(1.05) = 12.42$ $x = \frac{(75 \cdot 1.05)}{12.42} = 6.340$ Since the question asks you to round to the nearest hundredths, the exchange rate is 1 USD=6.34 Chinese Yuans.	Review the lesson on Extended Thinking.
21 1905	Thinking and dealing with one currency will help avoid errors in calculations. If she wants to purchase something for USD x using the Credit Card, she will be charged USD $1.05x$ including the fee. If she buys the Debit Card for 2000 Yuans, she would pay $(2000\ Yuans)/(\frac{6.34\ Yuans}{USD})$ = USD 315.46. So, she can purchase up to USD 315.46 using this debit card and her cost will be USD 315.46 since she has to prepay this amount upfront. That's how debit cards work. Make a table like shown below to see how this works.	Review the lesson on Extended Thinking.

	Purchase cost in USD	Credit Card 1.05 · purchase cost	Cost if using debit card	
	10	15	315.46	Credit card is cheaper than debit credit for this purchase
	100	105	315.46	Credit card is cheaper than debit card for this purchase
	x	$1.05x$	315.46	Credit card cost is equal to debit card's cost

A few values are shown – say for USD 100 in purchase cost, the cost using credit card is USD 105 and this is cheaper than the cost or purchasing this item using debit card which is 333.33. So, for some purchase that has cost of USD x, the cost using credit card is $1.05x$ and this is going to be more than the cost of paying it with a debit card, which is 333.33 USD. So, you can setup and equation to find this USD x.
$1.05x >= 315.46$
$x > \frac{315.46}{1.05} = 300.44$ USD. So, for a purchase price up to USD 300.44, the cost using credit card is cheaper than the cost using a debit credit card. After USD 300.44, the debit card will be cheaper than the credit card. Convert this amount to Yuans – 300.44 · 6.34=1904.78 and round it to a whole number – the answer is 1905.

22 C	$x^2 + y^2 = 185$ $x = -6y$ What is the value of y^2? $(-6y)^2 + y^2 = 185$ $36y^2 + y^2 = 185$ $37y^2 = 185$ $y^2 = \frac{185}{37} = 5$	Pause for few seconds to observe what is given and what is asked.
23 B	$\frac{9x^2}{3x+1} = \frac{1}{3x+1} + B$; Since you have to find B in terms of x, isolate B and simplify. B= $\frac{9x^2}{3x+1} - \frac{1}{3x+1}$	Review the lesson on Polynomials.

	$= \frac{9x^2-1}{3x+1}$; simplify numerator $a^2 - b^2 = (a+b)(a-b)$ $= \frac{(3x)^2 - 1^2}{3x+1} = \frac{(3x+1)(3x-1)}{3x+1} = 3x - 1$	
24 5801	The volume of the cylinder is $\pi \cdot 5^2 \cdot 10 = 250\pi$. The area of the base of the hexagonal prism is $3 \cdot 100 \cdot \frac{\sqrt{3}}{2} = 150\sqrt{3}$. So, the volume of the hexagonal prism $= A \cdot h = 150\sqrt{3} \cdot 10 = 1500\sqrt{3}$. The difference is $1500\sqrt{3} - 250\pi = 1812.68 \; cm^3$. The density is 3.2 grams/cubic cm. So, the mass of the prism is $1812.68 \cdot 3.2 = 5800.58 = 5801$ rounded up	Area of a hexagon is $\frac{3s^2\sqrt{3}}{2}$, where s is the side length. Review the lesson on Volume of Solids.
25 B	Let the center of the semicircle be the point O. Draw a line OC and OP. So, $OA = r \; OC = r$. OP is the distance between the chords. OPC is a right-angled triangle. $OC^2 = OP^2 + PC^2$. $r^2 = OP^2 + \left(\frac{r}{4}\right)^2$ $OP^2 = r^2 - \frac{r^2}{16} = \frac{15}{16} r^2$ $OP = \frac{\sqrt{15}}{4} r$	In problems like this, you will have to draw one or more lines and identify intermediate points and right triangles and then apply the Pythagorean theorem. Review the lesson on Pythagorean Theorem.
26 A		Review the lesson on Radians. You need to be familiar with unit circles, and trigonometric functions sin, cos, tan to answer these kinds of problems. You should also know how to find the values of sin, cos, tan when a point is reflected over the x and y axis and over the origin. Also, review the lessons in Trigonometry and Radians and know the difference between a reference angle and the positive and negative angles.

| | Note that the angles are in radians. The angle x is such that $\pi < x < \frac{3\pi}{2}$; so angle is in the 3RD quadrant. It is given that $\cos x = -p$. Mark a point P1 at an angle of x radians. Note that the reference angle of point P1 is $x - \pi$.
Since $\cos y = p$, and cosine is positive in 1st and 4th quadrants, the point in the unit circle for which $\cos y = p$ is in the 1st quadrant (P3) or in the 4th quadrant (P2). If it is in the 1st quadrant, the angle of the point P3 is $x - \pi$. This could be the answer but is not in the answer choice. If the point is in the 4th quadrant (P2), then its reference angle is $(x - \pi)$, but since the angle is measured counterclockwise, the angle of the point P2 is $-(x - \pi) = \pi - x$. So, $\cos(\pi - x) = p$. Since it is given that $\cos y = p$, it follows that $y = \pi - x$. This is given in the answer choice. | |

- Congratulations for completing the lessons and problems in this workbook. Hope you feel confident to take on the PSAT 10, PSAT/NMSQT, and SAT.
- The next step is to download the full length practice tests released by the College Board and practice them under test-like conditions.
- If you have siblings or friends in Grades 8 or 9, let them know that they can prepare for PSAT 8/9 using the FocusPrep's **PSAT 8/9 Workbooks**. Search for PSAT 8/9 in Amazon.
- Please visit http://www.GiftOfLogic.com for more information on PSAT and SAT workbooks.
- Good Luck!

NOTES

Made in the USA
Columbia, SC
14 May 2019